10/96

D0952369

ONE BOY AT WAR

PAUL A. SERGIOS

ONE BOY AT WAR

MY LIFE IN THE AIDS
UNDERGROUND

ALFRED A. KNOPF   NEW YORK

1993

THIS IS A BORZOI BOOK
PUBLISHED BY ALFRED A. KNOPF, INC.

Library of Congress Cataloging-in-Publication Data
Sergios, Paul A.
    One boy at war : my life in the AIDS underground / Paul Sergios.—1st ed.
    p. cm.
    Includes bibliographical references.
    ISBN 0-679-41839-3
    1. Sergios, Paul A.—Health. 2. AIDS (Disease)—Patients—United States—
Biography. I. Title.
RC607.A26S44 1993
362.1'969792'0092—dc20
[B]   92-18542   CIP

Manufactured in the United States of America
First Edition

FOR MADELINE, ALICE, AND ETHEL

Dr. Rieux resolved to compile this chronicle, so that he should not be one of those who hold their peace but should bear witness in favor of those plague-stricken people; so that some memorial of the injustice and outrage done them might endure; and to state quite simply what we learn in a time of pestilence: that there are more things to admire in men than to despise. . . . It could only be the record of what had . . . to be done again in the never ending fight against terror and its relentless onslaughts, despite their personal afflictions, by all who, while unable to be saints but refusing to bow down to pestilences, strive their utmost to be healers.

—Albert Camus,
The Plague

CONTENTS

PREFACE

In no other disease in history have patients taken such an active role in their own treatment. While one battle against AIDS had begun in mainstream clinical trials, another, more precipitous one was taking place in the laboratories and computer terminals of a group of individuals who found themselves at the center of the early AIDS underground, a movement that evolved surreptitiously, almost by accident. When referring to the AIDS drug importation and distribution network that forms the focus of this book, *underground* is a far-reaching term meant to include anything from holistic physicians prescribing nutritional therapies in Duluth, to more formalized underground studies conducted by group volunteers of imported medicines still considered "investigational" (even in their originating countries), to the informal research by patients who have chosen to self-administer experimental drugs procured from buyers' clubs, the progress and result of which were subsequently monitored by their individual physicians. Throughout the first ten years of the epidemic, these activities developed in part because of a system that prohibited patients with any life-threatening illness—and AIDS patients in particular—from having early access to drugs not yet approved by the FDA (Food and Drug Administration), and because of narrowly defined criteria for the diagnosis of AIDS that precluded many of them from taking part in mainstream research studies. It also happened because AIDS is a "high-tech" disease without precedent that struck a huge number of people living in a technological age of rapid communication.

Many of the people mentioned in this book are now dead. From early in 1983 onward, they fought valiantly to conquer AIDS on its own terms. They did not look only to healing circles or psychoneuroimmunology for answers. Rather, they became experts in the pathogenesis of HIV disease and obtained a broad understanding of immunological and virological pharmacology that rivaled and occasionally even exceeded that of many National Institutes of Health researchers. They networked with mainstream researchers, synthesized drugs in guerrilla clinics, staged informal studies, and rapidly evaluated large numbers of promising compounds. These underground researchers, and the renegade physicians who supported them, risked prosecution by federal officials and ostracism from the mainstream medical community. In going to extreme lengths to obtain and import a variety of drugs and subsequently find ways to analyze their efficacy and basic toxicity, they sometimes risked their lives. They were not politicians per se, yet they forged political change. Many of the changes occurring today with regard to the increased availability of experimental drugs are due to their pioneering efforts.

Through a series of chance encounters, I found myself becoming heavily immersed in the activities of the AIDS drug underground, at one point became one of the leaders of the Compound Q study, and developed friendships with almost all of the underground AIDS activists. Many of their efforts were never documented in magazine or newspaper accounts. On numerous occasions, several of them asked me, "Who will tell our story? Who will document our struggle?"

Ultimately, their efforts were inextricably linked to the larger infrastructure of mainstream AIDS research. I therefore found it impossible to write about the underground drug leaders without also discussing their mainstream counterparts.

This book is not intended to be an indictment of the mainstream medical system; in my experience, the system has worked many more times than it has failed. But it *does* raise a major issue that still exists: how to get promising drugs quickly into the hands of people with life-threatening illnesses, while at the same time completing formal and rigorous investigations of those compounds' safety and efficacy.

These pages do not claim to be without a personal viewpoint or to be exhaustive. Other books will surely be written about the underground battle to find a cure for AIDS. In my own, however, I have attempted to avoid writing a self-indulgent or overly colorful memoir, but rather, to integrate my own experiences and impressions of key events in the epidemic with a more objective overview.

Finally, this is not just a chronicle of the AIDS drug underground and its pioneers but the story of my own struggle with HIV, HIV dementia, and my reactions to seeing friends succumb at an early age to a modern-day plague.

Although I have attempted to describe in understandable terms the complex elements of the pathogenesis of HIV and the modes of action of the various drugs used, I have chosen not to do so at the expense of oversimplifying the disease's many facets. For the uninitiated, the medical and scientific vocabulary they will encounter can be overwhelming. I have used authentic medical terminology throughout and therefore suggest that, prior to reading the text, the reader first review the Glossary that comes at the conclusion of the book.

ACKNOWLEDGMENTS

When I first entered the Phase 2 AZT trial at UCLA, the study coordinator, Joan Lederman, urged me to keep a journal. I took her advice, and her appearance in these pages, along with that of her cohorts, is at least partially her own doing. I also recorded telephone conversations with underground and mainstream researchers, filed transcripts of meetings, kept copies of journal articles, underground and mainstream newsletters, conference abstracts, and unpublished manuscripts describing the results of many experimental therapies.

But these pages could not have been written without the aid and support of many who, like myself, participated in or witnessed the events related here. Some shared information on the condition that they not be thanked by name, a condition I hereby acknowledge and respect. They know who they are and are aware, I hope, of my gratitude to them. Others, whose names follow, were helpful in clarifying issues, situations, dates, moments, moods, and sometimes motives. They include Sam Murdoch, Margaret Fischl, the late Tom Hannan, the late Stephen Caiazza, Robert Mayer, Joan Lederman, Steve Gavin, Lenny Kaplan, Doris Feinburg, Stuart Blackburn, Joseph Sonnabend, Jim Corti, John Dwyer, and the late Rob Springer.

Others who were helpful include Shirley May, Alfredo Martinez, Troy Dickerson, Alex Conn, the late Jules Parnes, Steven Fowkes, the late Michael Gaffney, Jim Driscoll, the late Ron Woodruff, Derek Hodel, Dr. Anthony Lamarca, the late Nathaniel Pier, Michael Scolaro, and Stephen Hauptman. In some cases, family members of persons now deceased have requested that I maintain the anonymity of their relatives; in these cases, I have identified the persons by the pseudonyms that they created for themselves and used in the underground. These persons are David Wilson, Rick Andrews, Alan Field, Luiz Vasquez, and David Myers. Others still living asked that I maintain their anonymity and I have thus assigned them a pseudonym. These include Susan Drake, Scott Yageman, John O'Malley, Jack Gerhardt, Craig Loders, and Jason Adams.

In all but a few instances, I was either a participant in or witness to the conversations in this book. A few were obtained verbatim from transcripts, in-person or telephone interviews, and conferences.

I also wish to thank the following people and organizations for their generous extensions of time and help: Mitchell Speer of the American Foundation for AIDS Research, John S. James of the *AIDS Treatment News*, the late Barry Gingell of the Gay Men's Health Crisis in New York, Charles Henderson of the Centers for Disease Control *AIDS Update* and *AIDS Weekly*, Janet Martinez of AIDS Project Los Angeles, Bill Bow of the Shanti Foundation, the late Tom Jefferson of Project Inform in San Francisco, the Names Project in San Francisco, the public relations staff of the U.S. Food and Drug Administration, and the research staff and editors of the Pharmaceutical Manufacturers' Association. Also, James R. Lewis of the *Wall Street Journal*, Cecily Surace of the Los Angeles *Times*, Gina Kolata of *The New York Times*, Lisa Krieger of the San Francisco *Chronicle*, Elinor Burkett of the Miami *Herald*, Nancy McVicar of the Fort Lauderdale *News/Sun-Sentinel*, Lynn Seiffer of *Newsweek*, the research staff of the Roche/Roferon Oncoline, and the reference staffs of the University of Miami Medical Library and Florida Atlantic University.

Many of the experiences and insights included in these pages were written during a period of mild to moderate cognitive impairment. I am grateful to the following individuals for critiquing early drafts of chapters: Steven Bach, Andrew Holleran, Felice Picano, Arnie Kantrowitz, Robert Ellis, and C. F. Borgman. I am especially indebted to Harlan Greene, who provided invaluable assistance. In many ways, these people restored my narrative voice and allowed me to persevere. I owe them a huge debt.

I am grateful to Dr. Mario Isidron, Dr. Daniel Hamilos, and Dr. Jonathan Worth for providing a detailed and thorough medical edit.

I also wish to thank Julia Lewis and Carol Shookhoff for their invaluable clerical assistance.

Finally, I am proud to recognize my editor at Knopf, Robin Swados, who believed in the project from the start and intelligently guided it through its various incarnations.

PRINCIPAL PLAYERS

(an asterisk denotes a pseudonym)

DONALD ABRAMS, co-director of the San Francisco General Hospital AIDS Unit and a consistent critic of the work of the AIDS underground.

*JASON ADAMS, longtime survivor of AIDS and a subject in the Centers for Disease Control's Operation 577.

*RICK ANDREWS, a Kaposi's sarcoma patient in Robert Mayer's practice who tried many experimental drugs to save his life.

MICHAEL BRISTOW, a member of the original Shanti group who took his own life.

SAM BRODER, National Cancer Institute researcher and the chief proponent of AZT. Also, the principal investigator of the Phase 1 AZT trial.

STEPHEN CAIAZZA, New York–based physician who believed that AIDS was merely untreated syphilis.

MICHAEL CALLEN, long-term survivor of AIDS, author of *Surviving AIDS* and co-founder of the New York Buyers' Club, the PWA Health Group.

SALVATORE CATAPANO, New York–based independent researcher who claimed that typhoid vaccine was the cure for AIDS.

ELLEN COOPER, a mid-level manager in the Food and Drug Administration who was responsible for approving AIDS antiviral drugs.

JIM CORTI, the "James Bond" of the underground; the nation's leading importer of experimental AIDS drugs from all over the world.

MARTIN DELANEY, co-director of San Francisco–based information network Project Inform and organizer of the underground Compound Q study.

*SUSAN DRAKE, Robert Mayer's nurse, an ARC patient herself, who fought desperately to save HIV patients' lives—including her own.

JIM DRISCOLL, Shakespearean scholar turned AIDS activist; author of HR-2872, known as the Campbell bill.

PETER DUESBERG, a retrovirologist at the University of California at Berkeley who argues vehemently that AIDS is not caused by HIV.

JOHN DWYER, world-famous immunologist and virologist, author of *The Body at War* and innovator of thymic transplantation therapy for AIDS.

ANTHONY FAUCI, chairman of the National Institute of Allergy and Infectious Diseases and the nation's leading AIDS researcher.

*ALAN FIELD, Boulder PWA who imported Peptide T.

ROBERT GALLO, a retrovirologist at the National Cancer Institute, one of the discoverers of HTLV-III (HIV) and author of *Virus Hunting*.

MICHAEL GARSTEN, my lover in Los Angeles.

STEVE GAVIN, the "godfather" of underground drug chemists and researchers.

*Jack Gerhardt, underground chemist and researcher, who was among the first to synthesize complex compounds, and co-founder of DATA (Direct Action for Treatment Access).

Michael Gottlieb, Los Angeles immunologist, widely recognized as the physician who "discovered" the first cases of AIDS in gay men in the United States, and a principal investigator of the Phase 2 AZT study. Co-founder of the American Foundation for AIDS Research.

Tom Hannan, co-founder of the New York Community Research Initiative and the PWA Health Group.

Louise Hay, Los Angeles–based metaphysicist whose philosophy proposed that spirituality and positive imagery could heal AIDS.

Stephen Herman, developer of the experimental AIDS medication Viroxan and one of the only physicians to be arrested by state health officials for manufacturing and distributing unproven HIV medications.

Jeffrey Johnson, Carl Pommer's lover in San Francisco.

Lenny Kaplan, president of Fight for Life, a South Florida AIDS advocacy group, and manager of the Fort Lauderdale AIDS Buyers' Club.

*Stuart Kelly, leader of the original Shanti AIDS Support Group in Los Angeles.

Larry Kramer, founder of ACT UP (the AIDS Coalition to Unleash Power) and the Gay Men's Health Crisis (GMHC).

Mathilde Krim, co-founder of the American Foundation for AIDS Research and a major catalyst in the formation of the Community Research Initiative.

Joan Lederman, coordinator of the University of California–Los Angeles AZT study.

Alan Levin, an immunologist with a private practice in San Francisco, and among the first to advocate innovative aggressive interventions for AIDS; the principal investigator of the underground Compound Q study.

PRINCIPAL PLAYERS

*CRAIG LODERS, a longtime survivor of the original Shanti Support Group.

MICHAEL MAY, an AIDS patient who was among the earliest to receive AL-721 and who attempted to convince mainstream researchers of its value.

ROBERT MAYER, sympathetic Miami physician known for renegade treatments and a national innovator of ozone therapy. He helped pioneer the underground Compound Q study while I worked as a research assistant in his office.

*PAUL MCCLELLAN, Virginia AIDS researcher who joined forces with me to attempt an experimental protocol to cure the disease.

MICHAEL MCGRATH, San Francisco General Hospital AIDS researcher who established that Compound Q effectively reduced the number of HIV-infected macrophages *in vitro*.

LUC MONTAGNIER, leader of the Pasteur Institute team that first isolated HTLV-III (HIV).

*JOHN O'MALLEY, a close friend of mine in Los Angeles who helped me smuggle experimental drugs across the border from Mexico.

PETE PARSONS, my high-school lover.

CANDACE PERT, a National Institute of Mental Health researcher and innovator in peptide research who claimed that her discovery, Peptide T, was an effective treatment for HIV dementia.

CARL POMMER, my neighbor in San Francisco.

*KEVIN PRICE, a member of the original Shanti Support Group and one of the first to die of AIDS.

PHILIP RIEF, among the primary physicians to see the first cases of AIDS in San Francisco's Castro district.

MEIR SHINITZKY, Israeli researcher who developed AL-721 as an anti-HIV therapeutic.

Rob Springer, known as "the midnight chemist," and a pioneer in the national AIDS underground drug movement.

*Luiz Vasquez, Miami-based physician who attempted numerous experimental therapies to cure the disease.

*David Wilson, a heterosexual PWA who joined forces with me in importing and testing a wide variety of experimental drugs.

*Scott Yageman, south Florida AIDS activist and the first subject in the underground Compound Q study.

ONE BOY AT WAR

THE DUCK POND

The grass in the park surrounding the duck pond was very soft. As a child, I would lie there for hours, staring up at the sky through the interlocking branches of the seagrapes and poincianas that created a canopy, making me feel safe and warm. I'd dream and doze, listening to the sound of the Florida palms in the wind, watching the Muscovy and Peking ducks that paddled on the water.

I would cross the majestic bridge that led to the other side of the park. Green lawns, spotted brighter in the sun, sloped to an old gazebo of brown brick, Spanish tiles, and thick white wooden columns. In its shady recesses were a marble table, always cool to the touch, and two benches. Alongside grew a glade of bamboo, whose stalks, over thirty feet high, whistled and sounded hollow, like doves, in the breeze. Wild cherry bromeliad nestled nearby. On rainy days, drops fell from the roof of the gazebo and silently touched the surface of the pond.

There was a swing on the lawn that I often rode, pumping, arching over nearby oaks and water. Ilene and Jack and I played together. I remember them perfectly. But what comes back more powerfully now is the memory of the games we staged—not so much what they were, but the feelings they entailed. We must have been giants, of course—heroes and characters we had invented. We were at war with chimerical demons of our own creation. We projected our dreams and imaginings into our stories; we told each other tales of what we would accomplish and who we would become. Swinging out over the water, the world literally reeling at our feet, we were free to imagine anything and everything. It was as dizzying as the thrill of the swing.

That feeling came to imbue the duck pond for me, so that whenever I returned, I came upon that welcome sense of warmth and sun and the rush of possibility. Like the city beyond the bamboo and seagrape trees, everything else seemed unreal. So it became more than just a place; it was a space within me—of adventure, ritual and innocence, a place that I would come, in my day and night dreams, to visit regularly.

I was an only child and raised by my mother, Madeline Sergios (née Fekas). She was born in Cambridge, Massachusetts, the youngest of nine children. She was a precocious youngster who skipped the second grade, filled with dreams of becoming a writer and leaving behind the working-class life to which she felt inextricably cast. In 1941, when she was sixteen, she went to work in a defense plant for three years and managed to save enough to enter Boston University's School of Journalism. Four years later she graduated with honors, the only child in her family to attend college.

She worked for the Associated Press before returning to school to earn a master's degree in education at Hunter College. Several years later, she joined the civilian corps of the air force, teaching children of American servicemen on the island of Crete. It was there that she met George Sergios, a handsome architect. He came from a prominent Greek family of physicians, lawyers, and businessmen. The two moved to the United States and were wed in 1958. They moved to Florida and lived in a modest home in Fort Lauderdale.

My mother got a job teaching elementary school in Broward County. My father was employed in a large architectural firm in Miami, a job that frequently required him to travel. In January 1960, he was killed in a light-aircraft plane crash en route from Miami to New York. I was born eight months later, in August of that year.

In the heat of the summer, I was baptized on the eighth day of my life in the Greek Orthodox Church—at the time, nothing more than a converted storage room in the back of a local grocery store. Yards from where shoppers selected cabbage and brussels sprouts, I was dipped in sacred water and anointed with oil.

I grew up in Plantation, a city to the west of Fort Lauderdale. Plantation. The name conjures up images of expansive lawns and huge mansions. Actually it was a suburb of residential communities and businesses.

I had no sisters or brothers. My mother worked as a fourth grade teacher of science and math. When I was young we moved to a condominium, one of those nondescript places with a hibiscus in the yard and a row of crotons in the front patio.

When I try to recall the details of my childhood, it's all a complex jumble of events; the baseball cap I wore all year, the Lite Brite set I got for Christmas, coins collected with enthusiasm, weekends spent at a Fort Lauderdale beach. I was quiet and shy.

As I grew older, though, I became more outgoing. I was involved in a variety of activities as a youngster—Little League baseball, swimming at the beach, acting in children's theater productions, the Boy Scouts. I had unlimited energy. I did well in school and I liked to read, but I also liked to watch television. Images of Vietnam and Watergate were all part of my childhood.

From an early age, my mother often took me to the movies. We went to the university movie theater where foreign classics and American films were screened. Dreaming in the darkness, I was entranced by the images on the screen. I lived for the magic of those evenings in the darkened theater and dreamed of producing such movies myself.

I had surprisingly little conflict about being gay. Even from an early age, it seemed an innate and natural aspect of my identity.

In the wind-brass ensemble to which I belonged in high school was a beautiful boy named Pete Parsons; I had watched him since freshman year. In our junior year, he became the drum major of the marching band and student director of concert band. Our eyes met only occasionally, but I was certain he was aware of my fixation, especially during those afternoons when the ensemble would practice in the amphitheater outdoors. I stole copious but surreptitious glances at him, basking in his warm smile and good looks. I knew he must also be gay. There was a striking masculinity in his demeanor but also an unmistakable softness. And I knew that he too was secretly watching.

During Friday-evening football games, when our band attempted to outblast its opponent to the nonstop strains of "On, Wisconsin" from across the field, I removed my conspicuous white hat and cummerbund and made my way to the other side of the stands. From underneath the bleachers, I watched Pete as he sat between musical numbers occasionally polishing his saxophone, then rising to lead the brass section in another musical cheer. He looked radiant in his orange and brown uniform that molded his body in exquisite definition, all the while suggesting the nakedness underneath. I was aroused by the play of his muscles beneath his pants. I dreamed of lacing my fingers over his, feeling his strong arms around mine, tasting his wonderful lips.

Although in many ways we lived in separate worlds, I nevertheless managed to forge a bond with this young man. He played saxophone in a scene of one of the Super-8 films I produced in high school; I stayed late after band practice, helping him with miscellaneous tasks around the band room.

On the night of our junior prom, I arranged a double date with Pete and two girls from the band. We had fun that evening, dancing on the beach, roaring down Broward Boulevard, toasting our futures. At eleven o'clock, we dropped the girls back home and then drove to the Duck Pond.

Though shrouded in darkness, it seemed a natural place to be. In the distance, a twinkling of lights from houses glimmered through the trees. Instinctively, without saying a word, we found ourselves undressing. We touched our bodies, locking our fingers, our lips, our legs in the soft damp grass under the seagrape trees. We explored each other for hours, delighting ourselves with our discoveries. When we left, dawn was already lighting the city.

We continued to meet. We questioned nothing. Our ardor continued unabated, all through that summer and our senior year, consuming everything but the passion and the need we felt, until I went off to college and Pete joined the service. I couldn't possibly have known then how special that relationship would become—or why.

I hadn't formally admitted to my mother that I was gay. But on some level, I was certain she knew. Although we never discussed it, I was so transformed in those mornings when I returned from the pond that my mother understood implicitly what was happening between Pete and me.

I had graduated from high school with honors. Because of my particular aptitude for math and science, I could have pursued a wide variety of careers, yet there was only one I truly coveted, and at one school: film, at the University of Southern California (USC). Fueled by the meteoric success of such graduates as George Lucas and Francis Ford Coppola, hundreds of aspiring filmmakers from across the country vied for the small number of spots in a ferociously competitive program. Certain of only the slightest chance of getting admitted, I also applied to New York University and Stanford University.

Much to my surprise, I received letters informing me that I had been accepted to all three. I left Florida and boarded a plane for Los Angeles.

USC, which by some accounts was an acronym for the University of Spoiled Children or the University of Social Climbers, was in fact neither. It *was*, however, an island of relative wealth in a sea of poverty. The university and the surrounding village of shops, dormitories, apartments, and fraternity houses in which I lived was located not far from downtown Los Angeles in a low-rent district. In its heyday, the region had been one of the poshest in Los Angeles. But with the migration of the wealthy to the San Fernando Valley and the west suburbs, the area had changed radically in composition and economic character.

Every day, impeccably dressed students biked to school, past tenements, misery, and graffiti that externalized the hostility of inner-city warfare, toward a future that guaranteed freedom from such economic and cultural poverty.

It was in my introductory film theory class that I met John O'Malley, a brilliant young man, whom I instantly grew to like. He had a dark, brooding demeanor and, though only twenty, resembled a young Orson Welles. He came from an Irish-Catholic background and had been raised in an upper-class family in the Northeast. He was extraordinarily intelligent and well read. Like me, he had produced films in high school and won awards. With his appreciation of literature and background in silent comedy, John produced a series of *films noirs* that, combined with a technically slick editorial style, immediately set him apart and attracted me to his films. We often participated in discussions late into the night. I realized that John and I both had a propensity for making films that were at times controversial both in technique and in content, and as a result of our unorthodox filmmaking often incurred the disapprobation of our classmates. Despite his conservative background, O'Malley was not uncomfortable with my homosexuality. We spoke about it freely, and he accepted it as an integral part of my personality. There was an artistic bond between us that somehow transcended our religious and political differences, and we became fast friends, providing each other with emotional support in what was often a psychologically grueling environment.

One evening, after having listened to an especially brutal and divisive critique of one of my films, I sat alone in the back of the cafeteria, far from the whir of sprockets. It was eight o'clock and the place was deserted.

We had planned to attend a screening of a new Martin Scorsese picture but I was so affected by the comments of my peers that I ducked out at the last minute. John came looking for me and discovered me in the cafeteria, pining away like a wounded lion. He approached me but did not sit down.

"I wanted to make films that everyone would like, not throw darts," I said quietly. "I don't even know what I'm doing here. I feel like such an outcast."

"Don't give up!" John said, literally pulling me out of my chair. "You should be glad they fight. Don't you see? You're different," he continued, as though confronting the deeper, underlying reality that was perhaps the real reason for my depression. "We all are to some extent. That's why we're here. You have to become comfortable with that *difference.*"

He watched me brood a second more, then turned toward the exit.

"C'mon. We don't want to be late for the movie."

He was right, of course. Deep down, I felt even more comfortable even with homosexuality than I did with a "difference" that at times could only be described as creative madness.

I double majored in psychobiology, the study of how chemistry in the brain affects and influences human behavior. With a graduate student named James Cody, I designed and implemented an elaborate experiment on the dynamics of partner selection in gay male relationships that was ultimately published in the *Journal of Social Psychology* and the *Journal of Homosexuality.*

I buried myself in work for four years, staying away from the fast life of West Hollywood. I continued to correspond with Pete. He told me about the trials of military life, and I related the rigors of film school.

It was only natural that John and I should work together in our senior year. We had grown to be close cinematic allies and shared a similar dramatic sensibility. We spent hours in the editing room together, sometimes staying up all night, only to go to an eight-o'clock class the next morning with no sleep, our heads spinning with cinematic fervor. In those weary, languorous moments, we were constantly reminded of François Truffaut's statement that "film is more important than life."

In the early morning hours, the patio outside the editing room was redolent with the scent of jasmine. The smell filtered into the editing room, blended with the pungent odor of celluloid and splicing cement, and inspired us, making us continually attempt to improve our cinematic efforts.

We produced a short film that went on to win awards at several festivals and be shown nationally on cable. And we awoke on the morning following the first screening to read a positive review about the film in the Los Angeles *Herald-Examiner*. I called John and said, "It looks like we're off to a good start!"

In the months immediately following our graduation, we took our portfolio film, along with some samples of our writing, and arranged interviews with a wide variety of producers, independent production companies, and studio executives in Hollywood. Some of the interviews were set up by an agent who had attended the original screening of our film in our senior year; many we arranged ourselves. We found it relatively easy to get a foot in the door; it was the executives' business to search for young talent, and they couldn't afford to miss a bright possibility. It was harder to get two feet behind our own desks. The competition was intense. Graduates from numerous other film schools and talented producers of independent features were all knocking on doors with a vengeance, searching for the relatively small number of opportunities to produce or direct.

After almost three months of interviews, John and I were offered jobs as story analysts, he at Samuel Arkoff Pictures and I

in the development department of Focus 30 Productions, a rising
new company that had produced two successful feature films of
its own in the last three years and picked up half a dozen others for
distribution.

I was offered a salary of $30,000 a year and had an office in a
plush building in Century City. Although story analysts' work
would appear to be far removed from the actual production of
motion pictures, a surprising number of them had risen to execu-
tive-level positions over time. The work provided excellent exposure to numerous elements of the industry and provided an
opportunity to groom young talent. In addition to reading scripts,
I also attended "pitch meetings" and reported directly to the Vice
President of Development. In these meetings, writers would attempt
to summarize their screenplay or story idea as succinctly and elo-
quently as possible. Many talented writers seemed unable to articulate their creative concepts while other, less talented ones had more
masterful pitching abilities. A good pitch not only created a spark
of interest, it also encapsulated the essence of the story quickly and
in a way that was easy to understand. It was my job to take notes,
generate summaries of a writer's idea, and offer my opinion of its
feasibility.

John's manager told him on the first day of work that the
company he worked for offered numerous development deals to
writers each month. The vast majority of the finished scripts would
never be produced, though. The deals were arranged primarily as
a public-relations effort to nurture writers with a view toward future
projects. Both John and I were beginning to understand that development people did little else but *develop*—an end unto itself. It
seemed to us a wasteful and futile endeavor, though many insiders
defended the process as no more wasteful than, for example, the
research-and-development function of a pharmaceutical company,
which in any given year might pour large amounts of money into
testing and developing a variety of drugs that would never actually
see the light of day.

I was also disillusioned to learn that many executives appeared to know little about storytelling or the actual craft of movie making—a phenomenon that was not so unusual in Hollywood, 1982. Studio and production company executives spent their time in a variety of legal, financial, and administrative concerns. The executives most admired were not those who could write a script or edit a scene but those whose financial acumen could reduce a studio's risk and ultimately produce a chain of blockbusters.

In order to generate revenue simply to make more films, production executives in the 1980s had to be savvy market researchers, accountants, and lawyers more than storytellers and filmmakers. Unlike their predecessors—creative people who learned to be businessmen—the 1980s moguls were businessmen who learned to be creative.

I often read as many as ten screenplays or novels a week at Focus 30. In the course of a week, I read everything from a screen adaptation of Toni Morrison's *Tar Baby* to a soon-to-be-released murder mystery from New York. Yet I recommended only 10 percent of all material I read, about half of which ever actually went into development. The writers of these scripts got development deals and were paid handsomely for their time and effort. The result was a finished screenplay. Often, the script would be optioned by our company rather than purchased outright.

On more than one occasion, a script that John O'Malley and I recommended for development was turned down by the production companies where we worked; months or even years later, the same material was picked up for development at another company and sometimes even produced. This process gave us confidence in our own skills, enabled us to realize that we did possess insight into current taste as well as an eye for quality and that, at least in a few cases, worthy material did make it to the screen.

After nine months of reading scripts and sitting in on development meetings in which many of my comments inevitably fell on deaf ears, I grew restless and tired of playing the sage—and the fool.

I had been in Los Angeles for five years and needed a break from the relentless pace of the city. Several USC cinema grads had migrated to northern California. I decided to follow.

On July 5, 1982, I packed my bags, told John good-bye, and drove up Interstate 5.

CHAPTER 2

LIFE INSURANCE

My unfurnished two-bedroom apartment in San Francisco sat above a busy flower shop and overlooked Castro Street. It had hardwood floors, newly painted walls, a tiny kitchen, and a static view of a brick courtyard in the back. I could look out my bedroom window, however, and capture a panoramic view of the lively Castro street scene. The roof had been turned into a sundeck of sorts and afforded an even more expansive perspective of the western edge of the city, with the Mission district in the foreground and the Presidio in the distance.

Castro Street and an entire stretch of the Castro basin were a square mile composed almost exclusively of gay-owned restaurants, movie theaters, and dentists' offices. At five o'clock on a typical weekday afternoon, it was almost impossible to find even one single woman or heterosexual man arriving at the Castro Street subway station. A daily video magazine on gay events, produced by a gay ad agency on Castro Street, was broadcast from a kiosk on street level. The Castro Theater played host to gay film festivals and featured an international array of gay films. Distinctive multicolored flags, symbols of the "rainbow coalition" that represented homosexual liberation, hung outside many of the apartment buildings.

The buildings that lined streets with names like Noe and Fillmore sat tightly together, neatly stacked in layers—almost oppressively so. Yet they blended comfortably into the slope of the large hills.

At least a half dozen bars and lounges dotted Castro Street. In most of them, the decor was informal, the lighting dim, and the jukebox so loud as to prevent any intelligible conversation, reducing most contact to the purely visual.

The street was literally lined with men at certain hours, standing alone in doorways, sitting on steps, leaning against the railings of the subway terminal, or walking in pairs, some holding each other tightly. They took no pains to hide their obvious interest in each other, eyeing one another with a cool effortlessness, as if a possible encounter were merely a glance away. Many dressed suggestively in jeans and form-fitting shirts, often exposing tanned chests.

I was fascinated and intrigued by the overt displays of affection and freedom that Castro Street offered. With newly eroticized eyes, I looked at the trim physiques, firm thighs, and gleaming torsos that were on display everywhere. I caught the glances of some of the men. Many returned mine, and a sexual fling or one-night encounter ensued.

My next-door neighbor was Carl Pommer. He lived with his lover Jeffrey Johnson. Carl was a travel agent and had been all over the world. We had many conversations in his apartment that lasted late into the evening. "Most of us have five years of lost adolescence to make up for," he told me. "Gay men often indulge in wild sexual behavior late into their twenties. It's typical. Don't feel guilty about it."

I pondered his statement. If gay men were given the opportunity to be socialized from puberty, with appropriate socialization, training, and the chance to meet and date their gay counterparts openly, would they be less promiscuous than they were now? Somehow, I doubted it. There seemed to be a much stronger force at work, having nothing to do with environmental conditioning or learned behavior. Indeed, all across the country, young men and women were following the pied piper of sexual liberation. The collision between free love and the virus would have a deadly effect. But none of us could see this at the time.

On Halloween, a cadre of revelers danced on Castro Street, giving the neighborhood a Mardi Gras atmosphere. Amid the elaborate costumes and laughter, it seemed improbable that a sinister plague was in the making. I felt impervious to the possibility as I gazed down at the partiers from the apartment window of a handsome stranger I had met the night before. I turned away and felt myself become engulfed in his arms.

I never smoked cigarettes, used recreational drugs, or drank alcohol. Knowing their destructive powers, I had resolved to keep those elements out of my life. This made me somewhat of an anomaly on Castro Street.

Even in the summer of 1982, there were strong hints that something had gone horribly wrong in the Castro district. Jeffrey, Carl's lover, was suffering from a baffling array of symptoms that had also affected at least two dozen other men in the ghetto: weight loss, a dry cough, shortness of breath, and white patches of *Candida albicans*—a fungal infection known as candidiasis, or "thrush"—on the tongue. One group was dying of strange infections usually found in birds and mice. Another came down with purple and gray lesions that started on their lower legs and progressed upward, sometimes covering their bodies with ugly splotches. Kaposi's sarcoma (KS), a normally nonmalignant cancer originally found in elderly Mediterranean men, had started to get a foothold.

As early as 1979, long before the classic telltale symptoms of thrush and weight loss and Kaposi's sarcoma had become apparent, gay men were showing up at their doctors' offices with swollen lymph nodes, a syndrome that would eventually become known as persistent generalized lymphadenopathy. Physicians explained it as the activation of the immune system, a "useless response" mounted against some terrible but as yet unidentified invader. In time, many of the men developed symptoms of profound immune deficiency and life-threatening opportunistic infections. The most common was *Pneumocystis carinii* pneumonia (PCP), caused by a protozoan organism found deep in the trachea and lungs of healthy people and ordinarily innocuous. For some reason, it had developed into a lethal pneumonia in gay men.

The disease of KS and opportunistic infections had come to be known as GRID—Gay-Related Immune Deficiency, since it was found almost entirely in gay men and seemed to correlate with a loss of cell-mediated immunity resulting from a decimation of CD4 cells, a type of lymphocyte in the patients' blood.

No one had any idea what caused the immune suppression, although various theories abounded. As a result of their numerous sexual encounters, gay men had been treated for a wide variety of sexual diseases, including syphilis, hepatitis B, gonorrhea, and chlamydia. Perhaps the immune system, some theorized, had suffered an overload, with recurrent bouts of viral and parasitic infections leading to an exhaustion of its capacities. Gay men had been known to use the chemical amyl nitrate, also known as "poppers," to enhance sexual pleasure. (This drug dilates the blood vessels in the anal membrane, and induces a sense of euphoria, which may prolong orgasm.) Perhaps something in the amyl had turned deadly. Or perhaps a strain of another virus, herpes or cytomegalovirus (CMV), had mutated and turned lethal. Both were easily transmissible when seminal fluid made contact with the mucosal lining of the anus and intestinal tract of the passive partner in anal intercourse.

Throughout the Castro district, billboards started to go up warning gay men that a plague was under way and that certain sexual activities might prove highly risky. In subway stations and other public places, posters proclaimed slogans such as CONDOM SENSE and LIFE INSURANCE. They contained images of serious-looking gay men, resolutely encouraging their partners to heed the admonitory warnings. Although "safe sex" had not yet become an institutionalized concept, the rudiments of its law were already being formulated, even in the absence of the disease's exact cause. Yet an aura of denial and ignorance remained prevalent. "It couldn't possibly strike me," many gay men still reasoned.

I began using condoms and altering my behavior. On some level, though, like many others, I felt invincible, as though no harm could possibly come my way.

During my first two months in San Francisco, I interviewed at various film production companies and agencies throughout the city, finally landing a job as creative assistant at a midsized ad agency housed in a large tower on Market Street in the city's financial district. Every morning, I donned a three-piece suit, climbed aboard the subway, and rode downtown to my office.

It was a steady routine. But that routine was interrupted one morning in January 1983. I awoke short of breath. My sheets were drenched with sweat and I had a 100-degree fever. Lymph nodes were swollen like cherry tomatoes all over my body: beneath my arms, in my chest, on the sides of my neck, at the back of my head.

I went to the Castro Street Medical Center and saw Dr. Philip Rief. Without even examining me, he knew exactly what the symptoms meant; he had seen them time and time again in the last three years. It was he who revealed to me that GRID, from which I now probably suffered, had been given a new name: AIDS.

Rief did a complete physical exam, including a lymph-node examination, and ordered a specific battery of blood work, including a complete lymphocyte panel and tests for other viruses such as CMV and herpes. The lymphocyte panel was still considered an "experimental" test, but Rief had established contact with a lab that agreed to perform it.

As I walked down the corridor clutching a slip of paper with the word BIOHAZARD written on it, I felt a chill go through me.

"Having swollen lymph nodes—persistent generalized lymphadenopathy—is actually a good sign," Dr. Rief assured me coolly. "People with lymphadenopathy seem to avoid coming down with opportunistic infections for longer periods of time than those who don't," he revealed. "Get plenty of rest and keep your weight up," he advised.

That evening, I watched helplessly as Carl tried to make Jeffrey comfortable. Jeffrey had already been hospitalized with PCP; now he suffered from strange convulsions and tremors in his hands and legs. Toxoplasmosis—a fungal brain infection, the doctors at San Francisco General told Carl. There was nothing to be done. Carl held Jeffrey tightly, said comforting things, and tried to relieve the pain and suffering.

Three days later, Jeffrey died of complications from toxoplasmosis.

Up and down Castro Street, and throughout the neighborhood, gay men I knew were coming down with strange infections. Cryptococcal meningitis. *Mycobacterium Avium Intracellulare.* Increasing numbers of men began to die. And there was the business of that strange cancer . . . Kaposi's sarcoma, which had gotten a visceral grip on their internal organs. Dr. Rief often presided over the deaths of these early victims of AIDS.

●

I decided to visit the medical library at the University of California at San Francisco, where I began to read about the immune system. I learned that it consists of two basic components: the cell-mediated system, involving T lymphocytes and natural killer cells; and the humoral system, involving B lymphocytes and the antibodies they produce.

For both B cells and T cells, the path to maturity begins in the bone marrow, which produces pluriopotent stem cells—that is, cells with the power to develop or act in one or more possible ways, or to affect more than one organ or tissue in the body. These stem cells differentiate into both T lymphocyte precursor cells and B cells. B cells branch out of the stem cells and eventually come to maturity in the body itself. But T cells undergo further development in the thymus gland, an organ located behind the breastbone. The T lymphocyte precursor cells migrate from the bone marrow to the thymus. In the thymus, the surfaces of the T cells develop complex molecules called cell surface antigens or T cell receptors. Eventually, the T cells mature into one of three types of cells: "helper" or CD4 lymphocytes; "suppressor" or CD8 lymphocytes; and cytotoxic or killer T cells.

It is the number of CD4 cells that are deficient in AIDS. CD4 cells have the primary task of initiating an attack against a specific invading organism. When a CD4 cell detects the presence of an invader—in the form of an antigen that fits snugly into one of its receptors—it releases a chemical stored in its interior, called interleukin-2. This hormonelike substance transports messages from one white blood cell to another and assists in the recruitment of cells to destroy the invader.

The CD8, or suppressor T cells, have been referred to as the "brakes" of the immune system. These cells can determine that a virus or bacteria has been successfully attacked and, by secreting specific chemicals known as suppressor factors, ensure that the attack is halted at the appropriate time.

Cytotoxic or killer T cells directly kill cells that have been infected with invading viruses. They latch on to the cell and inject a chemical into the cell's surface, which makes the cell develop holes and die.

In the healthy immune system, each cubic millimeter of blood contains as many as 1,000 to 1,500 CD4 cells and 500 to 800 CD8 cells. In severe HIV infection, the CD4 cell counts can fall to zero, while the suppressor CD8 cell counts remain stable or become even more elevated. Ratios of CD4 to CD8 cells in AIDS can thus be as low as .01.

T lymphocytes reside throughout the body, mostly traveling alongside the blood vessels in a parallel circulatory system called lymph vessels, which carry only the white blood cells of the immune system. These lymph vessels are interconnected throughout the body by immune "stations" called lymph nodes, located in the groin, in the armpits, on the sides of the neck, in the back, in the upper arms, and in the abdominal cavity.

In AIDS and other infectious diseases, the lymph nodes may remain swollen for long periods at a time, as mine were—a sign that the immune system has become activated. AIDS patients with inadequate quantities of CD4 lymphocytes are unable to mount primary or even secondary immunological responses against the many microorganisms that are usually found in all humans but are prevented from causing a disease by a normally functioning immune system. Since a person with severe HIV infection has a diseased and helpless immune system, the AIDS patient dies from one or a series of such "opportunistic infections." Most opportunistic infections can be treated with various drugs with varying degrees of success. Ultimately, however, after one infection is treated, another one or a cancer rears its head weeks or months later.

While T lymphocytes can tackle viruses, parasites, and fungi with relative ease, they struggle with most bacteria. Nature therefore evolved a system capable of quickly dealing with invading bacteria. This humoral immune system involves B lymphocytes, also called B cells. In the human fetus, stem cells from the liver migrate into the bone marrow in a similar fashion to their movement into the thymus. In the bone marrow, certain cells become "educated" and marked as B lymphocytes.

B lymphocytes live for a few weeks at most, unlike T lymphocytes. Thus the bone marrow churns out B cells in great numbers every day. Each B cell has on its outer membrane almost half a million receptors for the specific antigen that it has been programmed to recognize. The B cells wait in the nearest lymph node for "their" antigen to come along. If it does, and becomes recognized by the receptor on the membrane surface, an immunological action will occur, but not before "permission" to attack the invading antigen is provided by the neighboring T lymphocytes.

A B cell can be ordered to attack bacteria or viruses by turning itself into a factory for producing and secreting antibodies. These antibodies—members of a class of proteins known as immunoglobulins—tag, destroy, or neutralize the harmful microorganisms. AIDS patients also show significant abnormalities in their B-cell function, including an inability to mount an adequate immunoglobulin M (IgM) response to antigenic challenge. This condition produces more severe problems in children, who have not had previous exposure to a variety of bacterial organisms and must rely on their initial IgM response to protect themselves against new pathogens.

Within days of my visit to the medical library, I visited Dr. Rief's office to learn the results of my blood tests or counts: my CD4 cell count was 350, percent of CD4 cells was 25, and CD4:CD8 ratio was 0.5.

"You have ARC, or AIDS-Related Complex. You're in the midrange of disease severity," Rief said. "That's where most of the people I see seem to be. Your immune system has been somewhat damaged but it hasn't been completely decimated. When the CD4 cells fall to below 100, it's time to be concerned about opportunistic infections. Even then, I have many patients who seem to go for long periods of time with very low lymphocytes. But all of them will probably develop an AIDS-related infection or Kaposi's sarcoma at some point."

"What's causing the loss of these helper cells?" I asked.

"We don't really know. Some kind of virus might be involved."

"Is there any treatment to bring the count up?" I asked him.

"There's a Dr. Robert Cathcart here in the city who is giving AIDS patients large intravenous doses of vitamin C, based on a protocol developed by Linus Pauling for cancer. And some doctors have tried using naltrexone and D-penicillamine, both approved in this country for other conditions. I haven't seen any improvement in patients who are taking these medications, however," he concluded. "How long do I have to live?" I asked him. "The information is limited," he responded. "I'd simply advise you to avoid stress, keep your weight up, and try to avoid any reexposure to the agent that could be causing this. That means *no* further passive anal intercourse without a condom. You also might be capable of transmitting whatever's causing this. It's probably best not to exchange your own bodily fluids, especially semen and blood. Understood?"

"Yes, Dr. Rief. And thank you."

At home, I contemplated the treatments Rief suggested. I could see why taking vitamin C might help: by neutralizing all unwanted free radicals and toxic oxidants, large doses of vitamin C might protect the immune system from whatever was causing its destruction. And naltrexone, I had learned, was an opiate antagonist used to treat opiate addiction. The drug increased serum levels of endorphin (a naturally occurring opiate in the central nervous system). This was significant because certain cells had opiate receptors that responded to endorphins. Perhaps naltrexone could stimulate the immune system and increase the CD4 cell count. Rief, however, seemed unimpressed with any of these treatments.

Later, I studied the surface of my tongue in the mirror, searching for the white patches of thrush that had troubled so many of my friends. I felt as though I was behaving like a child hypochondriac but the fear was based on something very real, very close. For the moment, though, my tongue remained unblemished.

That evening, I attended a community seminar on AIDS sponsored by the San Francisco–based Shanti Foundation. Shanti had been founded by entrepreneur Dr. Charles Garfield in 1974 to provide assistance and support to people facing life-threatening illnesses in the San Francisco Bay Area. The organization received national recognition in the 1970s for its ground-breaking work caring for the terminally ill. In 1981, when AIDS was still generally unknown, Shanti began providing volunteer-based emotional support to the first people diagnosed with the disease in the Bay Area. By 1982, when it became clear that the social needs created by the epidemic were outstripping available resources, Shanti turned its focus solely toward people with AIDS and their loved ones, providing one-on-one peer counseling, a wide variety of support groups, and comprehensive home care.

At the meeting I attended on March 1, 1983, several physicians and people with AIDS sat at a large conference table, answering questions from the audience. The discussion centered on suspected modes of transmission of the disease—probably through passive anal intercourse—and the need to use condoms and refrain from engaging in high-risk behavior. Mention was made of a DMSO (dimethylsulfoxide) treatment across the Mexican border, which one patient claimed had markedly improved his CD4 cell count. In addition to AIDS patients, there were a few young men who did not have symptoms of blood-count abnormalities; the "worried well" they were called. Another group seemed to romanticize death by AIDS, even revel in it. Overall, the tone was depressing and down-beat. There *was* a shared wave of understanding among many of those present that their behavior would have to change.

After the meeting, I returned to my apartment and sat on the steps of my building, studying the results of my blood tests and taking stock of my situation.

I was twenty-two years old, and I was being told that I suffered from a terminal illness for which there was no known cause or cure.

I was unprepared for the overwhelming fear and loneliness that suddenly came over me. I experienced a dreadful separation, as though I had become detached from the world. My growing sense of anxiety was punctuated by fast fits of denial and then replaced with a rising sense of alarm, which gradually gave way to numbness.

I was vaguely aware of the traffic outside, the noise of people returning in my apartment's corridor after a late evening at work, mailboxes opening, brief exchanges of words. It was all meaningless. I couldn't concentrate on anything but my feelings.

In addition to the fear and loneliness, there was a growing anger emanating from deep within me that blended into the other emotions I was experiencing and increased my confusion.

I knew I would have to find psychological resources that I had never called on before.

Within a few days, my fever and night sweats had completely disappeared, though my lymph nodes remained swollen.

• • •

The Centers for Disease Control (CDC) in Atlanta houses a massive bank of serum and tissue samples containing more than 250,000 specimens of registered pathologies. In fact, it provides a comprehensive record of *all* human indigenous diseases, from Asiatic cholera to Texas encephalitis. As its name implies, the CDC is charged with the task of monitoring and controlling the spread of epidemic disease in the United States. Since its inception four decades ago, it has been responsible for curbing the spread of such illnesses as measles and typhoid.

One month after the publication of Dr. Michael Gottlieb's article in the agency's own *Morbidity and Mortality Report* in July 1981, which detailed the first cases of five homosexual men diagnosed with unexplained *Pneumocystis* pneumonia, CDC Acting Deputy Director James Curran convened his staff. The mysterious disease AIDS was becoming more and more prevalent in the nation's largest cities. Curran was determined to learn how it was spread and what could possibly be causing it.

A team of epidemiologists, sociologists, computer statisticians, microbiologists, toxicologists, and venereal disease specialists decided it would be necessary to implement a "case control study" in which the behaviors, clinical profiles, and blood chemistries of a large number of victims of the disease would be compared against a healthy control sample. (Such a technique had enabled the CDC to discover the causal relationship between smoking and lung cancer, after all, and might reveal valuable clues about this new disease.) They further concluded that an important component of their methodology was the development of a questionnaire that could be submitted to both sick and healthy subjects, matched by certain demographic variables.

To start, Curran and his staff visited the cities where the disease seemed most prevalent: Los Angeles, New York, San Francisco, and Miami. They interviewed dozens of AIDS patients and in the process discovered that the majority of the affected men reported having had large numbers of sexual partners, often using amyl nitrate during sexual intercourse. The team also attempted to track down every case of Kaposi's sarcoma and PCP through telephone interviews with hospital administrators and physicians. On the basis of the preliminary information gathered in those early interviews, and using a methodology already in place for the screening of hepatitis B patients, Curran and his team developed an exhaustive questionnaire consisting of five hundred items.

It was dubbed Operation Protocol 577 and was one of the most ambitious epidemiological studies the CDC had ever conducted. The five hundred volunteers were referred by doctors and venereal disease experts at hospitals in the four cities in which the survey was conducted. The investigators also set up "headquarters" in hotels, where they performed physical exams and took blood and urine samples from the gay male subjects.

In December 1981, the field activities of Operation Protocol 577 concluded. The mass of data was fed into the CDC computers and a complex analysis performed. The researchers concluded that all the affected subjects had been more sexually active than the unaffected subjects and that the disease was probably sexually transmitted. The likely cause seemed to be a virus, perhaps transferred through semen and blood, that was capable of weakening the subjects' immune systems and hence allowing the cancers like KS and opportunistic infections to occur.

One evening I received a call from Jason Adams, an old high school friend. He revealed that since 1979 he, too, had experienced swollen lymph nodes and that he had recently participated in the Operation Protocol 577 study. Along with three dozen or so other subjects in Miami who had shown signs of immune deficiency for two years or longer, Jason had subjected himself to the physical exams and laborious questionnaires in an effort to help researchers discover more about the strange constellation of symptoms that had now become known as AIDS.

During one meeting at the CDC, according to Jason, the group was told that the cause of their mysterious illness was unknown and that researchers were not certain if patients represented a danger to others or even if other people posed a threat to their own health. They were advised to avoid large groups of people and to remain somewhat isolated.

Jason then explained that he and one other subject moved into a cabin in the Ocala National Forest, just outside Orlando, where they remained sequestered. He and his cohort maintained phone contact with a few of the subjects in the CDC study. Over time, Jason watched as one by one, the subjects succumbed to one infection after another. In March 1983, his friend died of PCP. Jason waited for his turn to come. It did not; throughout the entire period, he remained alive and apparently well. Clearly, there was something about his immune system that had enabled him to withstand the immune suppression also suffered by his peers.

"I feel great," he told me. "For whatever reason, I seem to have been spared."

"I seem to be holding my own as well," I told him.

The exact survival and mortality data had not yet been formulated and publicized. By 1987, researchers would establish that only one in ten people with full-blown AIDS would survive for three or more years, and only one out of thirty-three survivors five or more years. Furthermore, at least 66 percent of all people with ARC would progress to full-blown AIDS in eight years or less. The probability of progressing from ARC to AIDS in eighteen months was 58 percent for persons with total CD4 cell counts of 100 and 33 percent in eighteen months for persons with CD4 cell counts of 200.

Even without these figures, however—and the terms ARC and AIDS to go with them—I realized I had a disease that could instantly result in a life-threatening opportunistic infection or Kaposi's sarcoma. I no longer had the luxury of unlimited time. More than anything, I still passionately wanted a film career. I knew I would have to return to Los Angeles.

On June 15, 1983, I answered an ad in a trade publication announcing the opening of a position as Corporate and Marketing

Communications Manager for a large financial services organization. The job offered numerous benefits, including—most important
to me—flexible hours. After an interview, the company offered me
the position.

"Can you start immediately?" they asked.

CHAPTER 3

A KISS IS NOT JUST
A KISS

The temperature in Los Angeles had reached a record-high 104 degrees when I arrived on that oppressively hot and humid summer day. It was July 8, 1983. Despite my swollen lymph nodes I felt healthy and in no immediate distress.

John O'Malley now lived in the Bryson, an imposing apartment building on Wilshire Boulevard, just east of Hancock Park. It was one of the few original apartment buildings still standing along that stretch of Wilshire—in its day, one of the most elegant in central Los Angeles. Erected in 1890, the Bryson epitomized class and style in turn-of-the-century southern California. Originally, a famous industrialist had owned the place; it was later purchased by Fred MacMurray. In the 1930s, elegant garden parties, frequented by film and stage stars and fashion models, were held on its sprawling lawns. The building was just two blocks from the Vagabond, one of the oldest movie theaters in the city.

In recent years, the neighborhood had become populated by a mixture of yuppies, Mexican immigrants, art students, and elderly women, some of whom remembered the days when Jean Harlow and Fred Astaire walked from a premiere at the Vagabond to the Bryson for tea and publicity stills.

The Bryson stood proudly in all its faded grandeur, apparently unthreatened by the numerous business establishments crowding that stretch of Wilshire. I couldn't help but notice the air of grace and urbanity about it. As I walked up the long redbrick walkway in front of the building, I was confronted with a stunning view of two pairs of white marble columns framed by an archlike proscenium on which leonine gargoyles clutched a concrete sign bearing the building's black-and-white insignia. On the lawn, patches of marigolds and daffodils wove azure, red, and yellow patterns into the landscape. In the lobby, a massive crystal chandelier, a 1930s original, provided romantic illumination. Visitors were required to sign in at the front desk, just as they had in 1923. It was helmed by a large black woman named Martha, employed there for almost fifty years. She often recounted stories about the lavish Christmas balls to which the lobby had once played host, and the variety of famous guests who had frequented the place. A huge, ornate, mirror-paneled elevator, replete with an operator in uniform, carried residents to all nine floors. Because of its eerily authentic interior, the Bryson was often used as a location for feature films and television programs.

The top floor, where John lived in a two-bedroom suite, afforded a magnificent view of the city and the San Fernando mountains. An entrance foyer led into a spacious dressing room, living room, and kitchen. There was even a safe in the wall, one of the building's original accoutrements that had withstood the test of time and the challenge of renovation.

I moved down the hall from John, into a corner suite with a spectacular view of Silverlake and East Hollywood, and rekindled my intense friendship with him. We bonded in a profound and meaningful way, although we didn't always agree on day-to-day matters. There were significant philosophies and goals that made us tight and passionate friends, even inseparable at times. We had similar tastes in art and classical music. We shared a love of good literature. Above all, we passionately believed in the artistic potential of film.

John was now employed as a story analyst at CBS. We attended industry screenings together and frequently enjoyed silent-film retrospectives at the Vagabond. We went to the beach, sailed in Malibu, bowled, and took Saturday afternoon rides in Griffith Park and the Silverlake hills.

John was aware of my HIV status and consistently offered support and encouragement. "If you can just stay healthy for another five years, there's bound to be an effective maintenance therapy. In the meantime, don't let it consume you," he would say.

Within days of my arrival in Los Angeles, I started work at a large financial services organization downtown. During my orientation, I was afraid that my condition would be discovered as a result of the requisite physical examination that formed part of my reentry into the corporate world. After all, my lymph nodes were swollen and, although I seemed otherwise healthy, a detailed analysis of my basic blood chemistry would have revealed an abnormally low white count and slightly decreased platelet level. Nevertheless, I was waved through the physical without any problems.

As manager of corporate/marketing communications, I was responsible for supervising the production of a four-color employee magazine, wrote scripts for corporate training films and videotapes, and oversaw these projects' production. I worked in an office on the fifteenth floor of a skyscraper on Figueroa Street, a ten-minute ride from my apartment. I helped implement an internship program for young people interested in gaining experience in the world of corporate communications. Under my supervision, they researched and wrote stories, designed layouts, and participated in the creative and business aspects of magazine and corporate TV production. I felt certain that, had they learned about my HIV status, most of the people in my office would have been supportive. My reticence in openly revealing my HIV status stemmed less from a fear of reprisal or loss of benefits than from my conviction that my health was a private matter and not something to be widely discussed.

It would have seemed an ideal existence for someone else, but the notion of being a corporate clone remained unsatisfying for me. I yearned for the opportunity to work as a producer of feature films.

I befriended the entertainment editor of the now-defunct Los Angeles *Herald-Examiner*, a man who often lunched at the same downtown eatery as I. He was impressed with my knowledge of international film and encouraged me to contribute free-lance reviews to the *Herald-Examiner*'s entertainment section. Many of these also appeared in the New York *Native*. I renewed some of my prior contacts and occasionally did free-lance story editing for a variety of independent production companies. And I began work on a screenplay with John.

I avoided sex almost completely during this period of my life. It wasn't only that sex had the capacity to be creatively enervating; I also wanted to protect myself *and* my partners. At the time, no one was exactly sure how AIDS was transmitted, but some researchers had come to realize that it was through the exchange of bodily fluids—semen, blood, urine, vaginal secretions, perhaps even saliva. The Southern California Physicians for Human Rights and other groups established "safe sex" guidelines and disseminated these throughout the gay community. The guidelines warned against anal intercourse without a condom and oral intercourse—thought to be possibly unsafe for the recipient, since the mouth, throat, and gums often contained small cuts that could provide direct exposure of the bloodstream to semen and pre-ejaculate fluid. The guidelines encouraged the use of more creative sex, including "frottage, mutual masturbation, and tit play." It was not even certain that the agent of infection could not be spread through kissing. But even if it was not transmissible through saliva, a number of other agents *were*—including hepatitis B and mononucleosis, which could wreak havoc in an already depressed immune system and even be catalysts for the perpetuation and activation of whatever it was that caused AIDS.

A rising awareness began to take place in the gay community about the ways in which AIDS might be transmitted, and a rapid shift in behavior quickly followed. By January 1984, it was apparent that gay men, at least in New York, Los Angeles, and San Francisco, had modified their sexual practices. Health Department statistics from those cities showed that the rates of rectal gonorrhea had plummeted, a signal that unsafe anal intercourse had been almost completely phased out of the sexual repertoire. Moreover, the rate of other sexually transmitted diseases such as chlamydia and hepatitis B had also fallen sharply. A small faction of my gay acquaintances continued to indulge in their old ways, oblivious to the danger at hand. They continued to frequent the bastions of anonymous sex— the bathhouses. Many politicians in California believed that these places held the potential to greatly contribute to the spread of AIDS since unsafe sex was often practiced there. Even with intense campaigns on the part of gay community leaders to stem the spread of the disease, the high-risk behavior in the baths went on.

On October 9, 1984, San Francisco Health Department Chairman Mervyn Silverman succeeded in ordering the closure of the bathhouses in the city. Those in New York and Los Angeles, however, remained open. Critics of the ordinance cited gay men's behavior as the real problem, not the institutions that provided a haven for it. They argued that closure of the gay baths would merely force gay men to move their activities elsewhere—public parks and the Folsom Street warehouses, for example. "Out of the baths and into the bushes," they claimed. Opponents of the closings also argued that the baths could become forums for educating the public about safe sex.

These groups argued for funding directed toward massive educational campaigns, even "safe sex" workshops to be taught in the baths themselves. The techniques used to promote safe sex were both creative and disarming. The workshops were reinforced by pamphlets that made concretely clear which sexual practices were considered safe, which were risky, and which were definitely unsafe. The pamphlets also contained condoms, which were distributed free of charge to patrons. As Dennis Altman noted in *Aids in the Mind of America,* "The central dilemma that faced gay men as the epidemic spread was how to develop safe sex without feeding the traditional moralism that condemns both homosexuality and sex outside a committed relationship and so easily feeds into the heightened homophobia unleashed by AIDS."

In 1980, Dr. Robert Gallo showed that a human retrovirus could cause leukemia in humans. It was the first time that any virus had been linked to a cancer and the first time that the presence of a retrovirus had been definitely established in humans. His discovery of the first HTLV, a retrovirus, won him the prestigious Lasker Award. By the early 1980s he was considered one of the nation's foremost retrovirologists.

On April 23, 1984, I watched a television newscast in which U.S. Secretary of Health and Human Services Margaret Heckler announced, "Professor Robert Gallo and his team have discovered a new virus, HTLV-III, and furnished proof that it is the cause of AIDS." Gallo had been a fading star in the National Cancer Institute in the 1970s. But his career took a turn in 1980, when he showed that a human retrovirus could cause leukemia in humans. It was the first time any virus had been linked to a cancer and the first time that the presence of a retrovirus had been definitely established in humans. His discovery of the first HTLV, a retrovirus, won him the prestigious Lasker Award. By the early 1980s he was considered one of the nation's foremost retrovirologists.

Clearly Heckler's announcement was timed politically: it provided support for Ronald Reagan and proof that dollars allocated to AIDS research were working. Heckler also asserted during her news conference that government researchers would, within seven months, develop a test to eliminate all risk of contamination of the blood supplies used for transfusions. She went on to make the unlikely prediction that within a year or two, a vaccine would be widely available.

Yet two days prior to Heckler's announcement, the Centers for Disease Control in Atlanta attributed the discovery of HTLV-III to a team of French scientists led by Dr. Luc Montagnier. In her announcement, Heckler made only a vague reference to Montagnier: "Other research scientists in the world have achieved results in this field, particularly the efforts of the Pasteur Institute in France, who have worked with the NCI."

Montagnier, Director of Virology at the Pasteur and one of the world's foremost retrovirologists, announced the discovery of his own HTLV retrovirus in 1984 after a considerable exchange of information and biological samples between his own and Gallo's labs. Because of the striking similarity in viruses, Montagnier now charged that Gallo had purposefully or inadvertently claimed credit for discovering the HTLV-III virus the Pasteur team had isolated years earlier and had sent to the United States for further analysis. Gallo, for his part, insisted that his virus came from the blood of an American AIDS patient.

When Montagnier heard Heckler's announcement in Washington, he could not control his anger. "From the point of view of scientific ethics, the official announcement of this discovery was highly questionable. Having received the samples of our retrovirus, the American scientist should have compared the one he had just found with ours and published himself the comparison, in just the same way that we had compared it with his HTLV-I retrovirus." His indignation was intensified by Heckler's announcement that U.S. government lawyers were applying for a patent for Gallo's own test for the virus. This action would bar the ELISA (Enzyme Linked Immunosorbent Assay, or, HIV antibody) test, which the French had also developed one year earlier, from the American market. In order for the French to vindicate themselves and ultimately win the rights to the test, Montagnier knew they would be forced to take the U.S. government to court.

In 1985, the Pasteur Institute and Montagnier did sue the U.S. government, claiming the HTLV-III and its own virus, which it had renamed Lymphadenopathy Associated Virus (LAV), were the same, giving the French the right to the patent. The dispute was settled out of court in 1987 with an agreement allowing America and France to share royalties, but without determining whether HTLV-III and LAV were the same.

In the months following Heckler's announcement, other events seemed to confirm Montagnier's impression that the virus had been stolen. In the May 4, 1984, issue of *Science,* Gallo published several articles on the HTLV-III retrovirus accompanied by impressive pictures of HTLV-III in various stages of development. Two years later Gallo conceded that the articles published under his name did not, under any circumstances, show his virus, but were illustrative of the French scientist's LAV. And Montagnier later learned that Gallo had amended an official conference report, adding an introductory passage describing the HTLV-III retrovirus as if it had been discovered earlier. Montagnier wrote, "In defiance of all the rules of scientific ethics, Robert Gallo rewrote history to suit himself."

Yet while the French may have first discovered the virus, there was no question that it was the Americans who first determined the exact genetic code of the virus. In order to actually decipher that code, a sophisticated process of cloning and sequencing was required, which ultimately revealed an exact chain of nucleotides. In the months following Heckler's announcement, both French and American laboratories became engaged in a frantic race to determine those exact sequences. Ultimately, the American researcher Flossie Wong Staal beat the French by several weeks, publishing in the January 21, 1985, edition of the journal *Cell* an article that described the precise chain of 9,139 nucleotides that comprised HTLV-III.

Nonetheless, despite this apparent victory, most scientists would later agree that it was the French who first discovered the cause of AIDS.

Regardless of who first discovered it, the isolation of HTLV-III brought to light some preliminary conclusions about the modes of action the virus used to decimate the CD4 lymphocyte population.

Both Gallo and Montagnier knew that retroviruses such as

HTLV-III were composed of RNA—genetic material similar to DNA in the nucleus of normal cells. The scientists discovered that HTLV-III's outer envelope, its gp120, contained knoblike projections that were mirror images of the CD4 receptor on the T lymphocyte. This perfect fit allows the virus to bind to the surface of the lymphocyte.

After binding, the virus is then internalized and uncoated. Once internalized, the virus's RNA is transcribed to DNA by its enzyme reverse transcriptase. This proviral DNA, which can exist in a linear or circular form, becomes integrated into the lymphocyte's chromosomal DNA. A large amount of unintegrated viral DNA accumulates in the infected cells and leads to cell death.

After integration of the provirus, the infection may assume a latent phase until the cells are activated by some other bacteria or virus. Once activated, the proviral DNA transcribes viral DNA and messenger RNA, creating mature viruses. The mature viruses bud from the cell's surface, find another cell for entry, and the entire cycle repeats itself in another cell.

In essence, the virus seemed to have the capability of invading the genetic program locked up in the cell's nucleus, taking command or hijacking the program, and—with viral genetic materials—instructing the cell to use cellular raw materials to produce more virus.

But the HTLV-III retrovirus has other, even more destructive ways of perpetuating itself. Infected CD4 cells express numerous gp120 molecules, which have a high affinity for the CD4 receptor on healthy CD4 cells. Many uninfected CD4 cells can thus bind to the infected cell and merge with it. The resulting aggregate of cells, known as syncytia, is not a functional CD4 cell and is disposed of by the scavenging systems of the body. In this process, the original infected cell, as well as many healthy cells, die.

Macrophages, another type of white blood cells, can also be infected—but not killed—by HTLV-III. They can serve as long-term reservoirs for HIV infection and can also serve to transport the virus to various organs in the body, such as the lungs and the brain.

Macrophages do not have a CD4 surface receptor like lymphocytes, but HTLV-III is able to bind to a specific receptor on the macrophage, enter it, and sequester itself inside.

Lastly, in an insidious process, certain CD4 cells that express the HTLV-III gp120 envelope on their surface can be recognized as foreign by other healthy cells in the body and destroyed.

Thus researchers believed that through a variety of mechanisms HTLV-III was capable of crippling the immune system by systematically killing off the single most crucial element in its armory: the CD4 lymphocyte. A healthy person has 200 billion to 300 billion CD4 cells circulating in the body. Enormous as that number is, at least one immunological theory suggests that adults are incapable of producing any more.

Slowly but surely, the HTLV-III virus starts to destroy the CD4 cells in the blood. From having 1,000 or more CD4 cells in every cubic millimeter of blood, gradually there may be none left as the virus continues to replicate. This scenario does not occur overnight; it can take years. In some cases, the virus can lie dormant and cease replication, becoming activated later on by other viral infections, such as hepatitis B or herpes simplex type II.

Once the CD4 cells fall to a level of less than 50 per cubic millimeter, the risk of opportunistic infection or neoplasm increases exponentially. It is not the HTLV-III that actually kills the person with AIDS; it is, rather, the damaged immune system and the various infections and neoplasms that have taken advantage of a defenseless body.

Some people can remain healthy for years with only a moderately diminished CD4 cell count, their immune systems having apparently reached some form of equilibrium with the virus. It is almost as if the virus has run out of steam or entered a period of prolonged latency, allowing some CD4 cells to survive. To some extent, I had been one of those people. My CD4 cell count was 300 and appeared to be stable.

I also knew that an increasing number of patients with ARC, lymphadenopathy, or even no symptoms at all slipped into full-blown AIDS and life-threatening opportunistic infections. Studies had shown that up to two-thirds would progress from ARC to AIDS after eight years with the virus. I realized I could easily be one of them.

Still, the presence of lymphadenopathy itself was a good sign; patients with swollen lymph nodes and stable CD4 cell counts had tended to stay healthier longer than those without lymphadenopathy and fluctuating counts.

I also realized that the discovery of HTLV-III and a new understanding of how the virus causes AIDS allowed researchers to search for antiviral drugs intelligently, using laboratory tests containing live virus and lymphocytes. An understanding of such processes as reverse transcriptase and protease production permitted the evaluation of compounds with the potential of stopping the virus at various stages of its replication. Researchers across the globe were screening compounds for potential anti-HTLV-III activity. In August 1983, Congressman Ted Weiss's Subcommittee on Intergovernmental Relations and Human Resources had succeeded in increasing the federal budget for AIDS research from $17.6 million to $39 million. In short, there was every reason to have hope.

By April 1984, nearly thirteen hundred Americans had been diagnosed with AIDS. Two months later, the figure would rise to more than sixteen hundred. The disease had clearly become a full-blown epidemic, yet surprisingly little media attention was focused on it. Reporters and news producers seemed uncomfortable with dealing with a "gay" disease that might be spread through acts such as anal intercourse. Most newspapers relegated their stories on AIDS to the back of the news section. Television news broadcasts avoided the topic altogether.

Ironically, among the first groups in the media to pay close attention to AIDS were television evangelists. They reflected the attitude of a rising number of religious leaders across the country who contended that AIDS was God's way of incurring wrath upon homosexuals—a timely and just punishment for a promiscuous and immoral life-style. Jerry Falwell, for example, advocated not only closing bathhouses and backroom bars but punishing gay men who donated blood. A 1983 edition of the *700 Club* featured Pat Robertson, its publisher, condemning male homosexuals and asserting that through the modern-day plague God had finally found the means by which to force a change in that life-style.

It became obvious that these religious leaders wanted to use AIDS as an object lesson in morality. They wanted to bring as many people with a fundamentalist mentality as possible into their camp, securing money for their cause, convincing politicians of the value of their ideas, and moving the American public further to the right in the process. It was not difficult for Americans to adopt this belief. Gay men, after all, appeared generally to have greater discretionary incomes, to exercise few family or community responsibilities, and to be frivolous and hedonistic. In truth, a segment of the gay population *was* promiscuous and *did* engage in frequent anonymous sexual encounters. But many heterosexuals were equally promiscuous.

It was indeed possible that HIV spread first and fastest among gay men because it may have been unwittingly placed in their midst. In 1979 and 1980, large numbers of them had received injections of the hepatitis B vaccine as a prophylaxis against what was then the most serious disease among gays. The vaccine was derived from the serum of healthy gay male blood donors with a high concentration of antibodies against hepatitis B. Ultimately, some of the serum may have also contained HTLV-III antibodies—and antigens.

Exactly how the virus got into the blood of the "index" cases, who provided serum for the hepatitis B vaccine, is not known. Speculation abounded. Some theorized that American gay men visiting Haiti in the 1970s often had unprotected anal intercourse there with prostitutes who, as part of a tribal ritual, had been injected with blood from animals, and thus contracted the virus and spread it into the New York gay community.

Certainly, isolated cases of AIDS were documented as early as the Kennedy era. One report in *Lancet* speculated that a case treated in 1960 could have been one of AIDS. Physicians labeled the man's death—now thought to have been caused by PCP—as a freak and unexplained pneumonia. In 1965, a Ugandan man was infected with the virus (frozen samples of his serum confirmed this in 1981). And it is widely believed that an animal retrovirus in 1950s Africa entered the bodies of some already malnourished young African men unable to eliminate it with the ease with which they could have if their immune systems had been intact. According to Robert Gallo, the earliest report may have been that of a Norwegian sailor who developed an AIDS-like disease in the late 1950s after a visit to a central east African coastal city. Specimens from him were available and later tested positive for HTLV-III.

By October 1984, I began to realize the seriousness of my condition. My CD4 cell count hovered precariously around 300 and my CD4:CD8 ratio was down to 0.3. I knew that once the absolute CD4 cell count fell below 100, the chance for opportunistic infections to occur became more likely.

An underground network of AIDS patients and hand-printed newsletters was springing up across the country. I learned from one of them that there existed a handful of experimental drugs, antiviral and immunomodulatory agents not yet approved in the United States, that might be helpful in deterring HTLV-III and rebuilding the ravaged immune system. Two of the most popular were ribavirin and isoprinosine.

Ribavirin is an antiviral drug used in Europe and Mexico to treat a broad spectrum of viral diseases, including the respiratory syncytia virus, which causes a lung disease in infants. Early in 1984, researchers found that ribavirin inhibited replication of HTLV-III, in part by halting the process of reverse transcriptase. The drug appeared to be safe when given orally for other viral diseases, although it did cause slight anemia.

Isoprinosine was also a synthetic molecular complex, formed from inosine, a white crystalline powder. Since the early 1970s researchers had reported the drug to have a variety of restorative benefits in viral diseases and in cancer. Apparently, the drug enhanced lymphocyte growth and proliferation, natural-killer-cell activity, and gamma-interferon production. Except for slight increases in uric acid levels and the remote possibility of causing gout, isoprinosine appeared even safer than ribavirin. At least one study showed that ribavirin inhibited replication of HTLV-III in the test tube.

Through a fact sheet that I received from a friend, I learned that a small group of AIDS patients were taking the two drugs in tandem while being monitored by their private physicians for any signs of toxicity. The fact sheet pointed out the antiviral/immunomodulatory strategy of combining the two drugs. While ribavirin thwarted HTLV-III's replication, the author of the fact sheet speculated, isoprinosine would make new CD4 cells. Thus, a cure for ARC or AIDS could be effected.

The protocol fact sheet suggested using ribavirin *intermittently* while continuing isoprinosine for the entire six-month period. Ribavirin had the potential to sequester itself in red cells and produce anemia; it was designed to combat short-term viral illnesses, like an antibiotic. Taking it on an intermittent basis might avoid toxic buildup.

The fact sheet specified that the drugs were not available in the United States; neither had yet to receive approval from the Food and Drug Administration (FDA). However, both were available in pharmacies in Mexico, and the fact sheet went on to give the names of two or three such pharmacies in Tijuana and the price of the drugs in dollars, and instructions for smuggling them across the border. "Customs has been instructed to hassle anyone bringing in significant quantities of these drugs," the fact sheet warned. "Be prepared and work out, in advance of your trip, a scheme for transporting the drugs successfully across the border." No further advice was given on how to achieve this objective.

On October 20, 1984, I convinced John O'Malley to accompany me across the border and smuggle in the drugs. We left early that Saturday morning, pulling out of the Bryson parking lot in my car before dawn. We had dressed in jeans and T-shirts emblazoned with the Greek letters of a popular USC fraternity house, trying to appear as inconspicuous as possible, playing the role of uninvolved tourists. All the way down to the Mexican border, John and I did everything possible to keep our minds off the task at hand; we were both nervous, and although we had planned our course of action carefully, there was always the potential that something could go wrong.

As we arrived in Tijuana at ten-thirty a.m., I was confronted with a minor culture shock. The city seemed to me to be disorganized and poorly marked. We nearly careened into a passing vehicle at one point. Finally we pulled into a parking structure not far from the center of town and made our way on foot through the city streets.

The poverty was hidden and yet everywhere. The people here seemed intensely unhappy and displayed the kind of despair one did not see in the barrios of Los Angeles. Barefoot children approached and asked us for change at almost every corner. We passed through numerous open-air markets and bazaars, where vendors peddled everything from handmade jewelry to fresh fruit, with brightly colored piñatas prominently displayed. I purchased one, along with some gold cuff links from a vendor who seemed especially happy to have my business. As we walked through the market, vendors accosted us verbally and made dramatic gestures, hoping we would inspect their wares.

Finally, we arrived at the intersection of First and Revolution streets, where the major Tijuana pharmacy was located—the Regis Farmacia. Compared to the rest of the city buildings, the pharmacy was remarkably modern and clean. It had a high-tech look, a neon sign in the window, and a huge staircase leading to a second floor.

I perused the shelves of the apothecary and noticed a panoply of drugs for sale not available in the United States. Within seconds, I had found the boxes of ribavirin (packaged under its trade name Vilona) and isoprinosine. The price, marked in both American dollars and Mexican pesos, was higher than that quoted on the fact sheet: five dollars for a box of twelve 200-milligram ribavirin tablets and three dollars for a box of twenty 500-milligram isoprinosine tablets. Word had traveled fast in the underground; many AIDS patients had already made the journey. Many more would follow in the months to come, and the price would climb even higher.

I quickly performed some mental calculations and figured exactly how many pills of each drug I would need for a two-month supply. To satisfy the recommended dose of 1,200 milligrams a day of ribavirin and 2,500 milligrams a day of isoprinosine, I needed forty boxes of ribavirin and about twenty boxes of isoprinosine. I cleared the shelf of all the boxes and brought them to the front counter.

I had also promised two other ARC patients in Los Angeles that I would purchase the drug for them. This meant I would need an additional eighty boxes of ribavirin and forty of isoprinosine.

"Do you have any more?" I asked the young lady at the cash register, an attractive woman in her early twenties.

"We just received new shipment in this morning," she said in surprisingly good English. From the look in her eyes, I was certain she knew full well the true value of the medication and my obvious need for it. Within seconds, she had returned with the extra boxes I needed. I paid her $360.

John and I left the pharmacy and began the most difficult part of our mission.

I lay flat in the backseat of my car. While John spotted outside, I carefully and methodically removed each blue-and-white ribavirin capsule and each white isoprinosine tablet. I placed the ribavirin tablets in a large vial and then transferred this to the inside of the piñata. I also removed the isoprinosine, which looked like large American aspirin, from its packaging, and transferred it to an empty container that had once held prescription aspirin, a medication I had been given by my doctor in Los Angeles. I placed this container in the glove compartment. Even if it was discovered, I reasoned, no one would suspect I had exchanged the tablets. I hoped the border guards were not familiar with the color and shape of the experimental anti-AIDS drugs.

With John in the driver's seat, we maneuvered out of the cramped parking structure and back onto the streets of Tijuana. It was one p.m.

It seemed the line of cars waiting to cross the border that afternoon was interminable. We inched along for over an hour before advancing to the crossing booths. As we waited, Mexican children approached our vehicle, offering to sell us various wares and even to wash our car. I felt my pulse quicken as we approached the booths. At the entrance to the border, perched high above the booths, I could see a building with a glass panel, behind which federal agents worked and watched. I tried to stay calm. John was nervous too but maintained his composure like an expert smuggler.

The customs official who greeted us looked at each of us squarely in the eye. "Any liquor in that piñata, boys?"

Liquor! Of course. What else would two young fraternity boys crossing the border be smuggling?

"No," I said, laughing. "No liquor."

There was a slight pause as the agent pondered the possibility of actually checking the inside of the piñata and seeing for herself.

She thought better of it and said quickly, "All right then, drive on through."

I heaved a sigh of relief, then shot a conspiratorial glance toward John. Well into San Diego, I clutched the bottles of the precious medications I had so avidly pursued. We ate at a restaurant in Chula Vista to celebrate our private victory and then returned to Los Angeles before nightfall.

I began taking the drugs that evening and continued to do so for the next six months. I didn't notice any obvious reaction or negative side effect at any time. I was monitored by Dr. Claud Gravel, a doctor who had treated many AIDS patients and had agreed to monitor patients who were taking the two drugs. After the first three months, there was no change in my CD4 cell count. Although ribavirin would continue to produce contradictory results in clinical trials, the efficacy of isoprinosine in HTLV-III infection was later found to be limited.

By January 1985, AIDS had started to become something of a media hit. With the announcement of the discovery of HTLV-III and the mounting number of people infected, the American media began to regard the AIDS crisis as a story of emerging national importance and no longer relegated its coverage to the back pages. Nevertheless, it was not until the announcement of Rock Hudson's death the following October that AIDS would attain irrevocable legitimacy in the minds of the American public.

The first international AIDS conference took place in Atlanta in April 1985. Margaret Heckler announced that the disease was a growing threat to the American population and that the Reagan administration planned to battle the disease on many fronts. Of course, it was a lie. But most Americans hadn't yet been personally affected by AIDS, so the threat still seemed remote. At that stage, there was no reason for the government to remain true to its words.

It was Dr. Anthony Fauci, chairman of the National Institute of Allergy and Infectious Diseases (NIAID) who had become the controversial point man in the war on AIDS. Fauci obtained his M.D. from Cornell University in 1966, finishing his internship and residency there as well. He joined the Commissioned Corps of the Public Health Service as a clinical associate at NIAID, became its deputy director in 1977, and in 1985 became the Chief of AIDS Research for the National Institutes of Health (NIH).

Fauci convinced Dr. Vincent DeVita, chairman of the National Cancer Institute, to allow NIAID to run Phase 2 expanded clinical trials of promising drugs. DeVita had argued that NCI was the more logical place to perform the tests, since it had been running clinical trials of cancer drugs for almost two decades. Fauci argued successfully that AIDS was an infectious disease caused by a virus, not cancer, and that it was the institute he headed that should run the trials and be funded appropriately. Fauci set up a deal in which

DeVita's NCI would continue to screen drugs for possible effectiveness against HTLV-III in the test tube and would also supervise small Phase 1 trials of the drug's toxicity and basic effectiveness in humans. Fauci's NIAID would step in to perform larger, multisite Phase 2 studies.

Certain activist factions disapproved of Fauci from the start. They accused him of being too much the public-relations man, not enough the scientist, even of being an incompetent administrator. They later argued Fauci didn't do enough during key points of the epidemic, that he "grandstanded" findings in the press, had not delegated work adequately, and had not made his financial and staffing needs known to other executives and government officials. In a famous editorial, activist and playwright Larry Kramer actually called Fauci a murderer for his apparent complacency and managerial incompetence.

Fauci told *People* magazine in 1991: "No matter what you decide on, there will be people who praise you and those who will go so far as to call you a murderer. The saving grace is that, fundamentally, I am a scientist and science is the thing that is immutable. Do the science correctly and ultimately you will be doing good for people."

Activists argued that in fact Fauci did not "do the science correctly." They felt that AZT (azidothymidine), for example, had been studied to the exclusion of other promising agents and that the studies of it were, in their view, fatally flawed.

In the spring of 1985, I joined a support group sponsored by the Los Angeles Shanti Foundation. The group was led by Stuart Kelly, a gay man who was not HIV-positive himself. He had lost a lover to AIDS and had known many people who had succumbed to the disease, including a longtime companion. Organizing the group enabled Stuart to fight the disease in a profound way on the front lines, by trying to ease the suffering of those now affected by AIDS.

Stuart was a student in counseling at UCLA and had acquired

extensive experience in facilitating AIDS counseling groups. He knew instinctively when to be confrontational and when to offer unconditional support. He understood how to guide the discussion so that members of the group felt safe enough to express even their most frightening feelings. He inspired remarkable insight and served as a catalyst for members who wanted to change aspects of their behavior or personality at a point in their lives when change seemed unlikely.

At least six of us gathered regularly on Tuesday evenings at Stuart's West Hollywood apartment. Kevin Price was forty-two, a prominent record producer in Los Angeles and a "golden boy" in the southern California gay community of the 1960s. He had been stunningly handsome in his youth and his face had graced the cover of numerous fashion magazines. He wore expensive shirts and designer jeans to the group. The walls of his posh Hollywood Hills bungalow were covered with the gold records he had produced. He often traveled to Europe and still enjoyed the chic Los Angeles nightlife. He was diagnosed with AIDS in 1983. Recently he had suffered from an intractable colonic cytomegalovirus infection; his doctor had informed him that he had "one year, at best." Kevin was sardonic and cynical. He frequently made bitter comments that cut to the core of a conflict and in so doing sometimes forced the other members of the group to confront the tragic reality of their condition. Yet he also had an engaging sense of humor and, in his own way, was as much a catalyst for change as Stuart.

Craig Loders was a thirty-two-year-old gay real estate executive. He had early ARC, was basically asymptomatic, and lived alone in a Long Beach apartment. He had a cheerful, optimistic outlook that occasionally bordered on the saccharine. Some of us resented his bubbly, even cavalier demeanor almost as much as we did his relative good health. Our displeasure went deeper than mere envy, however: we viewed his sanguine, even unrealistic attitude as a disguised denial, a denial that interfered with his ability to experience the full range of emotions associated with having HIV.

Mark Waters was a traveling computer-parts salesman who had been diagnosed with PCP two years earlier. He was forty-four and had plain features and a bushy mustache. He dressed in low-key cardigan sweaters and jeans. He told us how he had participated in sadomasochistic sexual behavior with many lovers in countless cities across the country. He felt certain he had spread HIV to many of these people. He told us that he had typed a letter to each man about whom he had information, explaining that he had recently been diagnosed with AIDS and that if they hadn't already been tested, they should.

Michael Bristow was a pre-law student at UCLA, twenty-four, and bisexual. Like Craig and me, he had been diagnosed with ARC and, except for swollen lymph nodes, was asymptomatic. One of Michael's all-consuming issues was his anger and resentment toward his parents. They had not been supportive when he admitted that he was both gay and HIV-positive. Throughout his life, Michael revealed, his parents had been selfish and had never made any attempt to identify with his needs or goals. Michael's mood was by far the darkest in the group. He was extraordinarily intelligent, and he seemed introverted at times and often spoke of suicide.

Bob Gramley was fifty-five. Although he was gay, he had contracted HIV not from unsafe sex but rather from a dirty needle during a period of intravenous drug use in the early 1980s. He had been a nurse in a large Los Angeles hospital and remembered the days when he could steal methadone tablets from the pharmacy to control his heroin habit. CMV had robbed him of his sight in one eye, and he had suffered bouts of cryptococcol meningitis and toxoplasmosis, in addition to PCP. He walked with a cane and spoke in a hoarse whisper. His steps were slow and measured, but there was undeniable pride and dignity in his gait as well. Kaposi's sarcoma lesions mottled his face. His lover of ten years had recently died of AIDS. One of Bob's most pressing dilemmas was the guilt involved in the unfinished business in his relationship.

What follows is an excerpt describing a session at Stuart's. The date was April 2, 1985. (The session has been transcribed from a tape. However, the dialogue has been condensed and, in some cases, slightly altered for the purposes of publication.)

CRAIG: I heard that HPA-23 was going into Phase 1 trials in the United States.

KEVIN: So? It doesn't work. I saw Rock Hudson at the Pasteur the last time I went. He looked bad. And the rumor among all the subjects in the French study is that the drug isn't producing any long-term effect.

BOB: Rock Hudson has AIDS?

KEVIN: You heard it here first, folks.

BOB: What about those drugs from Mexico I heard about the other day?

PAUL: Ribavirin and isoprinosine. I got them several months ago. Neither seemed to up my CD4 cells at all.

MICHAEL: There's nothing at all out there. They just discovered the virus, and it'll probably take another five or six years to find the cure.

BOB: I don't *have* five or six years.

MARK: Few of us do. And to think this was all because we enjoyed sex.

KEVIN: We all did. To some extent, we were *all* promiscuous.

CRAIG: I knew one guy who was more promiscuous than anyone in this room and he still hasn't tested positive.

PAUL: You know, Kevin, they say "It's not the hundred, it's the *hundredth* that killeth." (Pause) Still, I don't want to believe that at some point in my life I did something wrong, that I got caught and am now being punished for it.

MARK: In my case, getting AIDS seemed unavoidable. I realize on some level that I always enjoyed playing on dangerous ground.

Even when I was aware of what I was doing, I found it hard to stop.

BOB: I *didn't* get it from sexual contact. I didn't even have sex with another man till I was forty-five. And that man was Jeff. I got it from a dirty needle in a shooting gallery in [the] Silverlake [section of Los Angeles]. Jeff begged me not to go that night, you know. Isn't it funny? (Pause) I feel so guilty about selling his record-and-tape collection. But there was no room for them in the new apartment.

MICHAEL: You could have put them up for auction and donated the proceeds to AIDS in his name ... or you could have given them to a collector who might especially value them the way Jeff did.

BOB: That's true. But they had become such a painful reminder. All I wanted to do was to get rid of them. To erase the pain. I gave all his clothes to the Salvation Army. (He begins sobbing.) I feel so guilty about taking the trip to Greece. He died two days before I returned. I wasn't even there to hold his hand or comfort him. He must have felt so abandoned.

CRAIG: You agonized over that trip for *months* before you finally went. You wanted to get away from the stress of having to care for Jeff. It seemed like the right thing to do at the time, and it was. You couldn't possibly have known Jeff was going to die before you returned.

STUART: Don't try to suppress the guilt you feel. It's O.K. to feel that. We all realize you wanted to be there in the end for him. It must have been a terrible disappointment when you weren't able to help him. I understand that you may feel guilty that you got away, perhaps even escaped from the stress his deteriorating condition also caused. But you needed that escape. You needed to do that for *you*.

BOB: I know. But there was so much I hadn't told him. So much I wanted to say—but didn't.

STUART: All right, I'm going to play Jeff. I want you to see me as your former lover. I want you to tell me, right now, everything you didn't tell him. Speak to me as though I am Jeff.

BOB: (After a pause) "I'm sorry I wasted so much of my life with heroin. In the hospital that time, I dragged my IV pole across the street. My lover John pushed a syringe of heroin into my pentam bag. I'm sorry I caused you so much pain in those moments. I feel so guilty about those fights we had over the drugs. I love you more than anything. I just want you to know that."

STUART: (Playing Jeff) "I know what you felt for me. And you have to realize that I loved you unconditionally. More than anything in the world. You can be secure in that." (A long silence)

STUART: Do you feel complete with that, Bob?

BOB: Yes.

MICHAEL: I certainly won't feel guilty when my lover dies. He claimed he was completely monogamous the whole time we were together. Then I found the bath card in his wallet. He admitted he had gone often and that he had contracted the virus. All that time he didn't even tell me. That sonofabitch. I gave him so much of myself. I surrendered so much. I really don't want to be with him now.

MARK: At least you had a lover. At least you knew intimacy. I never did.

STUART: Why do you say that?

MARK: My lovers were, for the most part, all men I met on the road. Some of them did develop into something special. But I would never describe those relationships as *intimate*. I suppose I was afraid of becoming intimate.

STUART: Why?

MARK: I was afraid of making myself vulnerable. Afraid of reciprocating affection, afraid of being hurt or abandoned. I can remember, as a child, being afraid of the dark and sleeping with my mom until I was eight years old. She provided a security. Then at summer camp I found a counselor who let me sleep with him. No one ever knew—nothing sexual ever happened between us—but I remember feeling so good and secure in his masculinity. I was looking for exactly what he had to offer. One night, he carried me into another cabin, when the heat had gone out in ours. I felt so good in his arms. I . . . I always wanted to find that security in another man, a lover . . . but I failed. I guess engaging in S & M gave me that security in some strange way. But in the long run, I was pushing away intimacy through that behavior.

CRAIG: You might have been trying to *achieve* intimacy.

MARK: I guess a part of me realizes it just might be me . . . out of my control. It's an innate trait. But I never learned to be fully comfortable with it.

MICHAEL: You're not comfortable because of the *dissonance*, Mark, not the behavior. It's because the gay and straight societies produced double messages. One said, Yes, be stable and find security and a full-time lover; the other, Go out, have a good time, and fuck your brains out. To some extent, it's part of being male. Most homosexuals—most men—have a promiscuous streak.

MARK: I know. But there are those who can still be promiscuous and come home to a lover. I never seemed to find that. And it's probably too late now. Dr. Long says I'll be due for another bout of PCP in a year or less—if I make it that long.

CRAIG: Don't telescope. No doctor really knows for sure what's going to happen to any of us, regardless of what the statistics say. Look at all the long-term survivors who've lived with this for six years. There are a lot of them out there.

KEVIN: They're actually the exception to the rule. Come on, Craig—you know the reality; it's undeniable. We've got shattered immune systems. As long as that's so, we're apt to get something—if not PCP, then crypto or toxo. It's inevitable.

CRAIG: But it doesn't do any good to telescope and try to predict the worst outcome.

STUART: No, *let's* telescope. If any of you knew that on March 31, 1986, you would die for certain . . . what would you do differently now? Bob?

BOB: I wouldn't do anything differently. I'm satisfied with my existence, for the most part.

CRAIG: Neither would I.

STUART: What about you, Mark?

MARK: I'd like to change somehow. I'm not exactly sure how. I wish I could lose my craving for the hunt. Even last night, as I approached the baths, I could feel myself getting wet. (He laughs a bit.) I'd like to try to enjoy the white picket fence and no more traveling. One man whom I loved very much. And who loved me.

STUART: How do you think you could make that happen?

MARK: I'm not really sure. There are some relationships I haven't cultivated that could lead to what I think I want. I probably should pursue those and quit my job. No more traveling—no more temptation. But it seems unlikely that I could reinvent my life at this point.

STUART: What about you, Kevin? What would you do differently?

KEVIN: I don't think I could even answer that. I feel like I'm floundering, without any direction. Even if I did reevaluate my current goals and decide on some new short-term objectives, I think it would be difficult for me to actually make them happen. It's hard for me to even think of short-term goals when I know I probably won't live long enough to see them come true. And I just don't *feel* right, you know? My energy's zapped. My concentration's shot. I'm even hesitant about forming any sort of love relationship at this point. Last night, I met this artist at Morton's. It turns out he designed a record cover for my company. We seemed to get along and he seemed to like me. I told him about my condition and he seemed to accept that. But . . . I don't know that I could even find it within myself to call him back.

STUART: Why?

KEVIN: For one thing, I'm insecure about what's happened to my appearance. I was standing in front of the mirror naked last night looking at my body. I studied the way it had changed . . . I've lost so much weight. And my face is pale. I felt so inadequate, just standing there like that, especially when I remember what I looked like even three years ago. Who would want me now?

STUART: You never know until you take the risk and find out.

KEVIN: Yes, but it's hard—hard to disclose. It's hard to be spontaneous about anything.

STUART: Kevin, you *did* take the risk of coming out and revealing your HIV status to that man. That was something positive. Has anyone else in the group found it hard to reveal their HIV status to men they meet who might be potential lovers?

MICHAEL: Definitely. There's still so much misinformation and paranoia afoot, even among gay men who supposedly have been educated about how the disease can be transmitted. It's almost as if they wonder, Can I catch it from his touch . . . or from a kiss?

KEVIN: It also has to do with how you feel about yourself. Deep down. In the beginning, I felt like "damaged merchandise." I gave up all hope of ever finding sex—never mind a lover. I almost felt guilty falling in love.

STUART: There's always the possibility that the other person will also be HIV-positive or have AIDS. Has anyone been in that situation?

CRAIG: I met a man in Long Beach last month. A marine. We got to talking and I told him I was positive. He said he had been HIV-positive for three years. We've been dating for the last several weeks. I was afraid to come out at first but now I'm glad I did.

MICHAEL: Listen to Ms. Pollyanna—all champagne wishes and caviar dreams.

CRAIG: You people don't have a monopoly on fear and rage, you know. My life isn't all cotton candy. But I try to see the bright side.

KEVIN: We do too, Craig. But you're not as sick as we are. It makes a difference. Besides, having someone who is HIV-positive can help somewhat, but it's not everything.

CRAIG: I know—but I still have my own issues. Having ARC can be as bad as full-blown AIDS. You live in this gray area, never knowing when an opportunistic infection or KS might come along. . . . You're suspended in a vacuum of uncertainty.

PAUL: I can relate. Not knowing what'll happen, but realizing you have swollen lymph nodes, makes me feel like a time bomb sometimes—a bomb that could go off at the least expected moment. Every time I get out of the shower and see a red spot on my legs, I immediately think it might be KS.

CRAIG: Exactly! Or when I become short of breath climbing the hill by my house, I immediately think I'm getting PCP. And there are other issues I share with you—like discussing my illness with my parents.

STUART: Have you told them yet?

CRAIG: No, I haven't. The other night my father asked me, "Do you have it?" I just stared blankly ahead. He told me how much he loved me and that it was all right if I had it. I still couldn't bring myself to say the words. I know I should. They have a right to know. But I'm afraid it would change our relationship somehow.

STUART: How, Craig?

CRAIG: They know I'm gay and all. But I think for one thing, knowing I was sick would cause them an added burden.

STUART: Do you think they would think any less of you, or that you had somehow done something wrong in any way?

CRAIG: No, not really. I just don't want to cause them any more grief, that's all.

MICHAEL: You should feel lucky you have an open enough relationship with your parents that you can discuss it. Mine are so selfish, it wouldn't faze them one bit that I had ARC. I could never communicate with them very well. I can't help feeling rage. I'd like to punish them in a way they'd never forget, even by ending my own life. I'd want it to be a long, slow death. I'd want to hear their agony.

PAUL: For God's sake—don't punish yourself for their inadequacies.

STUART: Michael, I hear your rage and your anger toward them. From all that you've told us, they must have made you feel very helpless . . . alone.

MICHAEL: Yes. They could never return my love.

KEVIN: You don't really want to kill yourself, Michael. You're just angry, that's all. You've got more of a chance to survive than any of us. Don't give up.

BOB: It's better than having a family that disowns you completely. My next-door neighbor's mom and dad won't even talk to him and have openly told me they won't until his will is to be contested.

MARK: You know, it seems like just surviving another year is a real goal. My friend Jonathan has had KS for six years. Every year a group of his friends throws a party to celebrate another year that he's managed to cheat death. I thought I might actually be able to cheat death . . . at least in the short run.

KEVIN: None of us can fully cheat death, Mark.

PAUL: Our culture doesn't see death as a natural thing. It never did. In some societies, the families of the deceased actually prepare the body for burial. But our culture seems to have a twisted, distorted view that death is wrong and taboo.

STUART: How do you feel about death, Paul?

PAUL: I'm very afraid. I know it sounds weird, but sometimes I'm afraid of falling asleep for fear I won't wake up. That must seem strange when put into words.

STUART: It doesn't sound strange at all. It sounds very real. What do you think is at the core of your fear regarding sleep and death?

PAUL: I guess they both represent a loss of control. It's like I'm relinquishing something. I'm afraid to do that.

STUART: (Rising and seating himself in a chair opposite Paul) I want to try a brief role play. I'm going to be death. I want you to picture me in the most ominous garb you can. A black shawl, perhaps. Carrying a sickle like the archetypical image of the grim reaper. Do you feel comfortable doing this?

PAUL: Yes.

STUART: I am Death, Paul. I am your death. I am extremely powerful and important, aren't I?

PAUL: Yes. You seem to be.

STUART: There's nothing you can really do to change me . . . or make me any less powerful, is there?

PAUL: No. I can try to wipe you out of my mind . . . But on some level, you'll always be there.

STUART: That's right. What is it you fear most about what I represent?

PAUL: Uncertainty. Eternal obliteration. Not knowing what you'll feel like. Losing the control I feel I have by being alive.

STUART: I can make you lose control, can't I? What else can I do?

PAUL: Make me feel alone . . . like there's no hope. But there are things I can do in the here and now to make you less powerful.

STUART: Like what?

PAUL: Live in the present, try to find happiness in the here and now. Find a new lover and write a short story. Then you won't seem so important. (Stuart returns to his original seat.)

STUART: Does anyone have any reactions to Paul's feelings?

KEVIN: On some level, his reaction is what we all do to keep going. It's the healthy thing to do and the only way to survive. But you also have to face reality. I've already made my burial plans. I don't dwell on it, but it's something we should all be prepared for.

BOB: I'm going to be cremated. I've already taken care of everything.

MARK: I'm more afraid of decay than death. I recall seeing this friend of mine with CMV retinitis in the process of losing his sight. He would go to the Blind Center at Cal State with his lover and the lover would learn how best to help a blind person see. How to maneuver spaces and even sit down. But late in the evening, his lover told me that Jeffrey would cry aloud, "Why me? Oh God, why has this happened to me?" He seemed so helpless. I don't want to experience that.

The group was often stirred up by intense emotions of profound depth. It was sometimes a painful place to be. But it was also exhilarating and liberating. It was a place where we could share our deepest fears and concerns in a safe and supportive environment and develop a network with other ARC and AIDS patients who were experiencing similar conflicts.

Kevin's reference to Rock Hudson provided a preview of what was to come. On October 21, 1985, the world watched a news broadcast in which doctors at UCLA Medical Center issued a press statement that Rock Hudson was ill with AIDS. I remember the headline that ripped across the front page of the *Herald-Examiner* and the reaction of an elderly lady in the street who had just heard the news. "I can't believe Rock Hudson ever slept with other men. It's unbelievable!" An American archetype of masculinity and heterosexuality had fallen victim to a homosexual disease.

The AIDS crisis would never be the same.

In late 1985, Congress allocated $20 million for a new government-sponsored AIDS clinical trial system. It was the NIH's Maureen Myers who was assigned the task of assembling a network of medical institutions and "principal investigators"—research physicians who would develop, design, and implement the clinical trials of promising AIDS drugs. The original group was composed of people from thirteen institutions across the country: Dr. Margaret Fischl of the University of Miami; Dr. Thomas Merigan of Stanford University; Dr. Michael Grieco of St. Luke's–Roosevelt Hospital in New York; Dr. Donna Mildvan of Beth Israel Medical Center in New York; Dr. Douglas Richman of the University of California at San Diego; Dr. Michael Gottlieb of the University of California at Los Angeles; Dr. Paul Volberding of the University of California at San Francisco; Dr. Jerome Groopman of Harvard–New England Deaconess Hospital; Dr. Oscar Laskin of Cornell University Medical College in New York; Dr. John Leedom of Los Angeles County–USC Medical Center; Dr. Martin Hirsch of Harvard–Massachusetts General Hospital; Dr. George Jackson of the University of Illinois at Chicago; and Dr. David Durack of Duke University Medical Center.

These sites became known as AIDS Treatment Evaluation Units (ATEUs) and were coordinated and linked by an outside private firm, the Research Triangle Institute of Research Triangle Park, North Carolina, conveniently located only blocks away from the Burroughs Wellcome Company, the manufacturer of AZT, one of the first drugs to be tested in the system.

Under the plan, Fauci's organization, NIAID, would actually provide the drugs to be tested at the ATEUs; drugs that seemed promising in the National Cancer Institute's screening program would be sent to NIAID, where a committee called the AIDS Clinical Drug Development Committee (ACDDC) would recommend those they felt were worthy of further study. These drugs would then be assigned to the principal investigators at the various ATEUs across the country.

The system was ultimately renamed the AIDS Clinical Trials Group (ACTG). The number of sites in the system grew in subsequent years. Today, there are fifty-two at various hospitals and medical centers across the country, each with its own principal investigator.

CHAPTER 4

THE SERENDIPITOUS STORY OF COMPOUND S

About a half dozen of Michael Bristow's family and friends stood in silence around the twenty-four-year-old ARC patient's open coffin, which lay in a room at the front of the Hollywood Funeral Home. Michael looked serene and not at all angry. His mother stared down at the face of her dead son. The funeral parlor had done an exemplary job of creating an almost robust and ruddy complexion for him; his lips had been tinted vermilion, his eyebrows darkened slightly. In his facial features, permanently and irrevocably etched, was an expression of serenity. At last, Michael Bristow was at peace with himself.

No one could have guessed the agony he had suffered in his final moments on earth or the pain he had inflicted on those who loved him most.

As he had promised, Michael had attempted suicide, on January 5, 1986. He meant to inflict "eternal guilt" on his mother and sister, who he felt had betrayed him. "They were selfish and never knew what I needed," he told me one week before his suicide attempt. "Not once did they ever really listen to how I truly felt. I could never trust them. Through my death, I want to punish them in a way they'll never forget!"

Rather than wait for AIDS to do the job, Michael swallowed two bottles of Nembutal and Seconal. He didn't die immediately; instead he lay in a coma at Century City Hospital for almost two weeks, connected to life-support equipment. Throughout the entire time, Michael seemed to be aware that his mother and sister had gathered at his bedside for what had become a twenty-four-hour vigil. "He seemed able to hear our sobbing and concerned voices, to feel my touch on his hand, even in his comatose condition," his sister said to me later. "It was almost as if he wanted to finish off his life with a dramatic finale that was meant to cast recrimination on us."

Nobody in the group believed that Michael was truly serious about his suicide threats. We somehow thought he reveled in the fantasy of killing himself but would never actually bring himself to do it.

Ironically, Michael's CD4 cell count was more than 500. His doctor seemed to feel he was relatively stable and might last another six years before progressing to full-blown AIDS. With any luck, he might even have lived to see an effective treatment for the disease.

"Michael's problem with his parents transcended HIV and AIDS. His suicide was more than simply a need to punish them," Stuart confided to me later. "The prospect of surviving and even getting well was far more terrifying for him than sickness and even death."

One evening, Craig, Stuart, and I marched in the first southern California candlelight vigil in honor of all those who had died of AIDS during the first five years of the epidemic. We were among a group of more than three hundred gay men and lesbians who walked slowly down Santa Monica Boulevard, which had been closed to traffic. We carried candles and sang hymns. As I looked back at the long trail of people in the march, the candles appeared as a mass of endless fireflies suspended in flight.

• • •

Among the most dedicated scientists in the early fight against AIDS was Dr. Sam Broder. A graduate of Stanford University, he began his career as a clinical associate at the National Cancer Institute and by 1982 had become the Institute's director for the Clinical Oncology program. In that capacity, he determined what drugs would be studied for cancer. When AIDS began to surface as a growing threat in the early- to mid-1980s, and with the discovery of HTLV-III as the probable cause, Broder became interested in studying the disease and was one of the first scientists to attempt aggressively to find an effective treatment.

It was the NIH's Robert Yarchoan who suggested to Broder that suramin be tried as a possible anti-HIV therapeutic. It was a reverse transcriptase inhibitor, after all, and had been in use for more than sixty years. The pharmaceutical firm Bayer had developed it overseas and the drug had been used by millions of Africans to treat and prevent river blindness and sleeping sickness. But while the drug cured some, it killed others. Researchers found that suramin was capable of producing kidney damage and even coma in a small subset of the patients who took it. Despite this finding, suramin continued to be used throughout the 1970s.

Broder and his assistants hunted through the index of scientific abstracts in the National Medical Library on the NIH campus. They found all the existing references to the pink sulphonic salt and learned that it had long ago been granted approval for human use in the United States by the FDA.

Broder had the drug tested in the NIH assay against HTLV-III. It worked beautifully. He filed for a government patent on the drug and rushed through the preliminary paperwork that proved its *in vitro* efficacy. The FDA moved amazingly fast. In less than thirty days, they gave Broder the green light to test the drug in humans.

The results of the Phase 1 trial, held under Broder's direction at the NIH Clinical Research Center and completed in 1985, were only mildly encouraging. Suramin did produce significant decreases in viral culture load levels of AIDS patients but otherwise produced no improvement. Broder, however, remained undaunted. Everyone connected with the study truly wanted to believe suramin to be a major breakthrough.

"Here was the first hint of a possibility on the horizon of an antiviral drug to treat this dreaded disease," Bruce Cheson told *Discover* magazine. It was Cheson who had coordinated a series of suramin studies sponsored by the NCI. "We were flooded with requests from patients, their relatives, and institutions asking us to release the drug on a compassionate-plea basis. But because of the drug's side effects—rashes, fevers, and changes in liver function—and uncertainties about dosage, we concluded that making suramin widely available to doctors wasn't a safe thing to do. Instead, we set up studies at six hospitals for only about a hundred patients in all."

In November 1985, at the beginning of the eighth week of treatment, Broder called together all the study's principal investigators in Bethesda. Many were in a state of euphoria. There was some early evidence that certain patients had experienced dramatic improvement while on the drug. Yet some were so certain the suramin would work that they had lost even the thinnest shred of scientific objectivity. At least one dissenting view was voiced at that meeting. Dr. Peter Wolfe, a co-investigator of the trial, revealed that the drug might be responsible for violent skin eruptions and other blood chemistry abnormalities. By the tenth week of treatment, Wolfe's fears were confirmed. At the end of the tenth week, several centers reported coma in some patients. Numerous cases of kidney failure were also documented.

"Suramin did have substantial antiviral activity," Cheson said. "But it produced no immunological improvement, and beneficial clinical responses were uncommon." Most important, more than a quarter of the patients who took it developed adrenal insufficiency, a potentially serious and completely unanticipated side effect. Suramin may even have killed a few patients, according to Cheson, by damaging their kidneys and livers.

Word got out to the media that the deaths of some AIDS

patients may have been accelerated by suramin. At least one researcher stated publicly that suramin was suspected of causing premature death in some patients.

Despite the negative publicity, patients continued to clamor
for the drug. It seemed to be the only hope, an oasis in a desert of
despair. Some physicians contacted the Bayer Corporation directly
to obtain suramin and then conducted their own research protocols.
The NIH announced plans to conduct expanded Phase 2 trials of
the drug in 1986 at six treatment centers nationally, one of which
was at UCLA. In time, it became clear that many of the twenty-four
AIDS and ARC subjects in the UCLA study experienced kidney
damage and muscle weakness. UCLA moved quickly to close the
trial as it became clear that the drug was too toxic, but the trials at
several other sites continued even as hundreds of patients begged to
get in. In the course of the study, many of the patients died, mostly
from opportunistic infections related to AIDS. But at least two died
from renal or liver failure that may have been linked directly to the
drug.

By January 1987, principal investigator Lawrence Kaplan announced in the *American Journal of Medicine*: "The lack of *in vivo*
virologic, immunologic, or clinical benefit of Suramin, coupled with
the drug's marked toxicity, precludes its use as a single-agent therapy for AIDS and makes it an unlikely candidate in further trials."
All clinical trials of the drug were closed. I had heard about the
suramin study, but by the time I contacted UCLA all the spots had
been filled, and negative publicity about the drug had already begun
to surface. It was one medication I was grateful I had *not* taken.

It was Craig who first introduced me to Rob Springer. In 1983,
Springer had suffered a bout of PCP and was diagnosed with full-
blown AIDS. Craig had told me that Rob was a bisexual who had
frequented the bathhouses in southern California and had confided
to him that he felt guilty that he may have inadvertently infected
a great many men and women in the early 1980s. In the spring of

1984, he enrolled in the suramin study at UCLA. Within weeks of starting the drug, he noticed, like many of the subjects, that his serum BUN (blood urea nitrogen) and creatinine levels (measures of kidney function) had markedly escalated, and his liver enzyme values had risen to unacceptable levels—a sign of liver toxicity. He felt nauseous and lethargic. At one point, his blood pressure fell to 90/60. He slept most of the day, and his muscles began to weaken. He could no longer manipulate a fork or spoon.

Springer discontinued his participation in the study and, over time, fought his way back to health. It seemed he had survived both suramin *and* AIDS. When I visited him in his modest Santa Monica apartment in February 1986, he appeared healthy and vibrant. He had been an economics professor at a large California university and possessed an impressive background in inorganic chemistry. For the last two years he had been on disability because of AIDS-related symptoms, which included increasing fatigue and short-term memory loss.

Springer, then in his early forties, wore small wire-frame glasses, which gave him a studious aura. He had brown hair and brown eyes and an inquisitive look stamped indelibly on his plain features. He dressed simply, in jeans and a sports shirt.

For the last two years, Springer had been actively involved in the acquisition and manufacture of experimental anti-AIDS medications that had shown promise in test tube and Phase 1 trials in Europe. He had written a protocol that described the theoretical advantages of implementing a combined regime of acyclovir, Imuthiol, and dextran sulfate. He shared the protocol with Dr. Michael Scolaro, a Los Angeles AIDS physician. Scolaro had tried the protocol on several patients in his practice.

It was hard to say what drove Springer; he did make some money from the underground pharmacy, but only enough to cover his expenses. I came to believe he was primarily motivated by the sheer will to survive, fueled by an aggressive intelligence.

During our initial meeting, he ushered me into a small laboratory at the back of his apartment. I studied the impressive array of beakers, test tubes, stoves, tableting boards, and other chemical manufacturing equipment that occupied a huge work table in the center of the room.

"This is Imuthiol," Springer explained, holding up a large capsule that looked as though it had been encoated with orange glue.

"It's also known as DTC, which stands for diethyldithiocarbamate. It's a metal-removing agent used for chemical and agricultural purposes and has been used in humans to treat nickel, mercury, cadmium, and copper poisoning."

The precision in the content and style of his speech impressed me immediately. He made no effort to simplify his often complex scientific language.

He continued his lecture while walking around the room. "In laboratory animals, the chemical has shown to provide protection against the immunosuppressive effects of radiation and chemotherapy. In the mid-1970s, French doctors treating stomach cancer with platinum added this chemical to remove the platinum and accidentally discovered an increase in T cells in the treated patients. In 1985, French researchers, searching for immunomodulators that would replace the depleted T cells in AIDS patients, treated a large number of ARC patients with DTC. They found unanimous clinical improvement in these patients and improvements in the total CD4 cell counts and skin test reactions. American trials will be starting in six weeks."

"I've heard that some immunomodulators actually make more fuel for the fire, so to speak," I said.

"That's the beauty of DTC. It's completely non-mitogenic. The French researchers established that there was no evidence that the drug encouraged replication of the HIV virus."

"HIV?" I asked him.

"The new name for HTLV-III. It stands for human immunodeficiency virus."

"How exactly does Imuthiol make more CD4 cells?" I asked.

"It doesn't actually *make* new ones," he replied. "It merely speeds the maturation of existing cells and thus increases their total number, perhaps by inducing the liver to make hepatosin, a hormone with thymiclike activity. It may also improve the function and viability of the *existing* CD4 cells. And Dr. Hutchinson in Paris has suggested that DTC might have an antiviral effect due to its metal-chelating properties. Metal-chelating agents have been shown to inhibit various types of viruses in the test tube. At least one study has shown that DTC can inhibit HIV in the test tube."

"How did you make that capsule?" I asked him.

He led me over to the lab table. "DTC is basically a chemical that can be obtained in pharmaceutical grade from numerous companies. If you were to simply place it in a gelatin capsule and swallow it, it would dissolve in the stomach and wouldn't effectively reach its site of action. It might also make you quite sick! The capsules need to be 'enterically coated' so that they bypass the gastric secretions of the stomach and dissolve in the intestines, where they can be effectively absorbed into the bloodstream. It's the same concept that the manufacturers of certain health-food products, such as encapsulated acidophilus, use in the preparation of their compounds.

"Using a modified technique pioneered by Dr. Ely Parrot in 1961, I create an extemporaneous enteric coating. I measure out about 150 milligrams of the DTC on this balance," he said as he actually placed a small amount of the white powder on the scale. "Then, I place it in a small capsule and dip the capsule in this mixture of cellulose phthalate, a photochemical which is nontoxic to humans." Springer held up the plastic bottle for my inspection. "I encoat each tablet separately. On a good afternoon, I can usually produce about twenty-five pills."

"How many of those do you take a day?" I asked him.

"Five a *week*," he corrected. "It is strong stuff.

"Some people dissolve the powder in liquid and take it as an enema. But I don't advocate taking it that way. It produces an offensive garbagelike smell, worse when it's given rectally. It can also damage the intestines in that method of administration."

"Are there things I can't take with this?" I asked him.

"You can continue on any regular American medication. But check with me first to be sure. And don't mix it with alcohol under any circumstances. DTC, in another form called Antabuse, is actually used to produce an aversion to alcohol in alcoholics."

"Have you noticed any changes since you've been on Imuthiol?"

"I've been on the drug for two years now. I'd say my CD4 cells rose by about 20 percent in the first six months I was on the drug. They've dropped down now. But I've got something in development potentially even better than Imuthiol." He led me over to another section of the table.

"This is AL-721." The drug was contained in a cellophane plastic wrap and looked like a thin orange Popsicle.

"AL-721 stands for active lipids in a ratio of seven to two to one. Technically, it's a trademarked name for egg lipids in a ratio of seven parts neutral lipids, two parts purified lecithin, and one part phosphatidyl ethanolamine."

The names rolled off his tongue. I committed them rapidly to memory.

"The seven-to-two-to-one ratio was arrived at by Dr. Meir Shinitzky and other cancer researchers at the Weizmann Institute of Science in Rehovot, Israel. They were investigating the use of egg lipids to increase the membrane fluidity of lymphocytes in subjects whose immune systems had been damaged by advanced age. It's been known for a long time that an important way in which cells communicate is through membrane contact. The Israeli doctors became engaged in the developing field of 'membrane engineering.' They realized that many normal cellular functions were inhibited when the lipid fluidity of the cell membrane was reduced, as it was in cancer and old age. But they observed that this loss of function was at least partially reversible with the use of AL-721, which operated by extracting the cholesterol that caused the cell membrane to harden. Since most of the electrochemical activity in the cell originates in its membrane, the researchers believed the fluidizing effect of AL-721 could be stabilizing and even de-age the cell."

Springer removed a large black binder from a workshelf and turned to a specific page. "This article published by researchers at the University of Virginia in 1978 establishes that some viruses need large amounts of cholesterol in order to infect cells and when the cholesterol was extracted, the virus stopped being infective," he said. "Many researchers today believe that HIV also uses cholesterol in this way and that AL-721 could be helpful in reducing its infectivity."

"How exactly?" I asked him.

"HIV can infect cells in one of two ways," he explained. He walked me over to a large easel that displayed a detailed drawing of the HIV virus attaching to an uninfected CD4 cell. "A free virus particle, called a viron, can attach itself to and infect a susceptible cell, like a CD4 cell. Also, an infected cell can attach to a healthy cell and infect it directly. AL-721 extracts cholesterol from both the cell membrane and the viral envelope and, in that process, reduces the receptor binding, halting both mechanisms of cell destruction. And in 1985, one researcher found that AL-721 inhibited HIV *in vitro.*"

"Have there been any human trials?"

"None in the United States, though they will be starting soon in New York. But the Baltimore *Jewish Times* reported that 52 of 60 people taking AL-721 in Israel last year have shown a decline in viral infectivity and an improvement in their general well-being, sometimes within days of embarking on the treatment. And an informal study of ten patients, conducted by Dr. Shinitzky himself, found that the drug induced improvements in clinical symptoms such as weight loss, diarrhea, and fevers and an improvement in the qualitative function, although not the number, of CD4 cells.

"I've just started taking the drug myself," he said. "One of these orange Popsicle-type spheres a day. If I find that it isn't harmful, I'll distribute it to some ARC patients here in Santa Monica."

When I asked him exactly how he created AL-721, he

launched into an incredibly complex and rambling explanation, which I only partly understood.

"Where did you find the formula?"

"From a chemist in New York."

We were interrupted by the doorbell. Springer left me in the lab for a moment and returned seconds later with a young man, no older than twenty-five. His face was covered with massive purple lesions—Kaposi's sarcoma. Springer strode swiftly to the refrigerator and produced a container of white paste.

"Here's the DNCB," he explained, removing the lid on the container of dinitrochlorobenzene and placing a smidgen of the gluelike substance between his thumb and forefinger. "You just rub a small amount over the surface of the lesions. Be certain to cover the entire spot." He moved his hand to the skin of the KS patient and gently rubbed the paste onto the purple lesion, erasing its purple color, blotting out the ugly vascular proliferation. It struck me in that moment that Springer had the power to heal.

"After a few seconds, the entire area is going to seem especially hard and red. That's normal. In forty-eight to seventy-two hours, you might notice a bright red bump over the lesion. That's to be expected also, so don't be alarmed, O.K.? Use it once a day and cover each lesion completely," he said as he replaced the cover of the box. "This much should last you thirty days."

"Thank you, Rob," the man said. "Thank you so much." Then he was gone.

"What was that drug?" I asked him.

"DNCB," he explained. "A photochemical I obtain in bulk and which has shown efficacy in treating wart virus infections and certain malignant lesions. There's some early data that suggests it might help KS. A San Francisco dermatologist named Dr. Mills began applying the chemical in a 1-percent concentration dissolved in acetone to the lesions of his patients with KS. He noticed an occasional responsiveness in the KS and a slight increase in CD4 cell counts when the drug was simply painted on clear skin. Soon thereafter, a buyers' group formed to purchase the compound in kilogram quantities from photochemical supply houses, produce the treatment solution in bulk, and then distribute it free of charge to individuals across the country who were interested in its potential anti-KS and immunomodulatory activity. A nationwide network of such groups has recently taken shape, of which I am a part.

"Although some promising results with KS have emerged, it's definitely not the cure for KS," he emphasized. "But it might be of some help."

"This is excellent," I said, examining the AL-721. "An entire AIDS drug synthesis lab right here in Santa Monica."

"It's hardly a synthesis lab," he said. "It's probably not even the most sophisticated underground lab in the country right now. Michael Myers in Pacific Palisades has one of the more advanced."

I had heard about Myers but had never met him.

"Would you like some Imuthiol?" he asked. "I can give you twenty pills for now."

"Yes," I said. "I'd like that." He removed the pills from a small bottle.

"Five a week taken at a single sitting. I've got to go to a meeting now, but perhaps we can get together again sometime." He walked me to the door of the lab.

"I'd like that very much," I told him.

"Remember, Paul," he concluded, "this is all our secret. No one must know about the lab, understand?"

"Of course," I assured him.

This "indoctrination" would be more meaningful than I could ever have imagined. In the days that followed, I rapidly became friends with Springer. I visited his lab on Saturday afternoons and helped him with miscellaneous tasks.

My "apprenticeship" with Springer not only taught me the fundamentals of an antiviral drug or immunomodulatory drug's pharmacokinetics and modes of action but also reinforced my knowledge of the principles of the pathogenesis of HIV disease, or the ways in which HIV actually destroyed CD4 cells, resulting in life-threatening opportunistic infection, and the methods by which various drugs inhibited those specific ways.

To be sure of its purity, I had the Imuthiol that Springer gave me tested at a professional lab. I did this without telling him, of course; I didn't want him to think my confidence or faith in his abilities was lukewarm. Still, I wanted an objective evaluation of the quality of his work. (As far as I knew, the pharmaceutical grade of DTC was not available anywhere in the world and Springer would not reveal exactly where he obtained the chemical. Later, I learned that Springer had developed a relationship with a large chemical company on the East Coast that supplied him with DTC as well as several other compounds.) The lab confirmed that the capsule was indeed pure pharmaceutical-grade DTC and that the enteric coating was also safe and effective.

In my first several months on Imuthiol, I noticed that my CD4 cells *did* rise by about 15 percent. My energy level also seemed to increase. But there was no change in the size of my lymph nodes.

In the following months, Springer became known as "the midnight chemist," and AIDS patients from across southern California visited his Santa Monica lab for a sample of the experimental anti-HIV medications he produced.

It was Springer who first informed me about a promising new drug that would soon be in clinical trials at UCLA. Compound S, or AZT, as it would become known, was soon to be the most important drug in the annals of the epidemic.

Its history was indeed convoluted and serendipitous. It was first synthesized and tested in 1964 by Jerome Horwitz of the Detroit Institute for Cancer Research. Rather than simply screen existing drugs, Horwitz realized that it would be more efficient to *design* a drug to stop the cancer. He envisioned that it might be possible to integrate a "phony" element directly into the DNA of the cancer cell and thus stop the DNA from reproducing. In the process, he reasoned, it might be possible to stabilize the cancer, if not completely arrest it. Through the process of designing his own experimental compound, Horwitz created azidothymidine (AZT). It substituted an altered form of one specific chemical, or DNA building block—thymidine—into the genetic series of chemicals that was needed for the reproduction of cancer.

Although the concept was elegant and seemingly workable, the drug failed miserably in practice. Studies with mice showed that it produced absolutely no decrease in tumor growth. AZT appeared so worthless at the time that Horwitz didn't even bother to get a patent for it. When further studies confirmed that it had no value as a chemotherapeutic agent, it was set aside in favor of more promising candidates.

During the early 1970s, a German group at the Max Planck Institute showed that AZT suppressed murine retrovirus (i.e., from mice) in humans. Because the existence of human retroviruses had not yet been identified, this work was virtually ignored in scientific circles. Indeed, AZT would perhaps have remained in obscurity had it not been for the work of Sam Broder and David Barry. Immediately after HTLV-III was identified as the probable cause of AIDS, Broder began formulating a plan to screen the most promising antiretrovirals he could get his hands on. Broder knew that HTLV-III used the enzyme reverse transcriptase to reproduce itself; so it made sense to evaluate compounds with the potential to block or thwart this enzyme.

Broder attempted to convince Burroughs Wellcome Company's president, David Barry, to launch preliminary tests on the company's antiviral compounds to see which, if any, held the potential to thwart HTLV-III. Burroughs Wellcome was actually one of about a dozen companies Broder visited in an attempt to gain support for the testing of anti-HIV agents. It was also one of the largest companies and one of the only ones that had a research-and-development mechanism in place for the testing of antiviral drugs.

Barry was hesitant at first. The development of any pharmaceutical product would cost millions of dollars. To guarantee the profitability of such an investment, Burroughs Wellcome's board of directors had set up specific criteria. Any new medicine must face a potential market demand of at least 200,000 patients. Anything below this level was listed as an "orphan disease." At the time, AIDS had claimed some 5,000 lives, but did not meet Burroughs Wellcome's economic criteria. (Some critics charge that even with more than 200,000 cases recorded today, this factor still plays a large part in why many drug companies are still reluctant to develop effective HIV antivirals and immunologics.)

There were also safety concerns, but Broder assured Burroughs Wellcome that he would personally supervise the testing of all potential antiviral agents in the NCI lab.

Finally, Barry agreed to search for anti-HTLV-III agents and assigned the arduous task of screening compounds at Burroughs Wellcome to a staff chemist who used an *assay* (a culture containing human immune cells that are capable of living outside the human body for as long as they are cultured, have the ability to react quickly to the HTLV-III virus, and can be used to screen drugs) that was developed by Broder's own laboratory director, Hiroaki Mitsuya. On December 20, 1984, the chemist saw the first signs that AZT might have substantial *in vitro* antiviral activity against HTLV-III.

Broder knew that BW509 (i.e., AZT) acted as a competitive inhibitor of reverse transcriptase. It became incorporated into viral DNA and resulted in a premature termination of DNA chain synthesis. Simply put, as the HIV virus instructs T cells to cement together the building blocks that will construct a new virus, the drug binds to one of the blocks, preventing the next piece of the virus from being correctly aligned.

Broder raced through experiment after experiment in his lab, compiling enough data by June 1985 to file an investigational new drug application (IND) with the FDA, which would allow for the commencement of human trials. The IND called for the drug to be administered in two places—at the NCI Clinical Research Center under Broder's direction and at the Duke University School of Medicine under the direction of Dr. David Durack.

The first patient received AZT in Broder's Phase 1 NCI trial on July 3, 1985. The protocol for the trial provided for progressively increased doses of AZT, which would be administered to thirty patients intravenously for two weeks, then orally for four weeks. The preliminary animal studies in rats and dogs had shown maximum tolerance levels of up to 40 milligrams of AZT per day per pound of body weight. The trial called for the intravenous dosage to increase from 3, 7.5, and 15 milligrams up to 30. The quantity would be doubled for oral administration.

As the days progressed, Broder's and the other principal investigators' hopes grew. The side effects, in the beginning at least, were negligible: slight anemia, headaches, and a decrease in some patients' total white-blood-cell count. The positive results were almost immediately apparent: a general weight gain averaging five pounds; a reduction of night sweats, fever, and chronic fungal nailbed infections; a reduction in viral activity within cells; and a modest increase in the numbers of CD4 lymphocytes. Two patients experienced dramatic improvements.

In the March 15, 1986, issue of *Lancet*, Broder and seventeen other scientists, including lead investigator Margaret Fischl, cautiously reported that AZT might be making some headway in the battle against AIDS. The results of the Phase 1 trial, Broder told *Discover* magazine, were unlike any he had ever encountered. Fifteen patients showed some improvement in their immune systems, as measured by CD4-cell-count levels and delayed hypersensitivity reactions. Two had chronic fungal infections clear up without any other treatment and six stopped running fevers or having night sweats.

Cell cultures no longer yielded any traces of the AIDS virus in several of the patients who took the highest doses of the drug. Side effects included headaches and a decreased red- and white-blood-cell count, but they were not considered severe enough to discontinue therapy. AZT appeared to cross the blood/brain barrier and seemed to cause an improvement in one patient's reported HIV-related dementia. By July 1985, between seven and twelve months after they had started taking AZT, sixteen of the original nineteen patients were still alive. Even though a few had become so anemic that they needed transfusions, most continued to use the drug. The results were good enough to justify further testing.

Encouraged by the early promising results, Broder championed the drug in the media and in scientific and political circles. When problems erupted that threatened to halt the study, including a shortage of thymidine—the essential building block of AZT—Broder quickly found a supply of the nucleoside within the NCI system.

I, too, was impressed with the results described in *Lancet*. After reading the Phase 1 study that Rob Springer had given me, I finally contacted Broder and spoke with him briefly. He told me he felt the drug might be something of a breakthrough and that a trial would be opening soon in Los Angeles for which I might qualify.

Shortly before the completion of the Phase 1 trial in the fall of 1985, approximately thirty Burroughs Wellcome investigators, including David Barry himself, convened at North Carolina's Pine Needle Lodge to determine if an appropriate study could be designed to delineate the strong and weak points of the drug. On November 15, 1985, they attempted to hammer out the specifics of the multicenter Phase 2 trial, which would be among the most ambitious in the history of the AIDS epidemic. Two months later, the Burroughs Wellcome representatives called upon twelve members of the AIDS Clinical Trials Group (ACTG) to put the final touches on the protocol originally formulated at Pine Needle Lodge. The outcome of this meeting was a 262-page protocol.

It specified that the Phase 2 trial would be a double-blind, placebo-controlled study. "Placebo-controlled" meant that 50 percent of the subjects would be receiving the active drug while the other 50 percent would be receiving an inert sugar pill, to provide a basis for comparison. "Double-blind" meant that neither the investigators nor the subjects themselves would know who was getting the active drug or the placebo until the conclusion of the study, when the "code of secrecy" would be broken and the results revealed. One objective of using double-blind trials is to avoid having physicians give any preferential treatment—consciously or not—to patients taking the active drug, since such special treatment could influence the outcome of the trial or bias the data in some way. Another objective is to minimize the positive effects experienced by any patient who takes a medication he or she believes might be helpful. Double-blind trials had become the hallmark of true objectivity in science, a method of preventing any deliberate or accidental special treatment of patients by their clinical or research physicians.

Half the subjects would be AIDS patients with a history of at least one opportunistic infection but no *current* infections or KS, while the other half would consist of ARC patients whose CD4 cell count was less than 200 and who had a history of thrush and anergy (or lack of response) on immune-response skin tests. The subjects would not be allowed to take any other experimental medication for the duration of the study, including drugs that could block opportunistic infections.

Twelve medical centers would participate in the study, which would involve 282 patients: 160 AIDS patients and 122 ARC patients. Investigators from the National Institute of Allergy and Infectious Diseases would help monitor and administer the study.

In Los Angeles, the study would be held at two ACTG sites, one of them UCLA, under the direction of Dr. Michael Gottlieb, whose early work in immunology involved research in graft implants in defective organs. In his Stanford lab, Gottlieb destroyed the immune systems of mice in an effort to discover a way of neutralizing the rejection phenomenon in humans that made organ grafting such a risk.

In November 1980, the thirty-two-year-old Gottlieb had been an assistant professor at UCLA for four months, when a graduate student reported the story of a young man who suffered from an esophageal candidiasis infection so devastating he could hardly breathe. Two days later, he developed pneumonia of unusual origin; the causal microorganism was a protozoan known as *Pneumocystis carinii*. Its consequences had been previously noted in persons undergoing immunosuppressant therapy for another illness, and whose immune systems had been undermined by cancer, or who were severely malnourished. But such symptoms were not typically seen in a healthy thirty-two-year-old man with no past history of illness.

Gottlieb originally thought that the strange disorder might represent a preleukemic condition or a severe disorder of the intestinal flora, perhaps caused by excessive consumption of antibiotics.

Gottlieb learned from a colleague who analyzed the blood that the patient's specimens contained hardly any CD4 lymphocytes. He rushed to the UCLA library and consulted the on-line computer database. All the articles documenting cases of *Pneumocystis carinii* pneumonia (PCP) in the last twenty years supplied a single explanation for the failure of the immune system that ultimately led to the illness: irradiation needed for an organ transplant, or a genetic deficiency. Yet the patient in both cases suffered from neither of these conditions.

Gottlieb realized he had discovered one of the first cases of AIDS in the United States. With Dr. Joel Weisman, he published a report in the *New England Journal of Medicine* in which they discussed the cases of the aforementioned man and five other homosexual men, all of whom suffered from PCP, and who were seen at the UCLA Medical Center.

In the months and years that followed, it would be Gottlieb who would spearhead much of the early research on the disease, organizing conferences of elite immunologists and virologists and finally working with Dr. Mathilde Krim to help launch the AIDS Medical Foundation, which would become the American Foundation for AIDS Research (AmFAR) in 1985.

• • •

Rob Springer encouraged me to contact Dr. Gottlieb's lab to try and get into the Phase 2 AZT study. Springer had already been accepted and would start within days. But by the time I reached Gottlieb in March of 1986, all twenty spaces in the Los Angeles branch of the study had been filled. Springer urged me to persevere, and I routinely kept in contact with Suzette Chafey and Joan Lederman, the protocol screening nurses and project co-coordinators, reminding them of my interest. Finally, on April 15, 1986, an additional three slots opened up.

"Could you come down this afternoon for screening?" Suzette asked me on the telephone.

Concocting a bogus story, I convinced my manager in the black tower to let me have the afternoon off. I drove from one end of town to the other—about twenty miles—in record time.

Suzette greeted me in the lobby of the UCLA Clinical Research Center and ushered me into one of the examination rooms. She explained that although I appeared to qualify for admission to the study on some basic points, I would nevertheless be subjected to an extensive series of tests to determine if I met more stringent inclusion criteria. Specifically, the study was admitting ARC patients whose CD4 cell counts were less than 200 and who were completely anergic on skin antigen tests. Furthermore, the ARC patients had to have at least one other symptom of progressive illness—specifically, oral thrush, persistent lymphadenopathy, or unexplained weight loss. Although I had no thrush or weight loss, I did have swollen lymph nodes and so qualified on that level. But only the blood and skin tests of my immune function would fully determine if I was in.

Suzette took me to another room and administered four needle sticks into my left forearm, each one containing a common recall antigen such as mumps or tuberculin. Next to each injection, Suzette wrote a number—one to four—that corresponded with the exact antigen that had been injected at the site. She explained that patients with advanced ARC often showed no response to the test. Patients with early ARC and asymptomatic HIV infection often manifested a response—a red bump of varying size also known as an erythema—at the site of the subdermal injection, a sign that there was still some immune function intact. I would be admitted to the study only if I showed *no* red bumps or erythemas at all four injection sites.

After I arrived home that evening, I realized that a large bump was beginning to form at the site where the candida antigen had been inserted. Crestfallen, I trudged down to John's apartment.

"What am I going to do? I'm basically too healthy to get in. But I feel certain that drug could buy me an awful lot of time," I lamented.

John thought for a moment. Then he asked, "Did they ever write down which arm they put the antigens in?"

"I don't think so," I said.

"Then it's simple. I'll draw four numbers on your right arm and make a small red mark after each to replicate where the needle went in. You just show them that arm and you'll be completely anergic!"

Two days later, I returned to the UCLA Medical Center and learned that my CD4 cell count was 199. I barely qualified on that measure of my immune function. And there was nothing in any of my other blood tests to exclude me from the study. When it came time for Suzette to check my arm, the phone rang in her office.

"Let me see your arm," she said quickly.

I rolled up my right sleeve, revealing the flat, bumpless skin.

"Completely anergic," she said, and hurriedly wrote down the results on the case report form. Then she rushed to get to her phone and deal with the myriad administrative details involved in running one of the most important AIDS studies in American history.

Five minutes later, I was led to an examination room. Within minutes, Dr. Gottlieb strode in. He wore a white UCLA lab jacket with his name inscribed in cursive letters over the left pocket. He had an authoritative air about him, a businesslike approach, but also a compassion that was unmistakable.

He reiterated many of the points involved in being in the

study and elucidated the possible side effects of the drug—migraine headaches, a potential decline in white and red blood cells. He then read me the informed-consent document, which explained my rights and responsibilities, and potential risks and benefits, as a subject in a medical experiment. I felt at once hopeful and afraid as I signed the form.

On June 5, 1986, I was enrolled in the study—the last person to be admitted.

The protocol called for us to take two of the white, generic-looking pills every four hours around the clock. This meant setting our alarms for three-thirty in the morning to take our dose of AZT. Suzette had explained that the drug had a half-life (the time required for half the amount of a substance in or introduced into a living system or ecosystem to be eliminated or disintegrated by natural processes) of less than four hours, and so continual administration of it was necessary to maintain constantly elevated blood levels. It was annoying to be awakened so regularly by that invasive digital beep at three-thirty every morning, but it was all part of the protocol.

Each week, I returned to UCLA to have more blood drawn, to have more skin tests and a complete physical and neurological examination. The protocol also called for us to undergo a heavy battery of tests of cognitive functions that measured short-term memory and concentration. They seemed ridiculously simple to me. I was able to recall ten words on the first try and could recall fourteen digits backwards with no effort whatsoever. But the entire exercise bored me; it simply seemed a necessary part of being in the study. How could I have known that even fifteen months later, I would have been glad to have accomplished such a feat?

Occasionally, Dr. Gottlieb would check on our progress, but I rarely saw him after our first meeting. Instead, my progress was monitored by the second protocol nurse, Joan Lederman. She had brown hair, brown eyes, and an electric personality. On days when I was depressed, she had the almost magical ability to bring me out of my doldrums with laughter and compassion. She also seemed to

me to be amazingly astute—as knowledgeable as certain HIV physicians I had known—and took the time to explain the meaning of my
laboratory test results in detail as they were placed into my case-
report form.

The study was a placebo-controlled trial. Half of us were
being given an active drug, the other half inert sugar. But it was
impossible to tell by examining the contents of the capsule who was
getting what. Springer attempted to perform an analysis of our own
capsules but was unable to determine for certain if we were both
getting the active drug. Some type of masking buffer had apparently
been integrated into the powder to create a slick, seamless appearance. In order to increase the odds that we were both receiving the
active drug, Springer suggested we swap halves of our capsules.
When Springer first made the proposal, I vacillated. "I've already
cheated to get into the study. This will really confound the trial,"
I told him. "It seems immoral—" "Immoral?" he shot back angrily.
"What about their twisted morality in giving half of us a sugar pill
for a year or two in order to see how fast we go to our deaths while
others get a drug that could potentially save their lives? Not only
that—this study prohibits us from taking certain drugs to prevent
opportunistic infections. The odds are stacked against *us*." His
points were well taken. Despite my feelings that we were possibly
corrupting the trial, I agreed to the plan. Needless to say, we kept
this fact from Joan Lederman, who would have immediately dismissed us from the study. (In the beginning of the experiment, no
masking buffer had been placed into the capsules. Numerous patients who were admitted into the trial between February and April
1986 opened their capsules to taste the contents. If the powder
tasted bitter, they continued the treatment. If it tasted sweet, they
threw the bottle away and rushed to catch a plane to try their luck
at getting an actual drug at another site. As a result, Burroughs
Wellcome chemists added the masking buffer, which prevented this
simple test.)

Both Rob and I could tell that something dramatic was happening in the first month of taking the white capsules, making us

believe that at least one of us had been designated to receive the real drug. My own CD4 cell count rose by approximately 15 percent; I also gained ten pounds. In addition, my p-24 antigen level, a surrogate marker of viral activity, fell to undetectable levels, and my beta-2 microglobulin level, a nonspecific measure of viral activity, fell into the normal range. Springer's CD4 cell count also rose slightly and the hairy leukoplakia on his tongue resolved completely. We both also experienced mild headaches, especially in the early evening. Later in the study, Springer developed a resistance to AZT, his p-24 antigen level soared, and the drug was no longer effective.

To participate in the study, I actually had to take a full afternoon off from work each week. No one at my office was aware that I was involved in a Phase 2 experiment or that I even suffered from HIV disease. I made up a variety of excuses that seemed to satisfy my superiors, but I knew that many in the office had grown suspicious.

By the time the Phase 2 study began, both the medical community and the general public had heard of AZT's potential for treating AIDS. Largely because a placebo group was being used in the study, media attention focused on the drug, and the progress of the trial was carefully monitored. As publicity about the trial gained momentum, advocacy groups and other watchdog organizations, impatient with what they perceived as an overly tedious and unnecessary process, began accusing Burroughs Wellcome and the FDA of delaying the drug's availability, arguing that withholding a potentially effective drug from AIDS patients was inhumane and unethical, as was the trial's use of a placebo group.

In May 1985, Mathilde Krim, who had taken up the cause of AIDS patients with special rigor, described the AZT study as "morally unacceptable." She cited the use of placebos, the small number of subjects, Burroughs Wellcome's refusal to release AZT for compassionate use, and the six-month treatment period, during which many of the subjects would die. "AZT currently appears to be the most promising treatment," Krim said. "Ten thousand victims are being denied the drug that they and their doctors believe holds the most hope. It should be possible to resolve the need for scientific data with justice and compassion." Krim went on, "The double-blind clinical trial of AZT is an insult to morality." She also criticized the restrictive criteria for eligibility and the six-month deprivation of any other treatment, including prophylaxis for opportunistic infections.

Krim had worked as a researcher at the Weizmann Institute in Israel. In New York in the 1970s, she was among the first to conduct experiments to prove interferon's value in treating cancer. In the early 1980s, she worked with Dr. Joseph Sonnabend in several early AIDS experiments. Shortly thereafter, with Gottlieb, she formed the AIDS Medical Foundation (now AmFAR) and later was a pioneering force in launching the Community Research Initiative. She also worked behind the scenes, staging fund-raising benefits and convincing then-Senator Lowell Weicker (now governor of Connecticut) to increase government funding for the newly formed ACTG system.

Krim suggested ways of testing AZT that surmounted the problem of leaving the control patients untreated. She argued for the use of "historical controls," i.e., using the medical records of past untreated patients whose immunological baseline characteristics were identical to those of a control group, or by comparing AZT with a drug whose toxicity had already been established, such as ribavirin. There was also the possibility of using a research technique popular in France: "crossover" experiments in which both the placebo and non-placebo groups received the actual drug at one point in the study.

Krim was adamant that AZT be supplied for compassionate use to patients who did not qualify for clinical trials or who had very little time left—people in the final stages of AIDS. "If a patient is willing to take a chance and wants it that badly," Krim told *Discover* magazine, "why not give it to him? They'll say, 'It may be toxic,

we've killed mice with AZT.' That's idiotic. We can kill mice with
sugar and salt and mother's milk. We're too paternalistic and in this
case, paternalism coincides with commercial interests."

In fact, she reasoned, AZT should be made immediately available for compassionate use in *all* HIV-positive patients. "If the
Burroughs Wellcome laboratories are not in a position to or do not
want to manufacture enough AZT, then the federal government
must sign contracts with other laboratories and distribute the medicine free of charge. With warships in all four corners of the globe,
the American government has the means to catch all the herring in
all the world's seas."

Krim presented her case on July 1, 1985, before a hearing in
Washington held by New York congressman Ted Weiss's House
Subcommittee on Intergovernmental Relations and Human Resources. But a Burroughs Wellcome spokesman defended the Phase
2 trial process, asserting that if placebo controls were removed, "it
could destroy the most modern and rapid clinical research plans
ever devised."

Indeed, many physicians and researchers agreed that there was
simply no methodologically cleaner way to evaluate a drug's toxicity and efficacy effectively than by placebo-controlled trials.

In spite of the placebo control, changes in the patients' blood
counts immediately tipped off both researchers *and* patients as to
who was on placebo and who wasn't. Rob and I saw it in our blood
chemistry reports, which Joan Lederman gave us every two weeks.
Like the others, we noticed changes in the mean corpuscular volume of our red cells—not a serious condition, but a red flag nonetheless. We also knew that certain patients were experiencing
anemias so severe that they were required to return to UCLA for
blood transfusions. We knew that simply the act of giving certain
patients blood transfusions alerted researchers to an apparent drug
effect and required that they implement different forms of patient
"management" for these people.

Because of these side effects, during the second month of the
trial the principal investigators at various sites across the country

began to put pressure on Sam Broder and the study's lead investigators, including Margaret Fischl at the University of Miami, to end the trial prematurely. Fischl and Broder held their ground, contending that the benefit-to-risk ratio of the drug might actually support continuation of the study, even in the face of apparent side effects.

Before the trial had begun, the debate surrounding the drug's possible toxicity and the controversy over giving certain patients placebos prompted Burroughs Wellcome to request NIAID to convene an independent Data and Safety Monitoring Board (DSMB). The DSMB consisted of AIDS experts not directly associated with the study. Its role was to review all patient data periodically in order to identify any significant trends in safety and efficacy, good *or* bad. If either of the two drug groups did exceptionally poorly *or* exceptionally well, the monitoring board was to recommend that the study be discontinued.

On September 19, 1986, some seven months after the start of the trial, the board became convinced that the patients receiving AZT had a significantly higher survival rate than those who did not. The nineteen-to-one ratio was undeniably impressive. Furthermore, the treated group showed a decrease in the number of opportunistic infections, as well as weight gain, increased CD4 cell counts, and improved immune functions. Nevertheless, some patients could not receive full doses of the drug because of its toxicity. As a result of these findings, the DSMB suggested that the placebo arm of the study be suspended on ethical grounds. The Phase 2 trial in which I took part was thus terminated after only sixteen weeks instead of the planned twenty-four.

When I arrived home that Friday afternoon, I received a message on my answering machine from Joan Lederman. "You were on drug all along," she told me. "And the code has been broken prematurely. The preliminary results are promising. Everyone will be converted over to active drug now. Please come in on Monday morning. Joan." Rob learned he had been on active drug as well.

In the Monday morning meeting, I learned that the effects of AZT had proven sufficiently successful that a traditional Phase 3 trial would not be necessary. To provide patient access to the drug, a study was designed to bridge the gap between the Phase 2 trial and marketing approval. Immediately, Burroughs Wellcome, in collaboration with representatives from the NCI, NIAID, FDA, and CDC, developed a protocol that would allow patients access to the drug under a treatment investigational new drug (IND) status. It was decided that we who had participated in the Phase 2 study would become part of the treatment IND and continue to receive the drug while being monitored at UCLA.

By the fall of 1986, my CD4 cell count had risen and I had gained even more weight. I wondered if my early participation in the AZT study, coupled with my consumption of underground immunomodulators, would keep the disease on hold, perhaps even push it back forever. It was optimistic thinking, but believable as well.

CHAPTER 5

THE MAKING OF AN UNDERGROUND AIDS DRUG CZAR

n April 1987, I came home to find a pamphlet in my mailbox from Surgeon General C. Everett Koop. Entitled *Everything You Should Know About AIDS,* the brochure gave basic guidelines on reducing the risk of acquiring the virus. The message, it seemed to me, was long overdue.

I checked my machine for messages. The carpet man wouldn't be able to come tomorrow; a story editor at Showtime, the cable TV channel, wanted to know if I'd completed a coverage for a development meeting Friday afternoon; and then Craig's excited voice. He had heard that researchers at the Weizmann Institute in Israel, considered one of four major medical research centers in the world, had been developing a promising new therapy for AIDS.

I called Craig and explained that I had already seen at Rob Springer's a prototype of the drug to which he referred. Craig told me all he knew about AL-721 from his own research. It was Dr. Meir Shinitzky who had actually developed the compound. His discovery emerged from his search for molecules with the potential to reverse senile dementia in the aged. The fifty-three-year-old Israeli knew what many in the field of aging had discovered: as people get older, the cell membranes lose their fluidity and grow more rigid. This is due partly to a build-up of cholesterol, the substance responsible for hardening of the arteries, and a possible factor in coronary disease. The membranes, Shinitzky knew, were a mixture of proteins and fats. Cholesterol was one of the fats. Scientists had found that the higher the ratio of cholesterol to the rest of the fats, the more rigid the cell wall. Shinitzky conjectured that if he could change the properties of the membrane, he could alter its fluidity and stop the hardening, not simply for cells in the body but for those in the brain as well. In this way, he might be able to reverse the senility associated with aging, perhaps even reverse the aging process itself.

Shinitzky hypothesized that certain compounds, particularly those found in egg yolks, held the potential to draw cholesterol out of the walls of human cells. With his laboratory manager, David Heron, he consulted on the best ways to harness egg yolks as cholesterol-extracting agents. Using an organic solvent and acetone, Heron devised AL-721.

The two men found that the substance induced significant change in the brain cells of aged mice, creating a distinct improvement in the animals' membrane fluidity. With a third scientist, David Samuel, Heron and Shinitzky found that the pain of heroin addiction withdrawal appeared to be sharply reduced in addicted animals, ceasing almost immediately after the drug's administration. The short-term memory of the mice improved as well. The three scientists patented their discovery.

Samuel then conducted a small study of the drug in six people and found that it could be well tolerated and produced no obvious toxicity. He then implemented a larger trial involving sixteen people, to determine if the drug could strengthen their immune systems, as measured by increases in their CD4 lymphocytes. Each was given 15 grams of AL-721 every morning for three weeks. All demonstrated significant improvement in their CD4 cell counts.

A businessman, scientist, and co-founder of Praxis Pharmaceuticals, Dr. Arnold Lippa saw the drug's value and convinced Robert Gallo to conduct *in vitro* studies with the substance. The studies showed that AL-721 did indeed interfere with HIV infectivity, although its exact mode of action could not be elucidated. Lippa worked with Drs. Michael Grieco and Michael Lange, specialists in infectious diseases at St. Luke's–Roosevelt Hospital in New York. With these men and Oxford Research, Inc., in 1986 Lippa succeeded in completing a Phase 1 study of the drug in six ARC patients. The drug did not produce any significant increase in CD4 cell counts, but subjects did gain weight. The FDA encouraged the researchers to wait until the ATEU system was up and running before continuing further testing. With Shinitzky, Lippa published a paper on AL-721's proposed mode of action and its effectiveness in the animal studies that had been completed to date.

Ultimately, a decision on how to proceed with the drug in the United States would have to be made by the AIDS Clinical Drug Development Committee, which met periodically and voted on every potential antiviral agent and immunomodulator thought worthy of study. AL-721 was brought before the committee. Because the preliminary Phase 1 study at St. Luke's–Roosevelt produced some clinical but no immunological improvement in the six ARC patients, no one believed that AL-721 was really very good. They unanimously voted against further testing of it.

Anthony Fauci also believed that the drug had limited value, but he saw the need to prove it once and for all. Beth Israel's Dr. Donna Mildvan agreed to test the drug in a Phase 1 dose-escalating trial that would satisfy the FDA's demand for a maximally tolerated dose and provide more definite data on its efficacy. In the trial, begun in February 1987, for up to eight weeks forty patients ate doses of up to 50 grams of AL-721 smeared on toast. Abbot Laboratories manufactured the drug, using the most sophisticated and expensive acetone-extraction techniques and the finest facilities. Numerous tests confirmed the drug's purity. But as of April 1987 the results were not yet known.

After Craig finished his story and explained that he had just purchased a case of AL-721, which was stored in his refrigerator, I told him I didn't think much of the drug. The entire concept behind it seemed hokey to me, and I had never gone out of my way to obtain it. But hundreds of other HIV patients would. AL-721 would continue to enjoy remarkable popularity underground. Few patients who took underground sources of AL-721, however, experienced the dramatic changes described by Shinitzky and the Israelis.

A year later, my early impressions of AL-721 would be confirmed. Ultimately, Mildvan's study showed that AL-721 produced "no objective evidence of an antiviral or immunorestorative effect in the treated patients." A British study confirmed her findings. After the results became known, several banks refused to fund further testing of the drug. A larger, Phase 2 trial never did materialize. Lippa disassociated himself from Praxis. Most researchers lost interest in AL-721's potential value as an anti-HIV therapeutic. I called Craig, who by that time had stopped taking the drug. We chatted about the remarkable demise of the egg-lipid-based compound. There was another, underground side to the AL-721 story.

Michael May was a talented New York concert pianist and choral director. He began to suffer from HIV-related symptoms in the summer of 1985: weight loss, debilitating fatigue, night sweats, painful sores. Through a friend, he learned about Shinitzky's work with AL-721 and that it might be making some headway against the symptoms of AIDS. May made arrangements with Shinitzky and Dr. Yehuda Skornick to try the material. There was no official clinical trial-in-progress at the Weizmann Institute at the time, but the doctors agreed to allow May to use the drug on a compassionate-use basis. With his mother at his side, he boarded a flight to Tel Aviv in April 1986.

The Israeli investigators were impressed as May's symptoms began to improve after the second week of therapy. He gained weight, his night sweats ceased, his diarrhea disappeared, and his rash vanished.

He returned to New York. By August, after he had been off the drug for several months, his symptoms slowly returned. He went back to the Weizmann Institute for another regimen of AL-721;

again his symptoms disappeared—this time, apparently, for good. He returned to New York and resumed work for the first time in a year. Triumphant, he published his story in the New York *Native,* the San Francisco *Sentinel,* and *AIDS Treatment News.* May wrote that, prior to taking AL-721, "I had developed painful sores. A fungus spread to my legs and arms. My skin was scaly, with red blotches. I had fits of perspiration at night, I had fevers. I couldn't eat and became thin. Worst of all was the generalized feeling throughout my body that I was dying. Indeed, I was dying. . . . In February and March my moribund condition had forced me to let go of my plans, my hopes, my loves, my career, my possessions and life itself. . . . As I write this, I have no more physical symptoms. The infections have gone; the night sweats have stopped and I have no more fevers."

May's own doctor noticed that his condition did improve somewhat, but he was not convinced that it was the magic bullet. Still, he and other doctors were willing to consider the possibility that AL-721 may have had certain benefits.

May convinced the researchers to share a copy of the formula for synthesizing AL-721. He sent it to John S. James, editor and publisher of *AIDS Treatment News,* who published it in the San Francisco *Sentinel* and later in his own newsletter. Simultaneously, May located a pharmaceutical company in New Brunswick, New Jersey, that agreed to make a small batch of AL-721. They used a sample May provided of the Israeli formula as a model for their synthesis.

May sent the New Jersey product sample of the compound to Israel to analyze its sterility and purity and to determine the correct proportions of the ingredients. The analysis proved that while Myers's product was pure, the New Jersey product was not. May then began a furious search for an American company to manufacture the true lipid product, with its complex ratios and extraction processes. With underground researcher Steve Gavin, he contacted a number of manufacturing firms.

Finally, in early 1987, Gavin found a company in Long Island, the American Roland Chemical Company, that represented a foreign firm that claimed they could make AL-721. For a reasonable fee, the company agreed to make a large quantity of the pure drug available. Simultaneously, Gavin succeeded in making a small batch of AL-721 from materials obtained from the Sigma Chemical Company. At this point, Gavin joined forces with Tom Hannan and the New York PWA Coalition. Gavin provided them with a sample of his drug and with information on American Roland. Ultimately, the coalition chose to purchase American Roland's imported product and distribute it as part of the launch of the New York Buyers' Club, the PWA Health Group.

May was upset that the lipids were not prepared correctly. He was afraid that bogus versions of the material would destroy the reputation of what could be a very valuable treatment. There was also the issue of availability of the drug for himself. After a visit to the Weizmann Institute by a United States undersecretary of state, May was unable to obtain any more of the drug.

May contacted a mysterious New Jersey chemist, known only as "Nick," who produced a version of AL-721 that was close to the Israeli formulation. More than twenty HIV-positive patients in New York took it. May attempted to gather efficacy and toxicity data on the various sources of the drug and provided this information to others in the underground.

Simultaneously, South African Drs. Barry Shoub, director of the Department of Virology of the Department of Health and Welfare in the Republic of South Africa, and Hymie Friedlander, a professor of medicine at the University of Witwatersrand in Johannesburg, attempted to open a clinic in South Africa (where patent rights would not be violated) to treat patients with AL-721 and other promising but unapproved therapies. They treated several patients in hotel rooms but were unable to obtain permission from their government to open a treatment facility.

By the time Michael Grieco's Phase 1 study of AL-721 was complete, the people at the center of the underground, like Grieco, knew that the drug was probably worthless or only marginally effective at best. Activist factions later charged that AL-721 was never properly evaluated either through mainstream American studies *or* in the underground. They argued that the underground sources that had sprung up in 1987 through various buyers' clubs varied greatly in quality and that the lack of positive results was simply due to defective manufacturing. This drug was extremely difficult to make; a cursory analysis of the buyers' club products revealed that few bore any resemblance to the real Israeli AL-721. And Donna Mildvan's study at Beth Israel could hardly be considered comprehensive or definitive. The activists further cited more recent research at the Weizmann Institute showing that the drug had some value in treating senile dementia of the Alzheimer's type; Shinitzky's *in vitro* data, which showed that the drug blocked HIV's infectivity in macrophages as well as lymphocytes; and studies establishing that AL-721 reduced circulating HIV antigens in seropositive patients.

The truth is, AL-721 was probably a loser; a handful of mainstream American scientists and underground researchers knew this in the end. Some formulations of the product did approximate the Israeli version, but neither produced any long-term improvements or even stabilization of symptoms in the patients who took them.

Michael May died of AIDS one year after traveling to the Weizmann Institute, despite continued AL-721 treatment. In 1990, the American Foundation for AIDS Research removed the drug from its quarterly treatment directory. The positive anecdotal reports of a few patients, it seemed, had blurred the distinction between scientific fact and the fantasy of efficacy. The real AL-721 is now manufactured by a German pharmaceutical company. Few AIDS patients order it, although it is still available through the New York PWA Health Group.

Rob Springer was not the only underground researcher working feverishly to find an effective AIDS therapy in the mid-1980s. In Pacific Palisades, David Myers had also become a major player.

Myers held a Ph.D. in biology from Harvard and had been a college science professor. He had a much more sophisticated laboratory than Springer and operated a small company synthesizing compounds for industry and research. Myers and his lover had been diagnosed with AIDS in 1981. It was Myers who made the first batch of AL-721 which Springer had shared with me.

But by far, the "godfather" of underground AIDS researchers in the mid-1980s was Steve Gavin. We grew closer as the epidemic progressed. A large man with tangled hair and a swarthy appearance, Gavin possessed a master's degree in math, taught computer science in New Jersey, and had worked for various corporations as a free-lance software developer. Like Springer, he had a heavy background in organic and inorganic chemistry in college, although he had never worked professionally in the chemistry field. Gavin helped compile information for the original treatment directory of AmFAR and wrote a regular column on AIDS treatments for the Baltimore *Alternative*. He was one of the first underground researchers to display a broad-based background in HIV pharmacology.

When his lover, Jim, was diagnosed with AIDS in 1984, Gavin searched the world over for something to help. He learned about AZT in 1985 when early reports about the promising results from Broder's Phase 1 study leaked out. One of Gavin's many residences was just minutes from the sprawling National Institutes of Health in Bethesda and he frequently consulted with researchers there on prospective therapies. He built an ongoing relationship with several, including Yehuda Skornick. These people indicated that AZT might be a major advance in the fight against AIDS. Gavin attempted to have Jim admitted to the Phase 2 trial at the NIH and at St. Luke's–Roosevelt Hospital, but no spots would be open until February 1986. It was October 1985 and Gavin wanted immediate access to AZT. Time was running out for Jim, who had already suffered one bout of PCP.

Gavin first contacted Burroughs Wellcome Company and spoke with the lead staff chemist there. Suspecting that Gavin was a reporter, the chemist gave no detailed information on how the nucleoside analog could be obtained or synthesized. So Gavin spent hours in the Johns Hopkins University medical library and finally found an obscure article in a Russian journal of organic chemistry that provided a simple method for making AZT. Gavin subsequently found a chemist at Queens College willing to try the synthesis but who was unable to produce the drug, since the "instructions" proved utterly inadequate.

Undaunted, Gavin located an article by researchers at the University of Michigan that provided a more detailed account of synthesizing AZT. He brought these articles to a chemist friend with a background in synthesizing nucleoside analogs. In less than one month, he produced 600 grams of the drug, which, upon independent analysis, proved to be pure. It was a small amount, just enough for Jim. Gavin mixed the drug in liquid and gave Jim 700 milligrams a day—a median dose he calculated as being reasonable from the Phase 1 NIH study.

In his first six months on the drug, Jim showed major improvements: weight gain, increased energy, and resolution of chronic fungal nailbed infections. After a year, however, he became anemic and leukopenic, so Gavin took him off AZT. Several months later, he developed a second bout of PCP. One year later, he succumbed to AIDS.

"There's no question AZT helped him," Gavin told me in a phone conversation years later. "It extended his life and improved the quality of what was left."

Gavin was not HIV-positive himself at the time, but he immersed himself in the underground drug scene and continued to help those who still suffered. A year after Jim's death, Gavin learned about a "second-generation cousin" to AZT called ddC (dideoxycytidine). According to preliminary reports, ddC was more powerful and perhaps as safe as AZT. Through David Myers, Gavin found the Ray-Lo Chemical Company in Canada (now defunct), which produced a pharmaceutical grade of the compound. At this point, Gavin joined forces with Ed Rogers, who had been HIV-positive for several years. Rogers's lover had progressed to full-blown AIDS, and Rogers believed that ddC held the potential to save his life. With Gavin's assistance, Rogers visited the Canadian company posing as a researcher. He managed to convince the company that he and Gavin were legitimate scientists. Gavin used a corporate account he had established for his computer business to handle the purchase of the material and to maintain a front for a bogus research firm that he called Rod Inc. Ultimately, Ray-Lo sold Gavin half a kilo of ddC, which Gavin distributed from his home in Maryland to more than fifty AIDS patients across the country—members of an informal buyers' group—along with detailed instructions on the drug's proper mixage and dosing, and information on all the *in vitro* data accumulated to date. Many of these people also ordered AL-721 from him; and, in monitoring patients' responses to ddC, he gathered valuable information on the drug's basic toxicity and efficacy, which he shared with Springer and Myers.

In addition to his work with AL-721, Gavin was the one who provided Springer with information on how to enterically coat the Imuthiol and also how to make dextran sulfate, another compound that showed promise in the test tube against HIV. And it was Gavin who first worked with David Wilson in obtaining ddI (dideoxyionisine) in what became one of the most ambitious distribution programs by any one person in the underground.

At one point, Gavin, Springer, and Myers formed a remarkably sophisticated underground network that functioned as a research, development, and small-scale manufacturing organization and which scrutinized the scientific literature, obtained or synthesized promising compounds, and provided experimental anti-HIV medications to a small number of PWAs across the country. In much the same way that mainstream researchers spoke with each other about a drug's potential value and toxicity, so too did these underground researchers engage in the scientific discourse that is the cornerstone of assimilating data and confirming impressions. Gavin, Springer, and Myers kept track of the effectiveness of the drugs they were supplying and the ones that seemed promising and nontoxic were referred to the likes of Tom Hannan and Jim Corti, individuals with the means to locate and import larger supplies of the compounds in international markets and then establish mechanisms to sell them to AIDS patients in the community. The patients' conditions were monitored by their individual physicians. These underground researchers were the forerunners to the underground studies and buyers' clubs that would emerge in 1988 and 1989.

In some cases, underground researchers shared their protocols with physicians in the community and provided them with small quantities of drug. The doctors administered the drugs to select patients, monitored their progress, and collected data.

Sam Broder mistrusted the activities of the AIDS drug underground. He had heard about Gavin and Springer and regarded them with contempt. In Bruce Nussbaum's *Good Intentions: How Big Business and the Medical Establishment Are Corrupting the Fight Against AIDS*, Broder is quoted as saying, "Science is being undermined. A number of people, for their own need to do something, took a number of approaches that basically were ad hoc self-experimentation. They were simply saying: 'I either don't trust or don't believe in or can't wait for the scientific method to work.' . . . They were saying: 'I will find a drug by myself and I will solve this problem. But I don't have to go through the scientific method.' "

What Broder failed to understand was that while many AIDS patients did lack true scientific understanding, a handful of individuals in the underground did know the scientific method, fully understood how to critically interpret journal articles describing the findings of clinical trials, could learn about the pharmacokinetics and modes of action of a drug, and, in some cases, could synthesize the compound. They came from a diversity of backgrounds and in conjunction with sympathetic physicians were able to pool their respective talents and implement monitoring trials of a drug's effectiveness. Ultimately, they rapidly and accurately gauged a drug's true short-term value in combating HIV-induced immune dysregulation. Although they could not match the precision of a controlled clinical trial, their efforts were more sophisticated than ad hoc self-experimentation.

And even though they lacked the means with which to search for novel compounds themselves, they scoured recondite articles detailing *in vitro* studies of compounds, some of which may have escaped the attention of government researchers. They then sought to obtain obscure drugs often not yet approved in the United States and evaluate them in similar monitoring studies.

As Broder himself pointed out, the underground emerged as much from mistrust as from impatience. Dr. Donald Abrams, one of the principal investigators at San Francisco General Hospital, wrote in the December 1990 issue of the journal *AIDS:*

> Many individuals—particularly those infected with HIV or at risk—have felt a sense of frustration at the pace of the research effort and the ultimate conquest of the disease . . . Among all concerned constituencies, perhaps the most vocal and critical individuals have been representatives from the male homosexual community, the group with the United States' highest incidence of HIV infection. It was within this community that the seeds were planted from which would grow an increasingly vocal and assertive alternative therapy movement.
>
> After HIV had been isolated in 1983 and 1984, there was a sense of elation, albeit extremely short-lived, because the face of the enemy was now known. Expectations ran high, both within governmental and scientific circles and among in-dividuals diagnosed with the disease, that a cure—or at least a vaccine—would be available within a year or two at the most. A society which had put men on the moon certainly should have no trouble devising the technology to combat a minute retrovirus.
>
> Disappointment and distrust began to emerge in 1985. HIV had now been recognized for a year. Substantial prog-ress had been made in dissecting the structure and function of the viral genome. Why was no progress being made in

discovering an effective antiviral agent? Why was it taking so long to investigate the agents that had demonstrated some *in vitro* activity against the retrovirus? Why were the clinical trials being launched enrolling so few patients, and in particular, why were the trials seemingly limited to only those patients with end-stage disease as opposed to those whose immune systems could potentially be preserved by an early intervention? It was out of this emotional climate of frustration and despair that the alternative therapy movement was born.

The growth of the AIDS drug underground was also linked to the slow process of approving drugs for licensing in the United States and the rigorous FDA approval process.

The system of American drug development begins with preclinical testing in which a promising agent is first subjected to extensive *in vitro* and animal testing to determine if the compound is in fact biologically active and safe in animals, even in high doses. Before human tests can start, the drug sponsor must file an investigational new drug application (IND) with the FDA, showing the results of all animal testing and how the drug is made. The IND also details the principal investigator's plans for clinical trials, and outlines the trials' methodology and outcome. The IND eventually becomes effective if the FDA does not disapprove the application in thirty days. Once the IND is approved, Phase 1 safety studies and pharmacological profiling may ensue. In this phase, the drug's pharmacological actions, safe-dosage range, method of absorption, distribution, metabolism and excretion, and duration of action are determined by administering it to a small number of healthy subjects. If the drug proves safe and biologically active, Phase 2 pilot efficacy studies proceed. In this phase, controlled multicenter studies are initiated, involving two hundred to three hundred subjects, mainly to assess the drug's effectiveness. This may take up to two years to complete.

In Phase 3, the testing is expanded to larger numbers of subjects in clinics and hospitals. The drug is administered to those actually suffering from the condition that the drug is intended to treat. Phase 3 trials are intended to confirm early efficacy studies and identify low-incidence adverse reactions. They can take up to three years. If the clinical trials of a drug are successful, a sponsor who wants to market it must file a new drug application (NDA) with the FDA, which then reviews all the data. Containing all the information the sponsor has gathered, an NDA typically runs into thousands of pages. The information includes the chemical structure of the drug, scientific rationale and purpose, animal and laboratory studies, results of human trials, formulation and production details, and proposed labeling. On average, *this* review process takes two to three years. To put a drug through the entire twelve-year system, a pharmaceutical company typically spends $230 million.

Only five out of every four thousand compounds screened in the lab make it to human testing, and only one of those is actually approved.

To further complicate the process, in addition to filing an IND, a sponsor and principal investigator are required to submit the protocol to an institutional review board (IRB) before starting clinical trials. The goal of an IRB is to protect the rights of human subjects in medical/scientific experiments. An IRB is composed of at least five people with varying backgrounds who are generally knowledgeable in the research areas likely to be considered. A range of racial, ethnic, and other interests must be represented on the board. At least one member must come from a nonscientific discipline, such as law or the clergy, and at least one other must not be affiliated with the research institute.

The IRB meets to review the protocol for the proposed research project and may approve or disapprove it or—as is most frequently the case—suggest changes before granting approval. The IRB also continues to review the protocol at least annually while the research is under way to ensure that procedures are used that are consistent with good research design and that do not expose the subjects to unnecessary risk; if any of the subjects is a patient, procedures are used that are already being performed on that subject for diagnostic or treatment purposes; the selection of subjects is fair and equitable; safeguards are in place to protect subjects such as the mentally retarded who may not be capable of looking after their own interests; any potential risks to the subjects are reasonable in relation to any expected benefits; it is able to gauge the importance of the scientific knowledge that may be gained; provisions are in place to protect the privacy of subjects and maintain the confidentiality of the data; and subjects have given their informed consent, by signing a form indicating that they have been given adequate information about the study and the opportunity to ask questions about any aspect of it. In short, the IRB provides ethical oversight.

There have been exceptions to this process. In 1962, a policy was added that allowed a doctor to treat a patient with a drug not approved in the United States, without applying for an IND permit or IRB approval. The permission was granted in the cases of some very rare diseases or when no standard therapy was available. In 1976, a "Group C Status" amendment was added that allowed cancer patients to receive the latest drugs, without participating in a clinical trial, if the drugs appeared safe.

In October 1988, the FDA announced an interim rule to speed approval of drugs for life-threatening illnesses and other serious disorders. Under the plan, known as "Treatment IND," if the drug showed efficacy and safety in Phase 2, it could be made available to large numbers of patients.

And in June 1988, the FDA approved a "personal import policy" that allowed patients to import a three-month supply of any experimental drug from anywhere in the world, provided that it was licensed or legal in its country of origin and was for the patient's own use, and that the patient would be monitored by a physician while taking the drug. The policy remained in effect even if the drug was being studied in American clinical trials and the monitoring physicians had not been required to obtain an IND permit or IRB approval.

Patients wishing to obtain an experimental drug manufactured in the United States and available only here could also file for a "Compassionate Use IND" permit and receive the drug while being monitored by a personal physician. This IND permit, however, required the cooperation of the drug company making the compound (sometimes difficult to obtain) and could take weeks to process.

In the May 5, 1989, issue of *AIDS Treatment News,* editor and publisher John S. James wrote that mainstream treatment research is based on a mind-set that supports the following notions:

— The first goal of clinical research is to prove, to a statistically stated degree of confidence, that a drug does work better than nothing (placebo), or better than some existing treatment.

— Above all, clinical trials must guard against the danger that a drug which is useless and perhaps harmful could become accepted and generally used in medicine, as has happened many times in the past.

— Since most drugs being tested will show only a small benefit, trials must be designed to distinguish a small benefit from none at all.

— The fact that a trial imposes an unrealistic environment which may never occur in practical use of a new drug does not matter. What is important is to learn about a drug in isolation, not a therapy in practical use.

— If for whatever reason (such as lack of national political will), it is impossible to arrange a trial which meets these and all other standards of pure research, then it is better to do nothing until such future time as trials may be done, instead of doing any other kind of a study, which could lead to error.

James added that in addition to ensuring the welfare of the research subject, this system also developed to serve the needs of the power players—pharmaceutical companies and the federal agencies.

He further wrote:

> The [pharmaceutical] companies want above all to get their NDA [permit], allowing them to market a drug which they have exclusive rights to and have chosen to push. The FDA, supported by consumer protectionists in Congress and elsewhere, wants above all to protect the public from unsafe or unproven drugs.... No one has the mission of making sure that trials which are critically important for saving lives get done quickly, or making sure that patients have access to treatments which are clearly beneficial but which for any of a multitude of reasons have not gone through all the steps necessary for full marketing approval. The smaller, more creative biotechnology and pharmaceutical firms simply cannot compete effectively in the current FDA overregulated marketplace. While they may be able to develop an innovative drug and put it through Phase 1 testing, they cannot afford to pay interest on that investment for ten years while simultaneously funding Phase 2 and Phase 3 trials.

Mark Harrington of the AIDS activist group ACT UP (AIDS Coalition to Unleash Power) and the Gay Men's Health Crisis in New York further outlined problems with conventional clinical trials and suggested means to resolve them in a statement presented at the third and final committee meeting of the Lasagna Committee Hearing (a national committee to review current procedure for the approval of new drugs for cancer and AIDS) in 1989. Specifically, Harrington pointed out that because of narrowly defined entry criteria, certain subjects were not eligible for government-sponsored trials. Trials should be designed to allow a broader range of people in, he argued. The use of placebos, according to Harrington, was as unethical as the practice in clinical trials of banning other drugs that could prevent opportunistic infections. Subjects should be allowed to continue to take such medications as pentamidine and

Bactrim and acyclovir, even in the setting of a clinical trial, and thus replicate "real world" conditions. And to use death as an endpoint through placebos was cruel and unnecessary. He argued that other outcome variables such as CD4 cell counts and clinical response should be used to gauge a drug's effectiveness in a clinical trial. Finally, Harrington noted that clinical trials were often designed by investigators in "ivory towers," isolated from a true perspective of their patients' problems. AIDS patients themselves, he emphasized, should be intimately involved in the clinical trial design process, not just by sitting on IRBs but by actively participating in the formulation of such detailed decisions as a drug's method of administration, dosage, and concurrently administered medications allowable in the trial.

At the epicenter of the conflict of AIDS drug regulation was Dr. Ellen Cooper, the manager of antiviral drug development in the Food and Drug Administration. She was a pediatrician and mother of four. She held a Phi Beta Kappa key from Swarthmore College, where she graduated with honors in political science in 1972. She attended Yale University School of Medicine for two years and then moved to Cleveland with her husband, John Michael Cooper, a lawyer, graduating from Case Western Reserve School of Medicine in 1976. She earned a master's degree in public health from Johns Hopkins in 1977 and spent five years at Children's Hospital National Medical Center in Washington, where she trained in pediatrics and infectious diseases. She joined the FDA on a research fellowship in virology in 1982.

By 1985, Cooper had risen to the position of director of HIV antiviral drugs, making her the single most important person involved in FDA decisions on drugs designed to attack the AIDS virus and the opportunistic infections associated with it. She had no jurisdiction over immunomodulators for HIV.

In 1987, at the time AZT was approved, Cooper was thirty-four years old—too young, according to the critics, to be given such massive responsibility. She was petite, had short, cropped hair, and wore conservative business suits. Some called her demeanor cold, others went so far as to label her "the ice queen." In addition to believing strongly in the scientific method and its unrelenting requirements, she also stated her views in plain language, without pulling any punches.

To her credit, Cooper was responsible for speeding the approval of AZT and gaining regulatory approval for marketing the drug to more than four thousand patients even before final approval for marketing. Her admirers cite this, along with her credentials and hardworking stance, when they maintain that she actually cares for the dying patient, and is compassionate and courageous.

Her critics have claimed that she was inexperienced and so determined to follow the strict scientific process that she needlessly denied drugs whose value had not been fully proven to dying AIDS patients who were willing to risk trying them. In 1985, Cooper led the FDA's decision to deny the widespread use of ribavirin on the grounds that the studies of its efficacy were fatally flawed. She restricted access of an anti-PCP drug, trimetrexate, to a narrow range of patients. Critics have also alleged that she vehemently insisted on the use of placebos in clinical trials.

After she stepped down from her position as the FDA's director of antiviral drugs in 1991, Cooper, referring to the early approval of ddI, told one activist: "The agency has become an advocate for the drug. It's lost its objectivity. That's wrong. The FDA's job is to decide whether the data submitted for a new drug meets the legal standard. It's not a question of whether researchers and doctors out there feel that it works. For a regulatory agency, you have to have data. If the drug company doesn't prove statistically significant efficacy, then the drug just doesn't get licensed. It's simple." Activists argued that it was not "that simple," and that other factors—including the positive clinical outcomes of patients in expanded-access programs, perhaps "softer" than the data Cooper had insisted upon—needed to be taken into consideration as well.

For her part, Cooper insisted that she was very open to alternative means for evaluating drugs, that she was merely one of a number of persons responsible for the actual decision-making process in approving AIDS drugs, and that she was being targeted as a scapegoat by frustrated patients and the advocacy groups that represented them.

AIDS patients across the country turned to the underground and the alternative therapies movement because of the slow pace of the medical research establishment as well as the apathy, frustration, and helplessness expressed by their individual physicians. Indeed, many doctors were simply unaware of the alternative therapies that existed or unwilling to monitor patients using them because of lack of knowledge about the drugs' modes of action, the possible toxic effects, and the illegality involved. And many patients questioned why they should trust a doctor who could offer them nothing, or only the most conservative therapy at best. Based on their own research and education, they felt they'd be better off trusting their own instincts, making their own informed decisions about potential treatments, and then finding a physician or health professional willing to support them in that effort. Indeed, a survey of patients attending an outpatient HIV/AIDS clinic in San Francisco revealed that 21 percent reported using at least one unapproved or unconventional treatment.

It was a conservative estimate. Other studies showed that up to 52 percent of all HIV-positive patients were taking some sort of unapproved therapy. The majority of them obtained the drug either through an AIDS buyers' club or a health-food store. A smaller number obtained the substance directly from an underground source or through a European pharmacy or buyers' club.

As the Phase 1 and 2 studies showed, AZT was not without its side effects. Both Rob and I realized that the drug was having an adverse effect on our white and red blood cell counts. By the second month of therapy, we realized that the 1,500-milligram-per-day dose was double or triple the optimum. We cut back to 600 milligrams a day without telling the researchers and noted that we were able to maintain the positive benefits of the drug without incurring any significant suppression of our bone marrow. Three years after we had decreased our doses, federal researchers would announce that 600 milligrams *was* the optimum dose and that the drug was effective at this level, with few side effects.

Others in our study group were not so lucky. Two ARC patients, whom Rob and I knew casually outside of the study, had remained on the 1,500-milligram-per-day dose and suffered serious anemia, requiring multiple blood transfusions. One of them became so sick he had to discontinue therapy for several weeks. He rapidly progressed from ARC and relative stability to AIDS, developed one opportunistic infection after another, and finally died.

Certainly, death was not uncommon among the subjects in the study as time marched on. By January 1987, four months after the study code had been broken, three AIDS patients and one ARC patient in the study had died. People in my Shanti group seemed to be dying in rapid succession as well. Bob and Mark had passed away within days of each other; Kevin was deathly ill. Craig and I visited him at Cedars–Sinai Medical Center one evening in February.

The hospital was clean and bright, and, unlike at others in the Los Angeles area, AIDS patients were given preferential treatment. Craig and I had heard horror stories about hospitals in Van Nuys where nurses left food trays outside the door, parading into rooms with masks and gowns like spacewomen, sweat at their temples. But no one here seemed afraid.

Kevin suffered from both CMV infection and PCP. Looking pale and exhausted, he lay propped up on his pillow. A tube had been placed in one of his nostrils, feeding him oxygen. A total of five intravenous "piggybacks" hung on a multihooked pole, dripping a variety of colored fluids into his veins. CMV had destroyed the retina in his left eye, leaving him totally blind in that eye. As a result, he moved his head constantly, needing to identify the source of sounds reaching his ears on his blind side. His shirt clung to his rib cage, over which his wasted arm flopped like a skeleton's. A few wisps of brittle hair sat atop his skull.

I did not recognize his face. I followed the line of his sharp, hollow cheekbones, the larger-than-normal violet eyelids stretched across his eyes, and the lips filled with tiny fissures.

But beyond his grotesque physical condition, I recognized my friend, and the revulsion slowly faded.

He tried to talk to us, but just the effort made him breathless from exhaustion.

He somehow mustered the strength to lift his hand and whisper hoarsely, "It's not fair that people like you have to go through this. I've lived my life, but you guys are too young. It's really . . . not . . . fair."

This once cynical and jaded man now displayed selflessness and compassion in his final hours. I was struck by the change in his character as I lifted my hand to touch his. His flesh felt cold and I almost pulled back, startled.

"You find a way out of this, you hear?" Kevin whispered. "You're smart enough."

I felt tears on my cheeks as I said, "You're going to be all right, Kevin."

He coughed again, then looked at me with genuine sadness in his eyes. A nurse came into the room and asked us to leave.

We learned that he died sixteen hours later from complications of colonic CMV.

The shock of Kevin's death was compounded by one even closer to home and far more personal, when I tried to contact my high-school boyfriend Pete Parsons. I had stopped corresponding with Pete after I moved to San Francisco in 1982 but had spoken with him by phone several times over the course of the last year. He seemed satisfied with his life in Indianapolis, where he lived with his lover, and seemed perfectly healthy. I placed a phone call to his home. His lover, whom I had never met, answered.

"Is Pete there?" I asked.

"I'm sorry, but Pete died two months ago. He had AIDS."

I was speechless. Finally I offered, "How long had he actually been sick?"

"For only a year. He developed tuberculosis and it spread. The doctors did everything they could."

"I'm sure they did. How old was he?" I asked.

"Twenty-five. Were you a friend?" the man asked.

I paused, considering the question. "Yes," I replied. "I was." It would have been impossible to explain the complexity of our relationship, the first serious one I had ever had, and which had lasted for a year. I wasn't even certain at that moment exactly what I felt for Pete myself. A strange combination of emotions churned inside me as I awkwardly attempted to bring the conversation—an all-too-familiar one being played out across the nation—to an end.

"Thank you for the information." I felt myself choking on my words as I hung up the telephone. There was a knot at the pit of my stomach.

It was nine o'clock in the evening. The streets in the Vermont–Wilshire district were hardly safe at that hour. Still, I felt a burning need to get to the nearest high-school-stadium field. I threw on a sweater and headed down Wilshire by foot. For some reason, I ran all the way, ran from the fear of my own mortality, of what would happen to me in the end, as it happened to Kevin and Pete.

The football field was deserted. I collapsed on the grass and cried for nearly an hour.

At six a.m., a security guard found me sprawled on the playing field.

I got up, brushed off my pants, and returned home.

On February 13, 1987, about a month before AZT hit the market, Burroughs Wellcome issued a short press release announcing that the price of the drug would be approximately $188 per bottle of one hundred 100-milligram capsules. At the recommended dosage of 1,200 milligrams a day, this amounted to $10,000 per person a year, making the drug among the most expensive of its kind. People who had been receiving the drug free through the treatment IND pro-

gram would have to begin paying for it on March 19. Luckily, Rob
and I continued to receive it free as part of UCLA's expanded
monitoring program of the patients in its original Phase 2 study.

Activists immediately protested the exorbitant price, which
was especially outrageous given the financial plight of AIDS and
ARC patients, most of whom were already devastated by medical
and hospital expenses. For its part, Burroughs Wellcome vehemently defended the $10,000 price tag, although it never explained
publicly exactly how it arrived at the particular figure. David Barry
did remind the press that Burroughs Wellcome had already spent
$80 million in direct costs to develop the drug and that the intro-
duction of newer, more promising compounds clouded the future of
financial returns from AZT. Even so, the figure still seemed outrageous to me, especially in view of *Barron's* prediction that Burroughs
Wellcome stood to earn some $200 million from AZT in its first
year on the market.

Although we continued to receive the drug for free, Rob and
I were nonetheless concerned. Ultimately, we—and our insurance
companies—*would* have to pay, and $10,000 a year simply seemed
unreasonable. We telephoned Representative Henry Waxman of
California, as did hundreds of other AIDS patients across the country. Waxman called a hearing of his Subcommittee on Health and
the Environment on March 10, 1987. He questioned the fairness of
the drug's price and asked Burroughs Wellcome to provide additional information on the costs of the distribution and manufacture
of the drug. Nearly two years later, through the combined results of
his hearing and the publicity generated by activists, Waxman succeeded in having the price reduced by 20 percent.

It was Jay from my Shanti group who first introduced me to Jim
Corti. A nurse, artist, and competitive bicyclist, Corti had already
lost his lover John to AIDS but was not seropositive himself. Like
Steve Gavin, Corti had fought valiantly to save his lover's life; when

the standard medications failed, Corti tried several innovative approaches, but John succumbed to another opportunistic infection weeks later.

Since the outset of the epidemic, Corti had carefully followed the emergence of every new drug that gained attention in the press and in the underground. He often spoke with Rob Springer and David Myers and got their early impressions about promising drugs. He was one of the first to import large quantities of ribavirin and isoprinosine from Mexico in the same manner that I had in 1984, subsequently distributing the drugs to other AIDS patients through an informal network in Los Angeles and northern California. In 1989, he was described by one reporter as "the point man in what had developed into an increasingly sophisticated international drug underground that imported a wide array of drugs from the four corners of the world and distributed those drugs to AIDS patients across the country."

Corti stood six feet, two inches tall and weighed 220 pounds. He wore large glasses with red frames that gave him a look of chic sophistication and worldly experience. While his outward appearance and demeanor brought to mind a college math professor, his lexicon was often punctuated with streetwise metaphors and colorful adjectives. He had traveled to almost every country in the world, attended art shows and openings in Europe and Canada, and been on bicycle expeditions throughout the United States and abroad. He had the ability to maneuver his way through any country. Acting as a courier for supplies of ribavirin and isoprinosine, he had survived confrontations at the U.S.–Mexico border. In the parking lot of a pharmaceutical company in Milan, Corti was accosted by thieves who attempted to steal a rare and hard-to-get thymic factor he had obtained, along with $2,000 in cash; he delivered two swift karate chops to his attackers, incapacitating them, and then sped off in his rented BMW. By placing himself in often unpredictable and even dangerous situations to obtain drugs and then devising and executing strategies to bring them into the country, he was truly the James Bond of the underground.

On May 5, 1987, I went to Corti's loft at the edge of downtown Los Angeles. The sky looked ominous; a rare southern California tropical storm loomed near. I paid the cabbie, checked the address Jay had given me, walked up to the front door, and knocked several times. After a minute, I was greeted by a friend of Corti's who ushered me into the spacious flat. Corti was on the phone, the young man explained, but would be with me in a minute. I surveyed Corti's apartment. The place was simply furnished and contained a record collection, modern art on the walls, and two expensive-looking racing bikes. From the next room, I could hear Corti's voice on the phone, explaining to someone the latest news about dextran sulfate—the very reason for my visit.

Dextran sulfate was developed in the 1950s as an oral treatment for hyperlipidemia, an elevation of fats in the blood. Researchers found that, given intravenously, a different preparation of dextran sulfate exerted an anticoagulant effect, similar to that of heparin. In Japan, it had been used for both purposes for more than twenty years. In 1986 an Osaka chemist, Dr. Ueno Seiyaku, published an article in *Lancet* reporting his findings that dextran sulfate had potent *in vitro* antiviral effects against HIV. Subsequent studies confirmed the initial report and further suggested that the drug might actually work by blocking the formation of syncytia (clumps of HIV-infected cells that fuse with uninfected cells) and, in so doing, compound the destruction of the CD4 lymphocyte population. If dextran sulfate worked as well in the body as it did in the test tube, it might prove to be a major advance as an anti-HIV agent. Ueno reported that he believed the concentrations of dextran sulfate that inhibited HIV could be easily achieved by nontoxic oral administration of the drug (although he had no proof of this). He further suggested that the drug might act synergistically with AZT, meaning that the effect of both compounds against HIV would be potentially greater than that of each drug taken separately.

Rob Springer had actually made enterically coated dextran sulfate flakes through an outside lab. But he could not produce the drug in large enough quantities and refused to reveal his source of production. Furthermore, Corti had heard complaints from PWAs that Rob was insisting on a minimum order of a one-year supply, at a cost of $1,200.

Corti was finally able to convince a West Texan PWA who had obtained the drug from Japan to reveal his overseas source. Corti established a relationship with the pharmacy that had sold the man from Texas the drug and persuaded its proprietors to sell him 15,000 pills at a cost of thirty-two cents a pill. Corti returned to Japan and imported an additional 16,000 tablets. He subsequently returned to Japan yet again, ultimately bringing in some 300,000 pills at a time. He found it safer to ship the pills directly into the country to sympathetic facilities rather than carry them on his person as a risky prelude to the inevitable confrontation with customs agents.

Corti hung up the phone and strode into the room.

I introduced myself as Corti shook my hand.

"Have a seat," he offered. "I'm sure Jay told you something about dextran."

"Yes, he did," I said. "A friend of mine expressed some concern that since the drug was primarily used as an anticoagulant, some side effects might be expected—problems with platelet levels, perhaps."

"I haven't seen that side effect in the first few patients who have taken the drug here," Corti assured me. "And I've followed their lab values carefully. Generally, you have to go up past 3,500 milligrams a day to see that kind of toxicity; 2,750 milligrams a day has been shown to be safe in human studies of the drug in Japan and that's the dose I'm recommending for HIV. Just about the only side effect you might experience is bloating or mild loss of appetite."

"I read that the lethal dose in animals is about a hundred fifty times the AIDS dose. Is that true?"

"That's what I've heard."

"It might be synergistic with AZT. Is *that* true?" I asked.

"Maybe," Corti said. "In any case, there's no harm in combining the two. Are you taking AZT now?"

I nodded. "I'm in the study at UCLA. Of course, I'd have to keep this from them."

"I've got three other guys in the AZT study at USC who just bought some this morning. There's no way they'll be able to detect that you're taking the drug through the blood chemistry tests they run. There's no overriding marker that could tip them off. You don't have any history of liver, kidney, cardiac, or neurological disease unrelated to HIV, do you?"

"No," I replied. "I was healthy as a horse before my HIV diagnosis. I'm still relatively healthy except for swollen lymph nodes."

"That's good. I generally don't sell any of these medications to persons with any history of concurrent illnesses. That's why I asked."

I could hear the unmistakable sound of thunder. Thick streams of rain pelted the roof of Corti's loft, sounding like distant darts hitting a target.

"Another gusher," he said. "Rare for this time of year."

"Yes, it is. Here's the blood work you wanted," I said.

Corti scrutinized the paperwork from the UCLA study. Finally he said, "Then it's a done deal. Here you go."

He produced a single aluminum foil–wrapped package with the name UENO FINE CHEMICAL COMPANY typed neatly on the outside and the statement, WARNING: NEW DRUG LIMITED BY U.S. LAW TO INVESTIGATIONAL USE.

"This is it. One package of a hundred pills will last you exactly a week and a half. Take nine pills a day—three, three times a day with meals and your normal dose of AZT."

"I'm also taking Imuthiol," I told him. "I obtained it from Rob Springer months ago."

"That's fine. There's no known negative interaction between dextran and DTC. In fact, several guys I sold dextran to are taking both."

"Are there any trials planned with dextran sulfate?" I asked.

"There's one under way at San Francisco General under the

direction of Dr. Donald Abrams. But you know how long things seem to take."

"I heard Dr. Scolaro is considering using the drug."

"I think he plans to try it in some patients."

"I also heard that dextran sulfate might work synergistically with heparin to inhibit HIV."

"That could be true," he said. "But I don't know of anyone injecting them together."

I felt certain that by this point Corti must have perceived me as an avid student of AIDS medications—and a pest.

"Thank you for all this information," I told him.

"No problem," he responded. "All I ask is that you keep me posted with your T-cell results. We need to start collecting some hard data on the drug. Why don't you start with three packages?" he suggested. "That should last you four and a half weeks. If you don't have any problems with it, come back next month."

"Fine," I said. "How much will all this cost?"

"The information *de nada*. Fifty dollars for the three packages," Corti said. "That represents a 15-percent markup from the actual cost of the drug in Japan. I don't make any profit on this," he said with real honesty in his eyes. "Just enough to cover expenses."

I wrote a check for $50 and placed it in Corti's hands. Then I pushed the pouches of the drug deep into the pocket of my raincoat.

He rose. "Did you drive here?" Corti asked.

"Actually I took a cab from my office."

"I'll drive you back. You can't wait in this rain for another taxi." He threw on a raincoat and grabbed an umbrella.

Outside, the rain was coming down in torrents. We made a dash for his minivan and hopped in. Corti was amiable and talkative before dropping me off in front of my office.

In the months that followed, I noticed that my CD4 cell count did rise slightly on the dextran sulfate. Clinically, however, I wasn't getting any better. In fact, my health was subtly starting to go downhill. Despite the Imuthiol, and the dextran sulfate, and the

AZT, I was plagued with intermittent bouts of increasing fatigue. A small patch of hairy leukoplakia had appeared on my tongue. The small lesions looked almost like patches of raised, white hair. The condition, I learned, was thought to be related to the activation of the Epstein-Barr virus and indicated that my immune system was becoming more depressed.

One evening in the summer of 1987 I awoke with a fever of 106 degrees, nausea, and diarrhea. John rushed me to the hospital.

I wondered if I was experiencing an opportunistic infection and had crossed over to AIDS.

CHAPTER 6

HAY RIDES

was out of the hospital and back to work within a week. Although I still suffered from fatigue, most of my symptoms had resolved completely. The final diagnosis: food poisoning, causing intense gastroenteritis. I had eaten seafood at a Chinese restaurant downtown the evening before. The doctors at Kaiser Sunset Hospital had concluded that the array of symptoms I experienced were likely due to the seafood and not to HIV.

I returned to Corti's loft for months to purchase more dextran sulfate. Yet the drug had not produced any positive effects on my CD4 cell count or impacted any of the clinical symptoms associated with HIV. Nor did it seem to create any significant side effects. Yet the combination of dextran and AZT did produce subtle changes on my standard chemistry panel—namely, a slight lowering of my platelets and a decrease in my total white blood cell count. Joan Lederman noticed the changes and questioned me about them during our semimonthly interview.

"Have you been taking any other HIV medications?" she asked. Her own patients had brought in copies of the *GMHC Newsletter* and *AIDS Treatment News* that described in some depth the latest new antiviral drug or immunomodulator available in the underground. She was well aware that many men were secretly taking the drugs.

When I entered the AZT study, I had promised the investigators that I wouldn't take any other experimental compounds. As part of the study, I had to "stay clean," as it were. Clearly, taking other drugs could vitiate the data that the researchers were gathering on the effects of AZT. Although the official Phase 2 study had ended, researchers continued to track data on the surviving participants. I was therefore hesitant to admit to Joan that I had been one of the cheaters.

"Come on, Paul, fess up," Joan said.

"I'm not sure I should tell you," I stammered. "I don't want to be thrown out of the study."

"Look," she said. "Everything you tell me will be held in the strictest confidence. But I have to know what else you're taking."

Slowly, I opened my white pillbox and produced a tablet of dextran. "This is dextran sulfate," I explained. "It's used as an anticoagulant in Europe and has shown positive anti-HIV effects in the test tube. It seems to be safe at the therapeutic dose I'm taking— 2,700 milligrams a day, or nine of these," I said, showing her the white pills. "And this is Imuthiol," I went on, "also known as DTC. It was developed in France by the Merieux Institute. In early French studies, it raised the CD4 cell counts of several hundred AIDS patients, delayed the progression of ARC to AIDS, and showed no toxicity. It seems to induce the maturation of immature CD4 cells, but it doesn't have the power to produce new ones. I take five of these 100-milligram tablets a week, all at a single sitting." I paused. "I can't reveal exactly where I got them. But they've been analyzed by a lab to ensure their purity."

Joan examined the pills for a long moment. She stared at them, looked at their color and texture, clearly fascinated.

"All of this explains why your white count and CD4 cells have gone up slightly over the last few months," she said, as though a startling revelation had come to light.

"Yes, and the change in my platelets as well. I didn't want to keep it a secret from you, Joan, really. But I didn't want to be thrown out of the study."

"Don't worry," she said as she handed the pills back. "We'll keep this under our hat now that the study's over. But you've got to tell me about every new medication you add into that pillbox. Understand?"

"Yes," I said, relieved.

Our relationship changed after that. Joan became my friend, my confidante. I revealed more and more about myself to her and even shared my day-to-day problems. During those dark days at UCLA, Joan provided remarkable support and guidance, radiating warmth and compassion. She offered courageous encouragement. She listened to my conflicts with a genuine interest and offered ways to improve the quality of my everyday life.

She revealed to me years later that, as the study progressed, it was difficult for her to maintain the cool objectivity that she was supposed to maintain. She and the other nurses came to see us not as nameless subjects in a medical experiment, but as human beings with individual problems and feelings.

"You need a diversion," Joan told me one day. "Don't dwell on your health situation."

"What happens when I meet someone I like and tell him I have the virus?" I asked her.

"You deal with it when the situation arises," she responded. "Each individual is different. Some people need to be up front from the beginning. Others wait until the relationship progresses before they feel comfortable revealing this information."

Two days after she offered this advice, I met Michael Garsten.

He stood by himself at a private party in West Hollywood. He was tall and slender, blond and fair, and his eyes blazed an almost electric blue. He wore Top-Siders, faded 501's and a blue-and-white-striped sweater stretched across his chest. He stood with one hand holding a Heineken, the other dug into his pants pocket. Like me, he was posing—he wanted to be seen. He had been feigning a look registering somewhere between arrogance and indifference, but he broke it off and grinned when he met my glance.

I smiled too, as if we had both witnessed something silly. We spoke for a bit and then went across to Sunset Boulevard. We sat down for a cup of coffee at a small bistro and launched into a conversation that seemed to go on all evening. We told each other the story of our lives. And I felt he understood me as completely as anyone I had ever met.

Michael had graduated from USC four years before I did. He now worked as the director of publicity for a production company and lived alone in a spacious, three-story town house in the Silverlake hills. He enjoyed attending Lakers games and listening to Rachmaninoff. He had had three long-term relationships. Although two of his lovers had tested HIV-positive, he had not. I told him about my condition and he listened with compassion. There was a sort of elective affinity that bound us instantly. We clicked.

I followed him back to his apartment. We undressed carefully, and fell into each other's embrace like two swimmers in a warm, sensuous sea. We surrendered to our senses all weekend. Afterward, we lay exhausted on the sheets and continued to talk. We were equally comfortable with our passion and our personalities. Being with Michael required no effort. As soon as he left my side or I his, I was lonely.

About a month after we first met, we moved in together. We attended screenings of films at the Directors Guild Theater and the Vista Cinema, to which Michael often received passes. We returned to our alma mater to view an Orson Welles retrospective. We took long walks on the beach and dined in elegant restaurants overlooking the ocean. It was idyllic. We had become friends as well as lovers.

Our lovemaking was passionate but safe.

When a person experiences some type of physical handicap, other senses become heightened. To a large extent, this is what occurs in safe sex. I found that other senses became more prominent in our safe lovemaking; there was the opportunity to experiment and the tenderness and novelty we experienced compensated for any limitations on our activities.

The specter of AIDS made it more difficult than ever before for gay men to get together—and stay together. The responsibility of dealing with the issue of one's HIV status honestly and up front could be overwhelming. There was always the fear of rejection on the part of an HIV-positive person becoming involved with an HIV-negative person, if his positive status came to light. Further, being involved with an HIV-positive person brought a whole new set of conflicts and problems into the lives of both people—conflicts that held the potential to destroy or to fortify the relationship over time. Some HIV-negative men were clearly reluctant to deal with this responsibility. In spite of these odds, however, many gay men surmounted these obstacles and remained happily ensconced in monogamous relationships for long periods of time.

I had purposely not told my mother about my condition. I still had hope that a cure would be found, and I didn't want to create worry and added stress in her life. On a visit to Los Angeles, however, she spotted my bottle of AZT, and she discovered my secret.

Because we had openly discussed my homosexuality since my senior year of college, my mother bypassed the double revelation that so many parents endure of simultaneously learning that their children are both gay *and* HIV-positive. My mom accepted the news of my illness with the same attitude with which she handled most seemingly insurmountable obstacles: she promised to help me fight to the finish in any way she could and offered unconditional support.

Together, she and Michael agreed to accompany me to a lecture by Louise Hay, a self-proclaimed "author, lecturer, and metaphysical teacher" who had a large cadre of faithful followers across the country, many of whom firmly believed that her sessions had helped cure them of AIDS-related infections.

Hay's parents had divorced when she was a toddler. Her new

stepfather was both emotionally and physically abusive. She was raped by a neighbor when she was five, and the abuse from her stepfather continued as well. As a teenager she ran away, became pregnant at the age of sixteen, and allowed a childless couple to adopt her newborn daughter. She returned home to guide her mother away from a destructive relationship with her stepfather. She moved to the Midwest and became a fashion model, bent on achieving the success she believed she deserved, working for Bill Blass and Pauline Trigère. During this period, she married a wealthy Englishman and hobnobbed with royalty at the White House and Buckingham Palace. By her own account, her material success had done nothing to improve her self-esteem. She divorced her husband and became disillusioned with the world of high fashion. Instead, she discovered a "metaphysical healing church" in New York City, the Church of Religious Science, which espoused a doctrine based on positive thinking and personal responsibility for one's own experiences. Ultimately, she obtained a doctor of divinity degree from the Science of Mind College.

In 1976, Hay was diagnosed with vaginal cancer. She put her own beliefs to the test and with the help of a neo-Reichian therapist, "released the anger and self-hate that had been locked inside of [me] since [my] childhood days of abuse." She forgave her abusers and gradually came to understand that they, too, were victims. She used colonics, reflexology treatments, and nutritional supplements to detoxify her body and engaged in visualization statements, many of the same ones that she uses now in her "Hay Rides."

After six months of this treatment, Hay claimed that doctors confirmed that her cancer was indeed gone forever. In 1980, she moved to Los Angeles and began working as a metaphysical counselor and teacher. She wrote and distributed pamphlets and audiocassettes in which she encouraged people to stop criticizing themselves, really love themselves, and assume responsibility for the despair and hopelessness in their existence. In 1984, she wrote the popular book *You Can Heal Your Life* and appeared on national talk shows and seminars across the country.

In January 1985, a group of six young men with AIDS asked her if they might meet once a week in the living room of her Santa Monica apartment. The group gradually expanded and Louise, now sixty, founded Hay House in Santa Monica, a place where people with HIV disease could come for support and counseling and learn more about the techniques of visualization and self-healing that she advocated. The operation soon included a successful publishing arm, a teaching unit, and a charitable organization that funds alternative healing programs. The entire operation involved twenty-two employees, a twenty-four-line phone system, an $11,000-a-month, 5,700-square-foot office complex, and a warehouse several blocks away.

Hay was most celebrated for her weekly "Hay Rides," which took place in a large West Hollywood auditorium, and during which she shared her insights and philosophies with HIV-positive people in the community. She also believed in a variety of practical healing techniques and demonstrated them at the seminars, which were free to the public and open to anyone. Unlike the hayrides of one's youth, however, Hay's were journeys through inner space. And it was frequently strangers, not childhood companions, who were at one's elbow.

Implicit in her philosophy was the notion that all people with terminal illness had somehow subconsciously *chosen* their condition. By taking responsibility for that choice, they now had the opportunity to "un-choose" it through appropriate thinking patterns and positive imagery.

By January 1988, Hay's following became so large that she was forced to move to larger quarters up the street. Inside, a banner drawn in poster paints proclaiming LOVE HEALS hung on the wall. Row after row of gay men sat before the platform stage where she stood. Balding middle-aged men sat side by side with youths barely out of their teens, many clearly in varying stages of illness. Those with advanced Kaposi's sarcoma had their faces dotted with broad bands of purple and blue; others looked robust and perfectly well. Newcomers appeared worried, wondering how they would face up to the disease that had already played havoc with their psyches and their bodies. Many sat forward in their seats, hovering over the slightest opportunity or richest expectation. Several clutched teddy bears they had brought from home.

Off to the side, men lay on tables while practitioners of "Reki" held their hands inches above the men's bodies, "transferring" a healing power that they believed was far more potent than any medicine. Other men sat before mirrors on a platform near the center. "Mirror work," the man next to me explained. "When you are looking at yourself, you don't fool yourself. When you say 'I love you,' you have to mean it. It's one of Louise's ideas." In the back of the room was a table where tapes of Louise's lectures and songs, along with New Age literature and healing crystals, could be purchased.

The lights dimmed as my mother, Michael, and I found seats in the front of the room. A prerecorded musical number rose up from the loudspeakers in the front of the room. A young man's voice sang the lyrics of "I Love Myself the Way I Am":

> I Love Myself the way I am,
>   there's nothing I need to change
> I'll always be the perfect me
>   there's nothing to rearrange
> I'm beautiful and capable
>   of being the best me I can
> And I love myself just the way I am.

"Welcome to tonight's Hay Ride," Louise said from her position on the platform. She was a stunning woman who looked much younger than her years. She had fair skin and chiseled features.

"Is there anyone who would like to introduce a guest?" she began.

Several men stood and introduced friends or relatives. Others offered announcements about upcoming events in the gay community.

After a dramatic silence, Hay finally began her sermon.

"I'd like everyone to close their eyes and listen." Pleasant background music played over the speakers. "We now acknowledge that your body is the divine expression of health of the universe and you accept perfect health for yourself. If there is any part of your body that is not healthy now, you are willing to release the pattern in your consciousness that is causing the dis-ease. The mind that created the dis-ease is the same mind that can and will heal your body, your mind. You now dissolve all patterns of resentment, anger, revenge, criticism, fear, guilt, and jealousy. You now allow your body to return to vibrant health, filled with energy ... beautiful and comfortable. Feel the bounce in your step. See your shining eyes. The radiant you is right here. Claim it. It does not matter how long you have had these negative patterns. Today is a new day. You can claim all that is good ... and know it is the truth for you. Now accept and affirm that the universe supports us in all of our beliefs and makes the necessary changes in our experience. All we have to do is think these thoughts, and acknowledge that we are willing to change.

"Let's try to paint some mental pictures of the dis-eased cells in your body. The doctor has told you that you don't have enough T cells to fight off the invader. Let us devise a way to make these T cells multiply. Perhaps a magician could walk through your bloodstream and touch each T cell with his magic wand and as he touches them, each T cell becomes twenty T cells ... and then those twenty become forty and the forty become sixty ... and the magician works faster and faster and the cells multiply and multiply until there are more than enough T cells to take care of any invader. Now let's see those thousands of healthy white T cells armed with buckets, brushes, and garbage bags, running around grabbing all the diseased cells that remain ... cleaning every nook and cranny so that there is nothing left. And all the dead cells are flushed out ... through the breath, and the urine and the stool. Going ... going ... gone! You can see your bloodstream getting cleaner and cleaner ... And now clean blood is beginning to flow into every muscle and tissue and pore and joint and cell in your body. Wherever there is any dis-ease or discomfort left in your body, just see the army of white blood cells rushing to that spot with all their equipment, cleaning and cleaning and making well. Lovingly give your body the command to feel itself. Now you are feeling a strength beginning to build in your body. Tell yourself, 'I am well, I am open, I am immune.' " At the conclusion of her speech, the music crescendoed to *forte.*

I was skeptical from the start. Like others present, I closed my eyes, tried to picture my white blood cells turning into magical scrub brushes successfully obliterating the enemy—the virus—with deft precision. I created my own positive imagery: the cells were electronic Pac-Men who neatly eliminated the virus and restored my immune system. I sang the strains of Hay's song over and over in my mind: "I'm beau-ti-ful and ca-pa-ble . . . of be-ing the best me I can. And I love myself . . . just the way . . . I am."

Even then, I knew that the contrived Western meditation on healing might be misguided. It was as if Louise had taken Eastern philosophy of Zen, combined it with psychological theories of visualization and healing, and transformed the entire thing repackaged into something practical in a setting of catastrophe and hopelessness. I was certain that the Far Eastern masters didn't meditate or visualize with a *goal;* they reveled in the *process* of their meditation, not the end result. Furthermore, people infected with HIV had not "chosen" their disease unconsciously. Certainly, people who had contracted the virus before its existence was even known or through blood transfusions could hardly be held responsible for their plight.

Still, Hay's beliefs on psychic healing were not without scientific precedent. The entire field of psychoneuroimmunology had been founded on the theory that the human brain, central nervous system, and immune system were all intricately linked in a complex matrix of chemicals and hormones and that it might be possible to effect changes in disease states of the body by producing repeated mental images and thought patterns.

But could the power of the mind be harnessed to positively

influence immune status as well? Was the human mind a giant, untapped pharmacy of neurochemicals and peptides? Scientific literature, I knew, was filled with stories—even clinical trials—of cancer patients who had healed themselves through visualization, and positive imagery, and other techniques. I also knew that numerous studies had disputed those findings, claiming that there was no reason to believe that one could cause a tumor to regress or cause the production of immune cells to increase simply by imagining their destruction or perpetuation. Further, if I didn't survive AIDS, I didn't want to think that it was because of some technique of visualization that didn't happen to work for *me*.

After several presentations by various members of the audience, the chairs in the room were methodically folded up and everyone formed a large circle and joined hands. Some who didn't fit into the circle sat at the center. The lights dimmed. A chorus of moans filled the room, for about ten minutes, rising and falling in volume. As the lights came up, Louise said, "We've done some fine work tonight."

After the meeting, I sat with Michael and my mother, who was visiting me on vacation, in a predominantly gay coffee shop on Santa Monica Boulevard.

"You know," my mother said, "Louise Hay does a lot of good for many people, whether you subscribe to her beliefs or not. Just for people to have the opportunity to interact with someone positive, someone offering hope, is a terribly important thing. In a sense, Louise Hay is giving people a sense of empowerment and self-determination."

"I know," I replied. "But I didn't *choose* to be sick, and *you* had nothing to do with it. I don't ever want you to think you did."

"I realize that. I don't believe I could have prevented you from liking men any more than I could have prevented you from getting HIV. I've always supported you and accepted you unconditionally. Even though I didn't always understand."

"Thank you," I said, reaching over and touching her arm. "I

don't know. The people who survive this thing aren't necessarily the ones who continually visualize their white blood cells becoming healthy or take better care of themselves by changing their diet or adopt better ways of coping or *any* of those things. It might all be due to your own physiology, over which you have very little control."

In point of fact, I *had* become one of the longer-term survivors. I had first been diagnosed with persistent generalized lymphadenopathy in 1982 and may have had the virus earlier than that. It was now 1987 and I remained relatively asymptomatic. My lymph nodes remained swollen and firm, a sign that some component of my immune system was working.

I thought my condition had plateaued. My CD4 cell count was stable at 350, and even though I did have minor fatigue and hairy leukoplakia on my tongue, I didn't suffer from any debilitating HIV-related symptoms.

But something else, something much more subtle and insidious had begun. Details were becoming slightly harder to remember. My short-term memory was not as sharp as it once was.

"It's just stress," Michael assured me. "It'll get better."

But it didn't. And I desperately continued to avoid giving in to the thickening haze that had begun to cloud my mind, leaving me stranded, powerless, alone.

CHAPTER 7

THE SANCTITY OF INTERNAL MONOLOGUE

A s Herve Guibert noted in *To the Friend Who Did Not Save My Life*, "HIV was an illness in stages, a very long flight of steps that led assuredly to death but whose every step represented a unique apprenticeship."

For Rob Springer, that apprenticeship ended in the spring of 1987, when he died from AIDS—specifically, from intractable bouts of diarrhea and subsequent dehydration caused by cryptosporidiosis. The cryptosporidium parasite, often found in the intestines of animals, had become an increasingly life-threatening infection in HIV disease. Through his international network of sources, Rob had obtained a wide variety of antiprotozoal agents to try to cure the infection, including spiramycin, an antibiotic used in Europe for malaria, and trimetrexate, a lipid-soluble drug, then available in Italy. None of them had been able to arrest the terrible progress of the deadly protozoan that had infected his intestines, nor had any of the immunomodulatory drugs he had obtained been successful in reconstituting his ravaged immune system.

There was speculation among some of our friends that Rob, realizing the hopelessness of his emaciating condition and his lack of response to treatment, may have actually consumed a lethal dose of barbiturates and brought about his own demise, even prior to the full onset of his opportunistic infection. The actual cause of his death was listed as AIDS.

Rob typified the consummate patient-fighter turned self-physician. He predated the formation of buyers' clubs and underground studies by almost two years and in his own way was a pioneer. In manufacturing and distributing experimental AIDS drugs to his small circle of friends while educating them about the drugs' modes of action and pharmacological effects, he served as a catalyst for the larger events that were to follow.

Joan Lederman, too, had been impressed by his spirit and incredible tenacity. The day after he died, she and I sat in silence in one of the examination rooms, staring out at the lush green garden on the veranda below. We were both at a loss for words, feeling the effects of a terrible deprivation.

Months later, I learned that David Myers, the other major underground chemist, had also passed away.

By April 1987, I was certain that there was something wrong with my memory and concentration. The problems manifested themselves mainly in subtle ways, but they had become so consistent that their presence was undeniable.

Ironically, I could recall the exact day and hour when the symptoms became extremely apparent. I was having lunch in the corporate cafeteria and was handing the cashier a twenty-dollar bill. She went to another register to get change and when she returned, moments later, I had forgotten the denomination of the bill I had just handed her. Certain that I had given her ten dollars, I attempted to return some change, but she insisted that I had handed her twenty dollars and that the change she had given me was correct. Later that day, I dialed the number of someone I had never phoned before—and immediately forgot whom it was I had attempted to reach. When the party at the other end answered, there was an awkward pause, I stammered that I would have to call them back, and then

I hung up. During the next week, incidents like these occurred with startling frequency.

Occasionally I would forget to bring items home from work and found myself inadvertently leaving personal possessions in other people's offices. It became increasingly difficult to memorize speeches, a task that had previously been effortless. And my verbal spontaneity in everyday discussions was impaired.

To compensate for the memory loss, I found myself engaging in mnemonic routines. At work, I began making detailed lists of tasks that needed to be completed in the course of a given day. This was unusual for me, since I had always been able to commit to memory a large number of tasks to be done and hold them there indefinitely. I also found myself making notes on yellow Post-it pads and sticking them to my computer, providing a salient cue of some ongoing job needing completion. And before leaving for work in the morning, I often had to gather items that I needed to bring with me that day one at a time to a central location, such as the couch or the dining table.

What I had taken for granted now became difficult: the swift and precise flow of thought that had enabled me to read and comprehend with accuracy and speed and to speak extemporaneously with accuracy and color. Instead, my reading speed had greatly slowed and the precision of my internal monologue was waning. Yet I was still able to write, and the overall quality of my thoughts was not greatly impaired. I experienced no errors in perception or judgment and had no difficulty learning new information.

During the early onset of these symptoms, I tried to reassure myself that the peculiar intermittent lapses in my memory and the difficulty I had in sustaining my attention were merely caused by stress. I had been HIV-positive for five years, and my cumulative knowledge of its presence in my life was bound to take its toll. Now, however, I knew that stress could not fully account for the problems I was experiencing. Perhaps, I reasoned, I was suffering from the short-term consequences of dextran sulfate or Imuthiol therapy, which would resolve once I discontinued the drugs. But the problems did not improve with the discontinuation of these experimental therapies. Or was it possible that I had been reexposed to a new virus such as HTLV-II, which was known to cause an array of symptoms that would become known as the chronic fatigue immune dysfunction syndrome (CFIDS), also referred to as the "Yuppie Flu"? I could not ignore the painful possibility that I suffered from the early onset of HIV-related dementia. I relegated this notion to the back of my mind, however, and tried to erase it completely.

Despite my lapses in memory and concentration, my intelligence and speech were almost completely spared. Thus, I spoke much more slowly but not much less accurately, and I was easily able to cover for the small mistakes I routinely made. No one guessed that I might actually be suffering from the early stages of dementia—not even one of the most prominent neurologists in Los Angeles, whom I visited in May 1987.

I described the changes I was experiencing to him and also produced a litany of other neurological symptoms that had simultaneously plagued me, even prior to the onset of dementia: a vague feeling of vertigo and dizziness; tinnitus in the right ear; occasional blurred vision. Subjecting me to an extensive battery of diagnostic tests, which included a lumbar puncture, a brain scan, an ophthalmological exam, EEG, and neuropsychological tests of my short-term memory and reasoning abilities, the neurologist found no major abnormalities. In a written statement of his findings, he concluded, "Mr. Sergios appears to me to have no major problems with memory or conceptualization. I wonder if, rather than having a serious or even subtle physiological or intracranial problem associated with HIV, that he is not, in fact, suffering from anxiety and depression. I will try to reassure Paul that he does not have AIDS dementia and is a stable ARC patient. I will refer him to the psychiatrist for counseling."

The psychiatrist's diagnosis echoed that of the neurologist. He prescribed antidepressants, which neither improved my memory nor made me any less depressed.

There is nothing more frustrating than to have a physician

deny the reality of symptoms that you know to be real—and, worse, attribute them to psychological causes. It was a mistake that many neurologists and psychiatrists made in the mid-to-late 1980s in HIV disease. HIV-related dementia, like other subcortical dementias, presented a complex and often mistakable array of symptoms in its early form. Attempts by neurologists and psychiatrists to "explain away" complaints of cognitive disabilities only increased the patients' feelings of anxiety, because the patients knew that their experiences were real.

Joan Lederman had seen HIV-related dementia in its earliest manifestations but was uncertain as to whether I was experiencing its classic symptoms. She knew that up to 30 percent of all HIV-positive persons, many of them asymptomatic, developed HIV dementia. The evidence was becoming increasingly strong that the cognitive problems of HIV could often be the first major manifestations of the disease, predating the occurrence of opportunistic infections by up to five years. Yet I was somewhat anxious about my condition. The symptoms of early HIV dementia paralleled those of depression and could be difficult to differentiate.

Joan referred me to a Veterans Administration neurologist, Elyse Singer, who was following the natural course of neurological complications in HIV-positive patients as part of a government-sponsored tracking study. Dr. Singer confirmed that in its earliest incarnation, HIV dementia could easily be misdiagnosed as depression. She further indicated that among particularly bright people and those with high motivational levels, the diagnosis of HIV dementia was difficult, if not virtually impossible. None of the widely used technologies, including routine neuropsychological screens, MRI (magnetic resonance imaging) brain scans, EEGs, or cerebrospinal fluid analyses could provide definitive evidence. Because HIV dementia's true etiological cause and pathogenesis were still a mystery, researchers could only look for surrogate markers, such as elevated levels of p-24 antigen, viral load in the spinal fluid, or abnormal IgG (immunoglobulin) antibody readings to determine that dementia was in progress. Singer herself had conducted such studies. She knew patients who complained of significant changes in their memory and concentration but otherwise appeared perfectly normal in every aspect of their neurological examination. None of her tests on me turned up any major abnormalities. She assured me that this was not unusual, since many of the symptoms I described were consistent with what she had seen in early HIV dementia.

"It's insidious," she told me over lunch one day. "It's not like an opportunistic infection that displays distinct symptoms and signs. HIV dementia is like a subacute encephalopathy. In its earliest stages, it's often undetectable. It can go for years without getting any worse. I suspect many of my patients don't even know they have it."

That evening I allowed myself to become engulfed in Michael's arms.

"I'm scared," I said. "I'm not as sharp as I used to be. I know something is wrong."

"I know you're afraid. And you may have lost something," Michael said. "But it's not that severe."

I felt his kiss at the back of my neck.

"You can't surrender to it," he said.

He continued to caress me before falling into a deep sleep. Yet I remained awake, my mind still at work. I knew I would not surrender.

By September 1987, all the original members of my Shanti group had died except for Craig and me. We were both, ironically, largely asymptomatic and stable. Both of our CD4 lymphocyte counts remained at about 200 and hadn't wavered since the time we joined the group.

One of the most significant events to occur in the fall of 1987 was the widespread availability of a reliable HIV test.

The most widely used test in 1987 to detect HIV was the ELISA (enzyme-linked immunosorbent assay), manufactured by several large companies, although others such as the Western blot would later become equally as popular. The tests were not 100-percent accurate, and the incidence of false positives and false negatives varied. The companies claimed that their tests were "reliable and had great sensitivity and specificity," but there was no public discussion about the legitimate scientific assessment of the tests, mainly because of the companies' unwillingness to present confidential business information. Many researchers recommended repeat testing to confirm one's HIV-negative status.

But it was the handling of the test results rather than their performance that produced controversy. A positive result not only informed an individual that he or she had a potentially life-threatening infection that might be transmissible to others through an exchange of bodily fluids; it could also greatly endanger the person's quality of life by creating discrimination in employment, housing, and insurance and arousing prejudice in the community at large.

It was hardly surprising, then, that a large number of gay men still chose not to be tested. Some preferred ignorance or denial. There was no cure; why have the burden of knowing one's imminent demise? Others were concerned about issues of confidentiality. Even under the most confidential of conditions, having an HIV-antibody test still represented a potentially accessible piece of information that might be used against a person in employment and insurance. Suspicion among insurance carriers that an individual might be infected with HIV had created a class of virtually uninsurable people.

Gay men didn't want to find themselves in that situation. And despite efforts to ensure confidentiality, test results in medical records have ended up serving as tip-offs to a patient's true condition. Many gay men who tested positive often sought the assistance of HIV specialists, who kept medical records of their patients' changing conditions and symptoms that might easily be identified as HIV-related by anyone with access to the records. It was also common practice for some blood banks to maintain a list of "deferred donors" that could easily be compiled into a federal register of HIV-positive people. Some political groups argued that gay men shouldn't take the test, pointing out that it could be used as a marker for homosexuality, drug abuse, or sexual promiscuity, with the potential for mandatory widespread blood screening and quarantining of anyone found to have tested positive.

As time progressed, however, most health professionals and political leaders agreed that anonymous HIV testing should be undertaken by anyone in a high-risk group: gay men; all recipients of blood transfusions in the last decade, including hemophiliacs; male and female prostitutes; and intravenous drug users. Health professionals hastened to add that, where voluntary testing programs are instituted, researchers have argued that high-quality laboratory services should be used, individuals tested must be informed about the results, sensitive and supportive counseling programs must be available, follow-up services that provide information about available treatments must be made available, and the confidentiality of tested individuals must be protected. Testing positively did not necessarily mean that a person would ever develop the full-blown disease. It did, however, suggest that the person should change certain patterns of behavior that could spread the disease to others. Furthermore, early interventions such as AZT and pentamidine seemed to buy time and improve the quality of life for HIV-positive persons, who clearly needed to know about options of treatment and the opportunity to take advantage of them. I agreed with activists that the risk of *not* knowing one's antibody status was probably greater than actually having the information become public record. I already knew that my test would be positive; the symptoms I had suffered for the last five years, including lymphadenopathy and a depressed CD4 cell count, were symptomatic of ARC. Nevertheless, in September 1987, with Michael accompanying me, I took the Western blot and confirmed my early suspicions.

In the fall of 1987, a growing faction of physicians and researchers argued that AIDS was merely untreated syphilis that had been allowed to flourish because of improper therapy and the overuse of antibiotics. In *AIDS and Syphilis: The Hidden Link,* Dr. Harris Coulter neatly laid out reasons supporting the still-controversial theory and offered a viable treatment alternative for HIV disease.

Coulter argued that one of the most fundamental and often overlooked rules of science had not been observed in identifying HIV as the cause of AIDS. It was true that almost all AIDS patients' blood showed positive antibodies to the HIV virus, but, as Coulter suggested, correlation hardly implied causation. *In vitro* tests had clearly established that HIV shows a tropism for CD4 lymphocytes, but so did a variety of other microbial organisms. Moreover, no one had fully and precisely defined the exact mechanism by which HIV could destroy an entire population of CD4 lymphocytes. A wide variety of theories attempted to explain the immune cell loss. Some blamed the formation of cell aggregates called syncytia; others implicated the HIV envelope protein gp120 or the production of certain cytokines—soluble, hormonelike substances that may upregulate the expression of HIV in lymphocytes, compounding their destruction—such as tumor necrosis factor. But more and more, scientists realized that if HIV was responsible, it might be causing its damage in an insidious and indirect way: most researchers agreed that fewer than one in four hundred CD4 cells were actually infected with HIV—even at the height of infection. Often, fewer than one in one thousand were infected. The number of infected macrophages, while somewhat greater, was still relatively small, less than 1 percent in the worst possible scenario. Certainly, some other pathogenic agent could easily be responsible for the massive decimation of CD4 cells. Coulter argued that syphilis was the agent and that HIV was merely a passive co-factor in the disease process.

Syphilis itself, after all, was known to be immunosuppressive. Studies had shown that the bacterium causing syphilis, *Treponema pallidum,* acted specifically against the thymus gland, the organ critical in CD4 cell maturation and development. Studies had also shown that in people who were not HIV-infected but who suffered from long-term, untreated syphilis, CD4 cell counts were somewhat depressed, much as they were in AIDS. "Like AIDS, syphilis makes the individual vulnerable to a host of opportunistic infections that a healthy person could easily ward off," Coulter stated.

Furthermore, gay men in particular represented an especially vulnerable population in which widespread undiagnosed syphilis could harbor. In a survey taken in San Francisco prior to the emergence of HIV, up to half the gay men were found to be infected with the treponeme. More important, Coulter pointed out, syphilis was impossible to detect in the presence of HIV. In arguing that the HIV virus might be introducing a factor of confusion, Coulter stated that HIV altered the body's ability to form antibodies against syphilis and thus kept syphilis from being detected on the standard diagnostic tests: the VDRL (venereal disease research laboratory test), the RPR (rapid plasma reagin), and—most reliable—the FTA (fluorescent treponemal antibody test). Coulter cited the experience of numerous physicians across the country who found that as patients became sicker with HIV, their test reaction to syphilis—which had repeatedly been positive before HIV infection—disappeared completely with the onset of AIDS. In an editorial written by Edward C. Tramont, M.D., Chief of Infectious Diseases at the Walter Reed Army Medical Center, Washington, D.C., in the June 18, 1987, issue of the *New England Journal of Medicine,* the conclusion was actually supported. "The antibody response to syphilis in HIV-infected patients, particularly in the later stages of the disease, may be severely compromised, and thus, the diagnosis may be obscured," Tramont wrote.

Coulter argued that because it *was* so difficult to adequately diagnose syphilis in HIV-positive men, a massive and growing pool of undiagnosed and untreated disease had silently invaded the gay community and it was *this,* not HIV, that was leading to the horrible array of life-threatening infections linked to chronic immune suppression. Syphilis, long known as "the great masquerader" because of its ability to mimic other disease states, had finally cloaked itself in an entirely novel disguise and had reemerged as a great new modern-day plague.

Coulter further argued that the presence of syphilis was masked by the widespread use of antibiotics in the 1970s—particularly in gay men, who were routinely treated for gonorrhea and nonspecific urethritis with massive doses of amoxicillin, tetracycline, and erythromycin. The short-term use of these oral antibiotics, according to Coulter, actually masked the presence of syphilis by temporarily decreasing the strength of the treponemal antibody response and eliminating an array of symptoms that might have immediately tipped off clinicians to its presence. Coulter cited the 1970 complaint of a California physician, who wrote: "The advent of oral antibiotics for other sexually transmitted diseases has shifted the concern of the physician from treatment to diagnosis, at least as far as syphilis is concerned. Indications are that far from eradicating syphilis, these antibiotics are driving the disease underground and increasing the difficulty of detection. Although the incidence of the disease has tripled since 1955, the canker and secondary rash are no longer commonly seen. Undoubtedly some of these lesions are being suppressed, and the disease masked by the indiscriminate use of antibiotics. The ominous prospect of a widespread resurgence of the disease in its tertiary form looms ahead." Coulter maintained that AIDS had indeed fulfilled that physician's apocalyptic prediction. Further, he argued, antibiotics were themselves immunosuppressive and their prolonged use (as often happened with gay men being treated for other sexually transmitted diseases) held the capacity to undermine the patients' immune systems, even without microbial involvement.

According to Coulter, even when adequately diagnosed, syphilis was not often treated correctly. Even with antibiotics, curing it required more skill than was currently possessed by the ordinary doctor "armed with a syringe and bottle of penicillin." Penicillin, he went on, acted on the treponeme only in the stage of replication and was maximally effective when administered immediately after in-

fection in the primary stage of the disease. However, the treponemes tend to spread rapidly through the body within a short time
after infection and eventually make their way across the blood/
brain barrier into the cerebrospinal fluid, the eyeball, and other
recesses in the central nervous system, where they cease replication
altogether or replicate very slowly. There, they become invulnera-
ble to the benzathine penicillin which was usually administered in
a single intramuscular injection. Although the syphilis treponeme is
usually found outside cells, it can also penetrate them and live
inside, where it is protected from penicillin. This is why ocular
syphilis and neurosyphilis can continue to progress clinically even
when no treponemes are detectable elsewhere in the patient's body.
The fact that treponemes have been found undisturbed in a patient's
body even after treatment with 100 million units of intramuscular
penicillin led one physician to comment, "Of all bacteria, *Treponema
pallidium* is one of the most sensitive and simultaneously the most
resistant to the action of penicillin." Had latent syphilis been treated
adequately in gay men, Coulter reasoned, AIDS might never have
become a plague of epidemic proportions.

Coulter argued that in treating gay men afflicted with HIV
infection and concurrent occult or detectable syphilis, an individu-
alized treatment approach was necessary. Like many physicians, he
suggested the use of intravenous penicillin—up to 20 million units
a day, given over a period of ten to twenty days. In certain cases,
other antibiotics might be necessary, such as intravenous ceftriax-
one, which had shown excellent results in neurological complications of Lyme disease. Follow-up treatment in six months or a year
would often be necessary. Coulter also advocated the use of Salvatore Catapano's typhoid vaccine therapy.

Chief among the proponents of the "syphilis causes AIDS"
theory was Stephen Caiazza, a Manhattan doctor with a large gay
practice. In 1985, he noticed that some of his HIV-positive patients
were also testing positive for syphilis. He treated them with intravenous penicillin and noticed not only that their syphilis symptoms
improved but that their AIDS symptoms did too. Some even experi-

enced massive increases in their CD4 cell counts, and others had normalization of their CD4:CD8 ratios. It never occurred to Caiazza at the time that he might actually be treating HIV and not syphilis. For when penicillin is effective against infection, it is largely due to the formation of bactericidal amounts of H_2O_2, when glucose is oxidized by oxygen in the presence of penicillium notatin. This combination might be somewhat virustatic at high doses, inhibiting HIV as well as the treponemes. Caiazza, however, perceived that in treating syphilis, he was actually treating AIDS.

He began treating large numbers of patients with twenty-day courses of intravenous penicillin or high doses of oral doxycycline, which he regarded as equally effective. Although he never conducted a clinical trial of the treatment's efficacy, Caiazza did keep meticulous records of anecdotal results he had obtained, and assembled patient profiles and before-and-after lab reports, which he reproduced and distributed at seminars and public forums. He also published his findings in *Quantum Medicine,* the journal of the Association of Eclectic Physicians. Sandwiched between articles on non-drug therapies for AIDS and holistic approaches to healing various diseases, Caiazza espoused the view that AIDS cannot be explained by a retroviral model and is more likely due to a chronic bacterial, spirochetal infection, and could be cured with megadoses of penicillin.

In 1987, Caiazza was himself diagnosed with ARC after accidentally sticking himself with an HIV-infected needle. Although HIV antibodies were present in his serum, there was no trace of treponemal antibodies either in his blood or spinal fluid. But he concluded that syphilis had been "on board" all along, only now it had become dormant and undetectable. Caiazza felt certain that the HIV antibodies were merely the tip of the pathological iceberg.

In order to prove that AIDS was really a result of syphilis, Caiazza experimentally infected himself with live treponemes. Within several weeks, he developed flulike symptoms—the same ones he had experienced several years earlier when he first perceived that he had been exposed to syphilis masquerading as HIV.

This time, however, he also noticed rapidly progressing neurological problems: an unsteady gait and severely declining short-term memory and concentration.

While on a business meeting with several German researchers in Europe, Caiazza treated himself with a twenty-day course of intravenous penicillin—the same one he had prescribed to the patients in his Manhattan practice. Within days, his symptoms almost completely disappeared. His memory returned to near normal and his CD4 cell count had climbed toward the normal range. HIV-related dementia, he concluded, was nothing more than untreated neurosyphilis. Caiazza went on talk shows and led seminars across the country, publicizing his theory that AIDS could be cured with megadoses of intravenous penicillin or oral doxycycline.

My own syphilis serologies were all negative. I found it difficult to bring myself to carry out the protocol Caiazza suggested. Several PWA acquaintances who also attended the lecture, however, *did* participate. They checked into a local hospital during a three-week leave from work and were hooked up to an IV twenty-four hours a day. Four million units of aqueous penicillin dripped into their veins every four hours for a full twenty days. Whatever syphilis was sequestered in their spinal fluid or other organs was certainly destroyed. But none of their HIV-related symptoms improved and none of their CD4 cell counts improved significantly.

Much of Caiazza's logic was later found to be fatally flawed. Many patients with syphilis, but not HIV, maintained near normal CD4 cell counts and did not die of AIDS. Moreover, many gay men who were treated with antibiotics for other STDs (sexually transmitted diseases) and who did not have HIV did not automatically die of AIDS.

In the spring of 1989, plagued with increasing bouts of fatigue, and oral candidiasis, Stephen Caiazza announced that he would drastically reduce the size of his Manhattan practice. In January 1991, he died of complications from AIDS.

If it is true that science advances from funeral to funeral of researchers adamant about their views, then no event more than

Stephen Caiazza's death helped to so completely end speculation that AIDS was merely untreated syphilis, curable with megadoses of penicillin.

By September 1987, it was becoming clear that dextran sulfate was also useless in the treatment of HIV disease. My own CD4 cell count hadn't changed appreciably while I was on the drug, and most of the patients Jim Corti was following hadn't experienced improvements either. Later, studies would establish that dextran sulfate in oral form did not reach sufficient blood concentrations or even its site of action. The government-sponsored trials of the drug at San Francisco General Hospital, led by Dr. Donald Abrams, found that not only was the drug poorly absorbed, but it did not produce significant increases in CD4 cell counts or declines in beta-2 microglobulin levels or HIV antigen levels. Studies presented at the Fifth International Conference on AIDS, in Montreal in 1989, showed that the drug proved of little value even when given intravenously. Other drugs in the same family, known as sulfated polysaccharides, were being evaluated for their anti-HIV potential. Drugs such as heparin, pentosan polysulfate, glycyrrhizin sulfate, and ribofuranan sulfate might have more powerful *in vitro* anti-HIV effects than dextran sulfate, and would be far more available and perhaps even less toxic.

There was similar disappointment with Imuthiol, since researchers in the United States and Europe were unable to replicate the initial positive European results with that drug.

After evaluating the data that had been accumulated to date, and seeing that neither Imuthiol nor dextran sulfate was significantly impacting on my own blood work, I stopped taking both of them.

In spite of the evidence against their effectiveness, AL-721, dextran sulfate, and Imuthiol would continue to enjoy a remarkable popularity in the AIDS underground for at least two more years. Months after Tom Hannan and Michael Callen offered AL-721 as part of the launch of the New York AIDS Buyers' Club, several private companies offered it for sale as well. In fact, by the fall of

1987, at least three generic versions of an all-egg AL-721 became available as health-food products. Some individuals continued to prepare home formulas of AL-721 based on instructions that had been disseminated in alternative treatment newsletters and pioneered by Steve Gavin. Following a recipe that required 75cc of lecithin to be combined with 180cc of water and subsequently whipped together with melted butter, they began to produce their own AL-721 "workalikes" on their kitchen stoves. Most were wildly inconsistent in quality and texture. American AIDS patients continued to obtain dextran sulfate through Jim Corti's underground pharmacy and through such companies as Polydex Pharmaceuticals in Toronto, which filled mail-order requests for the drug. Others traveled to Japan, where it was available from at least a dozen companies. Imuthiol later became available for sale through the New York PWA Health Group.

Opportunity finally knocked for me in the television industry in October 1987. Through a fellow USC graduate, I learned of a new cable television network, the Health Television Corporation, which was hiring producers and associate producers to head narrative-style and magazine-type programs. Housed in a sprawling series of offices and soundstages, and occupying a large portion of the old Hollywood National Studios lot, the network was a twenty-four-hour "basic" cable subscriber service that would be seen in every major market in the country and would feature programming in the areas of health and fitness, personal improvement, entertainment, and fashion. I was hired as senior producer, responsible for supervising the creation of two daily programs. A staff of five writers created the scripts for each show and reported directly to me, as did three associate producers and an associate director. I worked on scripts with them, cast the on-screen talent, worked with composers in the scoring of original music, and supervised tapings and editing sessions. I hired John O'Malley as my associate director. We had, of course, both attended USC and shared similar philosophical and practical insights into the elements required to make good television. Because we were the youngest producers hired, we found ourselves working doubly hard to prove our mettle.

While gazing out of my office window overlooking Sunset Boulevard, I felt somewhat satisfied. I was producing material with substantial budgets and working with professionals whom I liked and respected. But it was all tarnished by my cognitive decline. At the very point in my career when I most needed my creative faculties, I'd been hit with a curveball that prevented me from performing at my best. Occasionally I would substitute an incorrect word when speaking extemporaneously, and often I would forget where I'd placed a stack of papers or filed an unlabeled videotape. But my dysfunction became most problematic in editing, a task that required the sequential juxtaposition of images. In film school and in various editing jobs, I had been able, with little or no advance preparation, to swiftly design and cut complex montages that neatly and concisely advanced plot and characterization, editing entire sequences in my head. Now, I had to view takes over and over again and rely on "paper cuts"—editing plans that had been mapped out in advance in writing. More important, because of my increasing inability to visualize and retain images, I was unable to associate disparate images from unrelated sequences that when cut together would create a seamless flow of images. Editing requires a sort of innate rhythm—a sense of visual tempo. This inner cadence now seemed all but lost to me.

John was aware of my problem and helped me rectify the occasional minor error. We often drove to work together and found some of our most creative ideas resulting from conversations in the car, ideas we followed up in early-morning meetings with writers and producers.

Ironically, it was while doing research for a show on biofeedback that I learned of Dr. Candace Pert, a scientist at the National Institute of Mental Health. Rumor had it that she had discovered a cure for HIV dementia—a drug that she called Peptide T. Peptides are the essential hormones that govern communication between the brain and body cells. Their structure and composition, short strings of amino acids, set them apart from the brain's other well-known chemicals, neurotransmitters. Neurotransmitters are the medium neurons use for "conversations" with other neurons. Author Joseph Light created this metaphor: "Neurotransmitters operate like lines connecting individual telephones to one another, while peptides are more like a television broadcast, which can be picked up by anyone with the right receiver. . . ." The sixty to seventy currently known peptides transmit information in a sophisticated game of telephone tag played by the brain, the immune system, and other organ systems.

The peptides, Pert knew, result in a message as unambiguous as pain or thirst or even sexual arousal. In addition to being involved with emotional states, moods, attitudes, and tastes, peptides might also be linked to the acquisition and maintenance of new behavioral patterns. In 1986, Pert mapped out the pattern of peptide receptor molecules in the brain, concentrating on the CD4 receptors, which seemed to trigger immune response and were the same receptors to which HIV bonded in the peripheral blood. Pert immediately realized that her research might help find a way to block HIV's path toward healthy CD4 cells. It must join up with healthy CD4 cells *some*how; perhaps she could stop the process.

Using a computer model to compare peptide structures with the shape of the gp120 on the HIV virus's outer coat, Pert developed a string of eight amino acids that appeared capable of blocking the gp120 from getting into the CD4 receptors. Pert's theory was that this sequence, Peptide T, would prevent the CD4 cells from "taking the bait" offered by HIV's gp120 molecule. Positive test-tube studies with the drug led to a series of clinical trials that suggested the drug might have value in improving the symptoms of HIV-related dementia and peripheral neuropathy. I attempted to gain admittance to the Phase 1 trial of Peptide T under way at USC–Los Angeles County Medical Center but did not meet the inclusion criteria.

I learned that the underground AIDS researcher David Myers had obtained a quantity of the drug from a lab in northern California. He had since died, but through his lover, I was able to obtain a four-month supply of the drug. "Just snort it like cocaine," he advised. "About forty milligrams twice a day seems to be an effective and safe dose."

Each morning and evening, I measured out 40 milligrams of the substance on a balance scale. I then smashed it into tiny crystals on a metallic plate, shuffled it into thin lines with a razor blade, and snorted it into both nostrils through a dollar bill, feeling much like a cocaine addict going for a fix. I experienced no adverse effects from the drug.

By June 1988, I had been taking the drug for three months, yet I hadn't noticed any significant improvement in my memory or concentration. Other researchers in Europe I had contacted suggested that the peptide be placed in sterile solution to produce a mist. This was the more recent technique used to administer vasopressin and other peptides and was also the method to be used in the protocol of Peptide T at Fenway Community Health Clinic in Boston. Another two months of treatment using this technique failed to produce any improvement.

I was one of the first patients to self-administer the drug in this way. In 1990 Alan Field, a PWA from Boulder, Colorado, set up a distribution system. He imported the drug from a Scandinavian biotechnology company and sold it to four dozen PWAs across the country while monitoring their progress.

As luck would have it, Candace Pert was slated to be a panelist at a conference on "AIDS, Medicine, and Miracles" in Boulder in the spring of 1989. Field approached her after the seminar and the two wound up chatting over lunch. Pert revealed that Peptide T was being manufactured at the Carlsburg Biotechnology Company in Copenhagen and that perhaps an agreement could be reached with the company for Field to import a quantity of the drug—pharmaceutical grade and certified pure—for a reasonable price. After all, the FDA Personal Import Policy, then approved, would allow for individuals to accomplish this.

In the days that followed, Field managed to reach an agreement with Carlsburg to purchase a tiny quantity of the drug—a mere 2 grams—at a cost of $1,000 per gram. He supplied this amount to the PWA in Boulder who had first requested it. Field was subsequently able to purchase 200 grams of the Peptide T at the greatly reduced cost of $730 a gram. He sold it to forty-two PWAs across the country, along with instructions on procedures for its proper mixing and reconstitution for subcutaneous administration, and tracked their blood chemistries, profiles and clinical progress. They self-administered Peptide T at doses ranging from 2 to 5 milligrams per day and for treatment durations lasting from two to eight months. While it produced consistent improvement in HIV-related peripheral neuropathy, Field reported to me that he saw none of the immunological or virological improvements in HIV dementia claimed in the European and American studies with the drug.

In the winter of 1989, Field ceased distribution of the drug and turned information on his Danish source over to Ron Woodruff of the Dallas Buyers' Club and Jim Corti of the Los Angeles Buyers' Club. In the months that followed, both men obtained larger quantities of the compound and offered it for sale through their buyers' clubs at the reduced price of $500 per gram. Woodruff ultimately credited the drug with partially reversing his own AIDS-related dementia and constitutional symptoms. When fear of international disclosure compelled the source in Denmark to discontinue supplying Woodruff or Corti with more of the compound, Woodruff continued to obtain small quantities for his own personal use from Peninsula Labs in Belmont, Texas. Ultimately, federal officials cracked down and prohibited Peninsula from selling the drug to Woodruff—or anyone else—and he became embroiled in a court case to obtain access to the medication. The conflict was resolved out of court and Woodruff became the first PWA in the country to be granted a compassionate-use IND permit for the drug.

• • •

In July 1988, the Health Television Corporation was on the verge of bankruptcy. We were given two weeks' notice.

Although I remained relatively stable, I realized that as my CD4 numbers decreased, I would be more vulnerable to opportunistic infections and full-blown AIDS. The AZT, which had produced some apparently positive effects during the first two years I had taken it, had now bottomed out in its benefit potential.

Through a friend at Kaiser Sunset Hospital, I learned of Ampligen, a drug being tested in clinical trials around the country. It had produced promising results in a Phase 1 study with eight ARC and AIDS patients. Further, the Ampligen molecule appeared to be able to cross the blood/brain barrier and might be effective in reducing HIV viral load in the cerebrospinal fluid, thus helping fight HIV-related dementia. There were no investigation sites on the West Coast, but the drug was being studied in Miami, in a physician's office about twenty-five miles from my home in Fort Lauderdale. No underground supply of the drug existed at the time.

I said hasty good-byes to Michael, Craig, and Joan as I left Los Angeles to obtain what I hoped would be an effective anti-HIV treatment in Florida.

John drove me to the airport. We hugged in the terminal. All around us, businessmen rushed off with briefcases, finalizing contracts, chasing careers, and closing deals. I remained oblivious to them. There was an awkward pause as John looked into my eyes. "Do you think you'll ever come back?"

"I don't know," I replied.

We hugged again, and then I was off, away from the pace of Los Angeles and the companionship of the best friends I had ever known.

CHAPTER 8

THE IRREPRESSIBLE
DAVID WILSON

U nlike the Phase 2 AZT study, which was held in the drab, institutional halls of university hospitals, the Phase 2 Ampligen study was staged in gracefully appointed physicians' offices and high-tech research centers. In Miami, it was conducted in a modern Coconut Grove office building nestled in a hospital plaza minutes from the chic art deco boutiques of Sunset Drive. Beams of sunlight refracted off the building exterior's massive metallic panels, creating patterns as engaging and offbeat as the art in the Grove galleries just minutes away. It was oppressively hot and humid during those long summer days. The long drive from my apartment in West Fort Lauderdale to South Miami was often an unpleasant one.

Ampligen is a mismatched double-stranded RNA molecule. RNA, I knew well by now, is one of the substances found in every cell as part of the "genetic code" of the cell. The genetic material of HIV is also composed of RNA. When a cell is infected with a virus, such as HIV or viral RNA, many of its responses are triggered to thwart the virus's replication. These responses include interferon synthesis, production of specific antiviral substances, activation of natural killer cells, and generally enhanced immune responses. Ampligen is a form of synthetic RNA that acts as a "phony virus" and stimulates these same components of the immune system. Various double-stranded RNAs (including Ampligen) were investigated in the 1970s for their anticancer effects. Some beneficial results were noted, but severe toxicity limited their use. There was renewed interest in Ampligen in 1987 when AIDS researcher William Mitchell found that, in the test tube, it significantly inhibited replication of HIV and triggered key enzymes to "chew up" foreign RNA, an important antiviral mechanism in the body. Later that year, Ampligen was given to ten HIV patients at Hahnemann University in Philadelphia, under the direction of principal investigator Dr. David Strayer. A report detailing the findings of the study, published in the June 6, 1987, issue of *Lancet* suggested that Ampligen had the "dual ability to restore immunological function and to control HIV replication in ARC patients."

While Ampligen didn't seem effective in patients with advanced AIDS, and some researchers cautioned that even its positive effects in ARC patients involved too small a sample to allow for a comprehensive analysis, the report spurred undisguised excitement. Within weeks of its release, the Du Pont Corporation announced it had formed a joint venture with HEM Research, the Rockville-based company that had developed and tested the drug in Philadelphia, to fund and oversee a placebo-controlled Phase 2 clinical trial of the drug: a massive test of three hundred patients with ARC to be held in seven cities at physicians' offices and hospitals across the country. Du Pont produced Ampligen for the study and provided the up-front cash needed to implement and keep the trial going.

Like the AZT trial I had entered in 1986, the Ampligen study was placebo-controlled. Unlike the AZT experience, however, the placebo was not in the form of a sugar pill; half the Ampligen subjects were actually being given a useless bag of saline. In subjecting ourselves to potentially ineffective twice-weekly needle sticks, the impetus and ultimate payoff for me and many other patients were that if the drug proved it could delay the onset of AIDS, then at some point—perhaps even before the study's scheduled conclusion—we would *all* be switched over to the active drug group and receive Ampligen free of charge for up to one year. As in all double-blind studies, neither I nor any of the subjects or the doctors involved would know who was on the active drug or the inert saline. Each of the subjects on Ampligen received 250 milligrams of the drug. This was determined to be an optimum dose based on results from the earlier studies.

The principal investigator of the Miami study was Dr. Stanley Cooper, a venerable physician who had spent most of his career working as an internist at South Miami's Victoria Hospital. He had a warm smile and a pleasant though unengaging demeanor. Cooper himself had been diagnosed with terminal lung cancer and was often absent on trips to the Bahamas receiving experimental therapy for it.

The drug was administered in a single, large infusion room with chairs and IV poles situated along the walls. After we were seated, one of the protocol nurses would draw blood and then begin the barrage of quality-of-life questions, concurrent medication log, and recent-symptom history queries that were endemic to a carefully monitored clinical trial. We also periodically filled out lengthy and tedious psychological questionnaires, aimed at assessing our coping skills and levels of depression.

After the battery of questions, the IV was inserted in a peripheral vein, and the slow, twenty-five-minute drip would begin. I spent those arduous moments reading or chatting with the other patients. After the drip was concluded, we were given copies of our T cell counts and basic blood chemistries from the last draw—depressing reading for the long drive home.

Although we were discouraged from speaking about our symptomatic changes or lab values with the other patients, it was inevitable that conversations about our impressions of what the drug was or wasn't doing to us would ensue in the corridors, in the elevator, or even during telephone discussions between visits. I knew at least a half dozen of the subjects enrolled in the trial, and we routinely shared information. What we all seemed to discover was that the drug was neither producing significant changes in any of our symptoms nor having any significant impact on our virological or immunological conditions.

Between Ampligen infusions, I often attended information-exchange seminars and lectures at Miami's Body Positive Resource Center, which contained a gym where people with HIV disease could excercise and socialize. There were also meeting rooms for Positively Sober and Narcotics Anonymous groups, and a large auditorium in which a variety of lively lectures and discussions took place. In cooperation with the PWA Coalition, Body Positive also sponsored "Positive Tea Dances"—social events open only to HIV-positive people in the community. The center was founded by Doris Feinburg, a woman of seemingly limitless energy who had lost two sons to AIDS and who had given selflessly to the cause for years. She converted the cavernous health club she operated into the Body Positive Center.

At one of Body Positive's board meetings, I met a remarkable young man named David Wilson. He was twenty-seven, attractive, and had the demeanor and youthful energy of a Michael J. Fox combined with the power and authority of a young Donald Trump. Heterosexual, he had contracted the virus through a blood transfusion two years earlier.

David was born in Kansas City, Kansas, and had moved to north Florida when he was thirteen. Both his parents had died while he was a teenager and David was faced with the responsibility of helping raise and support his younger brother and manage a household from the age of fifteen. "It gave me character," he confided over one of our early dinner discussions. "I'm not sorry I had to work as a teenager. I learned the techniques for success in the business world early." David had married when he was twenty-one and had one child, a girl. He found his immune system on a precipitous decline and his health steadily failing. Thrush bloomed at the back of his mouth, his energy level was waning, and he often had night sweats.

However, he had not experienced any opportunistic infections and thus, like myself, remained in the interminable gray area of ARC. Despite his gradually worsening and sometimes debilitating symptoms, David continued to manage a highly successful Jacksonville commercial real-estate investment firm.

He was unstoppable in his quest to find an effective treatment for his condition, which he regarded as merely temporary; he radiated a tenacity and drive that was rare among the AIDS patients I had known. When I first met him, he was carrying a twenty-pound satchel, filled to the brim with articles and reviews of potential antiviral drugs and immune modulators. For the last six months, from the time he was first diagnosed, David had traveled to almost every major city in the nation, assembling information on protocols and speaking with principal investigators. Almost every AIDS doctor in the country knew him.

We traveled to San Francisco and Los Angeles during the second week of August and met with some of the most prominent AIDS researchers on the West Coast. In San Francisco, we stayed not far from Castro Street, and while walking through that familiar place, I was struck by how much it had changed; the bustling thoroughfare, which had once been filled with men in cutoffs and tank tops hurrying to some destination or those in business suits returning home after a long day at the office, now seemed deserted. Those who remained seemed preoccupied, unfriendly. There was not the casual exchange of glances or the friendly cruise that had been so common in 1981. It reminded me of a scene from a Western ghost town. Clearly, many men who had spent much of their lives in San Francisco's gay community were now dead, and many more had migrated out of the area, away from cold reminders of their fallen friends. The bars that lined the strip were empty; monogamy was "in." The intimate dinner party had replaced the raucous night on the town. This fact was also mirrored in the plummeting rate of sexually transmitted diseases among gay men from 1985 to 1986, assembled by the San Francisco Department of Public Health—a sign that unprotected anal intercourse was rapidly becoming obsolete and that anonymous, one-night encounters were decreasing in popularity as well. Gay men were rapidly and methodically adapting their behavior to deal effectively with the crisis at hand.

David seemed comfortable in the openly gay environment. He joked about the multicolored flags that seemed to dot the landscapes of certain homes. "Does that mean 'Gay man lives here'?" he asked me.

I even dragged him into one of the bars on Castro. He was fascinated and intrigued, and when a handsome gentleman tried to pick him up, he replied diplomatically, "I'm with my boyfriend!"

We met with Dr. Donald Abrams, one of the directors of the San Francisco General Hospital AIDS clinic who, with Dr. Paul Volberding, was among the first in the Bay Area to see the devastating effects of the disease in the city's young gay men. An openly gay man himself, Abrams had graduated from Stanford University Medical School and, after his residency, studied the relationship between viruses and cancer under Nobel Prize–winning researcher Harold Varmus. Later, in Seattle, he studied bone marrow transplantation. Abrams had become acquainted with Volberding on one of his fellowships. When Volberding took over as chief oncologist at San Francisco General, he invited Abrams to join him there on staff. Together, the two helped establish one of the first dedicated AIDS wards in the nation with specialized nursing staffs and treatment protocols. The program became a model for other cities across the country. Abrams impressed me as one of the most compassionate and intelligent mainstream HIV physicians I had met.

We also saw Dr. Alan Levin, an immunologist and allergist who had once worked with Volberding and Abrams at San Francisco General and who now maintained a large HIV private practice in downtown San Francisco. Levin had served as a Marine Corps combat surgeon in Vietnam, and later testified on behalf of soldiers hurt by Agent Orange. He had amassed a huge number of commendations and publications in his thirty years of practice. Levin's wife was Dr. Vera Byers. She was widely regarded as an authority on bacteriology and microbiology and, with Dr. Baldwin at the University of Nottingham in England, had developed effective and novel treatments for breast cancer. Byers was also the director of new product development at the Berkeley-based Xoma Corporation.

Levin's clinic, Positive Action Healthcare, occupied a large space in an office building on Sutter Street. It was clean, high-tech, and very organized. Unlike some physicians who were treating HIV disease, Levin believed that the patient should know about the intricacies of the disease process. He had produced a thirty-minute videotaped presentation in which he explained all that was known about the pathophysiology of HIV disease and the most logical therapeutic interventions based on what was known. The tape was shown to all prospective patients.

In his talk, Levin stressed the importance of monitoring specific laboratory parameters, known as surrogate markers, laboratory values that could indicate the progression and severity of certain diseases and could also be used in evaluating a treatment's efficacy. One of these is the p-24 antigen level, which measures reverse transcriptase activity and is considered a surrogate marker for viral replication. Another is the level of beta-2 microglobulin, a protein tightly bound to the surface of many nucleated cells. Beta-2 microglobulin levels are elevated in a variety of cancers and other diseases and seemed to be elevated in poor-prognosis ARC and AIDS patients—although there is no complete correlation between this marker and the progression of HIV disease. A third surrogate marker that Levin assessed in his patients is serum neopterin, a protein secreted by activated HIV-infected macrophages. He also ran viral culture tests, which measured levels of viral load in the blood, and ordered a complete lymphocyte panel, which included not only the CD4 and CD8 cell counts and CD4:CD8 ratio but the natural killer cell and B-cell level functions as well.

Levin advocated aggressive early intervention with antiviral drugs and immunomodulators long before such a view was fashionable; he suggested the custom design of a protocol based on an individual's specific needs. He was among the earliest AIDS physicians to advocate using a much lower dose of AZT—400 milligrams, instead of the original 1,200. Levin also suggested the use of dextran sulfate when beta-2 microglobulin levels were elevated, DHEA (dehydroepiandrosterone) when neopterin levels were elevated, and an immunomodulator called transfer factor when CD4 cell counts fell below 200.

Levin offered the optimistic prediction that HIV would be a chronic, manageable disease, similar to diabetes in the very near future, and that a cure would be found within five years. He further posited his own version of the cure for AIDS: the creation of monoclonal antibodies linked to a toxin that specifically sought out and killed HIV-infected lymphocytes and macrophages. By eliminating the reservoir of viral load completely, both in peripheral blood and tissues, Levin explained, such immunotoxins may well represent an effective maintenance therapy for AIDS. He indicated that he was developing the drug in his own lab and that it would be available to his patients within the next two years. He also believed that some people who were HIV-positive, but whose immune systems contained certain as-yet-undiscovered genetic differences, would never develop AIDS.

David and I gave Levin copies of several journal articles that detailed promising therapies, including one on passive immunotherapy. He seemed impressed with our enthusiasm and assured us that he would look into the treatments. David received an injection of transfer factor; I did not, since I was a subject in the Ampligen study and was forbidden to take any concurrent experimental immunomodulatory drugs for the duration of it. The study coordinators had assured us they would perform blood levels to detect any taboo medication and that any subject who cheated would be dropped from the trial. I doubted that they could actually detect blood levels of the transfer factor, but the drug had the potential to affect certain chemistry values that might arouse suspicion.

What was remarkable about Dr. Levin in the spring of 1988 was that he was one of the first AIDS physicians openly to administer investigational therapies in his private practice. Levin made available experimental drugs and appropriate monitoring in the setting of a private physician's practice, and he was open to monitoring patients who were taking medicines that they had discovered through their own research and personal initiative. Equally impressive was Levin's philosophy of educating the interested patient about even the most subtle detail of his or her illness.

While David and I were in San Francisco, we also met with Martin Delaney, president and co-founder of Project Inform. The organization had been providing information on experimental therapy to AIDS patients through fact sheets and its *PI Perspective* newsletter since the mid-1980s and offered comments and interpretations of promising findings. Years before, Delaney had entered the seminary and was well on his way to becoming a Jesuit priest when he suffered a crisis of faith, and instead became a highly paid marketing consultant—a profession that he incorporated into his involvement in the AIDS crisis. Cold but perceptive, he, like Levin, consistently advocated that the patient has the right to decide if a particular treatment is in his or her own best interest and to intelligently gauge the risks involved and then have the option to pursue that therapy.

In his meeting with us, Delaney cited his own treatment in the mid-1970s, when doctors told him he had terminal hepatitis and had, at best, two years to live. Delaney enrolled himself in a risky experimental treatment program at Stanford. Within five months, his health was amazingly restored. Then, in the sixth month, the drug that had cured his hepatitis produced a debilitating side effect—an acute neuropathy, which caused an excruciating burning sensation in his feet. It was a pain so intense, Delaney told us, that he would wake up with nightmares about leopards trying to gnaw off his feet. He began taking methadone daily to relieve the pain, and became aware that he might have to stay on methadone for the rest of his life. In the wake of the side effects that he and others experienced, Delaney recalled, the study was closed and the drug made unavailable. Six months after the trial was closed, five of

Delaney's friends—all of them also suffering from terminal hepatitis—approached him, begging for access to the drug that had apparently saved his own life. But the clinical trial was closed, and there was no underground market for the substance. Delaney watched as, one by one, the friends succumbed to the disease that he himself had survived. This was one of the many experiences that made him angry and disillusioned with the mainstream system of experimental drug testing.

Delaney noted that trading sore feet for a prolonged life was his own choice, one that he would do over if given the chance. "Others have been deprived of that decision," he told me. "Since that time, I've watched five friends die of chronic hepatitis because some bureaucrat decided that the risk of side effects outweighed the benefit." By founding Project Inform in 1985, Delaney was helping AIDS patients make informed choices about their own treatment options. He was among the first AIDS activists to establish contact with FDA Commissioner Frank Young and NIAID Director Anthony Fauci. He maintained an ongoing rapport with Ellen Cooper, the FDA's manager of antiviral drug development. Delaney hired Tom Jefferson, then the administrative director of the San Diego AIDS project, to be the acting administrator of Project Inform. Shortly thereafter, Delaney's organization spearheaded the Bay Area Ribavirin Interest Group (BARIG), a major program monitoring the drugs ribavirin and isoprinosine. Under Delaney's direction, Project Inform published a monthly newsletter and operated an eight-hour-a-day hotline where up-to-date information on conventional and alternative HIV treatments could be obtained.

In the spring of 1985, Delaney and his partner Joe Brewer met with representatives of the manufacturer of ribavirin, ICN Pharmaceuticals in Newport Beach, California. The two reached an agreement with the company in which even larger quantities of ribavirin could be purchased directly from the wholesaler in Mexico City and then shipped to Tijuana for importation. They also developed a questionnaire that would assess the drug's basic effectiveness and toxicity and which PWAs and their doctors could fill out and return to Project Inform. ICN agreed to pay for the analysis of the questionnaires and to provide the drug in bulk quantities at a reduced cost. Thus, the Bay Area Ribavirin Interest Group was born. By the spring of 1986, there were Ribavirin Interest Groups in many major U.S. cities, which obtained both ribavirin and isoprinosine from California and which independently returned their completed questionnaires to Project Inform. With Jim Corti, the two imported large quantities of both ribavirin and isoprinosine.

Delaney compiled and analyzed the data on the drugs and sent the results to dozens of interested PWAs and their physicians around the country. He also presented the data to the FDA. Delaney argued to Fauci and other government officials that there should be a floating standard, depending on the threat of the specific disease. "The standard of proof for a new headache pill should be different from standards for a fatal disease where there are no effective remedies. You ought to be able to put a drug on the market on conditional approval, to be reevaluated in a year, or only in certain circumstances," he said.

After exchanging histories, David and I spoke with Delaney about the possibility of pursuing a treatment program using passive neutralization, or passive immunotherapy (PI). We discussed the mechanics of actually manufacturing the product: plasma that was rich with antibodies from healthy HIV-infected individuals and that had shown *in vitro* neutralizing potential against HIV.

Also present at the meeting was John S. James, editor of *AIDS Treatment News*. We left the meeting feeling certain that some effective treatment would soon be found and that we would be among the first to take advantage of it.

A physician friend in Los Angeles had heard that I was becoming more and more involved in the research of alternative medicines, that I had obtained ribavirin and isoprinosine from Mexico, and that I was a subject in the Ampligen study. He invited me to speak before the Southern California Physicians for Human Rights, some of whom treated HIV. I created a brief compendium describing alternative therapies, duplicating and distributing it to the audience in advance of the meeting. I brought along those drugs I had in my possession and explained how they could be obtained. Some of the physicians expressed a willingness to monitor their own patients who wanted to try the drug. After the meeting, several activists asked me to speak at their groups.

In the months that followed, I also spoke to high-school groups and college audiences in Florida. I discussed the need for safe sex, the growing threat posed by the epidemic, and which treatments were proving most effective. It occurred to me that many of the young men and women to whom I spoke had never known a time when sex existed without the threat of disease or the fear of infection constantly chipping away at their unconscious, shaping their attitudes, and influencing their behavior.

When I returned to Florida from California on August 28, I learned that Du Pont had announced it would pull out of its joint venture with HEM Research in developing Ampligen as a potential AIDS therapy. The chemical maker said it would continue to supply the drug and continue to support the study in progress but wouldn't back any further trials after the venture was dissolved in mid-November.

There were rumblings that Du Pont had conducted its own analysis of the Hahnemann University pilot study and that its review had produced a less positive picture of the drug's ability to boost the immune system. Rumors also circulated that Du Pont officials had early access to results from the Phase 2 trial of which I was a part and had determined that there were no significant improvements in the patients who had been treated with the drug.

This rumor was confirmed days later when the FDA ordered the Phase 2 trials of Ampligen closed. An objective evaluation of the data by a review board had concluded that Ampligen failed to produce any significant immunological improvements in the treated patients. Just as many people on the drug arm of the study developed AIDS as on the placebo arm, if not more. The clinical trial's code of secrecy was broken and I learned that I had actually been on the placebo arm of the study; for five months, I had been traveling forty miles to have a useless bag of saline pumped into my veins.

Ironically, some patients who had received the active drug in other cities felt that it actually *had* helped them, and they threatened to bring lawsuits against Du Pont for pulling out of the study and withholding a lifesaving treatment.

David and I continued to call researchers around the world to obtain information and journal articles on a wide variety of experimental drugs, both of the antiviral and immunomodulator type, that had shown promise both in test tube and in preliminary human trials.

We even obtained a small supply of MM1. "MM" purportedly stood for Mubarak and Mobutu, the leaders of Egypt and Zaire (where the researchers who developed the drug originated). The exact identity of the compound remained a mystery; but, according to its inventors—Egyptian surgeon Ahmed Shafik and African researcher Zirimwabago Lurhuma—it was without a doubt the "cure" for AIDS. They announced at an international press conference in December 1987 and in subsequent articles published in the *Egyptian Medical Journal* that MM1 restored the underlying immune deficiency in eighty AIDS patients in a trial in Africa but that its mechanism of action was as yet undefined. A medical consulting agency in Tampa was actually arranging for American AIDS patients to travel to Zaire to obtain the medication. The thirty-one-day expedition would cost each patient $50,000 and drew attacks from community leaders who feared that the agency was practicing the most harmful kind of deception and exploitation. Several friends of ours in north Florida sold their homes to raise the money for the trip, convinced that the drug would restore their health. It didn't. When they returned to Florida, they were forced to declare bankruptcy.

We learned about the huge worldwide pharmacopoeia of AIDS drugs through industry trade publications such as the American Foundation for AIDS Research's *AIDS Targeted Information Newsletter*, *Antiviral Agents Bulletin*, the Centers for Disease Control's *AIDS Update*, *AIDS Research and Human Retroviruses*, and the journal *AIDS*. We obtained Medline on our computer systems and performed our own on-line literature searches using a variety of key words and, in the process, found articles on immunomodulatory and antiviral drugs that were not referenced in any of the AIDS publications. The articles filled an entire room, with information on thymic factors with potential immunomodulating powers, biologics, antiviral agents of every conceivable sort and with varying modes of action. We obtained only those drugs that appeared to hold the most promise and had demonstrated the least toxicity. In the process, we established contact with research-and-development executives at pharmaceutical companies around the world.

We grew to have an expert understanding of the drugs' pharmacological modes and actions. Some we obtained directly from the manufacturer. For others, we contacted the researchers in Europe at the medical centers and clinics where the drugs were developed. We identified ourselves as knowledgeable American AIDS patients who were interested in taking the medications under the supervision of a monitoring physician. Occasionally, Jim Corti obtained the drugs for us. Others, however, we procured on our own.

Perhaps the most remarkable journey was one that David made himself, in Germany, alone. He was there on a business-related venture but was also seeing a doctor in Munich, Dr. Vetter, who was using a variety of nutritional and vitamin-based approaches in treating AIDS patients along with a German version of the American drug immune globulin. "It was potent stuff," David revealed to me later. "It gave me all kinds of energy and I found myself climbing mountains and going on hiking expeditions every afternoon!"

David's real interest, however, was a drug called Resistocell. It was originally created and manufactured in Heidelberg by Dr.

Karl von Weldt. It was a freeze-dried concoction of animal bone marrow, which when reconstituted with dextran sulfate, showed preliminary efficacy in treating certain cancers and in boosting both the red and white blood cell counts of cancer patients. David had heard about the drug and was determined to get it. His own red and white blood cell counts had gone down from taking such medications as AZT; Resistocell held the further potential to raise his CD4 cell count.

He drove to a location in Heidelberg, Dr. von Weldt's last known address. After a five-day search, David learned that the controversial physician had been driven underground and was now operating in a 400-year-old castle in the midst of the Black Forest, far outside the city. David drove for miles in inclement weather through the Black Forest and finally arrived at the clinic. He purchased ten ampules of Resistocell and returned to Munich with the drug. Dr. Vetter was amazed and impressed that David had tracked down von Weldt so methodically, and made the substance so readily available to him.

In our marathon worldwide search for literature on possible AIDS remedies in the summer of 1988, we consistently avoided the obvious scams: catnip enemas . . . horse urine therapies . . . hokey cancer elixirs . . . treatments that were not backed by scientific evidence or a sound basis in antiviral or immunological theory. We also avoided the less obvious scams, which, though less obvious, we knew to be useless nonetheless—"immune formulas" and amino acid combos advertised in the back of certain magazines, for example. We were independent and objective in our evaluation of the many drugs we learned about in our research and reading. We crossed the boundaries of traditional Chinese medicine and Ayurvedic (Indian) medicine and pursued compounds from as far as away as Australia and New Zealand.

We eliminated the most toxic compounds up front and concentrated on those with the most efficacy data and theoretical reasons to their credit. We tried a few of the most promising ourselves, while carefully monitoring our blood work, and always under the auspices of sympathetic physicians. Those we didn't try were distributed to the Central Florida Buyers' Club, informally led by an Orlando AIDS patient named John Scafutti and a local physician, who were carrying on the tradition pioneered by Springer and Myers. They led some of the earliest underground trials in the Southeast, trials in which groups of patients volunteered to test a new drug outside the confines of mainstream academic research. Scafutti often fed the data to me via modem and I kept a massive computerized database. It was more sophisticated than ad hoc self-experimentation but certainly not as sophisticated as a clinical trial.

Scafutti's mini-studies established that, contradictory to basic dogma in AIDS research, meaningful data could emerge without the use of placebo controls and that a variety of clinical indicators and laboratory markers—rather than death—could be used as meaningful outcome variables and endpoints. Furthermore, we knew, subjects could continue to take other drugs to protect themselves against opportunistic infections without significantly skewing the data.

Three major advantages immediately became obvious to us in implementing informal monitoring trials of a drug's basic toxicity and efficacy. Unlike the classic clinical trials, informal studies could rapidly incorporate new information and change the details of a protocol at any time once the trial was under way. The conventional studies were forced to follow a strict protocol, which was established prior to the first subjects' entry, and could not alter a drug's dosage, method of administration, or concurrent medication log, even if such changes seemed clearly advantageous. Second, underground trials allowed monitoring physicians and researchers to observe patients for a longer period of time than the traditional studies that typically had preestablished end dates, after which time subjects were often lost to long-term follow-up. In addition to allowing doctors to follow patients for longer periods of time than in classic trials, informal research allowed them to obtain more detailed background histories, since many of the patients were registered in the doctors' own computer databases. Clinical and immunological information—in some cases dating back years—was therefore available to other researchers.

We also sent several compounds with unclear or contradictory *in vitro* data to the National Cancer Institute's Drug Synthesis and Chemistry Branch. The NCI screened the compounds for free and determined their efficacy in their own HTLV-III assay. We also screened certain compounds for toxicity and efficacy in a private lab in Boston. Many of these compounds were drugs that we knew had been overlooked by the establishment.

The real problem with contemporary science, we came to understand—especially in the realm of AIDS—had nothing to do with old-fashioned investigators insisting on placebos or using death as an endpoint. The real problem was that scientists pursuing their various specialties and individual labs often worked with blinders on, and sometimes blind*folds*. Using a narrowly defined range of criteria that often lacked creativity and ingenuity, they rarely saw the "big picture" when evaluating a compound's potential. They were not familiar with research in other, similar but unrelated areas, and they frequently missed the more far-reaching implications of the data they had gathered.

In our worldwide search, we found Dr. Stephen P. Hauptman at Philadelphia's Thomas Jefferson Memorial Hospital. He had recently completed a Phase 1 clinical trial with lymphocyte transfusion therapy and had garnered marginal short-term success. Hauptman's work was significant, since it represented some of the earliest attempts by researchers to achieve full-scale immune reconstitution in AIDS. It became clear to us early on that HIV was not only a persistent pathogen, it might have the potential to permanently destroy the immune system. Somehow, it seemed to destroy some fundamental mechanism, perhaps by disrupting a critical feedback loop between cytokines and lymphokines or forever destroying key thymic precursor cells. Beyond a certain point of damage, spontaneous immune reconstitution in an AIDS patient seemed unlikely, even with the help of the most sophisticated antiviral. The damage would not be reversed, we felt certain, even when the viral invasion was fully stopped. Even if all this were not true, there was still the immunological theory suggesting that CD4 lymphocytes were quite possibly a nongenerative cell line. Thus, Hauptman's work was especially relevant and meaningful. In his procedure, CD4 lymphocytes were harvested from AIDS patients' parents, brothers, or sisters and then transfused into the AIDS patient in much the same way that red blood cells are during surgery.

The concept itself was a very logical one. AIDS patients lacked CD4 lymphocytes; why not simply replace them the way you would red blood cells or platelets through transfusions of these cell lines in conditions such as anemia and thrombocytopenia? Unfortunately, there were numerous practical problems that undermined the treatment's potential success.

Hauptman knew what all immunologists knew: that anyone who has a transplant of organ tissue or blood cells must be tissue-typed prior to selecting a candidate organ in order to prevent rejection of the tissue. In the process of being typed, the patient's biological trademarks, represented in cell-membrane-bound proteins, are genetically characterized. With the help of computers and monoclonal antibodies, these markers are given names. On chromosome number six, there are four places, or loci, where the genes that produce these markers reside. The loci are designated A, B, C, and D. There are many different genes that can occupy each locus, but only one will be present at each locus in any one individual. Since chromosomes are paired, therefore, there will be a total of eight genes involved in this spectrum, known as the major histocompatibility system. Humans inherit one set from each parent, producing the total of eight markers—two on each locus.

When it comes to organ or plasma donation, a perfect donor match must have all the same eight HLA (human leukocyte antigen) markers that the recipient has. A perfect match is *required* in most major organ transplant operations—including heart, bone marrow, and liver transplants—since intact immune systems are capable of recognizing mismatched antigens as foreign and rejecting them. Alternatively, intact lymphocytes within the donated organ can reject the tissue of the recipient, thereby creating a disease called graft-versus-host. In that disease process, many tissues can be attacked simultaneously and become dysfunctional or destroyed, and the transplant recipient can die.

Hauptman hypothesized that since AIDS patients' immune systems were not intact, the chance of their getting graft-versus-host disease from lymphocyte transfusion was much more remote. Therefore, the need to transfuse identical HLA-matched lymphocytes from relatives was less crucial than in other types of transplants. Hauptman also reasoned that transfusing HLA-identical lymphocytes might help make a patient even more immune-suppressed from HIV. Therefore, he used donor lymphocytes that shared only two of eight antigens with the patient. In this way, he conjectured, the newly transfused lymphocytes might resist attack by the virus and prevent the development of full-blown AIDS. Other immunologists we spoke with expressed surprise that no graft-versus-host disease would occur, since the infusion of immunocompetent lymphocytes into a mismatched immunosuppressed recipient—even an AIDS patient—would be expected to produce some graft-versus-host reaction.

In 1986, Hauptman performed a pilot study with eighteen AIDS patients. Using a Fenwall CS-3000 blood cell separator, Hauptman harvested a yield of one billion lymphocytes from the donors—parents and siblings (who were, of course, negative for HIV, hepatitis B, and the herpes viruses)—and then reinfused the cells into the patients via a peripheral vein over a period of one hour. The transfusions were performed once every four weeks for six months.

After five months of treatments, Hauptman found a somewhat modest increase in CD4 cell counts in the treated patients and a significant increase in responsiveness to interleukin 2—a sign that their immune systems were improving. Most patients showed weight gain and a significant abatement of fever, fatigue, and malaise. Despite the immunological improvements, twelve patients died in the months following the study's conclusion. The remaining six survived for thirty-six months after cessation of therapy, but their lymphocyte numbers and immune status returned to baseline levels. There was no graft-versus-host disease in any of the treated patients.

Although the study was closed, Hauptman agreed to make the treatment available to us. Despite the disappointing results, David chose to pursue the therapy. Fortunately, he found an appropriate match in his younger brother and the two of them flew to Philadelphia for the monthly transfusions. After two months, David noted that his CD4 cell count did rise slightly, from 56 to 88. But the improvement was not sustained over time, even with repeated transfusions. After twelve treatments, his CD4 cell values had dropped below baseline levels.

Hauptman partially blamed the failure on the ineffectiveness of the antiviral cover used to protect the newly transfused lymphocytes; he conjectured that the new cells became infected by the virus and were killed as fast as they were introduced, despite concurrent AZT therapy. Hauptman argued for the more frequent transfusion of lymphocytes and perhaps for the use of completely mismatched donor lymphocytes. Also, we later learned, the equipment that he used to harvest the cells may not have been capable of harvesting the maximum numbers of CD4 lymphocytes. And it could well be that one person's lymphocytes—identically matched or not—simply could not survive in another's immune system.

One evening, just after David and I had concluded a telephone conference with a researcher in Bangkok, I received a call from my high school friend Jason Adams. I hadn't heard from him since our last discussion in San Francisco six years earlier. He told me he was living in Fort Lauderdale. Although he suffered from bouts of fatigue and energy loss, he maintained that he was basically stable. We met for lunch at a Las Olas deli and I was impressed by how healthy he looked. It was now close to a decade since he first manifested lymphadenopathy and had been exposed to the virus. He had yet to cross over the line into full-blown AIDS.

In the eyes of AIDS drug activists, one of the most salient examples of the FDA's bureaucracy was the lack of speedy action to approve ddI, a second-generation nucleoside analog that was a "fourth cousin" of AZT. In preliminary Phase 1 human trials, the drug appeared to produce the same efficacy at a safe dose as AZT but without AZT's bone-marrow-suppressive side effects. As early as August 1988, AIDS patients across the country were clamoring for the drug. But under the current FDA guidelines, it would be almost two full years before ddI would become widely available.

David Wilson correctly assessed the drug's importance. Rather than lead a demonstration against the FDA to get it approved, however, he took more direct action. As early as the fall of 1988, David learned that the drug was manufactured by Ray-Lo, the same Canadian chemical company from which Steve Gavin had purchased ddC two years earlier. He joined forces with Gavin and AIDS patients Jules Parnes, Rick Schwartz, and Charley Donnelly, and formed a small buying group to obtain the drug. Eventually, one of the buyers lost interest in the group; Gavin did too. David took over the project himself.

He managed to convince the Canadian company that the drug was needed for research purposes. From his own savings, he sent the company a money order for $37,500, enough to purchase one kilo of the drug at approximately $37.50 per gram. Along with the money, he sent a letter explaining that the drug was going to be used "to thwart a chicken virus on [his] associate's poultry farm." Certain that his request would be discovered to be bogus and his money returned, David simultaneously enrolled in a Phase 1 clinical trial of the drug at Bellevue Hospital in New York. David knew, of course, that if Ray-Lo agreed to supply him with the drug, the company was not only violating Bristol-Myers/Squibb patent rights for human use of ddI, but that it was also violating government laws that forbade the sale of nonapproved drugs in large quantities.

On the same day that the hospital called to inform him that he had been accepted in the study, the kilo of ddI arrived at his doorstep! He talked his way out of the hospital trial and began taking the drug he had purchased, using a median dose he calculated from the clinical trial in New York—500 milligrams a day. He also sent a small sample to Jules Parnes, Rick Schwartz, and four other members of the original buyers' group—AIDS patients who had consistently been among the first to try new therapies and who had educated themselves thoroughly about a drug's potential toxicity, benefits, and mode of action. Along with the drug, David sent a certificate of analysis along with instructions for its proper mixage: the powder was to be dissolved in sterile water, and then a designated amount was to be drawn into a syringe and squirted into six ounces of apple juice (which was used in the formal clinical trials of the drug both to disguise the taste and help maintain the drug's stability). The liquid was to be taken with an antacid, since stomach acid held the potential to destroy the drug's effectiveness.

Both Jules and Rick reported excellent results in the first few weeks of taking David's underground ddI. They didn't seem to suffer the drop in their red and white blood cell counts that they routinely experienced with AZT. Their CD4 cell counts rose slightly, Parnes's p-24 antigen level fell sharply, and both had more energy than ever before. Their physicians were impressed. Through these two patients, Jim Corti learned about David's "buy" and flew to Jacksonville, where he purchased 200 grams at a cost of $7,000. Within a week's time, Corti had sold the entire supply to ARC and AIDS patients in Los Angeles.

David continued to purchase the drug from the Ray-Lo Company and was eventually able to negotiate the price down to $26 per gram. Corti returned to Jacksonville several more times in the following months to purchase more of the drug. Sales were brisk in Los Angeles. Everyone, it seemed, wanted ddI.

At one point, Ray-Lo became aware of David's true motivation for purchasing the chemical and refused to sell him any more. He could have stopped then and there; most people in his position probably would have. With enough to last himself at least a year, he wasn't running low on his own supply of ddI. But he knew that there were other people who needed it and for whom it was genuinely helpful, and who did not qualify for or live close enough to sites of the early clinical trials.

Two weeks after the company cut off his supply, David established a phony corporate identity with a Canadian post office box and street address. He then invented an outrageous but believable cover story: he told the company officials that he represented a corporation called "Pal Research" that was conducting hydroponics experiments to see if various nucleoside analogs such as ddI could cure viral diseases in plants grown under special conditions. David had actually found a hydroponics expert in Virginia who agreed to act as his "scientific director" and legal front man. The two obtained a Confidential Disclosure Agreement and through the "corporation" purchased the drug from the company at the reduced wholesale cost of $15,000 per kilo. This brought the price down to $15 a gram. David then hired a confederate to receive the drug when it was delivered to the Canadian address and forward it—all three kilos— to his home in Jacksonville. He saw that ddI was a relatively expensive drug, affordable to only the richest PWAs, and so he made efforts to reduce the price.

Simultaneously, an AIDS activist stood up at a gathering in Los Angeles, told the huge group that a man in Jacksonville had real ddI, announced David Wilson's Jacksonville post office box, and quoted the price of $17 a gram. Insiders speculated that David himself had "arranged" this convenient event, but he vehemently denied it. "I have no idea who this person was or how he got the information," he confided to me later. "My identity was an absolute secret throughout the entire affair. I had intended merely to keep a steady supply of drug flowing for Corti's established customers."

Within days of the Los Angeles announcement, hundreds of orders for ddI from across the nation arrived at David's Jacksonville address. With the help of Orlando AIDS activist Alfredo Martinez, he distributed all three kilos of the drug to hundreds of AIDS patients across the country at the quoted cost of $17 a gram, using what was left over to pay for postage and other expenses. Prior to distributing the drug, David had each batch tested by a New York chemical company through a sympathetic physician, Dr. Nathaniel Pier. Pier indicated that the chemical company confirmed the drug to be as pure as the one being developed for the Bristol-Myers clinical trial. And afterward, David kept in continuous touch with many of the patients who took the drug, and collected data on its basic efficacy and toxicity.

"I had no intention of directly distributing the drug myself," he told me later. "I was perfectly happy to let people like Jim Corti sell the compound to people in the community. Through a fluke, I ended up taking on that responsibility as well."

Ultimately, officials learned about the scheme, tipped off by an anonymous source. U.S. customs officials confiscated a final shipment of the drug at the post office—ten kilos of it—on August 6, 1989, but not before hundreds of ARC and AIDS patients across the country had gained early access to it. Shortly thereafter, the Canadian chemical company was purchased by a larger firm. Neither Wilson nor Corti was able to obtain any more ddI, despite repeated attempts to procure it from other sources, and it remained unavailable for a time. But the entire process provided a dramatic example of how AIDS patients were capable of taking care of their own needs without waiting for the establishment to respond.

Ironically, about six months later, the FDA and NIH became convinced of ddI's potential value. It was the first drug to be placed into a fast "parallel track" under a new program, which afforded

AIDS patients access to investigational drugs before they had completed Phase 2 trials.

On April 28, 1988, during a hearing of a Subcommittee of the Committee on Government Operations, the NIAID's Anthony Fauci assured Chair Ted Weiss that the government-run AIDS Clinical Trials Group had implemented thirty protocols of new, promising anti-HIV drugs, sixteen of which did not involve AZT.

Congressman Henry Waxman challenged Fauci on the progress of the trials and specifically asked Fauci why the ACTG had no study in place for aerosolized pentamidine (a drug that had shown early promise in the treatment and prevention of one of the most common AIDS-related infections, PCP), which his own drug-selection committee had placed at the top of a priority list for development. (Ultimately, it would be the New York Community Research Initiative, an organization run heavily by PWAs themselves, that would conduct the trial.)

Fauci responded that he simply did not have the staff to conduct the pentamidine study and in that process, admitted what he had been denying to the committee for years: that the NIAID and ACTG were grossly underfunded and that the OMB (Office of Management and Budget) had failed to allocate the promised funds.

Weiss suggested to Fauci that, in fact, as far as drug development for AIDS was concerned, very little had actually been achieved and that he and his staff needed a tremendous amount of assistance to help them move forward.

Shockingly, that assistance was not forthcoming. And on November 7, 1988, exactly eight months after the conclusion of the hearings, 77,994 cases of AIDS had been reported to the Centers for Disease Control in Atlanta, of which 43,888 were known dead. Still, the disease had not yet achieved a broad and enduring impression in the minds of government officials.

And most Americans remained unaware of the gravity and relevance of the plague. Indeed, the distribution of cases by risk group illustrated that over two-thirds of AIDS patients were still bisexual or homosexual men. Another 19 percent were heterosexual drug users. Even as late as the fall of 1988, the popular conception was that AIDS was an illness that simply could not happen to just anyone. The full impact of the epidemic had not yet hit home.

CHAPTER 9

BEHIND THE COUNTER AT
DR. MAYER'S DRUGSTORE

T hrough a physician in New York City, I learned of a
pediatrician in North Miami Beach, Dr. Robert Mayer,
who for the last six months had been quietly treating AIDS
and ARC patients with ozone therapy. His office was located between a Jamaican grocery store and a beauty salon in a medical
plaza buried in a low-rent shopping mall.

Mayer had been using ozone therapy for decades to treat a
wide variety of childhood illnesses. In the 1950s, he injected it
directly into the spinal fluid of infants to cure such disorders as
pediatric viral encephalitis. He also used more conventional treatments in his practice with two other pediatricians. But when the
standard remedies failed, he turned to ozone. He had built up quite
a reputation in the Miami community of the 1950s, and parents from
all around brought their children to his office for the unusual treatment. Mayer achieved amazing success using ozone with children;
he became something of a local hero and his work was written up
in several journal articles.

As a therapeutic agent for human disease, ozone had histori-
cally shown undeniable efficacy. It had been used for decades in
Germany to treat a broad spectrum of viral diseases including

herpes and hepatitis A and B as well as certain cancers. But it was not until Dr. Horst Kief published a remarkable study documenting the effects of ozone in twenty ARC patients in 1986 that the procedure's true potential in HIV disease became apparent. In Kief's study, the patients treated with a thirty-day regime of ozone experienced almost complete alleviation of various HIV-related symptoms, including night sweats, thrush, and oral hairy leukoplakia. More important, their CD4 lymphocyte levels rose dramatically. Many were able to return to work.

Of course, Mayer had read all the literature. With an engineer partner, he custom-designed and built his own ozone generator and with minor modifications had been using it for three decades. Like the German researchers, Mayer practiced the major autohemotherapy technique of ozone, not the rectal insufflation method, which was thought to be less effective. In the autohemotherapy procedure, a single pint of blood was removed from a vein in the patient's arm, and siphoned into a 500-milliliter bottle containing vitamin B-12 and heparin to prevent clotting. Then a large glass syringe, linked to the ozone-generating unit, released 10,000 micrograms of ozone into the pint of blood, and the ozone-enriched blood went back into the patient. The same procedure was repeated each day for thirty consecutive days. The theory was that as the ozone molecules dissolved in the blood, they gave up their third oxygen atom, releasing an energy that destroys all lipid-enveloped viruses. Over a thirty-day period, all the patient's blood would be processed.

In 1987, the Medizone Corporation in New York City designed and built its own ozone generator and completed studies showing that ozone had moderate *in vitro* antiviral activity against HIV. Another researcher also found that ozone was capable of inactivating 99.01 percent of HIV at free concentrations of less than 0.5 milligram per liter. This same researcher also performed a small trial with ozone using the rectal insufflation method and produced promising results. But it would be years before Medizone and others would get the green light from the FDA to pursue full-scale human tests with ozone; an elaborate battery of tests and animal studies would have to precede the human trials. It was only natural, then, that pragmatic practicing physicians with a background in ozone therapy would attempt to use the process in treating AIDS, out of the limelight and scrutiny of regulatory officials.

Mayer was actually one of a handful of such doctors in the United States who had set up ozone clinics in the late 1980s. Others included Rodney Hoffman in New York and Robert Battle in Houston.

Mayer's office was situated at the end of the second-floor corridor of the Norwood Medical Plaza, a nondescript office space that contained medical and dental offices. Across the hall, substance-abuse patients sauntered in for their daily methadone treatments, unaware that they were but a stone's throw from an AIDS treatment center. An aura of secrecy and mystery surrounded Mayer's office. There was continuous speculation among the other physicians in the building about what actually went on there.

Inside, Mayer's office was colorless but extraordinarily clean. The metallic smell of ozone was barely detectable. Imitation wood-grain paneling covered the walls, and the floors were tile. The lobby contained an old couch and a coffee table. In one room, a personal computer, circa 1975, idled at low speed.

When we met we developed an instantaneous and solid bond. He was seventy-seven but looked far younger. He had been married three times, and had six children and many grandchildren. He looked rather distinguished, with graying hair that was neatly parted, penetrating blue eyes, and a quiet, kind demeanor. He was intelligent yet somewhat eccentric. He often spoke in colorful meta-phors. And he wore a small ceramic butterfly pin on his lapel. "It makes the children feel comfortable," he explained.

There was unmistakable compassion in Mayer's eyes, a com-passion I had not encountered in the eyes of many other AIDS physicians in south Florida. Mayer vowed to save the lives of as many AIDS patients as he could with his innovative treatments, although he never promoted the alternative therapies or made ex-travagant claims about their efficacy. He never turned away a patient who was unable to pay for the drugs or his services. Financially secure and well past retirement age, he easily could have chosen to withdraw from public life comfortably. Instead he chose to spend every day working with AIDS patients. His practice rarely turned a profit; in fact, he barely broke even. He seemed genuinely interested in improving the quality of life and health of every patient he treated. He was a tremendously hard worker, often staying in the office late into the evenings to see patients. Some HIV physicians had a tendency to abandon those patients they considered to be "beyond hope"—those with chronically depressed immune systems, or whose opportunistic infections no longer responded well to treatment. They often relegated these patients' care to other doctors and/or home health-care agencies, preferring not to deal directly with the terminally ill. Dr. Mayer, however, stood by every patient to the end, never ceasing to offer encouragement or allowing them to lose hope.

He was also a bit disorganized. His files were in a state of perpetual disarray and his accounting procedures outdated. I offered to help organize his practice in exchange for free ozone treatments and a modest weekly salary. Mayer agreed, and in a period of months, I became the research assistant of the Mayer HIV Clinic.

At the time, Mayer was using ozone in combination with a single immunomodulatory therapy known as typhoid vaccine. In the 1960s, a New York medical researcher and former Navy hematology laboratory supervisor named Salvatore Catapano had evaluated a large number of vaccines as potential cancer therapies. Among others, he tested vaccines against candida, mumps, and tetanus in animal models. After nine years of experimenting with every vaccine he could get his hands on, Catapano found that infinitesimal doses of typhoid vaccine effectively shrank tumors in hamsters. Through further studies, Catapano learned that the cell wall of the vaccine contained an unusual number and combination of proteins and complex carbohydrates, whose surfaces bore distinctive sequences of atoms called prosthetic radicals. Catapano conjectured that when injected subcutaneously in animals, the vaccine reached the lymphatic system, where its unusual surface activated CD4 lymphocytes and B-cell macrophages. In the mid-1980s Catapano began using the vaccine to stimulate the immune systems of two hundred New York AIDS patients. He found that many of the patients experienced significant clinical improvements, and he wrote up his findings in an unpublished manuscript. Encouraged by those early results, he obtained a patent for the use of typhoid vaccine in AIDS and began issuing licensing agreements to physicians across the country to use his vaccine for the treatment of AIDS. Mayer was one. Typically, the doctor charged $40 to $65 per vaccine injection, and gave half of that to Catapano, who owned the patent on the vaccine's application to AIDS. Catapano kept the exact protocol a secret and released the detailed information on dose escalation only to those doctors who signed licensing agreements.

The vaccine was initially given in very small doses and then gradually stepped up, depending on the patient's immunological response and adverse reactions. The protocol called for the vaccine to be given weekly for at least six months, then monthly for another six-month period. It typically produced high fevers and malaise—signs, according to Catapano, that the immune system was being activated.

The use of vaccines to stimulate the immune system was hardly a new concept. The history of experimental cancer therapy was filled with such adjuvant treatments, which included the poly-antigenic immunoregulator (PAI) developed by Julio I. Colon at the University of Puerto Rico, the staphage lysate vaccine, and—for AIDS—the polio vaccine treatment developed by Alan B. Alan.

Catapano, of course, was most familiar with the literature describing the use of vaccine adjuvants in oncology. He had spoken by phone with many American researchers in the field and had corresponded with others in Europe. The general purpose of using an adjuvant, he knew, was not simply to temporarily stimulate the production of new CD4 cells but to provide an optimal and long-lasting state of immunity, classically measured through antibody production against a specific antigen. In addition to boosting the CD4 cells, Catapano suggested that perhaps the typhoid vaccine might increase the antibody response to HIV and thus in the long term confer lasting protection against HIV. After six months of injections, Catapano reasoned, certain patients would be "cured" and not need further treatments.

As proof that his vaccine therapy worked in AIDS, Catapano cited several cases of HIV-positive patients who, before his treatment, had consistently tested negative for syphilis on all the standard measures. After three months of typhoid therapy, the patients began testing positive for syphilis. According to Catapano, they had syphilis all along; HIV had diminished the ability of their immune systems to mount an appropriate, detectable response to the treponeme that causes syphilis. With the administration of his vaccine, the immune system was now functioning and the response against syphilis simply became detectable. (It did not occur to Catapano that some, if not all, of these subjects may have been exposed to syphilis for the first time in the days immediately following the start of his typhoid treatment.)

Catapano, who had earned neither an M.D. nor a Ph.D. himself, forbade his contract physicians from using other treatments, including AZT, which he regarded as a "toxic compound." He was utterly convinced that his typhoid vaccine application was the cure not only for AIDS but Kaposi's sarcoma as well and insisted that his medical followers maintain a singular loyalty to his discovery.

Mayer had used typhoid vaccine to inoculate children against the disease throughout his career as a pediatrician. Now he was using it in AIDS patients.

From my own experience, I realized there was something grossly wrong with Catapano's research and reasoning. He claimed that only one AIDS patient of the two hundred he had treated had died. I knew it was common practice for cancer researchers at the periphery of their field to mention the total number of patients they had treated and use it as a basis for evaluation. Even in the best-designed clinical trials, though, numerous subjects are lost to follow-up. The truth, I suspected, was that Catapano didn't really know what happened to many of the two hundred he had treated.

In spite of his written report, Catapano was elusive about the specific immunological benefits he observed in patients. He dismissed CD4 cell changes as unreliable and irrelevant and instead made unsupported claims about the importance of the "differential" count. However, no study that I was aware of had identified the differential as an effective predictor of clinical outcome or HIV progression.

I also knew that people at varying stages of HIV infection often experience periods of apparent remission in which they are "symptom-free," with or without treatment. When they experience this change concurrent with the use of a particular treatment, they are easily convinced that the treatment is responsible. A San Francisco doctor who reported early data on his use of the vaccine claimed that 25 percent got better, 50 percent showed little change, and 25 percent actually got worse. These were actually the expected changes experienced by any group of patients with or without treatment, monitored over a given period of time.

Most important, I knew from my own reading—and through more specific immunological tests that we ordered on five of Mayer's typhoid-treated patients—that typhoid was a potent stimulator of macrophages. Thus, it might actually *worsen* the disease process by inappropriately activating and stimulating macrophages and monocytes infected with HIV, which could eventually lead to the decimation of more CD4 cells. Moreover, there was no evidence to support the claim that typhoid increased the antibody response to HIV. Even if it did, there was conflicting evidence that such an increase was actually helpful or that it could delay the progression of the disease.

I shared my observations with Mayer and encouraged him to add other therapies to his list, including many that seemed to show promise in preventing opportunistic infections and which were increasingly available through the buyers' clubs. I organized a means for tracking patients' virological and immunological parameters through a computerized database and contracted with a Miami laboratory that was capable of performing more detailed measures of immunological blood tests. And if any patients wanted to try a novel compound that they had discovered through their own re-search, Mayer agreed to monitor them on that drug.

Unfortunately, I found that over time few of the drugs—even ozone—produced significant and consistent improvements in pa-tients' CD4 cell counts.

"How could a cure for AIDS not emerge from such a variety of drugs?" my mother asked me one day while visiting me. I had returned from Mayer's office and showed her some disappointing numbers and graphs reflecting CD4 cell counts from patients taking a new immunomodulator. The answer is multifaceted.

Certain drugs showed excellent anti-HIV activity in test tube and even animal studies. However, they often had poor-to-low bioavailability in humans—that is, they were not able to reach sufficiently high blood levels at nontoxic doses to be effective against HIV. Oftentimes the drugs did not efficiently reach their site of action, the specific cell line or target tissue containing diseased cells, or the brain. Many of the drugs stimulated other components of the immune system—B-cell production or natural killer cell function—but not the component of the immune system primarily attacked by HIV: CD4 lymphocyte function and production.

Some but not all of the foreign human studies lacked the methodological integrity of scientific design and execution that characterized American trials, and so certain data were actually bogus. Kief's ozone trials and the French Imuthiol studies both fell into this category.

HIV infection represented a broad range of disease severity, and patients in different stages responded differently to a variety of possible treatments, depending on their mechanism of action. Pa-tients with early HIV infection and ARC who did not have thrush and who had more than 200 CD4 lymphocytes often also manifested elevated sedimentation rates, lymphadenopathy, night sweats, and other signs that their bodies were still capable of fighting and mounting defense activities. Patients with poor-prognosis ARC and full-blown AIDS who had a history of opportunistic infections, thrush, fatigue, and chronically low CD4 lymphocyte counts had transcended the "acute phase response" and entered a stage of immune exhaustion. There was some early speculation (based on the immunological theory that a person receives all the CD4 cells he or she needs for a lifetime by his or her late teens) that once the CD4 cell count fell below 50, recovery of those key immune helper cells was impossible, even given the best of antiviral or im-munomodulatory therapy. Thus certain drugs, such as Imuthiol and levamisole, were most apt to help the early ARC patient but likely to be ineffective in AIDS.

HIV is highly mutagenic; that is, it has the potential to change its characteristics once inside the body, mutating into other strains. Thus, a drug that might work against one strain might be totally ineffective against another. This is one of the reasons why develop-ing such a vaccine against HIV has proven to be such a challenge; the vaccine would have to work against *all* variants of the virus.

Few anti-AIDS drugs were actually designed specifically for HIV. Unlike such substances as Peptide T and recombinant soluble CD4—both of which were made specifically to combat HIV—most of the other agents that have been tested against the virus are drugs that were originally conceived for use in fighting cancer or other diseases, though most had shown efficacy *in vitro* against HIV.

Finally, the exact pathogenesis of the disease process had not been fully and completely determined. In 1988, there existed no decent animal model for the disease. Thus, while a drug might work in a given assay or animal model, it might have no bearing on how the disease actually attacks the human body.

However, some of the drugs we used did produce significant and permanent improvements in other, related areas. For instance, iscador, in our experience, while having little impact on the CD4 cell count, did bring up the total white blood cell and granulocyte count, also often depressed in AIDS patients; it also raised the natural killer cell count, another part of the immune system sometimes deficient in HIV. Resistocell, while showing little of its promised impact on the lymphocyte count, did consistently raise the red cell count and hemoglobin of anemic HIV patients. Although ozone, thymosin and hypericin did not improve CD4 cells greatly, they increased patients' overall energy levels. They also lowered liver enzyme levels in patients with chronic hepatitis B. This was important, since researchers had shown that the activated hepatitis B virus was capable of secreting an "x protein" that could serve as a catalyst for HIV proliferation. *In vitro*, the drugs also worked against other viral co-factors including the human herpes virus known as type 6.

Therefore, although none of the drugs offered a cure for AIDS, they did create positive benefits in other areas of immune response and in the general blood counts of patients. When used in combination with low doses of AZT and pentamidine, the drugs even bought valuable time. Indeed, other physicians in the Miami area frequently observed that Dr. Mayer's AIDS patients seemed healthier, had fewer opportunistic infections than the average AIDS patient, and had better overall blood chemistries. Several actually referred their own patients to Mayer for ozone therapy.

Through early intervention with the appropriate antiviral drugs, controlling viral co-factors, maintaining his patients' blood cell counts, aggressively protecting them from opportunistic infections, and trying to boost their immune systems with experimental immunomodulators, Dr. Mayer was among the earliest AIDS physicians to practice an intelligent effort to improve the quality of his patients' health and life.

One of my closest friends and allies at Mayer's was Mayer's longtime nurse, twenty-seven-year-old Susan Drake. She had full lips and ivory skin. She learned that she was HIV-positive in 1986, and that she had contracted the virus through sexual contact. She currently had a boyfriend with whom she practiced safe sex. In addition to being HIV-positive she was also a diabetic and routinely took insulin injections. She now assisted Mayer in the clinic, helped with the ozone therapy, and drew patients' blood, hoping that Mayer's renegade treatments would buy her the necessary time to find a full cure. She radiated enthusiasm and had a wonderful rapport with the patients.

I also found myself forming emotional bonds with many of the patients. One of these was fifty-seven-year-old Rick Andrews, a former New York University English professor who had moved to Florida a year earlier after being diagnosed with Kaposi's sarcoma (KS).

Unlike a typical cancer, KS has the ability to grow in many places of the body simultaneously and to infiltrate a mixture of cell types: lymphocytes and macrophages, endothelial cells (cells that line the surface of all blood vessels), and a proliferation of small blood vessels underneath the skin's surface. It is this proliferation of vessels beneath the skin that gives KS lesions their characteristic purple color. KS also contains spindle cells, derived from endothelial cells and smooth muscle cells, which are the true tumor cells of the cancer.

KS seems to be reversible in its early stage because in that phase, it is not a true cancer and KS lesions resemble normal-growth healing. At this stage, the lesions depend on a continuous supply of stimulating cytokines to keep growing. After mutations occur in the spindle cells, however, there is the chance that the lesions will grow autonomously. At this point, the lesions become classified as a true malignancy, are called a sarcoma, and are no longer reversible.

Although KS is most often seen in patients with AIDS, it can occur in HIV-positive patients with relatively high CD4 cell counts. It has also been found in at least six gay men who were neither HIV-positive nor immune-suppressed. This has led some researchers to believe that another co-factor virus or agent may be linked to the development of the lesions, entirely separate from HIV, or that certain factors (the use of amyl nitrate, for example) could predispose some persons to the cancer. As for its true pathogenesis, scientists are still uncertain. Robert Gallo has speculated that certain cytokines and lymphokines are activated and somehow promote the spindle cells to mutate in certain persons.

When associated with HIV infection, Kaposi's sarcoma becomes aggressive, with visceral involvement. Lesions often form in internal organs such as the lungs as well as on the surface of the skin. The internal lesions often lead to death through organ obstruction and damage.

Bald, with dark eyes and bushy eyebrows, Rick Andrews was one of Mayer's earliest and most aggressive patients. A gay man, he maintained a positive attitude and even a sense of humor, in spite of his grim situation. "I used to be a regular at the St. Mark's Baths—now I'm a regular at Dr. Mayer's," he once joked.

Kaposi's sarcoma had already riddled his skin with ugly purple patches and was beginning to get a visceral grip on his internal organs. Mayer tried everything with Rick, from massive doses of intravenous vitamin C, to the daily ozone treatments, to anticancer drugs that helped other sarcomas. Rick also tried the more conventional treatments such as chemotherapy, vinblastine, and vincristine at the University of Miami. Nothing seemed to work. With every passing day, his lesions became more intractable.

Susan, Rick, and I formed an odd trio. We often sat in the lounge in the back of Mayer's office talking about our lives and the ways we coped, knowing we might not live to see our next birthday, or the one after.

One day, Rick began discussing his will and what he hoped would appear in his obituary after his demise. "I hope they remember how hard I fought," he declared. "I don't want people to think I went down without a struggle. Damn . . . I wanted to beat this thing," he said, as if resigning himself to the notion that it was already too late, that nothing Mayer or any other doctor could do held the power to save his life.

"I know," I said. "I wish I could find a drug to help my memory loss."

Just then, a courier from the Immunodiagnostics Laboratories arrived and placed a stack of envelopes on the table by the door. Susan moved quickly to retrieve one of the envelopes as Dr. Mayer joined us in the room. She knew the envelope contained her recent CD4 cell counts, results from a blood sample drawn by Mayer just days earlier. She quickly scanned the page. A look composed in equal parts of anger and fear swept across her face. Tears streaked her pretty face. "The last lab report says my CD4s have fallen to 212. They've never been below 300, Bob. I don't want to die," she said softly.

Mayer stopped what he was doing and embraced her. With power and strength in his voice, he said, "The lab values vary from day to day. You haven't had your ozone treatment today. Don't forget about the lentinan we just got in." He took her into one of the ozone treatment rooms and summoned the best weapon he had. He began assembling the bottles of heparin and vitamin B-12, the butterfly needles and IV lines that were the props in the drama of ozone. He quickly found a vein and began the procedure. The blood flowed smoothly into the large glass bottle, turning candy-apple red as it hit bottom. Mayer positioned the syringe into the bottle top and pressed hard. Bubbles erupted in the blood-heparin mixture as the ozone concentration made contact with the static oxygen and blood.

(Mayer almost always wore special gloves when performing the procedure. But on several occasions, he didn't put them on. Twice he accidentally stuck himself with a needle containing HIV-infected blood. Yet he never developed HIV. "Until you all are cured, I will remain in perfect health," he told us.)

In the midst of dealing with our individual psychological conflicts, we also faced the problem of which treatments to pursue in that vast, diffuse armamentarium. Almost weekly, a new drug would capture our attention and be touted as an effective treatment. Nearly all of them had side effects of some kind, and we had to become experts in immunological and virological pharmacology, gauging the benefit-risk ratio of each drug, scrutinizing the European literature on human studies, and making informed decisions based on our individual blood chemistries and specialized needs. For Rick, any drug that resulted in a significant rise in his SGOT or SGPT levels—measures of liver enzyme functions—was taboo since, in addition to HIV, he suffered from chronic persistent hepatitis B and had elevated liver enzyme levels to begin with. And a single drug that might lower the SGOT and SGPT levels, enabling him to tolerate a medicine that was harsh on the liver, might also interact negatively with that medicine.

Furthermore, any drug that promised to boost the immune system held a significant risk for us all. Since it was thought by many researchers that fresh, uninfected lymphocytes might provide a renewed reservoir for viral proliferation, any immune-stimulatory drugs had to be administered in conjunction with potent antivirals—AZT and ozone among them—to guard against activation of target cells and possible reinfection. And combining drugs of any sort could produce unexpected side effects. Taking more than one drug simultaneously can make one of them stronger, weaker, or cancel each other's effect, often by altering the body's rate of absorption and elimination of one or both of the compounds. There was almost always a reason *not* to take a drug as well as one in favor of taking it.

The entire process was further complicated by distortions about a drug that resulted from inaccurate and incomplete reporting in the media. An item on television, a clip on the wire service, or an article on the front page of an AIDS treatment publication typically reported—albeit cautiously and with many caveats—that an effective maintenance therapy or even a cure for the disease had been discovered. People with AIDS and ARC often began a furious quest to obtain the treatment. But over time, the initial positive results that had generated so much enthusiasm were not reproducible in further studies, and careful scrutiny of the original data revealed that the "groundbreaking" reports were blown out of proportion or even entirely bogus.

We were not among the newly diagnosed HIV patients who

immediately leaped to embrace every reputed cure or any and every new drug. We forced ourselves to develop an objectivity that was rare among people in our position. Through our growing understanding of immunological and virological pharmacology, we were able to intelligently interview principal investigators, speak with patients who had undergone therapy, and subsequently make informed choices based on the information available to us. Finally, though, we did make choices about which drugs to try and which to postpone. The choice resembled walking on a mine field at times but was one that we actually learned to maneuver well.

I was restless and searching. Like David, I knew that most of the therapies we were using were at best only marginally effective. Few actually held the potential to buy time, and none represented a cure for AIDS. We needed a breakthrough.

One day at Mayer's office, I saw a brown envelope on my desk with the return address "U.S. Patent Office." I had almost forgotten that I had requested a copy of the patent months earlier, after having read an intriguing *New York Times* article in which it was reported that Drs. Michael McGrath at San Francisco General Hospital and Jeffrey Lifson at GeneLabs in Redwood City, California, had discovered a Chinese medicinal herb extract called trichosanthin. Nicknamed Compound Q, trichosanthin actually killed HIV in the test tube while leaving uninfected cells intact. More significant, the drug appeared to kill macrophages infected with HIV. McGrath and his colleagues believed that HIV infection could be greatly moderated if the infected macrophages could be destroyed and replaced with healthy ones, which in turn could be protected from reinfection with drugs such as AZT and ddI. Thus, the drug promised to be an important advance. The patent explained in great depth the techniques that researchers had used to discover the compound and also described a series of related drugs that had similar effects. It further stated that McGrath and his colleagues, working with the University of California and GeneLabs—a company financed by

Sandoz—had jointly synthesized and patented their own version of the drug, which they called GLQ223.

It was like taking an oncological approach to AIDS: the therapy tried not only to block the spread of the virus but also to kill as many of the infected cells as possible, in much the same way as chemotherapy kills cancer cells.

Was trichosanthin the magic bullet for AIDS? Did it hold the power to cure the disease as efficiently as the immunotoxins upon which Levin had theorized a year earlier? More important, if it *did* work, how could proof of its efficacy be obtained quickly and accurately?

CHAPTER 10

THE CUCUMBER HAS
ITS DAY

Word from San Francisco General Hospital in December 1989 was that when veteran AIDS researcher Paul Volberding saw the lab work on trichosanthin, the hair on his arms stood up. It was not Volberding, though, but Michael McGrath who, after conversations with Dr. Hin-Wing Yeung of Hong Kong, first realized that ribosome-inactivating proteins, and particularly a group of plant and bacterial cytotoxins (many of which had been in use for centuries in Chinese medicine) held the potential to destroy HIV-infected macrophages. Yeung began studying herbal extracts in the small medical institute he ran in Hong Kong. He catalogued hundreds of traditional remedies; when AIDS emerged as a modern-day plague, he was prepared to evaluate each one for efficacy against its culprit: HIV. It was Yeung who first identified trichosanthin and a related series of compounds as having potential anti-HIV activity.

McGrath had developed a unique screening system that allowed him to test compounds for their anti-HIV activity in macrophages. Prior to experimenting with the Chinese plant proteins, he had considered creating his own anti-HIV drugs by taking lipid vesicles—fatty globules called liposomes—and putting toxins in them. One of the characteristics of macrophages, McGrath knew, is that they will eat particulate things, including liposomes. By causing specific macrophages to eat the toxin-containing liposomes, a method of killing those macrophages might be realized.

Through a serendipitous encounter, McGrath met with Dr. Yeung. Yeung opened his briefcase and produced a series of Chinese plant proteins that he knew held the potential to destroy HIV-infected cells. McGrath screened many of the compounds Yeung discovered, including Momordica charantia inhibitor and gelonin. He found that the proteins all seemed to work by inactivating the eukaryotic ribosomal structure within cells—the cells' power plant—thus killing them. In his hands, trichosanthin had emerged as the plant protein with the most potent action against HIV.

The copy of the patent I had obtained summarized McGrath's basic research on macrophages. Unlike CD4 cells, macrophages did not quickly die once infected but lived as long as a year and a half, always able to produce new virus. Some scientists believed that they were the missing reservoir of HIV that kept the infection going, despite the rapid death of infected CD4 cells.

McGrath suggested that a large percentage of macrophages may harbor HIV, even though viral antigens may be actively expressed in a relatively small percentage of them. McGrath reasoned that HIV infection could be greatly moderated if the infected macrophages could be destroyed and replaced with healthy ones, which in turn could be protected from reinfection with more conventional drugs such as AZT.

McGrath showed that trichosanthin also demonstrated the ability to eliminate the expression of gp120 and gp41. Researchers had long speculated that gp120 might play a key part in the fusion of HIV-infected CD4 cells with uninfected cells to form the giant clumps called syncytia. Thus, the drug held the potential to address a number of important aspects of HIV pathogenesis.

The patent also indicated that trichosanthin proved more effective in reducing HIV-infected cells than AZT, ribavirin, or phosphonoformate and other antiviral agents that had been tried in the search to find a cure for AIDS. The researchers suggested that trichosanthin might be beneficial against later stages of HIV, where progression to serious clinical disease would be most likely. In other words, it held the potential to keep ARC patients stable for an extended period of time, delaying the onset of such life-threatening opportunistic infections as *Mycobacterium avium.*

The researchers also confirmed that in addition to trichosanthin, a series of drugs—all plant proteins, including momorcharin and gelonin—also strongly inhibited HIV replication in macrophages and appeared to hold the potential to halt the disease's progression. The researchers suggested that people who initially demonstrated an allergy against trichosanthin might benefit from these other drugs; or, they conjectured, the two drugs could be used interchangeably.

The patent stated that trichosanthin was a protein that had been in use in China for years, mainly to induce abortion, particularly during mid-trimester. As an abortifacient, the drug, an extract from the root tubers of the Chinese cucumber *Trichosanthes kirilowii,* selectively destroyed the wall of the placenta and the syncytiotrophoblast. It was also used in China to treat choriocarcinoma, a cancer of the placenta, producing only minor side effects that included muscle aches, hives, and a mild transient immune suppression.

Trichosanthin appeared to be capable of crossing the blood/brain barrier. This was crucially important to me, since it suggested that the substance might well be helpful in treating HIV dementia. If (as many researchers suspected) chronically infected macrophages were even part of the cause of HIV dementia, trichosanthin might eliminate those cells in serum, cerebrospinal fluid, and brain tissue and improve those symptoms related to the terrible brain disease.

The patent's inventors indicated that they had synthesized their own version of trichosanthin, GLQ223, with protein sequences and peptide patterns nearly identical to those of the Chinese drug. It was owned and developed by GeneLabs, where Jeffrey Lifson worked as research development director and Michael McGrath acted as consultant. From the moment it was first discovered in 1988 to the date it was officially granted a patent in January 1989, there was an official "informational blackout" on trichosanthin and its related proteins. Exactly why is unclear; insiders speculated that the researchers in San Francisco wanted to keep their discovery a secret until human trials of the drug were under way.

GLQ223 would soon be entering a Phase 1 ACTG study at San Francisco General Hospital, under the direction of Dr. James Kahn. However, the study called for subjects to be given only a single, infinitesimal dose, and for the drug to be administered to only one subject a month. The researchers planned to carefully escalate the dose with each additional subject. The entire project, which would ultimately produce only minimal information on the drug's toxicity and pharmacokinetics and shed little light on its true efficacy, would take a total of two years to complete. For an AIDS patient, there was no other alternative than to obtain a small personal supply and be given the drug under the supervision of a sympathetic physician.

I telephoned Dr. Kahn, the principal investigator in the San Francisco General study, in order to obtain additional information on the compound. Kahn wouldn't even reveal the identity of the drug, which he referred to only as GLQ223, and indicated only that he was currently recruiting subjects.

McGrath and Lifson were both unavailable. I realized that, in any case, I would probably garner little valuable information from the American researchers on how to obtain the drug in its originating country. So I telephoned Hong Kong and spoke with Dr. Yeung, who had shared his original observations with McGrath two years earlier, and whose name appeared on the patent. He was at first hesitant to give any detailed information about the drug, but after some discussion, he revealed that it had been studied in clinical trials for abortion by Dr. Jing Cui, a gynecologist and researcher at the Second Shanghai Medical University. I obtained the hospital's number from Shanghai directory assistance.

There was something of a language barrier in communicating with the Chinese, but I managed. When I first contacted Dr. Cui in Shanghai on February 20, I referred to the drug as "tri-cho-santhin," not realizing the "ch" was pronounced as "k."

"Dr. Cui, my name is Paul Sergios. I'm a research assistant in the office of Dr. Robert Mayer in Miami," I began. "We're interested in obtaining some trichosanthin for use in a research project."

"How you get my name?" she asked.

"Dr. Yeung suggested I contact you. We need the Chinese medicine trichosanthin . . ."

"Trichosanthin?" she asked, still unfamiliar with the drug I was referring to.

"Trichosanthin," I kept repeating stupidly. "We need many ampules of trichosanthin . . . the drug used for abortion."

There was a pause on the other end of the line.

"Trikosanthin," Dr. Cui said. "Yes, I have trikosanthin. You want make abortion?" she asked.

"No, we need the drug to treat cancer. I hear you've attained good results with this disease in China."

I was extremely hesitant to divulge that the drug was really needed to treat AIDS. Such a revelation might invite unnecessary attention.

"Oh yes," Dr. Cui said. "How much trichosanthin you need?"

"As many ampules as you can supply," I answered.

After a short pause, the doctor said, "I can send you eighty ampule. Forty red and forty blue. The red makes test dose, the blue is true dose. You see when I send instruction."

"Yes, yes, Dr. Cui, eighty ampules would be fine. How much money do you need for the trichosanthin?" I asked, speaking slowly, trying my best to enunciate every word.

"You send me five dollars for one ampule. You tell me address. I send you drug," she assured me.

The deal was closed.

"I'll send you the money immediately, Dr. Cui. Please tell me the address where I should send it."

She gave me the address of the university where she worked.

"Thank you—thank you so much," I said, trying not to sound overly obsequious as I hung up. Yet I was extraordinarily grateful to the magnanimous gynecologist in Shanghai. The next morning, I obtained an international money order for $400 and sent it to Shanghai by Express Mail.

A large brown box inscribed with Chinese characters arrived at Dr. Mayer's office on March 23, 1989. Inside were four blue boxes and four red boxes of trichosanthin. The red- and blue-striped boxes contained ten ampules each and displayed the insignia of the factory where the drug was produced along with dosage and indication instructions in Chinese. There was also a six-digit serial number at the bottom right-hand corner. We learned that the drug was considered a controlled substance in China and released to a tightly knit group of physicians and researchers.

Dr. Cui had graciously translated the instructions into English, along with several journal articles that summarized the Chinese experience with the drug in inducing abortion and for treating choriocarcinoma. One of the articles included detailed information on trichosanthin's pharmacokinetics and rates of absorption in humans when given by intramuscular injection. As she had already told me, the red ampules were "test" doses. The instructions that she provided explained that they contained 0.9 milligram, smaller amounts of the drug which were to be given prior to the administration of the blue ampules. The red ampules provided an indication of any potential allergic reaction a subject might innately have against the protein and gave a realistic barometer of how well the full dose might ultimately be tolerated. The information further specified that the drug commonly produced muscle aches, soreness, pain at the injection site, and hives when given to women and cancer patients. Cui suggested that the anti-inflammatory steroid compound dexamethasone, given prophylactically, could relieve many of these symptoms. The package insert also indicated the typical dose and method of administration: for cancer, between 1.2 and 2.4 mg per treatment, which amounted to one or two ampules of the drug, given by intramuscular injection.

We realized, of course, that we needed to assess the purity and authenticity of the drug, at least three versions of which had been manufactured in China over the last decade for abortions. Some contained harmful proteins, called lectins, which held the potential to cause blood clots and stroke if injected intramuscularly or intravenously. More important, even if the drug was pure, was it the same version being used in San Francisco? Did it represent the same compound, the same amino acid sequence that McGrath and Lifson originally tested at GeneLabs? The Health Department of China provided specifications which indicated that the product was 99 percent homogeneous, as defined by a process called SDS-PAGE, and not dissimilar to an American process of the same type. To be certain, we sent a single ampule from each box to Martin Delaney, who I heard had established contact with Dr. McGrath. Delaney forwarded the samples to McGrath's lab, where they were analyzed. Subsequent analysis showed the drug indeed to be the correct and pure version of trichosanthin. It was structurally similar, though not identical to, the version developed by GeneLabs.

We were faced with the problem of selecting an appropriate subject for the first pilot treatment. Susan and I were tempted to go first but as much as we wanted to try the therapy ourselves, we knew we had to maintain our objectivity as study monitors and thus decided to wait. David Wilson also chose to wait. We collectively decided that the initial pilot treatment should be given to a stable ARC patient who still had some immune system intact but who nevertheless manifested certain clearly HIV-related symptoms such as thrush and fatigue. Second, we wanted someone who had not taken a wide variety of other experimental medications in the last month. Finding someone who fit the first criterion was easy; identifying one who fit the latter, less so. Most of Dr. Mayer's patients were currently taking various combinations of drugs.

Ultimately, we found Scott Yageman, a longtime friend of

Mayer's and the transportation coordinator of Broward County's AIDS service organization, Center One. Scott drove ARC and AIDS patients to doctor's and dentist's appointments. Occasionally, when I would feel fatigued and not up to making the long drive to North Miami Beach, he would offer to drive me. He frequently transported other patients (including Rick Andrews) to Dr. Mayer's at the same time, and I enjoyed their company on that long trip.

Scott knew I had obtained the drug and quickly volunteered to be the first subject. At the time, he was a stable ARC patient with a CD4 cell count of 400. Except for a constant tingling and numbness in his extremities, he was relatively asymptomatic. And with the exception of AZT two years ago, he had not taken nor was currently taking any other experimental drugs. He represented a good candidate.

Scott himself was a character. He had bushy brown hair and a neatly trimmed mustache. He wore prescription sunglasses, had an earring in his left ear, and could often be seen combing his hair vigorously while driving patients to their appointments. His 1975 Ford station wagon had racked up an impressive 300,000 miles on the odometer—the same vehicle he had driven for years, often to collect bric-a-brac items for sale at the weekend swap shops.

Scott found himself on the front line of daily dramas. Often, he would be required to drive an indigent patient suffering from a toxoplasmosis-induced seizure or cryptoccocal-related attack to the county hospital emergency room. Hospital staff in the county medical system were notoriously irresponsive to AIDS patients, and Scott would sit with the patient in the emergency room, saying comforting things while trying to gain the attention of the ER supervisor and physicians on call, and help with the patient's admission.

He had moved from New York to Fort Lauderdale in January 1985, a year after learning that he was HIV-positive. His brother, who had also been diagnosed with the virus, died during a kidney transplant. And his lover of three years took his own life because

AIDS was about to take it from him: a few months after being diagnosed, he killed himself at his mother's house in New York.

In 1987, Scott contracted bronchial pneumonia. By year's end he weighed only 147, a drop of almost 50 pounds. He felt certain he was crossing the line from ARC to full-blown AIDS. But he fought vehemently. He took high doses of vitamin C, ate everything in sight, and put his weight back on. His pneumonia cleared up and he felt as though his health had been restored.

Since coming to Florida, Scott had worked as a systems analyst for a Fort Lauderdale law firm. On December 31, 1987, the firm fired him, claiming that, although he had been an excellent employee, they were faced with budget cutbacks and found his position to be the most expendable. Scott believes that he was fired because his bosses knew of his illness and didn't want to spend insurance money on his treatment, which at the time included AZT and monthly pentamidine therapy.

In June 1988, a law was passed in Florida that made it illegal for employers to fire employees because of catastrophic illnesses. The law was retroactive to January 1—one day after Scott had been fired. He suspected that his company's lawyers knew about the upcoming law and fired him one day short of being forced to keep him.

Even while working for the law firm, Scott had been doing volunteer driving for an AIDS service agency in Fort Lauderdale. After his dismissal, a staff position opened and he became the agency's transportation coordinator and lead driver.

Scott vowed to fight the disease on his own terms. "I'll be damned if I'm going to die just because the CDC, NIH, and FDA say I have a fatal illness," he swore. He backed up his angry words with action. He marched in demonstrations and helped organize "phone zaps" in which hundreds of people simultaneously called a government switchboard at a prearranged time and virtually shut down the phone system. And like the New York ACT UP activists, he participated in "chalk talks," in which outlines of bodies were drawn in chalk on sidewalks outside federal agencies, similar to the technique used by police to designate a fallen victim's location at the scene of a crime.

He would have to draw a lot of chalk marks. Since 1981, he claimed, he had known more than 750 people who had died of AIDS. He drove patients to Dr. Mayer's office—considerably out of the way—because he believed that Mayer was one of the few people trying to make a real difference in a generally conservative and apathetic climate.

On March 31, 1989, Scott and I drove to Mayer's office. Mayer ordered a complete battery of blood tests on him, and then at two-thirty administered the first dose of Compound Q to be given in the United States. Mayer first administered the red test ampule as per the label indications and, an hour later, since no immediate adverse reactions had occurred, gave Scott a shot of 2.4 milligrams of the actual drug, half in each buttock. He was not pretreated with dexamethasone or any other anti-inflammatory since we wanted to observe the natural course of the drug's side effects. Scott had agreed to this, fully aware that the compound's short-range effects could be unpleasant.

He reported no adverse experiences at all when he returned home or at any time during the evening. At three o'clock in the morning, however, I was awakened by the ringing of my phone. It was Scott. His voice sounded hoarse and husky.

"My temperature keeps shifting from 96.6 to 102 . . . It's been fluctuating like that for an hour now. And lymph nodes have started to pop up in places I never knew I had them! I've got night sweats. And muscle aches—*bad* muscle aches. There's a rash on my back," he whispered.

I knew the muscle aches and the hives were part of the side effects that Cui had warned about, but the lymphadenopathy, night sweats, and fever fluctuations concerned me. They could also have been part of the constellation of an allergic prostaglandin-induced arthralgia. But perhaps the lymph nodes and night sweats reflected an immune response—a sign that Scott's immune system was being "jump started" and that the virus was being destroyed.

I also knew from my reading that in the immediate short term, trichosanthin had the potential to be immuno*suppressive*, actually lowering CD4 cell counts as one of its temporary side effects. This phenomenon was documented in the Chinese medical literature. Possibly, Scott's swollen lymph nodes and night sweats were compensatory responses against this short-term immunosuppression. In any event, he needed immediate attention.

"I'll be right over and take you to ER," I told him.

"No, I've been taking warm sitz baths and I seem to be doing better. I don't want to go to ER. I think I'll be all right. It's scary, though—really scary."

"We'd better get you to Fort Lauderdale General," I insisted.

"No, I'll be all right," Scott said. "Father Fred Tondalo is coming over to do my vitals and to be with me. Everything'll be fine." Fred Tondalo was the former director of the local AIDS service organization and was currently a registered nurse. He often found himself helping AIDS patients in unique ways.

"All right," I said, "but I'll call you in an hour, O.K.?"

Scott agreed, and we stayed in constant touch for the next twelve hours.

The following evening, Scott and I had planned to attend a spring concert of the South Florida Gay Men's Chorus in Plantation. I suggested that he stay in bed, however, given his current condition. He insisted that his symptoms had abated and he wanted to hear the chorus perform. He claimed that in spite of the arthralgia, he had an abundance of energy, something he hadn't had in quite some time.

He picked me up at seven-thirty and I could immediately tell that he was not completely recovered. He walked with a limp, his complexion was pale, and he had a fever of 100 degrees.

"How long have you been limping?" I asked.

"All day long. It's the muscle aches. My legs feel like logs."

Despite my vehement objections, we drove to the concert. When it was over, we attended a small coffee party given by the chorus. Only Rick and several other patients "on the inside" at Dr. Mayer's office knew that Scott had received the drug. I had sworn them to silence. The rest of the crowd that night knew that something was going on, that he had taken *some*thing; they could tell by his limp and complexion. But they weren't sure exactly what. Rumors began circulating about the true cause of his condition. I was tempted to quell the speculation with the truth, but I knew it would be best to keep the experiment a secret for the time being.

On the way home, Scott confided that in the wake of the unpleasant side effects the night before, during the few hours that he had actually managed to sleep, he was struck with a recurring and vivid dream image—a soothing scene of his late mother hanging laundry on a clothesline. In the dream, he was a child again, watching pure white clothes flap in a gentle breeze against an azure sky.

"Do you think the child watching white linen signifies some sort of redemption?" he asked me. "Do you think the virus has actually left my body?"

"Only the blood work will say for sure," I told him. "But it does suggest that the drug may have crossed the blood/brain barrier and stimulated the cerebral cortex to some degree," I offered. "It might be valuable to repeat your MRI brain scan soon."

Like many ARC patients, Scott had shown small patches of increased high-signal intensity in the brain's white matter on the MRI scan taken at the University of Miami study a year earlier, suggesting that the virus had infiltrated microglial cells and brain macrophages. If Compound Q really did kill those cells, as some suggested, a new MRI might actually show improvement.

"We should probably repeat your memory and concentration tests," I concluded, as he dropped me off at my apartment.

By Monday morning, Scott's muscles were still a little sore, and there was a trace of hives on his back. But the worst of the aches had passed and his complexion had returned to normal. At one o'clock we drove to Dr. Mayer's and he repeated the tests Scott had had on Friday. I called the lab in advance to make special arrangements for the Sunday pickup.

The results arrived the next morning. At first, we couldn't believe what we were seeing. Scott's white blood cell count, typically at 4,000 to 5,000, had jumped to 22,000! The lymph count on his differential was reduced. His p-24 antigen level, which had hovered at 100 picograms for the last year, suggesting reverse transcriptase activity and HIV replication, had fallen to zero.

Five weeks later, we repeated his lymphocyte panel and found that his CD4 cell count had risen by 15 percent.

We figured that the leukocytosis—the massive increase in white cells—was a side effect of the drug. But the decrease in p-24 antigen and increase in CD4 cells, especially given the short-term immune-suppressive nature of the drug, was impressive and appeared to be a direct assault on the virus. These results were undeniably encouraging. And despite the adverse side effects, Scott's basic blood chemistry values remained unchanged. Furthermore, he reported that for the first time in a year his peripheral neuropathy had cleared completely. In the days that followed, he reported feeling renewed energy and vigor and was thinking more clearly than ever.

As Dr. Mayer and I continued to track Scott's blood chemistry over the next several weeks, we realized that there might be genuine promise in trichosanthin.

"Look, his beta-2 microglobulin, which soared immediately after the infusion, has now also fallen," I pointed out to Mayer one afternoon. I had plotted the numbers on the computer and created a color graph.

"Yes, and his CD4 cells have risen by another 8 percent," Mayer added. And we all observed that his lymph nodes, which had swollen greatly immediately after the injection, were now actually smaller than they had ever been throughout his illness.

"Plus he says he has more energy than ever," Susan commented.

At that moment, Dr. Mayer and I realized an immediate need to implement an organized and highly controlled means of gathering and assembling information on trichosanthin, that the informal tracking and monitoring trials we had executed for typhoid and ozone—and that David Wilson and I had led for other drugs—would be inappropriate for this compound. If the drug worked, or even produced marginally significant long-term improvement in ARC or AIDS patients, we needed irrefutable, verifiable evidence to convince regulatory authorities and other researchers about its value. Such data on the drug's optimal dosage, method of administration, and mode of action—sound enough to withstand even the harshest scientific analysis—was also needed to guide with intelligence what was sure to be a burgeoning underground and community use of the drug.

How could we obtain this information quickly and cleanly without submitting an IND and participating in a hospital-sponsored Phase 1 clinical trial? We contemplated the possibility of bringing the project to the Community Research Initiative in New York but realized that it could take months to develop in that milieu. There was only one answer: We needed to design and implement an underground Phase 1 clinical study that was every bit as rigorous and well executed as an NIH-sponsored effort, and we needed to do it quickly. The study of Compound Q that plodded along at San Francisco General Hospital would not reach completion for up to two years and would provide only minimal information on the drug's efficacy.

Our pilot study had to use a realistic dosage and scheduling of the drug. It had to define meaningful outcome measures clearly and use professional data analysis in its examination of the results. It would have to be capable of withstanding the scrutiny of the adjudicator.

After much deliberation, Dr. Mayer and I decided to design a study with eight ARC patients, all of whom had identical baseline characteristics and histories. We chose to give three injections of the drug, one every four weeks, a schedule actually suggested in

McGrath and Lifson's patent. We decided on 1.4 milligrams (20 micrograms per kilogram of body weight) as a viable starting dose, about 0.8 milligrams less than Scott Yageman had received. It was close to the maximum dose used in China and close to the median dose of the San Francisco General Hospital study.

We agreed not to give any concurrent medications with the trichosanthin. We wanted to observe the natural course of the side effects, just as we had with Scott. The subjects would have to be free of any prior experimental HIV medication for five full weeks before taking the drug. And they would have to agree to subject themselves to the same rigorous questioning and tests included in traditional HIV drug trials.

We chose to include CD4 cell counts, p-24 antigen levels, beta-2 microglobulin levels, and PHA (phytohemagglutinin) values as the major outcome variables. We also gave the subjects skin tests of four common antigens to further assess their changes in immune function—the same tests I had taken in the AZT study in Los Angeles.

We neither filed for an investigational new drug permit nor passed the study through any institutional review board. Following that traditional protocol would have taken at least six months—time we knew we couldn't afford. One person was dying of AIDS every half hour. And the total number of cases officially reported was thought to be extremely conservative.

Each of the subjects signed an informed-consent document witnessed by an attorney and an HIV-positive patient. By so doing, the subjects acknowledged that they understood the risks involved in taking trichosanthin. Later, each patient also selected a personal friend or witness to join him or her in a videotaped consent. The half-hour talk included the patient, the witness, the treating physician, and a "patient advocate" who led the discussion. The advocate's duty was to make sure that the patient understood the risks, the lack of any proven benefits, and the availability of other treatments. The patient's experience with other treatments and the reasons for their failure were documented. The witness was present so that everyone could determine that the patient was of sound mind in making the decision to seek treatment with trichosanthin. When all points were clear, and after the advocate challenged the patient on each key point, the patient made a closing statement to his or her loved ones or relatives, staring directly at the camera and briefly explaining why he or she had chosen to participate in an unorthodox protocol conducted outside the realm of traditional research. Ultimately, the protocol was reviewed by a board consisting of a patient advocacy group representative, two HIV-positives, a layman, an attorney, and two physicians.

In our study, the patients were actually given their own ampules of Compound Q, which they subsequently brought with them on the day of treatment, presenting them to Dr. Mayer for injection. In this way, the subjects made a gesture, a statement that they had learned about the drug through their own research, had obtained a three-month personal supply, and were interested in being monitored by a sympathetic physician.

We believed that conducting an underground trial requiring patients to undergo informed-consent procedures would simultaneously protect them and provide information quickly, surmounting many of the bureaucratic obstacles endemic to traditional research. In essence, we had launched a combined Phase 1–Phase 2 trial designed to measure the drug's basic toxicity and efficacy in a multimodal patient population and suggest intelligent dosing schedules, dosages, and prophylactic medication logs for use in future, expanded trials. The study would be completed in one-third the time of a classic trial and cost one-third as much.

In any professional clinical trial, a thorough and comprehensive documentation of the subjects' histories and responses to a drug is needed. This is accomplished through lengthy case-report forms, filled out by the principal investigator or protocol nurse at each office visit. The forms are designed to assess a patient's complete medical history, list any concurrent medications the patient is taking and every symptom he or she has ever experienced in relation to the disease state being studied, assess any adverse effects the patient might experience from the present medication, and of course, monitor improvements or changes in a patient's symptoms throughout the study.

Through a friend who worked in Dr. Stanley Cooper's office, I was able to obtain a set of blank case-report forms from the Ampligen study, which I adapted to meet our specific needs with trichosanthin. On my home computer, I designed and printed out an all-new set. It was an arduous task; I frequently found myself working up to sixteen hours a day. The forms were reviewed by a colleague of Mayer's, and modifications were made based on his suggestions. In spite of my impaired memory, I had been a subject in two major clinical trials and had carefully observed every administrative detail. Like the title character in the movie *All About Eve,* I had seen the play so many times from the wings that I could act it perfectly, line for line.

We realized that adverse reactions, including allergic responses more serious than those encountered by Scott Yageman, were to be expected in some patients and that immediate emergency medical treatment might be necessary. Dr. Mayer's office was at least twenty minutes away from any emergency room in a hospital. Furthermore, we needed a secure location where we wouldn't be disturbed by aggressive reporters if news of the study leaked out. Mayer's office—even a private home—would have been too obvious. Instead, we chose to hold the study in the Howard Johnson's across the street from Parkview General Medical Center in North Miami, where Mayer knew physicians on call. The hotel provided us with a secret, central location that was close to an emergency medical facility.

In essence, we transformed an entire floor of the building into a study ward for weekends at a time. The hotel was clean, and convenient to the major freeways. Most important, we were able to reserve rooms in a section of the hotel where our actions would not be under scrutiny by hotel personnel or other guests.

A team of four volunteer registered nurses agreed to help monitor the subjects, administer the drug, and help with the completion of case-report forms.

On Friday evening, April 20, we checked four subjects in at the front desk, then quietly moved our supplies in the elevator to the third floor. A curious security guard in the back lobby asked us about the tall, metal IV poles we carted along as casually as luggage. Our story: We were visiting Miami for a garment exhibitors' convention and needed the poles to display our clothes on the convention-center floor. The explanation seemed to satisfy the man, although he later gave us a suspicious glance or two.

Inside the rooms, we carefully laid out the syringes, the gauze, the antiseptic solutions. We positioned the IV poles close to the beds and started hanging saline bags. The nurses and I then set about questioning subjects and filling in the case-report forms. The subjects had been briefed by Dr. Mayer a day earlier, but there were still items in the forms that required completion. Hours earlier, we had methodically scrubbed the rooms down and disinfected them with aerosols.

By nine o'clock that evening, the patients had been given their first injections and were in bed. We attached IVs of saline to ensure that the subjects were properly hydrated. The nurses retired to their rooms.

The side effects that first weekend were mild compared to Scott's reaction. Two of the subjects experienced muscle aches, low-grade fevers, and hives. We discovered that 500 milligrams of intramuscular Benadryl and/or 300 milligrams of ibuprofen lessened the severity of these side effects, and were much safer than dexamethasone. Two of the subjects showed dramatic red streaks along their arms where the Compound Q had crossed into their vein, an irritation that would become known as a "Q track." The nurses took vital signs on the hour, and we had complete blood cell counts drawn daily. By Monday morning, the subjects were well enough to return home.

On Tuesday afternoon, the preliminary blood test results crossed my desk. As in Scott's case, the four patients had experienced reductions in p-24 antigen levels and modest increases in CD4 cell counts. Curiously, all related that each evening following a treatment they experienced vivid and peaceful dreams.

At Jim Corti's request, two weeks before we treated our second group of patients at the Howard Johnson's, I had sent a copy of the trichosanthin box cover to him in Los Angeles, providing him with the name and address of the factory where the drug was manufactured. Dr. Cui, the gynecologist in Shanghai, had agreed to send us fifteen more boxes of the drug—hardly enough to meet the burgeoning demand nationwide. On May 1, 1989, Corti, with $19,000 in $100 bills and accompanied by his friend Edward Chan, boarded a plane to Hong Kong.

He wound up driving sixty miles to the factory that produced trichosanthin. When Corti arrived at the doors of the drug's exclusive manufacturer, the Shanghai Research Institute's pharmaceutical arm, factory officials listened politely to his request for five hundred ampules of trichosanthin for AIDS patients in the United States. They then produced stacks of letters and requests from around the world, received in the wake of promising reports published in the scientific press about trichosanthin's anti-HIV potential.

At first, the Chinese were hesitant to hand over any amount of the drug at all. After some prodding and negotiation, however, they agreed to sell Corti one hundred ampules for a staggering $100 apiece and a pledge from Corti to send them gifts—American VCRs and TVs. Outside, students and workers had begun to mobilize against a regime. Days later, the events in Tiananmen Square would rock the nation and the world. Corti paid $10,000 for the one hundred ampules and smuggled them in his suitcase back to American soil. At his request, I sent Martin Delaney a copy of our protocol, along with the instructions we had received from the Chinese gynecologist and the preliminary results we had obtained with the first four patients we had treated.

Within days of Corti's return from China, Delaney had convinced Alan Levin to open a multicenter underground study with the drug. Forty ARC and AIDS patients would receive the drug in San Francisco, twenty more in Los Angeles under the direction of Dr. Paul Rothman, and twenty more in New York under the direction of Dr. Barbara Starrett. Rothman, who worked for the relatively conservative Pacific Oaks Medical Group, was more open to alternative therapies than his partners, who included Dr. Joel Weisman, a member of the AmFAR board of directors. Ed Winger at San Leandro's Immunodiagnostics agreed to donate the blood work.

Levin's wife, Dr. Vera Byers, was affiliated with the University of Nottingham in England, where she had performed experiments with other ribosome-inhibitory proteins like trichosanthin, including ricin a chain. She conducted preliminary animal studies on trichosanthin there and in a week's time determined how far the drug penetrated into the bodies of balboa mice, how long it took to get there, and how long it remained. From this, she extrapolated trichosanthin's half-life in humans. She calculated that it probably stayed in the body in effective quantities for only forty-five minutes. By contrast, McGrath's human extrapolations from his animal studies showed that GLQ223 stayed in the body for seven hours. His studies also confirmed that the drug could produce muscle pain and arthralgic-like symptoms.

With Dr. Larry Waites, Levin and Byers designed a new set of case-report forms for the national trial and suggested a protocol of 1.2 milligrams (16 micrograms per kilogram of body weight, given intravenously) once a week for three weeks. No one would receive a placebo.

On May 15, 1990, we were added as a fourth site of the national trial. We would treat twelve additional patients using Levin's newly designed case-report forms and a central laboratory for processing the blood work. We would conform to the national effort in every way.

Our first eight subjects had been treated by intramuscular injection. This sometimes produced tissue death and pain at the injection site. Furthermore, it was different from the intravenous method used in the "official" San Francisco General Hospital trial. More important, giving the drug intravenously held the potential to maximize its impact, since greater blood levels could be achieved more quickly. Levin correctly assessed that in the Project Inform study, all subjects should be treated intravenously.

Injecting the drug intravenously also posed new and greater risks, however. With an intramuscular injection, a "safety barrier" existed, since the drug did not directly enter the bloodstream. Because trichosanthin had never been administered intravenously in China, little experience existed with this method of application. Amazingly, the first four patients who received the drug intravenously under our direction suffered fewer side effects than their IM-treated counterparts. No doubt, the heavy anti-inflammatory premedication helped greatly. But we hypothesized that the drug was probably excreted faster with the IV method and thus held less chance for long-term harm.

We all agreed to keep the underground study from the press until its conclusion; there might be a groundswell of hysteria from desperate AIDS patients if news of the trial leaked out. Yet ultimately five reporters around the country were allowed to monitor the study on the condition that they report nothing until the trial was completed.

We already faced the problem of fair and impartial subject selection. Almost all of Mayer's patients had heard about the study, and they all wanted in. Yet we could add a total of only twelve new subjects in addition to the eight already chosen. One of the most adamant was Rick Andrews. In his view, he had been one of Dr. Mayer's longest-running and most dedicated patients. He had taken major risks by subjecting himself to unproven therapies in the past.

Now, a drug had emerged that he perceived as having the potential to genuinely help him, and he was being denied access to it.

Dr. Mayer saw the situation differently. Rick was deteriorating rapidly. His Kaposi's sarcoma had spread into his lungs, and he had already been hospitalized once to have fluid drained from his left bronchial tube, a KS-induced hemoptysis. Moreover, Mayer had a hunch that Kaposi's sarcoma was not caused by HIV-related immune suppression. He had seen too many patients die of KS with relatively high CD4 cell counts and preserved skin test reactions. Clearly, these patients' cell-mediated immunity was still intact. They were dying from complications of internal Kaposi's sarcoma, which Mayer felt was triggered by some as-yet-unidentified pathogen or mechanism, unrelated to HIV. The odds were that trichosanthin simply would not help Rick and might even exacerbate his already precipitously declining condition. Moreover, our protocol called for the treatment of patients who were not that sick. Rick's visceral KS was rapidly progressing, and his condition—despite a relatively high CD4 cell count—was terminal, according to his own oncologist. Mayer firmly told him that he would not be allowed to participate in the study. Angry and frustrated, Rick attempted to make arrangements to be treated by Barbara Starrett in New York, but all the spots in her study had been filled.

One evening, a desperate Rick Andrews called my mother. I suspected he actually wanted to talk to me and have me persuade Mayer to include him in the study, but he hadn't been able to reach me at my apartment.

"Please, Mrs. Sergios," he cried, "they won't let me in. They're keeping me from getting Compound Q. Please talk to Paul."

"That's not fair, is it?" my mother replied. "I'll talk to Paul. Don't worry. Everything will work out."

My empathy with Rick's dilemma came from firsthand experience. I well remembered the time when I wanted to get into a trial but couldn't because of narrow entry criteria. The following day, Susan and I convinced Dr. Mayer to admit Rick into the study. He was the ninth patient to receive the drug.

We knew that the risk of a subject's experiencing serious toxicity from Compound Q was great. In truth, with each patient who got the drug, with each needle stick, our hearts leaped with apprehension. Still, there was a pervading sense that the treatment held the potential to be better than anything we had in our arsenal and so we pushed on.

A despondent AIDS patient in Kansas, perhaps even more desperate than Rick, had read the preliminary *in vitro* reports about trichosanthin. He found a health-food store in Topeka that stocked the fresh cucumber root. Not realizing that the trichosanthin used in the study had undergone a complex extraction and purification process, he crushed up the raw root, passed the pulp through cotton, and injected the juice into his veins. The next day, a friend found him in his apartment writhing in pain. His liver was close to failing. In the emergency room, doctors diagnosed his condition as a stroke. After three days in intensive care, his condition stabilized, but his doctors noticed a personality change. "Emotionally labile" is how one described the patient—in plain English, squirrelly. No one knew whether it was the effect of HIV, the toxicity of the unpurified root, or the ordeal of one more hope that had been dashed.

Alan Levin also knew the chances for harm were great. He told a reporter on the National Public Radio show *All Things Considered*, "This is a poison. Not only that, this is a disease where the infected cells are all over the body, so we never know what the ultimate outcome of a treatment is going to be. I'd be very surprised if somebody didn't die of the treatment."

In fact, San Francisco patient Tandy Belew slipped back into HIV dementia three days after his third infusion. Levin and Waites wondered if it was simply a remanifestation of an earlier HIV condition, or if the symptoms represented some type of neurotoxicity from the trichosanthin. Waites related the man's dementia to a thyroid condition he had suffered, unrelated to HIV; after he was given thyroid medication, he returned to normal. Still, Levin and Waites were impressed that in spite of the neurological problems he had suffered, Belew's p-24 antigen fell from 1,100 to 170 in seven days.

But three weeks later, one of Levin's patients did, in fact, die. On Friday, June 16, 1989—two days after his first Q infusion— Robert Parr was hospitalized with dementia-like symptoms. Levin met Parr at the emergency room of Mount Zion Hospital in San Francisco and immediately ordered him treated with Decadron. Parr seemed to recover and several days later was moved out of intensive care. When Levin visited him again, the two of them traded small talk. The following morning, while still asleep, Parr apparently vomited, sucked the stomach fluids into his lungs, and suffocated. Because his family refused to allow an autopsy to be performed, the true cause of his death was never fully established. However, circumstances uncovered later revealed that trichosanthin was not the cause. After Parr began experiencing problems with his lungs, the hospital staff inserted a tube into his throat and were able to clear his lungs. It appeared as though he was once again on the way to recovery. But the tube was removed at the request of a family member who held power of attorney, and Parr died shortly thereafter. Levin noted that at no time did the resident caring for Parr even consult him before removing the tube; nor should Parr have been transferred out of the intensive care unit so rapidly.

Still, Levin had his own hunches about the cause of the neurological problems that some subjects experienced. Trichosanthin was not known to disturb the mental functions of patients who took the drug in China, yet this seemed to be a factor here. Something in the physiology of the AIDS patient must have interacted with the trichosanthin to produce the effect. HIV infection, Levin knew, came into the brain in cells called microglial cells. One population of microglia, the resident microglia, migrates into the brain before birth and remains there. Another, called perivascular microglia, migrates in and out of the brain as a normal physiological process throughout adulthood. These perivascular cells are transient, moving rapidly through the brain and are not part of its permanent structure. While in the brain, they provide nutrients and act to some sort of degree as insulators. Levin conjectured that in the cases of Parr and another patient who had suffered a coma but who had recovered, trichosanthin had successfully crossed the blood/brain barrier, killing large numbers of infected glial cells either in the patients' spinal fluid or serum. Both perivascular and resident microglia, Levin knew, expressed CD4 receptors when they are activated, as in viral infections and other types of stimulation. Thus, Compound Q may have activated the HIV-infected microglia and caused them to be neurotoxic. The rapid killing of glial cells or activation of this "nerve glue" may have contributed to enough neural dysfunction to result in coma. Alternatively, Levin knew, the drug may have liberated the release of cytokines—hormonelike proteins released from infected, activated macrophages in the brain, some of which were neurotoxic. In any case, the drug appeared to pose a special risk to persons with HIV-related brain disease or dementia and with fewer than 100 CD4 cells. After the incident, Levin revised the protocol to exclude patients with fewer than 100 CD4 cells and, moreover, to exclude all patients with abnormal MRI scans. This meant that all future subjects would have to present us with a recent, clean MRI of their brain—a considerable expense.

Six other patients in the San Francisco and New York arms of the study also experienced changes in mental condition ranging from brief periods of confusion or disorientation to reversible coma and seizures. All responded to dexamethasone. The patients with these complications had abnormal or suspicious MRI brain scans, or evidence of strokes.

One patient in the official study of GLQ223 at San Francisco General Hospital also suffered a coma from which he only partially recovered. In this instance, however, the patient was not immediately treated with dexamethasone. He remained semicomatose for more than ten days before treatment with dexamethasone was attempted, and he awoke forty-eight hours later. The patient ultimately died, although whether his death was due to the drug or not was never made clear. When asked about the patient, doctors involved in the trial had no comment. Insiders speculated that Kahn and the other doctors conducting the trial "wanted to observe the natural course of events involved in the drug's toxicity." The insiders revealed that the patient might well have died sooner were it not for pressure exerted by the patient's family and friends to intervene with the appropriate antidote.

The following day, I watched on television as Paul Volberding of San Francisco General Hospital criticized the methodology and soundness of the underground study, and Martin Delaney attempted to defend it. I also caught part of a press conference in San Francisco in which Delaney asserted that Project Inform had no intention of stopping the trial because of Parr's death; that his demise could not be directly linked to trichosanthin; that many people had died with far less fanfare in FDA-sanctioned studies; and that in some of those cases, other patients in the trials were not notified of the deaths. He assured the group that all subjects in the Compound Q study were made aware of Parr's death and given the option not to continue.

Two and a half days after Parr's death, NBC reporter Robert Bazell went public with the story of the underground trial. He was one of five other reporters, including the Fort Lauderdale *News/ Sun-Sentinel*'s Nancy McVicar, who had been permitted to monitor the study. With Parr's death, Bazell chose to break the agreement.

The *Sun-Sentinel* carried the story on the front page; Scott Yageman was mentioned as being the first patient to take the drug. When I arrived for work at Dr. Mayer's office on June 27, I spent the entire day speaking with reporters from across the country who wanted early data on Compound Q and with desperate AIDS patients willing to do anything to get into the study.

On my way out of the office for lunch, I was intercepted by a camera crew on the steps of the Norwood Medical Plaza.

"Being such an advocate of Compound Q, Mr. Sergios, why have you not chosen to take the drug yourself?" the reporter asked.

"As the Miami study coordinator, it would not be appropriate for me to take the drug while monitoring others in the study," I answered.

The reporters pressed me for early proof of efficacy, but I

stood firm in my contention that the results from all four sites would be released at the conclusion of the study in September.

Backlash from the mainstream scientific community was awesome and swift. Most AIDS researchers denounced the study. Some charged Levin and Delaney with unethical behavior and warned that "cowboy medicine" could turn patients against dedicated researchers who had devoted their careers to finding a cure for AIDS.

Donald Abrams, Volberding's colleague at San Francisco General, echoed these other researchers' sentiments. He asserted that the underground tactics we perpetuated had threatened what he regarded as the most important bond in medicine—the trust and confidence that binds a patient to his physician. Abrams quoted the ancient Greek physician Galen—"He cures the most successfully in whom the people have the most confidence"—and suggested that our study may have abolished that degree of confidence.

William Reiter, a prominent AIDS physician and researcher in south Florida, told the Miami *Herald,* "This assertiveness of PWAs is patient autonomy run amok. The whole atmosphere is frightening. This is self-medication, and suspicion of the medical establishment [is] out of control."

Volberding said, "What [the underground study organizers] have done is a real disservice to volunteers in the official study and to a drug that might be interesting. It doesn't take a genius to hand out drugs to people without controls, but it takes a certain amount of discipline to ask questions in a rigorous way."

But Larry Kramer defended and praised Martin Delaney. "I think Martin is one of the greatest heroes in the country right now. This is really historic."

The FDA announced an immediate investigation, suggesting that Delaney, Levin, and the other physicians involved (including Mayer) may have violated criminal laws against drug importation and human experimentation.

Even in the face of this criticism and potential litigation, we stood fast. We continued to administer the drug and were close to reaching the conclusion of the study. To us, of course, it was our right to choose and even implement the most effective therapy for our own conditions. We didn't believe we could morally withhold or interrupt a promising treatment from persons who were of sound mind and willing to try it.

On September 21, 1989, after AmFAR's Mathilde Krim was quoted in several news articles as doubting the accuracy of the Compound Q data, Delaney wrote a pointed memo to her:

> Questioning our credibility now, in the midst of what is an already unfair and unprincipled media barrage instigated by longtime New York critics, steps over the line of propriety and adds salt to the growing wound within the community.... We had innocently hoped that the urgency of the AIDS epidemic would have helped our people overcome their seemingly instinctive and endless appetite for internal bloodletting.... I am angry with the hypocrisy and dishonesty present in the current debate and will no longer continue to turn the other cheek in my Jesuit way.... I can only say that I will defend our people and our program to the utmost of my capability, whatever it costs in the light of broadened public disclosure, discussion and accountability.

Citing safety concerns, the FDA banned the importation of trichosanthin on August 4, 1989. By this time, however, more than 3,000 ampules of the drug had successfully made their way into the country. A former associate of Alan Levin had succeeded in obtaining more from the factory in China and was selling them through buyers' clubs across the country.

On August 10, 1989, Carl Peck, director of the FDA's Center for Drug Evaluation and Research, sent a letter to Martin Delaney. The letter invited Delaney and the other doctors involved in running the study to discuss their findings with the FDA at a meeting in the near future and recommended against the continued use of trichosanthin until the meeting was under way. "We feel that you should discontinue any further unapproved experimentation with

Compound Q and should not initiate any new use of the drug," Peck wrote. Ironically, representatives of the FDA had known about the secret trial since its inception and, according to one source, had even given Levin and Waites advice on how to organize the clandestine research. FDA officials had actually visited Levin's office during the week of July 30 and expressed interest in reviewing the preliminary data. And Delaney himself had sent a copy of the protocol to an FDA official as early as the third week of the study.

By the time the FDA issued its warning, our trial had already concluded and we were analyzing data and preparing the results. Meanwhile, the "official" study of GLQ223 at San Francisco General had admitted its twelfth patient.

"It's all about power and turf and responsibility," one California AIDS specialist told *In Health* magazine. "It's about who is anointed with the privilege of using those drugs, those treatments which in the pursuit of a cure may also kill. In this society, only certain people are granted that privilege and there are certain rituals they have to perform before they can get it."

In essence, we who lacked experience in such rituals as medical training and traditional clinical trials had seized the privilege and power and even transferred it to others. In so doing, we established new and unprecedented bonds between unlikely partners. We violated a tradition set in granite. Now we would have to face the music.

On September 1, nearly three weeks after the conclusion of our study, Rick Andrews died of complications from intractable Kaposi's sarcoma.

I led a preliminary presentation of the Miami study's results to a cluster of interested physicians, patients, and the press at a banquet on September 19. Simultaneously, Delaney led a similar conference in San Francisco on the findings there and in New York. (The Los Angeles data had not yet been analyzed.)

I reported that in our twenty-patient arm of the trial, eight had experienced increased appetite and energy levels after the first dose of the drug. Five patients gained between five and ten pounds during the study, two had substantial reductions in peripheral neuropathy, four had significant decreases in p-24 antigen levels—two fell all the way to zero—and all had reductions in beta-2 microglobulins. Four had improvements in their DTH (delayed type hypersensitivity) skin tests.

Eight of the twenty subjects, all ARC patients, had modest percentage increases in their CD4 counts—an average of about 15 percent. We concluded that the drug appeared to help alleviate HIV-related symptoms and produced minor CD4 cell increases in healthy ARC patients, but it produced no significant immunological or virological improvement in cases of full-blown AIDS. We further acknowledged that the drug was potentially dangerous, especially for AIDS patients with HIV-related dementia.

In his presentation in San Francisco, Delaney defended the unorthodox research. "Frustrated by the glacially slow pace of new drug development and the years of empty words and broken promises from the system, we felt compelled to act, not just talk," he told a crowd of three hundred at the Metropolitan Community Church.

Summarizing the data of the underground study, Delaney indicated that nine of fifteen patients with elevated p-24 antigen levels showed sustained reductions averaging 42 percent one month after their first infusion, compared to their baseline levels. The findings suggested that the drug does have a definite antiviral effect, and that it is well sustained after the drug is withdrawn. Furthermore, in patients with more than 50 CD4 helper cells at baseline, levels of those cells indicated a mean increase of 28 percent after two months of treatment.

Subjects also experienced decreased sedimentation rates (a nonspecific measure of infection) and increased platelet counts. Severe but reversible fatigue and muscle pains (myalgia) were the major dose-limiting side effects. The myalgia typically began within thirty-six hours in the shoulder girdle and arms and radiated into the neck and throat before progressing to the whole body, and lasting about one week. Fever was also seen thirty-six to sixty hours after infusion. The drug also produced a significant increase in the total white blood cell count. Delaney further remarked that toxicity to the central nervous system was noted in seven of fifty-one patients, ranging from temporary mild confusion to one case of coma. The temporary mental confusion and disorientation resolved with the steroid dexamethasone. All of the patients with neurologic toxicity had abnormal MRI brain scans and low CD4 counts.

The November 1989 issue of Project Inform's *PI Perspective* reported these findings and further warned that Compound Q "should definitely not be used by those with active opportunistic infections, CD4 cell counts below 100, any evidence of HIV infection of the nervous system or the brain, or by patients who are severely debilitated."

Several physicians in the community were quick to criticize the methodology and soundness of the data generated in our trial. They cited the fact that the trial did not contain a control group with which to compare possible drug-induced changes. Surrogate markers, including p-24 antigen and beta-2 microglobulin, were not reliable markers of disease progression or severity, they argued. The CD4 cell count percentage increases were modest, at best, and could have been due to random fluctuation. Moreover, the statistically significant increases in the CD4 cell values in the San Francisco and New York study participants were based on absolute CD4 cell count values, not *percentage* of CD4 cells. Since trichosanthin, as one of its side effects, affected a rather significant leukocytosis, or upward shift in total white blood cells, this could have falsely skewed the absolute cell counts upward. Most important, the study failed to provide any definitive data on the drug's tissue and cellular penetration and pharmacokinetics, although some of this data was established in Kahn's study. And, critics argued, the drug undoubtedly held the potential to produce significant neurotoxicity in certain patients, some of whom could not be identified or "screened out" in advance.

Finally, a few of the early patients treated in the underground study were given the steroid prednisone—not ibuprofen—to counter their myalgia. Prednisone is known to increase the CD4 cell count in certain patients.

Dr. William Reiter publicly stated, "There's nothing here that would make me want to recommend Compound Q to any of my patients."

Martin Delaney, Dr. Levin, Dr. Waites, Dr. Starrett, Dr. Mayer, Susan Drake, and I met with the FDA on Friday, October 6, 1989. Ellen Cooper and Carl Peck were present along with James Bilstad, director of the FDA's Office of Drug Evaluation. Also in attendance were GeneLab's Jeffrey Lifson, a representative from Sandoz (the company that held the rights to the drug), San Francisco AIDS advocate Jesse Dobson and Tom Hannan. There were also people present from the agency's antiviral, statistical, and pharmaceutical divisions.

At the time, the FDA was housed in a labyrinth of offices scattered throughout the Department of Health and Human Services Building in Rockville, Maryland. The meeting was held in the FDA's Drug Evaluation and Research Center conference room. Pictures depicting pioneering discoveries in the history of medicine and pharmacology decorated the high walls.

Peck opened the meeting by assuring us that no one was on trial. His goal, he made clear, was to bring the event into compliance in order to bring the questions to an end. Delaney began the presentation by providing background information on the project and introducing the principal investigators. Drs. Waites and Levin then provided a summary of the data collected in New York, San Francisco, and Miami. (Data from the Los Angeles arm of the study was not reported by Delaney since it was never received. Beyond a certain date, the L.A. group broke compliance and failed to continue reporting data. Not a single case-report form was supplied to Project Inform. And certain lab work, such as p-24 antigen assays, was diverted from the central lab, Immunodiagnostics in San Leandro, to be processed at a local facility in Los Angeles, thus rendering the p-24 data inconsistent and useless.) Graphs and charts, depicting the collective virological and immunological changes experienced by subjects who took Compound Q, were placed on an overhead projector.

In their critique of our presentation, the FDA expressed concern over several points. The officials doubted that the drug had such a short half-life and rapid elimination phase in the body, as Levin and Delaney claimed. They also doubted that the drug was capable of crossing the blood/brain barrier. The molecule was too big, they argued, and could not cross in its entirety. Any neurological side effect it produced would have to be due to activity that originated in the blood, not the cerebrospinal fluid. They allowed, however, that some subjects may have had abnormal blood/brain barriers and that this had permitted trichosanthin unprecedented access to brain tissue.

Despite their reservations about some of the details of the trial's results, the FDA officials seemed impressed with the quality of the research and the comprehensiveness of the data presented. They agreed to meet with Levin again in ten days to further discuss ways of speeding the approval of trichosanthin.

After the meeting, Dr. Mayer, Susan, and I went to see the NAMES Project AIDS Memorial Quilt on the final day of its 1989 exhibition on the lawn of the Ellipse.

The idea for the quilt was first conceived in November 1985 by Cleve Jones. A longtime gay rights activist, Jones helped organize the annual candlelight march honoring Harvey Milk and George Moscone, the San Francisco politicians assassinated in 1978. As he planned for the 1985 march, he learned that the number of San Franciscans who had died of AIDS had reached 1,000. To mark this terrible milestone, Cleve asked each person joining in the march to write down the names of their friends and loved ones who had died of AIDS. At the end of the march, shrouded in a sea of candlelight, Jones and others stood on ladders taping the names to the walls of the San Francisco Federal Building. In the midst of the process,

Jones stepped down from his ladder to view the growing tribute and was struck by the image of the names on the side of the building. The individual squares, each with a name, looked to him like a patchwork quilt.

Inspired by this sight, Jones started to formulate plans for a larger memorial. A little more than a year later, Cleve created the first panel for the AIDS Memorial Quilt, in memory of his friend Marvin Feldman. More panels were added, and an enormous quilt began to grow. Jones joined forces with several others to formally organize the NAMES Project Foundation in June 1987. That summer, the Foundation helped initiate a four-month national tour of the 1,920-panel quilt, which raised nearly $500,000 for hundreds of AIDS service organizations.

Lovers, parents, brothers and sisters had created brightly colored panels out of the most unlikely materials. Feather boas, Mardi Gras masks, records, and ribbons were assembled together with all sorts of fabrics in meaningful collages. Each stitch in the tapestry wove a rich story. We could tell so much about each individual by the symbols and materials used to celebrate their lives.

Now, two years later, we were seeing an even larger quilt on the lawn of the Ellipse. We noticed a stretch of the quilt with blank panels, and Magic Markers and paints strewn about nearby. Visitors were busily creating their own panels. Susan and I joined them and made a panel for Rick Andrews. We knew how much he had loved his record collection, so we drew a stack of shiny vinyl records and a turntable. Susan drew a picture of Rick's classroom at NYU, complete with the faces of his admiring students. Yet the endeavor seemed to me so feeble, so inadequate a representation of Rick's life, which had been so complex and rich.

For a long moment, Susan, Dr. Mayer, and I stood by the panel, watching, holding each other's arms tightly. At a podium to the side of the area, people read the names of individuals they loved who had died of AIDS.

In stark contrast to the somber tones of the people reading names, a chorus of angry voices rose up in the distance. About fifty members of ACT UP New York marched around the perimeter of the quilt carrying placards and shouting slogans such as "History Will Recall—Reagan and Bush did nothing at all!" and "Health care must be free—we need more than AZT!" Founded by playwright and author Larry Kramer, ACT UP's singular mission was to use every weapon at its disposal to fight for the release of promising experimental drugs for AIDS. If that meant civil disobedience and protests, so be it. Meetings with high-level FDA and NIH officials to effect permanent policy change were high on their agenda.

In September 1989, Peter Staley, a former New York bond trader, and six other ACT UP members donned blue pinstripe suits and, bearing bogus name-tags, crashed the New York Stock Exchange, protesting Burroughs Wellcome's pricing of AZT. One minute before business was about to begin, they chained themselves to the banister of the balcony overlooking the trading floor. Unfurling a banner that read SELL WELLCOME, they then made obstreperous noises with foghorns and metal "crickets." They were eventually removed by police, but thousands more continued to march in protest outside the stock-market doors. The firestorm of activity—designed to generate change—worked. Burroughs Wellcome cut the price of AZT by 20 percent, to about $8,000 a year.

Months later, Representative Henry Waxman succeeded in having the price of AZT reduced even further, to about $6,200 a year. In the next several months, ACT UP chapters sprang up in many American cities, staging demonstrations and protest marches and becoming catalysts for important changes in AIDS patients' care. ACT UP compiled a treatment registry that documented all clinical trials in progress throughout the country and distributed it nationally to AIDS patients free of charge. And in the weeks that followed, the organization would be responsible for some of the most sweeping changes and reforms in the drug development process.

The group members wrote a critique showing that a series of protocols aimed at testing the drug ganciclovir's efficacy were coercive, unnecessary, and even cruel. Thousands of patients had used

ganciclovir under special compassionate-use exemptions, and doctors reported universally that the drug helped arrest the blindness
associated with CMV retinitis—an increasingly common opportunistic infection in AIDS—and that it also produced improvements in
other manifestations of CMV, such as colitis. But the FDA continued to demand placebo-controlled studies before it would license
the drug. This meant that subjects in the placebo group, who had
active CMV infection in their eyes, would go blind and perhaps
succumb to an early death—all in an attempt to prove that the drug
was worthy and should be licensed. Activists charged that this was
inhuman and immoral. Under pressure, ganciclovir was finally licensed for use in CMV retinitis. Partly as a result of ACT UP's
persistence, the FDA approved the drug for sale to PWAs with
CMV retinitis, without passing the drug through a formal clinical
trial. It was more than a mere bending of the rules; it was a rewriting
of the rules.

In 1989, at the third and final meeting of the Lasagna Committee hearing, ACT UP members James Eigo, Dr. Iris Long, and Mark
Harrington delivered an incisive critique that summarized the
FDA's inadequacies and, in particular, how its supervision of AIDS
drug development and clinical trials of anti-HIV medications was
grossly inappropriate. Harrington then read twelve demands from
what would become a historic manifesto—among them, requisitions
to permit prophylaxis in government-run trials, ban the use of
placebos, choose endpoints other than death as outcome variables,
focus on the evaluation of immunomodulators as well as antiviral
agents, and incorporate the patient as an active participant in the
design of clinical trials.

Now, as the ACT UP members marched around us, the anger
in their voices stirred our own rage, making us feel the hurt in our
souls even more intensely. Susan and I stared at the panels. We
couldn't help but envision our own names inscribed there. And
we couldn't help but imagine which of our objects and mementos
our loved ones would choose to symbolize our lives.

CHAPTER 11

THE FIGHT FOR LIFE

B y April 1990, it seemed clear to me that not only was Compound Q not the cure for AIDS, but it probably held little potential to improve the condition of most ARC patients significantly. I continued to monitor those in Mayer's study and others who received the drug in the underground. Like AZT, Compound Q reduced p-24 antigenemia and beta-2 microglobulin levels. (However, these surrogate markers had recently been disputed as especially meaningful or predictive of disease progression by numerous researchers.) In patients who were asymptomatic with higher CD4 cell counts (300 or more), it did produce some marginal but often transient improvements in immune function. It did not, however, create a resolution of the various symptoms that were hallmarks of profound and sustained cell-mediated immune suppression in ARC and AIDS patients—symptoms such as oral thrush, hairy leukoplakia, molluscums, chronic candidiasis infections, and diarrhea. Nor did it produce improvements in the more consequential measurements of immune function, including DTH and PHA blastogenesis. And it did not seem to vastly reduce the symptoms of HIV-related dementia, as earlier reports had speculated. It also remained unclear whether the drug reached its site of action at

effective, sustained concentrations. Independent physicians direct-
ing underground Compound Q clinics reported that the most significant and lasting changes in surrogate markers such as p-24
antigen levels occurred at doses of 50 micrograms or higher. But
even if the drug did reach its site of action effectively at specific
doses and methods of administration and did selectively kill HIV-
infected cells, I realized that it probably failed to address the true,
underlying pathogenesis of the disease: the exact mechanism by
which HIV laid claim to the entire CD4 cell population. It seemed
to produce a similar response pattern as AZT—and why not? After
all, the drug was based on a model similar to that of AZT: the
destruction of a virus or the inactivation of a virus within a given
cell line. Perhaps it had no direct impact on other, more significant
facets of the disease's pathogenesis, such as cytokine-mediated immune suppression or autoimmunity. If infected macrophages did
represent the larger slice of the pathological pie, then the potential
toxicity of trichosanthin would be worthwhile. But this had not been
proven.

Without question, a small subset of patients, all of whom
started with higher CD4 cell counts (above 300), did seem to benefit
from the drug, at least in the short term and at higher dosages of the
medication. Exactly why these patients (and others who started with
even higher CD4 cell counts) benefited was unclear, although I had
my own hunches. Many of the people who saw rises in CD4 cells
after several Compound Q treatments might have been recently
exposed to HIV. Perhaps they had a larger population of infected
macrophages that would be more susceptible to cell killing by
trichosanthin. Or perhaps there was some other factor in these
people's immune systems that permitted a response. But this was
pure conjecture on my part.

I hadn't yet taken the drug and did not intend to. Aside from
the fact that it would probably do little to boost my immune system,
I knew that it also had potentially significant side effects in people
with HIV dementia. I couldn't help but realize how ironic it was that

I had never taken advantage of a drug I had worked so hard to acquire and evaluate.

I was also faced with the dilemma of the ethics of the underground trial, which, after all, I had helped pioneer. Had we violated the first rule of the Hippocratic oath, "First, do no harm"? In administering the plant protein to patients as rapidly as we did without filing an IND application or using a standard IRB, we wrought harm as well as healed. Patients who experienced myalgic side effects and reversible changes in mental status and sometimes saw no improvement in their immune function had suffered for the benefit of another group, some of whom *did* experience modest if only temporary increases in their cell counts and improvements in specific clinical symptoms. But did the drug's margin of efficacy justify the harm brought against the justifiably frustrated minority? Morally and ethically, were we justified in proceeding as we did?

Indeed, critics alleged that rather than elucidating the failures of the standard methods of drug testing, the underground study may have wound up demonstrating why such methods, with their deliberate pace and safeguards, are ultimately necessary.

Dr. John Fletcher, who heads the Center for Biomedical Ethics at the University of Virginia, told the *New York Times* that he was "shocked and chilled" by the underground study, which "violated the very first ethical principle." Fletcher explained, "In any study, you begin with a question, 'Should this study be done at all?' Then you submit the study to a disinterested group who could put themselves in the places of those who would be in the study. The premise of secrecy [that governed the underground Compound Q study] violated the impartial review by others that is the greatest protection for human subjects."

Ronald Bayer of the Columbia University School of Public Health confronted these and other questions in an editorial in the December 1990 issue of the journal *AIDS*. He pointed out that the research protocol undertaken by Project Inform was not examined by a standing IRB. Instead, it was subjected to analysis by a board consisting of members of a patient advocacy group, two HIV-positive laymen, an attorney, and two physicians with expertise in ribosomal inhibitory proteins. Bayer called into question the "committee's" capacity to judge the study's ethical and scientific merits independently. He went on to assert that Project Inform should have filed a general assurance with the FDA. This document would have stipulated the methods for choosing the committee members, fully delineated the proceedings of the review, and increased the odds that an independent and truly unbiased critique of the protocol could emerge.

Bayer further noted that the study did not start with a very low dose of the drug to monitor for evidence of side effects, and that the release form signed by subjects stipulated that they forgo the right to sue for damages resulting from negligence. He argued that it represented an unethical demand to waive such a right and that it bordered on coercion. He was quick to add that Byers, Levin, and Waites—as well as the other doctors involved in the national study—*were* professional in their conduct and knowledgeable about the drug and HIV disease. Under less conscientious medical leadership, Bayer noted, the potential for patient abuse would have been far greater.

Levin countered that the protocol was reviewed by an impartial jury of physicians, lawyers, and clergy, not dissimilar to a standing IRB, and that the secrecy was justified, given the nature of the study. He told the *New York Times,* "We are empowering the practicing physicians, we are empowering the family physicians. The underground study kept the university physicians and the FDA out of the loop because the FDA-approved protocols just aren't going to be able to provide answers quickly enough."

The truth was, subjects were *not* coerced into participating. AIDS was, and still is, a desperate situation. Rules are often meant to be broken. Subjects of sound mind who were willing to risk trying an unproven medication ought ultimately to be given the opportunity under the best possible monitoring conditions. We had provided both the conditions and the opportunity. And some activists argued that our "secret" trial was in fact no more secret than certain ACTG studies, which were conducted in relative anonymity and received little public attention.

Finally, the goal of all physicians was to pursue the best possible course of treatment for all patients, particularly those with life-threatening illnesses. Had we not achieved that goal? Yet the scientific method demanded the use of placebos, the inclusion of an IRB, and less flexible protocols—none of which we had done. Science, it seemed, was in irreconcilable conflict with medicine.

Although I tried to discourage him, Scott Yageman continued to receive more than two Compound Q treatments a month, some containing of up to 50 micrograms—double what he received in the underground study. By January 1990, he had received a total of twenty infusions. Yet his condition, which initially had shown signs of mild improvement, now steadily deteriorated. His CD4 cell count fell to an all-time low, his peripheral neuropathies returned, and he complained of marked energy loss. And he was bothered by a new and disturbing symptom: molluscums. Caused by the virus *Molluscum contagiosum,* molluscums appear as small white or clear bumps on the skin with umbilicated, or crater-shaped, tops. Inside, the bumps hold vesicles containing virus and are often itchy and painful. Molluscums were not an uncommon condition in PWAs with low CD4 cell counts.

"Why do you keep taking the drug when you see that it's not having any real impact?" I asked him one day, observing the red "Q track" along his arm.

"Because it helped me more than any other medicine I've ever tried," he insisted. "I never felt so good as after that first injection. I want to get back to that level of health."

Scott was not the only one who still believed in the Chinese cucumber's potential. Martin Delaney also believed it might have real value. He, along with Larry Waites and Alan Levin, worked with GeneLabs and Sandoz to create a Phase 2 study of GLQ223. Sandoz agreed to fund the project, which would be conducted in Los Angeles, New York, and San Francisco and would cost up to

$250,000. The new protocol called for 100 subjects to receive two initial doses of the drug, followed by monthly doses of 36 micrograms for up to twenty-four weeks (this to allay the discomfort and to allow time to recover from the common myalgic side effects of the drug). The original version of the study would include four treatment groups: the first would receive AZT; the second AZT and Compound Q; the third Compound Q alone; and the fourth—an AZT-intolerant group—would receive Compound Q alone.

Waites and Levin also continued to administer Chinese trichosanthin, using the modified protocol to treat patients in their practice and to monitor the results. An analysis of the data of the Compound Q patients who continued to receive treatment under their direction showed that over time, 60 percent stabilized or increased their CD4 cell count. And a statistical analysis on data gathered between December 1989 and March 1990 was performed by Levin and his associates. In 62 patients with an average follow-up time of 128 days, there was a median CD4 increase of 0.9 cells per day of individual patient follow-up. The median change across the entire group was an increase of 43 cells.

Meanwhile, the drug continued to enjoy substantial popularity in the AIDS underground during the months that followed. Ron Woodruff of the Dallas Buyers' Club and Jim Corti continued to sell Compound Q at $50 to $100 per ampule. AIDS patients from across the country purchased the drug from these and other sources, then convinced sympathetic physicians and nurses in their communities to administer the medication and monitor their progress while following the guidelines suggested by Project Inform.

In February 1990, I decided to stop working at Dr. Mayer's office. My energy level had waned considerably and the long commute to Miami had become extremely tiring. More significant, the specter of tuberculosis loomed ominously over the Miami area. More and more of Mayer's patients were contracting the disease, which is highly contagious at certain stages. I felt that the risk of catching TB and other diseases was too great. And so one afternoon I packed my boxes of research materials, charts, and graphs into Scott Yageman's station wagon and quietly told Dr. Mayer and Susan good-bye.

During the months that followed, I spent time alone at the beach, reading a wide variety of journal articles and abstracts. Although my reading speed had decreased somewhat with the onset of my dementia, I was still able to get through a sizable amount of material in a day and comprehend much of what I read. It was becoming strikingly clear to me that the true pathogenesis of HIV disease had not been fully elucidated. Direct viral infection of CD4 cells as the cause of the massive immune destruction seemed unlikely, since at any one given time as few as 0.001 to 1.0 percent of the lymphocytes and macrophages were infected.

Some theorists hypothesized that AIDS was actually a bizarre autoimmune disease, that HIV infection was merely an early catalyst that set off a complex cascade of immunological events in which the body actually destroyed itself. One theory, even supported by Anthony Fauci, suggested that the virus set off the production of certain cytokines—non-antibody proteins that are produced and released by lymphocytes. Such proteins as tumor necrosis factor and interleukin 6 were present in healthy people but temporarily elevated during illness. In HIV infection, certain theorists reasoned, the cytokines became *permanently* activated, perhaps binding to specific receptors of non-HIV-infected CD4 cells, hence targeting them for destruction by healthy macrophages, the body's scavenger cells that specialize in the destruction of harmful bacteria. According to this theory, the targeted receptor actually caused the CD4 cells to be recognized as "foreign" by the still healthy macrophages, which attacked and destroyed them. Researchers speculated that up to 20 percent of the body's dendritic and Langerhans cells (found in the skin) could also be infected with HIV, and this could contribute to the disease's pathogenesis. There was also the theory of "superantigen infection," according to which HIV marked the CD4 cells for destruction well in advance of their death—a process that researchers called "programmed cell death."

And Luc Montagnier announced that he believed that the real cause of AIDS might be HIV acting together with a small viruslike bacteria known as the mycoplasma incognitus. This organism's association with HIV was originally discovered by Dr. Shuh-Ching Lo at the U.S. Armed Forces Institute of Pathology. Montagnier believed it to be a hidden co-factor capable of rendering HIV infection lethal. A lack of mycoplasma in the blood of certain persons with HIV infection, he conjectured, was why some of them remained asymptomatic for so long.

As early as 1987, Peter Duesberg, a chemist and molecular virologist at the University of California at Berkeley, was arguing that AIDS could not possibly be caused by HIV. Among the reasons he gave was that HIV violates the "classical conditions" of viral pathology, i.e., that viruses cause disease quickly and after much replication. In contrast, HIV is associated with disease only after infection, "when the virus is not replicating" and when an antibody is present. Furthermore, people with AIDS, he suggested, could not lose their CD4 cells due to any retrovirus, including HIV, because viruses are never cytopathic. Duesberg also pointed out that HIV is found in fewer than one of every 10,000 CD4 cells it kills; that HIV-infected CD4 cells grown in culture continue to divide; and that it is impossible that any retrovirus would be capable of killing only its natural host with a 50-to-100 percent efficiency. Finally, Duesberg argued that Koch's famous postulates—requisite conditions for proving a causative relationship between an agent and a disease—were never fully established with HIV, since many people who have HIV still do not have AIDS, HIV isn't present in the tissue site of disease, and HIV does not produce AIDS in animals.

Gallo and other researchers challenged every one of Duesberg's assertions. Although HIV *is* associated with disease long after the virus is replicating, it has managed to wreak havoc on the immune system; what's left in the end are small amounts of virus and a devastated immune system. Moreover, many viruses cause disease after a long period of dormancy. Such "slow" viruses include measles encephalitis. Second, Daniel Zagury, the controversial French researcher, Gallo, and the Whitehead (Cambridge, Mass.) Institute of Biotechnology's David Baltimore have each independently shown that HIV *is* capable of infecting and killing CD4 lymphocytes and that it is indeed a cytopathic retrovirus. More important, it may catalyze the release of cytokines and thus be indirectly responsible for the damage. As for Koch's postulates, Gallo shows that they have all been proven inaccurate in recent years: Expression of disease is the *exception* for the majority of infectious microbes. Almost every microbe can be found in asymptomatic carriers with minor infections. Many people, for instance, are exposed to and infected with tuberculosis bacilli but never become sick with tuberculosis. In answer to Duesberg's criticism of Koch's second point, it is true that HIV does not *infect* every organ it seems to *affect*. For instance, although it may not directly infect neurons and cannot be cultured directly from specific regions of the brain, it does seem to produce mental dysfunction. Indeed, the virus itself may not have to be present in those tissues: it may instead provoke the release of toxic proteins and cytokines in the blood that contribute to the death of neurons. Diphtheria is found only in the membrane tissues of the throat, but it too can produce a disease of the brain; it produces a neurotoxin that gets into the blood and crosses the blood/brain barrier into brain tissue. Finally, many viruses that cause disease in humans do not produce disease when introduced into a different species of animal because they cannot, under any circumstances, infect that species. For instance, the bacillus that causes leprosy in humans can only be grown in the footpads of armadillos, the only other species susceptible to the disease. HIV can be tested for disease production only in chimpanzees, gibbons, and pigtail macaques; it cannot produce disease in chickens or cows.

In February 1990, ddI was approved for use in a new program that would broaden access to the drug. Conceived by the National

Institute of Allergy and Infectious Disease's Director Anthony Fauci and officially implemented on June 23, 1989, the parallel track program is an administrative process through which promising new drugs are released for treatment use without waiting for the completion of research studies. Studies of a drug would thus proceed on one track while the drug was also being used for treatment on another. The drugs would be made available to patients through their physicians, who would take responsibility for monitoring their progress and reporting data to the drug company.

Some investigators objected to the program, claiming that parallel track would prevent patients from enrolling in early clinical trials of ddI—the first drug to be put into the system—or any other new drugs that went into the system. But proponents of parallel track assured them that the clinical trials would open first; only patients who didn't meet the inclusion criteria for the clinical trials would have early access to ddI through parallel track and their doctors. Thus, there would be no danger of the trials' not filling up. Moreover, the trials would not use placebos but would instead test ddI against the already approved treatment, AZT. This would, according to proponents, be an added incentive for people to join the clinical trials.

The parallel track program came as a boon to the patients, including me, who had first received ddI from David Wilson's underground pharmacy. Many of them had benefited from the drug but had been forced to discontinue its use after the supply was halted in November 1989. By April 1990, parallel track allowed many of them to resume use of the drug.

In January 1990, Fort Lauderdale AIDS activist Lenny Kaplan quietly revealed plans to open his own underground clinic in Fort Lauderdale. For the last six months, Kaplan's Fight for Life organization had disseminated information about experimental HIV medications in monthly meetings that took place in his home. In a style not dissimilar to those of ACT UP in New York, Kaplan's meetings also provided a forum for political debate on issues of HIV treatment care and political policy. Memos streamed into his fax machine from New York and San Francisco announcing such events as "national die-ins," in which PWAs lay down in front of their local FDA offices as a reminder of what extreme caution and overregulation had wrought. Kaplan rounded up local AIDS patients at his meetings to add Fort Lauderdale to the list of participating "die-in" cities. Through the fax and through his on-line computer system, Kaplan also received information on promising experimental HIV drugs and where they could be obtained. He also set up Fight for Life offices in several European countries, including one in Scandinavia. These satellite branches, staffed by volunteers, collected "inside" information on promising new therapies—some of which had not been released to the mainstream scientific community—and forwarded it to Kaplan. All of this information was photocopied and passed out at the monthly meetings.

"We have the spontaneity of the yuppies, but we aren't afraid to throw in big business techniques as well," he told the Miami *Herald*.

Now, with the announcement that he would actually be treating patients and not merely informing them about new therapies, Kaplan crossed the fine line dividing those who only expressed concern and those who actually provided care. It was a transformation similar to the one experienced by Project Inform, which in 1989 went from distributing newsletters containing information about promising HIV therapies to implementing treatment protocols with such drugs as Compound Q.

Kaplan, who had an epicene appearance and had performed as a female impersonator, reached an agreement with a gay-owned hotel located on Fort Lauderdale's popular tourist strip, the Federal Highway, to set up his clinic there. Under the agreement, Kaplan would have complimentary access to two hotel rooms each weekend—to be used for Compound Q treatments—and a full-time office in which to conduct Fight for Life and ACT UP business. Like our operation at the Howard Johnson's, the entire affair was kept quite clandestine. Potential patients learned about the clinic through word of mouth. Each would be charged $125 for the first ampule of Compound Q and $50 for each additional ampule. A nominal fee was charged for supplies. Each treatment would wind up costing about $225. Two other volunteer registered nurses agreed to help administer the drug.

Kaplan also announced plans to import various other experimental drugs and sell them through a local buyers' club, the PWA Health Alliance, which he would operate. All profits from the club would go to Fight for Life. He also announced plans to hold a conference in the fall that would feature speakers such as Martin Delaney and representatives from various pharmaceutical companies, and which would offer the latest information on a wide variety of potential therapies. A monthly newsletter would provide updates on these and other events.

The Fight for Life Clinic would ensure that patients who wanted Compound Q could get it at a reasonable price and under professional medical supervision. I agreed to act as a consultant to the clinic, providing Lenny with vital information on toxicity management and intervention.

Kaplan's was not the only underground Compound Q clinic to emerge. "CliniQs" sprang up all across the country, with the dosages, methods of administration, clinic setups, and choice of premedications varying as widely from city to city as the personalities of those running the clinics. Some CliniQs would not infuse persons whose CD4 cell counts fell below 100; others gave the drug even when the count was down to 0. Some required CT (computerized tomography) or MRI brain scans prior to treatment to rule out neurological problems at baseline. Dosing schedules ranged from 16 micrograms all the way up to 100. Some dripped fast, some dripped slow; others fast, then slow. Groups who premedicated to guard against Q-induced myalgia usually used antihistamines, non-steroidal anti-inflammatory drugs, or steroidal anti-inflammatories. Essentially, each adapted a protocol based on its own experience with and understanding of trichosanthin.

Ironically, while Lenny Kaplan was successfully piloting an underground clinic with an unapproved drug for AIDS, another group of medical innovators was being castigated for just such a venture. On January 20, 1990, investigators from the California Medical Board and the State Department of Health Services arrested Dr. Stephen Herman and his son Jim on felony charges for the illegal manufacture and distribution of a drug they claimed had the potential to cure AIDS: Viroxan. The warrant for Herman's arrest charged that he was manufacturing and selling "an unapproved, unadulterated, dangerous drug" to AIDS patients with the intent to "defraud or mislead."

Admittedly, the drug had both "bad press" and theoretical disadvantages working against it from the beginning. Dr. Michael McGrath's *in vitro* analysis of the drug showed that at specific dilution factors, it had no substantial anti-HIV activity. Furthermore, at the time, the therapy required daily intravenous infusions for up to six months and the installation of a Hickman catheter, making it rather impractical and potentially hazardous.

An extract from the bark of the lemon tree, Viroxan was part of a family of chemicals known as superoxides that had long been used in Europe to treat certain tumors. According to the Hermans, Viroxan had the unique ability to activate polynuclear neutrophils, making them virucidal and capable of phagocytizing or "eating" HIV as well as other viruses, including herpes and Epstein-Barr. The Hermans also claimed the drug was capable of stimulating the production of new CD4 lymphocytes as well as neutrophils. In short, Viroxan purportedly worked by mimicking the process by which the superoxide anion from white blood cells, especially neutrophils, inactivated viruses.

The fifty-three-year-old Stephen Herman developed the drug with his son Jim, a biochemist. Another son, Ken, had died in 1987 after contracting AIDS. The Hermans had originally developed the drug in an effort to save Ken's life, but he died before the project reached completion. The senior Herman, who suffered from lymphoma, took the medication on a regular basis and told some of his patients that the drug had kept his lymphoma in remission.

The father-and-son team manufactured the drug in a laboratory behind their Villa Park home and distributed it to local AIDS patients for a nominal fee—about $300 a month. In some instances, the Hermans also provided intravenous supplies. Because the drug required daily infusion, they advocated that certain patients have Hickman catheters inserted by a local surgeon to facilitate the drug's administration.

The Hermans had not obtained an IND or Human Subjects Review Board approval prior to treating their patients, many of whom were monitored by Valentine Birds, a doctor who maintained a sizable HIV practice in southern California. Birds himself was known for renegade treatments in a style not dissimilar to those used by Robert Mayer, one of the doctors who adopted Salvatore Catapano's typhoid treatment to combat AIDS.

Birds and the Hermans claimed that the group of ten AIDS patients they followed for 22 months, each of whom received daily intravenous infusions of Viroxan for six months, all experienced significant increases in both the percentage of CD4 and total number of CD4 cells, reductions of lymphadenopathy, and clearing of thrush, oral hairy leukoplakia, diarrhea, and pulmonary congestion. The Hermans also claimed that the drug produced total remission in a group of seven patients with mixed forms of polyarthritis. Since the Hermans perceived polyarthritis to be, like AIDS, an autoimmune disease, they concluded that Viroxan could benefit HIV-induced immune dysfunction. In an unpublished manuscript, the Hermans wrote, "Viroxan is a broad spectrum agent capable of curing a wide variety of chronic, degenerative diseases involving immune dysregulation and associated with chronic inflammatory infections of bacterial, fungal or viral etiology." Responding to McGrath's analysis, the Hermans argued that the drug worked in a manner that could not be fully assessed in a standard assay, and furthermore, that his dilution factors skipped over an important range.

I had heard reports that, in fact, few of the treated patients experienced such an improvement in CD4 cells or a resolution of symptoms. A study by one underground drug researcher found that in some cases Viroxan was capable of producing mild but sustained liver and bone marrow toxicity, side effects that obviated its long-term use. The drug sometimes also created severe tissue death at the infusion and injection site.

There were also allegations of death attributed to the product. On December 3, 1989, Los Angeles floral designer Mark Snider was found lying in three-day-old bathwater, a Hickman catheter in his chest and bottles of Viroxan on the bathroom sink. He was rushed to a local hospital, where he was diagnosed with meningitis, blood poisoning, and dehydration. He died four days later. His lover argued that toxicity from a contaminated batch of Viroxan had contributed to his demise. (Later tests would show that Viroxan was not responsible.)

On January 11, 1990, Stephen Herman was lecturing to a small group of AIDS patients in a guest building behind his home, which had become a regular practice. An undercover medical board investigator sat among the listeners, posing as a patient. Questioning Herman about the drug's efficacy, he then purchased a one-month supply. After the seminar, a team of eleven state investigators descended on Herman's home, placed him under arrest, and carted him off to the Orange County jail. The Hermans' entire supply of Viroxan—along with their confidential medical records—was confiscated. Herman was later released on bond.

Although he was arrested in January 1990, Herman was not officially charged until February 13, 1991. The charges consisted of sixteen felony counts, including the false advertisement, sale, and misrepresentation of an unproven AIDS therapy and grand theft by taking money under false pretenses. Investigators further noted that some vials of Viroxan were not properly stoppered and might have become contaminated. Prosecutors had also contemplated filing manslaughter charges against Herman but later determined that there was not enough evidence that the drug caused the deaths of the patients. (Autopsies revealed that the true cause of death was AIDS, not the medication.) Kathleen Schmidt, a senior investigator with the California Medical Board, told the Los Angeles *Times:* "Herman experimented on people before he sought any laboratory tests. Not only is the drug not FDA-approved, it is unapproved, unproven and even potentially dangerous."

Herman insisted publicly that the charges were groundless innuendos and attacks by politically motivated city and state officials. "Viroxan and drugs with similar modes of action have been openly understood and accepted by the medical community outside the United States for years," he told reporters. "I tried everything possible to work with the system here in the States, but because the mechanisms were not there, I had to do it my way."

At a hearing in Orange County on July 3, 1991, Herman pleaded not guilty to all sixteen counts. A trial was set for October 8. His arraignment came on the heels of civil charges filed on July 1 by the California Medical Board. The charges alleged that Herman was negligent, incompetent, and dishonest in selling the unproven drug to AIDS patients. Although Valentine Birds was not charged, the board eventually revoked his license.

In the months that followed, Herman and his research team continued to persevere. They presented their results at the Sixth International Conference on AIDS in San Francisco and at a conference on alternative treatment methods in Berkeley. They assembled their data in IND form for FDA approval. For reasons never fully explained, the IND was denied. Whatever potential Viroxan held as a therapy for AIDS, arthritis, or any other disease seemed to be crushed under the weight of a system that had neither tolerance for scientifically unproven treatments nor for the physicians with the courage and initiative to try them.

A group of Herman's patients who believed that Viroxan had genuinely improved their health rallied around him, led most notably by Scott Beatty of Palm Springs. Through fund-raising dinners, they raised the money to pay his court costs and to have the drug tested in mainstream European research circles. In January

1991 Viroxan entered clinical trials at the University of Normandy in France. However, these studies never reached completion, and Herman subsequently joined forces with a clinic in Tijuana. Patients traveled across the border for their weekly doses of Viroxan, in a manner not dissimilar to the DMSO treatments of the early 1980s. Several physicians at the clinic informally collected data. Reportedly, the price of intravenous Viroxan had increased to more than $550 a month. It was also available in suppository form through a pharmacy in the Bahamas at a unit cost of $12. Herman also opened clinical trials of the drug—which had a new formulation and a new street name, VX-2—at an undisclosed university center in Kenya.

Scott Beatty, among others, continued to argue fervently that the drug had saved his life. "There's no question I would be dead if it were not for VX-1 and VX-2," he told me. "I want every PWA to have the same chance I did."

Like Michael May, who had strongly defended the efficacy of his AL-721 treatments in Israel, Beatty was a concert pianist. When he began the treatment in the spring of 1988, he was diagnosed as having ARC, with a CD4 cell count of about 300. Since starting the treatment, his CD4 cell count had soared to 800 and remained there. He claimed he had more energy than ever. He passionately defended the drug to me in numerous conversations, even though he couldn't fully explain its mode of action or offer any more recent data on its efficacy. And he steadfastly championed Dr. Herman. "If Herman goes to jail, so do I," he told me.

Ultimately, Herman did not go to jail. In July 1991 he agreed to surrender his medical license after state prosecutors dropped civil charges of gross negligence, incompetence, and dishonesty. On January 8, 1992, he pleaded guilty to ten misdemeanor counts, and was sentenced to three years' informal probation and fined $12,000. But he vowed to continue studies of Viroxan overseas and promised to publish the results in a major medical journal.

• • •

Craig called from California. He had enrolled in the parallel track program for ddI and had suffered one of its unexpected and potentially life-threatening side effects: pancreatitis. Although he fully recovered after discontinuing the drug, five people in the expanded-access program and one in the official study died from the condition. In May 1990, the FDA sent a letter to all physicians participating in the parallel track program, alerting them to the problem and advising them to routinely check certain chemistry markers for all patients on ddI.

I experienced good and bad days during the spring of 1990. During periods when I felt stronger, I spent time reworking the script that John and I had completed in Los Angeles three years earlier. I eventually managed to sell it to a small production company in Orlando. The company liked my work and hired me to rewrite several scripts they had in development. Yet I couldn't help wondering—if the projects ever did see the light of day, would I live to see the final result? And I wondered what would happen when the producers, who I knew were conservative, learned that I was HIV-positive and had been one of the ringleaders of a controversial underground study.

CHAPTER 12

ORGANIZED COMBAT

The Fight for Life Buyers' Club formed by Lenny Kaplan was not the only institution of its kind. Since mid-1988, at least fifteen buyers' clubs had sprung up across the country, including the Healing Alternatives Club in San Francisco, the Dallas Buyers' Club, and the Carl Vogel Club in Washington, D.C. These clubs provided PWAs with the opportunity to purchase many of the experimental drugs that David and I had discovered years earlier, as well as newer compounds, many of which had not yet been approved. The buyers' clubs were not-for-profit institutions. They sold anti-HIV medications to PWAs under the terms of the Personal Importation Policy, which allowed the individual patient to import a three-month supply of a medication from anywhere in the world, provided the drug was for his or her own personal use and that it would be taken under the supervision of a physician. The buyers' club presidents found sources in international markets for unapproved drugs, purchased them in quantity, and redistributed them to American AIDS patients. The clubs also imported drugs already approved in the United States but whose prescription price made them economically prohibitive for many PWAs. Typically, the clubs published product and price lists in addition to newsletters that explained the methods of action, suggested dosages, and provided background for the drugs they sold. A patient could review this material and then send a check or money order to cover the cost of the drug in question along with a signed release form confirming that it was for the patient's personal use. Pending its availability, the drug was shipped within a few weeks.

Perhaps the largest and best known of all the clubs was the New York People With AIDS Health Group, founded by Michael Callen, Dr. Joseph Sonnabend, and Tom Hannan. Hannan, a young man with superb organizational skills, spearheaded the operation. An AIDS patient himself, Hannan probably would not have become nearly as involved if not for his lover, Stephen Roach, a graduate student in chemistry at Columbia University who had ARC. Like Steve Gavin and others in the mid-1980s, Roach had read every article published on potential anti-HIV therapeutics. In May 1987, he saw the letter in the *New England Journal of Medicine* by Drs. Robert Gallo and Arnold Lippa, and several months later he noticed the article by Michael May in the New York *Native*, both of which extolled the virtues of AL-721. Roach contacted May, who gave him a list of references on AL-721's potential efficacy in treating chemical addiction and dementia, as well as more general references on lipid chemistry and cell membrane fluidity engineering. Roach obtained almost every paper on May's list from the medical library and read them voraciously. He then met with Sonnabend to talk about what he had learned.

Sonnabend agreed that AL-721 appeared to be interesting, and that it might be worthwhile to distribute the compound to the gay community and collect efficacy data on it. Yet how could they accomplish this? Neither had the time or organizational abilities to mount such an ambitious effort. Roach immediately thought of Tom, and introduced him to Sonnabend. After that, the three met regularly to discuss how to obtain and distribute the drug.

They first approached Praxis Pharmaceuticals, the company that had sponsored the early American trials of the drug, and attempted to convince Arnold Lippa, its president, to release it to the gay community by marketing it as an over-the-counter "food supplement." Lippa refused, claiming that he couldn't take part in such a scheme because he was waiting for an IND approval from the FDA to conduct further clinical trials.

So Sonnabend, Roach, and Hannan explored methods of manufacturing the drug themselves. With several medical students, they assembled generators, vacuum pumps, and pressure cookers, and brewed the foul-smelling concoction of flammable acetone and egg yolks by hand in Hannan's bathtub. The process yielded nothing of value. AL-721 was indeed difficult to make. For the large quantities they had in mind, the drug would almost certainly have to be produced by major pharmaceutical firms with quality-control standards. Even then, batch contamination or inaccuracy of the drug's ratio was likely.

Meanwhile, Steve Gavin located a small company in New Jersey that was able to produce a small supply of the compound and ultimately found a source that could produce a larger quantity. Hannan convinced Michael Callen to lend his public relations and promotional skills to the project.

Hannan and Callen chose the name "People With AIDS Health Group." They decided it would be structured as a nonprofit institution. Shortly after founding the club, Hannan and Callen collected $25,000 from hundreds of New York PWAs who wanted AL-721. It was distributed to them on May 4, 1987, from a refrigerated truck located in a church parking lot.

Through word of mouth, hundreds of AIDS patients nationwide began requesting information on obtaining AL-721. In its first year of operation, the PWA Health Group of New York sold $1 million worth of AL-721. At its peak, the buyers' club was handling several hundred kilos a month. By the fall of 1987, at least three companies in California were offering their own version of AL-721 for sale as a nutritional health product. Such products as "Eggstract" and "Lecithat" each adapted a different extraction method in their syntheses.

By mid-1988, the group had added other products to its list

and by 1989 had set up offices in the same building as the PWA Coalition on West Twenty-sixth Street in New York, and was supplying more than 1,500 customers in almost every major American city.

Hannan, Callen, and Sonnabend had a vision, and the purity of that vision prevailed. The trio believed that PWAs and their doctors had the right to decide their own courses of treatment, including the right to purchase substances that had demonstrated manageable degrees of toxicity, whether or not they had proven effective. Even if no winning antiviral existed now, chances were good that an effective drug would eventually emerge. When it did, PWAs had the right to early access to that medication through an institution already in place, without having to await the outcome of traditional clinical trials. The group's mission then, as it is now, was to deliver the highest quality and most up-to-date products at the lowest possible price. The PWA Health Group was able to pressure manufacturers and distributors into lowering their prices and refining the quality of their products at the same time. And by buying in volume, the group was able to exert substantial influence on the market price of experimental drugs.

Hannan became less involved in the group in 1988 in order to expand his participation with the New York Community Research Initiative (CRI) with Callen, Sonnabend, and Mathilde Krim. The CRI's mission was to perform research on promising anti-HIV medications outside the walls of traditional clinical trials and university settings but with the same precision and accuracy and with the legal sanctions of the IND and IRB, unlike the underground studies. It was the CRI that was responsible for a trial that ultimately led to the approval of using aerosolized pentamidine to prevent PCP. And most recently, the CRI was responsible for the completion of a multicenter trial that showed the drug rifabutin (Ansamycin) to be effective in the prevention of *Mycobacterium avium*, which had become among the most common of the AIDS opportunistic infections. On some level, our underground studies were akin to guerrilla warfare—an aggressive bid by PWAs and their doctors to gain formal control over the research process, and to decide what drugs would be developed, to whom they should be given, and under what circumstances, and then to evaluate them quickly. The CRI was more like civilized combat, through which doctors and patients would also gain control over the research process, but by observing the rules of mainstream protocol.

When Hannan relinquished leadership of the New York Buyers' Club in 1988, the group came under the executive directorship of Derek Hodel. Under Hodel's direction, the club was the first to offer for sale fluconazole, an antifungal drug useful in the treatment of candidiasis and cryptococcal meningitis. Most notably, the club made available pentamidine at a substantially reduced rate. Since the demand for the drug had burgeoned in the fall of 1989, the American company manufacturing the product had raised the price to an all-time high, charging as much as $100 for a single ampule. Hodel managed to find a source in London that manufactured the drug and was willing to sell it at a greatly reduced price. He offered it through the buyers' club for $40 per ampule. People who would otherwise have been unable to afford monthly pentamidine treatments were suddenly given access to the important therapy; many of them purchased nebulizers and rented pumps, and self-administered the medication at home.

By 1991, the PWA Health Group of New York had grown into a mainstream service provider serving more than 3,000 PWAs across the country. The organization maintained a list of 5,000 clients and operated an advanced distribution system, a sophisticated mail-order operation, and full-time staffers. In 1990, Jim Corti announced the formation of the Los Angeles Buyers' Club and named himself as president. In that process, he made official a role that he had informally assumed since the beginning of the epidemic.

The buyers' clubs were not formally regulated by the FDA or any other governmental agency. The potential for charlatans and profiteers to take advantage of unwitting AIDS patients with contaminated products, shoddy manufacturing, or even outright fraud was therefore great. Amazingly enough, most of the major clubs were run by committed, conscientious individuals, many of them PWAs themselves who often possessed a more thorough understanding of the HIV pharmacological scene than certain research-and-development executives in private industry. Their primary goal was to ensure the safety of the PWAs they served, to have all batches of internationally obtained products tested for purity, and to encourage all PWAs to take the drugs under the supervision of an experienced physician.

In September 1991, an FDA representative told activists at a San Francisco meeting that "the FDA had become increasingly concerned about buyers' clubs and had decided to conduct inspections." He emphasized that the agency did not intend to shut down the clubs and acknowledged that they performed an important function within the AIDS community.

The FDA expressed more specific concerns in only the broadest terms. The agency was supposedly concerned about the distribution of potentially dangerous or contaminated drugs, or those that had been obtained or synthesized in underground labs and had not yet been approved for Phase 1 testing. There was also concern about "promotion." Although most of the buyers' clubs never advertise and are listed only in the phone book, the FDA's mandate was to ensure that any promotional activities were truthful, balanced, and not misleading. The FDA was also concerned with excessive profiteering. The PWA Health Group of New York, for instance, is a not-for-profit organization but it still makes money—money not distributed to individuals connected with the organization. Reportedly, the FDA's inspection would include an examination of a buyers' club's assets, liabilities, and balance sheets. Finally, the FDA seemed unhappy when buyers' clubs undercut American manufacturers' prices on drugs already approved. For example, Fujisawa's NebuPent (aerosolized pentamidine) retails for $100 to $175 per ampule, while another brand of the product is available through the PWA Health Group of New York for $44 per ampule.

Perhaps one of the most significant contributions of the buyers' clubs was the early access to ddC that they provided for thousands of patients.

In the fall of 1990, ACT UP Golden Gate and Project Inform simultaneously called upon the FDA to license both ddI and ddC by December 31 of that year. Project Inform launched an initiative and quietly recruited the support of more than 150 AIDS groups. ACT UP Golden Gate took to the streets in two major demonstrations targeting the FDA and its antiviral chief Ellen Cooper and congressional watchdog Congressman Ted Weiss of New York, who died in October 1992. More than two dozen demonstrators were arrested.

ACT UP's Barry Freehill, who was among those arrested, took a more intellectual approach by drafting a citizen's petition to the FDA. The burden of proof of a drug's efficacy, Freehill argued, should not be based on its superiority or even equivalence to AZT. Moreover, efficacy need not be proven for monotherapy, he insisted, citing Margaret Fischl's research, which established that AZT worked much better and longer if combined with ddC. Despite activist pressures and Fischl's impressive research data, Cooper and other FDA officials insisted on comparing ddI and ddC monotherapy with AZT monotherapy, all the while discounting the potential value of combinational therapy. For AIDS patients, however, combining ddC with AZT offered new hope; but because the FDA insisted on dismissing combination therapy as "unproven," patients were not permitted access to ddC for combinational use from Hoffmann-La Roche's expanded-access program. They had nowhere to turn but to the underground.

Fortunately, ddC was a relatively inexpensive chemical, available in pharmaceutical grade in at least a dozen U.S. supply houses. As early as 1987, Steve Gavin had obtained a small batch and distributed it to his buyers' group. In 1989, Ron Woodruff of the Dallas Buyers' Club sold a version of ddC obtained through underground researcher Jack Gerhardt.

In the spring of 1990, a small Santa Cruz company named

Intrend, which had previously distributed AL-721 and DHEA, began supplying capsules of ddC to all the major buyers' clubs at a cost of $25 per bottle. Jim Corti eventually took over the distribution-and-manufacturing operation from Intrend. For several months, he continued to obtain ddC in bulk from Intrend—an arrangement that resulted in some 20,000 bottles being sold at a cost of $45 each. In July 1991, Corti found a less expensive bulk source than Intrend, and his total product cost dropped from $15 to less than $10.60 per bottle. He reduced his price to $35 a bottle. He continued to search for an even less expensive bulk supplier of ddC and eventually found one in Düsseldorf. He again lowered his price—this time to $30 a bottle.

While ddC continued to be available through Phase 2 clinical trials, many more patients were obtaining the drug from Corti or through the New York PWA Health Group. Rather than refer their patients to Hoffmann-La Roche's expanded-access program or to the ongoing clinical trials, many doctors simply gave the patients one of Corti's fifteen buyers' club phone numbers. The demand for ddC had burgeoned nationwide exponentially.

Everything seemed to be going smoothly until January 1992. Hoffmann-La Roche had recently heard from doctors and patients who had purchased ddC through buyers' clubs that the drug was inducing swelling in their hands and feet—side effects that should not have been characteristic at the stated doses. Hoffmann-La Roche's own chemists discovered that the underground ddC contained between one-half and three times the stated doses of the drug—significant because ddC has a narrow "therapeutic window": too little could be ineffective, and too much could prove toxic. The scientists hypothesized that some of the side effects reported could have been due to improper dosages, and they reported their suspicions to the FDA.

On January 15, 1992, apart from its general inspection of the buyers' clubs, the FDA asked the clubs' permit inspectors to collect samples of the underground ddC in order to verify the reports independently in their own labs. Ten days later, the FDA's tests of ddC from three buyers' clubs revealed variations in potency of between 0 and 230 percent—that is, some ddC capsules contained over two times the declared amount of the drug and some contained none at all. Based on these tests, the FDA strongly urged the buyers' clubs to discontinue their distribution of ddC and to alert patients to its potential hazards. In conjunction with other clubs across the country, the PWA Health Group in New York immediately discontinued distribution and informed both clients and doctors of the situation.

By May 1992, a newly formulated ddC was created, "quality-controlled," in the words of one buyers' club, "to an inch of its life," and once again began distributing the drug. One month earlier, the FDA had finally recommended approval of ddC for combinational use with AZT.

Hoffmann-La Roche, meanwhile, broadened its expanded-access program and made the drug available free of charge for combinational use with AZT to people whose CD4 cell counts had fallen below 300.

Why had the underground ddC temporarily gone bad? According to one activist source, Corti's second supplier was not as conscientious as the first; ddC was electrostatic and had a tendency to clump, and without proper monitoring during mixage it could easily create pockets of extremely high or low potency—very likely what occurred in the second batch.

The buyers' clubs did not fulfill the same role as such activist organizations as ACT UP. They didn't directly lobby for legislation in FDA drug policy or become involved in lawsuits. For the most part, the clubs maintained a low profile, yet they had the capacity to be even more litigious than the activist groups. The PWA Health Group, for instance, sued Burroughs Wellcome to break its strangle-hold on the AZT patent. Woodruff himself personally became involved in litigation over the acquisition of a still-investigational drug, Peptide T.

Although I occasionally obtained products through buyers' clubs, more often than not I obtained them elsewhere. As a highly active member of the drug underground myself, I had over the years established my own sources for purchasing experimental medications.

It must be noted that like parallel track, the buyers' clubs and the CRI posed a very real threat to the established ATEU clinical trial system. Enrollment in the principal investigators' clinical trials had already been steadily declining; with the formation of the buyers' clubs, fewer and fewer AIDS and ARC patients were entering the ATEU trials—which often included placebo controls and sometimes required an extensive commitment of time—choosing instead to purchase experimental medications or enter a CRI trial to obtain them. It came as no surprise, then, that certain principal investigators denounced the buyers' clubs and the CRI just as they had castigated the underground studies of trichosanthin.

On March 15, 1990, David Wilson was diagnosed with colonic cytomegalovirus infection (CMV). The virus had become entrenched in his intestinal tract and was causing diarrhea and intense stomach cramps. Astonishingly, a leading AIDS physician in south Florida had been unable to diagnose the virus; it was only after David was examined by the Mayo Clinic in Jacksonville that the pathogen was discovered.

The new diagnosis meant that David had crossed the line from ARC to full-blown AIDS. Several weeks later, he was told he had CMV retinitis; the CMV had disseminated to his left eye. The odds were that he would lose the sight in it.

"I'm moving to San Francisco," he told me. "I'll be staying in Pacific Heights with my wife and daughter. If this is the end, I want us all to be together in a place where I can get the best treatment."

He explained that he would have the opportunity to enter an experimental protocol there evaluating the effectiveness of intravenous ganciclovir in CMV retinitis. If the therapy began early enough, perhaps his sight could be preserved.

He also knew that the longer his immune system continued to

be chronically and profoundly suppressed (his current CD4 cell count was 23) the more likely he would suffer still more opportunistic infections—even in addition to CMV. He desperately needed to get out of the hole, to find some way of bringing his CD4 cell count out of the danger zone.

In much the same way that a burgeoning underground market for experimental anti-HIV drugs had emerged in the early 1980s, a similar one was now developing for drugs with the potential to help memory disorder diseases such as Alzheimer's.

Alzheimer's is primarily a cortical dementia, so-named because it affects the brain's neocortex, or outer covering. Its clinical hallmarks include *aphasia,* a loss of the power to use or understand words; *apraxia,* the loss of ability to manipulate objects; and *agnosia,* the loss of ability to remember familiar objects or people.

HIV dementia, from which I suffered, is a *sub*cortical dementia, affecting structures such as the basal ganglia and hippocampus, and clinically manifested more as difficulty with sequential tasks and concentration, errors in reasoning, and diminished analytical skills than by any deficiencies in language or global intelligence. In certain respects, subcortical and cortical dementias are related; there is some overlap, and I realized that drugs being used in Europe for Alzheimer's and available through mail-order pharmacies there held the potential to help my own condition.

Pharmacies and buyers' clubs such as In-Home Health Services in Zurich and Interlab in London offered memory-enhancing drugs and "cognitive enhancers" with names like Nootropil and Lucidril for sale, much as their American counterparts did. As in the field of immunomodulators and antivirals, there existed various classes of cognitive enhancers with specific modes of action and effects. Indeed, I obtained detailed literature and information on many of these drugs and tried a few of the most theoretically promising. Unfortunately, none demonstrated the power to reverse the condition that had befallen me.

According to Camus, there is but one truly serious philosophical problem: suicide. Suicide among the *well* poses an even more complex problem than suicide among the *sick*, whose physical and mental well-being may have been robbed by an insidious illness, especially at an early age.

I thought about the AIDS patients I had known who had taken their own lives—a Miami physician whose mind had been decimated by dementia. He sat in his car as carbon monoxide fumes streamed in, bringing a painless death. Then there was the pre-med student who progressed from ARC to AIDS. He read literature published by the Hemlock Society, and when he began to suffer excruciating bouts of neuropathy, he committed suicide. There was also the case of the AIDS patient who begged his lover to end his life with a single gunshot. The lover did, and was ultimately tried and convicted of manslaughter. And there was Michael Bristow from my Shanti group in Los Angeles, whose drug overdose kept him in a coma for almost two weeks prior to his demise, a suicide that was deliberately intended to inflict guilt on his family. And still I wondered: at the moment just before the end came, if there was an *awareness* during that final irreversible stasis, would any of them have wished they could have it all back? I knew that there was at least no more extended coma, cognitive decline, blindness, or indignity for those who chose to end their own lives.

I tried to picture myself as one of life's lucky survivors, but the image didn't play very convincingly. In the early stages of my illness, I had been able to understand its emotional component—the depression of being chronically ill—deal with it effectively, and get on with my life. Now, however, I was constantly reminded of the pathology that was mine. With every derailed thought, every blunted emotion, every spark of motivation that was extinguished, I found myself confronting a problem larger than any I could ever have contemplated or prepared for. Overwhelmed by depression, I no longer felt fulfilled, whole. I'd been robbed of the one weapon I most desperately needed to win this unwinnable war: my mind. Whole aspects of my personality and even identity were affected. I felt I had become an intellectual cripple of sorts, unable to perform analytical reasoning and creative thinking with the speed and clarity that had once been innate. At the height of my cognitive powers, I could read a passage from the most complex textbook and immediately grasp its full implications. More important, I could instantly commit it to long-term memory while simultaneously analyzing its content. Now, I had to re-read passages over and over to make them stick and even then, they were not easily assimilated.

I found that because of my reduced "working" short-term memory, my reading span had decreased. I was unable to store the first portion of a sentence in my mind; by the time I reached its conclusion, I'd forgotten the gist of the thought.

My mental flexibility and fluidity were also affected; I lacked the ability to interpret a written or spoken thought as I once had. When following a news broadcast or scientific lecture, I had always been able to guess the next logical thought and the one after, long before the presenter had spoken them. Now it was a chore to keep up with the immediate line of reasoning, never mind anticipating the logical progression. I found myself having to "catch" my thoughts, which were fleeting and short-lived.

I also noticed a disruption in my visual/spatial and linear sequencing abilities. I found it difficult to absorb an image as simple and striking as a stop sign.

While I slept, my dreams had been filled with strangely logical, creative stories that were populated with colorful characters. Now my dreams were muddled and senseless.

I'd often had intense daydreams in which images, stories, and solutions to problems would emerge as if by magic. I was able to develop, evaluate, and verify those stories, analyzing and improving upon them in seconds. There were no more daydreams now, no more solutions to problems, no more creative stories.

Prior to June 1990, I had been able to compose intelligent expository text, but not true prose. Yet with the help of editing, taped transcripts, and my journal—much of it completed prior to the onset of HIV dementia—I was able to write this book.

All the cognitive deficiencies I describe here are related to the function of the hippocampus, basal ganglia, and other subcortical structures, structures rich in such neurotransmitters as norepinephrine, acetylcholine, and substance P, all of which showed decreased blood flow on my SPECT (single photon emission computerized tomography) brain scan. Ironically, elements of my general language, speech, global intelligence, and reasoning were left intact; consequently, few people suspected anything was wrong or even believed me when I attempted to tell them the truth. Thus, while I spoke far more slowly, I still spoke accurately. Few diseases, I thought, held the diabolical ability to erode parts of the mind while leaving others intact to record the phenomenon.

Speed of speech was not the only element of my demeanor affected. My tone of voice shifted downward, and my inflection changed perceptibly. It was as if I had adopted the characteristics of a different person.

In addition to cognitive changes, I also experienced dizziness and mental lethargy, which did not show up on tests of balance or equilibrium or sinus series. They were always with me and contributed to my lack of energy and stamina. I became unmotivated and apathetic. I was no longer easily excited when confronted with novelty. Friends who visited me in Florida described me as "less charismatic" and "eccentric." I enjoyed fewer peak experiences and became more solitary, often withdrawing from group activities.

I watched as many of my peers from college climbed the ladder of success and achieved significant accomplishments in their lives and careers. The disease had robbed me of the talents and gifts upon which my career had been based. I felt as if I had been hurled into a twilight existence.

There were new and more advanced theories to explain HIV dementia: an excess uptake of calcium, a neurotoxin called quinolinic acid which overstimulates certain receptors, the drug NMDA. But there were far fewer possibilities to erase the condition's horrible effects and I found myself sinking into a gray mire.

In the summer of 1990, I went on strike from life. It happened one evening. As I drove down a street in a low-rent district of Fort Lauderdale, it seemed as if I was suddenly transported to a different planet: the strangeness of all things and my alienation from the world hit me in an epiphany. The tenements I passed seemed to me no more than anthills or caves with people cowering in them; civilization had given way to poverty and misery. I became afraid of what I suddenly perceived as the primitive nature of street lights. Here we were in the latter half of the twentieth century and all we could really do was mount simplistic lights on sticks to try to illuminate the darkness. I could see it was not going to work. Biotechnology was still too crude and was going to fail me. It all seemed so clear to me.

I came to a stop. I changed directions and backtracked hurriedly to my apartment. I felt caged in there, vexed and worried. I was tired, but insomnia also plagued me. It would take hours for me to fall asleep, only to suddenly wake up, dazed and unhappy.

I lay on my bed, my head on the pillow, barely aware of the silken breeze from the window that brushed my arms. I felt I had become someone else; since I felt the person I had been was already gone, there was no reason to continue as a stand-in, a ghost of the original. The simple logic of this argument won me over. So did fate. To fight it would be silly. I swallowed the contents of my bottles of Nembutal and Seconal, given to me by a friend in Miami. And before I passed out, I remembered to take acetaminophen to prevent vomiting.

It didn't work. I woke up, still a part of my life, feeling groggy and disoriented, unable to appreciate the irony that even now, medicine had failed me.

CHAPTER 13

COLD CHOICES

I didn't get out of bed for what seemed like days, and not just because I had lost all feeling in my right leg. A paralysis of the will was really what pinioned me. The phone rang but I didn't answer it. Why respond to anybody, I wondered. People drifted in and out of my room like specters or figures from a dream. But I couldn't concentrate on what they said.

Time meant nothing until one morning I felt the sun on my cheek and a breeze drifted through the curtains to caress me. I was shocked to find that a world still existed outside my numbness and self-pity. I realized that if I wanted anything from it, no one was going to bring it to me. I got up, showered and got on with the business of living.

Luiz Vasquez was a Miami physician diagnosed with ARC. Born in Cuba, he emigrated to America as a teenager. He obtained his medical degree at the University of Salamanca in Spain, and trained at Jackson Memorial Hospital in Miami. Eventually, he became an anesthesiologist and a part-owner of a Miami hospital. He was handsome, with an athletic build, expressive eyes, and a masculine

Latino presence. Luiz seemed to have what so many spend a lifetime striving for—good looks, an expensive home, an attractive lover. He had been in the process of ascending to the pinnacle of his career. Over the course of the last year, however, he had watched in vain as his CD4 cell count plummeted. No antiviral drug or immunomodulator seemed able to stop the decline.

He had gone on disability in March and now saw a small number of HIV-positive patients in an office in his South Miami Avenue home, where he and his lover, Stuart, lived. Even six months ago, it seemed, he had much to look forward to, despite his HIV-positive status. Now all that had changed. He was plagued by bouts of fatigue, diarrhea, and malaise, his career unceremoniously interrupted.

I met him at a seminar at the University of Miami. We quickly became friends and scoured the latest literature for new approaches to treating HIV. In the abstracts to the Sixth International Conference on AIDS, we paid particular attention to new *in vitro* discoveries; one of them was a series of traditional Chinese medicines discovered by David Ho and his colleagues at Cedars–Sinai Medical Center in Los Angeles. One of Dr. Ho's colleagues had worked as a pediatrician in Beijing and had used the medicines to treat such ailments as hepatitis, pneumonia, and heart disease. In Ho's assay, ten of the fifty-six compounds screened were found to have dose-dependent inhibitory activity on HIV replication.

Luiz and I located a cardiologist at the Beijing Institute of Traditional Chinese Medicine who agreed to send us a large supply of three of the compounds. Following label indications and dosages—but, in some cases, using slightly higher doses—we conducted an underground tracking study in some of Luiz's patients with the medicines, but no positive benefits were noted.

Luiz, David Wilson, and I were among the 12,000 people to attend the Sixth International Conference on AIDS, which was held in San Francisco in 1990. It appeared to us to be more a clash between activists and scientists than a dignified exchange of information among researchers. Throughout the four-day event, members of ACT UP staged demonstrations outside the Moscone Convention Center. About 120 people were arrested as they blocked entrance-ways, lay down on the sidewalks to symbolize those who had died in the epidemic, and clashed violently with police.

Inside the convention center, conflict between the mainstream establishment and activist researchers brewed on an even more complex scale. Dr. Arnold Relman, editor of the prestigious *New England Journal of Medicine*, lambasted Martin Delaney's Compound Q data, saying, "We mustn't resort to black magic." He also called Delaney "irresponsible" for releasing data on Compound Q prior to its publication in a review journal. (The data was not slated to be published for another three months.) For safety reasons, Margaret Fischl, who had been universally vilified for her seemingly singular support of AZT, was escorted onstage by a group of burly men.

Luiz, David, and I were virtually inseparable. We sat in on the various plenary sessions and presentations of abstracts, carefully choosing those we found most relevant to our own situations. We also arranged to meet with several top researchers, three of whom we knew from extensive conference calls on the phone.

One of these was John Dwyer, head of the School of Medicine at the University of New South Wales in Sydney. Dwyer realized the significance of the dysfunctional thymus in AIDS and ARC. In 1986, while head of the Yale University Division of Clinical Immu-nology, he successfully transplanted human thymic tissue into fif-teen AIDS patients. He obtained the thymic tissue while performing surgery to correct congenital heart defects in young children. Since the thymus gland of AIDS patients is infected with HIV and degen-erates after death and since it is essential in the maturation of CD4 lymphocytes, Dwyer reasoned that thymic tissue transplantation was an essential element in any attempt to reconstitute the immune system of AIDS patients. Unfortunately, Dwyer found that none of the patients experienced significant increases in CD4 cells three months after the transplant. Only two developed an improved capacity to produce a delayed hypersensitivity response. There were, however, modest increases in CD8 cells and slight improvements in blastogenic responses.

In the short term, however, the therapy did result in some clinical improvement. In one patient, severe CMV retinitis cleared spontaneously. Two cases of tuberculosis improved, resistant PCP cleared within hours of the transplant, and previously intractable diarrhea of unknown origin vanished in another case as well. However, the apparently impressive clinical results were not borne out in the long run. In the months to come, most of the subjects developed opportunistic infections; eighteen months after the transplant, only three were still alive.

Dwyer concluded that transplanting thymic tissue alone was probably not enough to achieve full immune reconstitution. The thymus needed a healthy population of stem-cell lymphocytes to act on, and thus the transfer of bone marrow stem cells, liver, spleen, and perhaps even lymph node cells might be necessary. Furthermore, HIV and its cytokines were persistent pathogens, and some type of effective antiviral therapy needed to be given concurrently to prevent the thymocytes from being attacked again. The simultaneous early administration of interleukin-2 (IL-2) would also greatly aid in the rapid activation and proliferation of CD8 cells and induce the production of CD4 cells that might mature in the transplanted thymus.

Finally, by the time they reached eighteen years of age, most adults had dysfunctional thymuses. Despite this fact, those who experienced immune suppression because of intensive chemotherapy all showed a normalization of their CD4 cell counts after the negative stimulus to the immune system was removed or a behavior altered. Even if these patients' CD4 cell counts had fallen to levels as low as those of some AIDS patients, the CD4 cells often managed to rejuvenate spontaneously—without a thymus to "educate" them. This fact hinted that HIV infection was doing something other than merely destroying the thymus.

Still, Dwyer believed that thymic transplantation therapy—in combination with other therapeutic modalities—held great promise for AIDS. When we met, he revealed plans to conduct a Phase 2 trial of epithelial fragmented thymic transplantation combined with IL-2 and AZT among ARC and AIDS patients in Australia. He told us he believed that the combined therapy might well provide an effective maintenance therapy for AIDS.

As we concluded the meeting, Dwyer put his arm around David's shoulder. "Don't worry," he said. "I'll make sure you're one of the first to be in my study. You're a courageous young man and I admire your tenacity."

We talked to Dr. Joseph Cummins, whose early experiments with oral interferon had shown promising results in treating HIV.

We also met with researchers from Palo Alto who had recently announced a stunning achievement: the successful transplantation of a human immune system into laboratory mice. The researchers accomplished this remarkable feat by using a mouse strain with severe combined immunodeficiency (SCID), a defect that prevented the mice from producing functional CD4 or B cells. The mice readily accepted the grafts because they could not distinguish between self and non-self.

The transplanted grafts included blood precursor stem cells, thymus, and lymph nodes, all harvested from human fetal tissue. The appearance of mature human CD4 cells and human antibodies in the blood of the graft-recipient mice showed the implanted tissue to be intact and functioning.

The mice with the human immune systems, which became known as the SCID/HU mice, provided an invaluable model for medical research. Rather than test promising experimental agents in animals with nonhuman immune systems, researchers could now evaluate compounds in animals with human immune systems. But the scientific advances also suggested a striking implication for a cure for human AIDS. If a human immune system could be built into a mouse from the ground floor up, why couldn't it just as easily be built into immunosuppressed humans?

Later it occurred to us that it would be feasible to attempt

full-scale immune reconstitution in humans with AIDS by transplanting not just fetal-cell thymus plus IL-2 but bone-marrow precursor
cells *and* liver and spleen, in a manner similar to the SCID/HU mouse
model. Theoretically, the developing precursor cells would migrate
to the newly transplanted thymus and spleen, achieve differentiation
and identity, learn "self" recognition, and ultimately become attached
to already immunocompetent cells of the host. I even suggested this to
the SCID/HU mouse researchers and, although they agreed it might
be possible, they pointed out that such an experiment would have
overwhelming logistical and theoretical barriers. As in Dwyer's own
thymic transplant experiments, it would be necessary to select tissue
with compatible HLA typing for the recipient. The odds of finding
such compatibility might be slim. Second, if fetal cells were used, it
would be crucial to determine the most appropriate stage of maturation of the fetal cells prior to harvesting to ensure the cells' best
viability *in vivo*. Third, it would be necessary to establish an optimum
process for transplanting the cells, including the scheduling and
placement of the cells. Much could be learned from the SCID/HU
mouse experiments, but the best methodology in humans would still
be unknown. More important, even though the AIDS patient's cell-
mediated immune system is devastated, other components of his or
her immune system—including CD8 cells, B cells, and natural killer
cells—are often intact and even functional. It would certainly be
necessary to temporarily suppress those components prior to the
operation to prevent graft-versus-host or host-versus-graft disease.
Of course, some effective antiviral treatment would have to be given
prior to the procedure, and continue permanently after it, to ensure
that the new immune system was not reattacked by HIV and the
body's cytokines. Finally, there would be the difficulty of harvesting
and obtaining human fetal tissue, due to the virtual embargo in
America on its use for human experimentation.

The tiny noses of the small white rabbits looked to me like moving
powder puffs. There were four of them in the cage, situated on a

platform in the back of David Wilson's home. As the animals breathed, their sides moved, almost in unison.

Transfixed, I watched as David gently smoothed liquid preparation into the rabbit's eyes. The creature made no attempt to avoid human contact but merely twitched its ears. I stroked one of the animals gently.

"Is that the HPMPC?" I asked.

"Yes," he said. "It was prepared by the chemist in Seattle. An intra-ocular dose. Just like humans get."

Despite the ganciclovir treatment, the sight in his left eye had deteriorated. Even intra-ocular doses of the ganciclovir had failed to control the virus's growth. David had spent countless hours relentlessly tracking down new therapies for CMV. He had heard of a new drug, HPMPC, which, *in vitro*, outperformed ganciclovir and Foscarnet and appeared to be safe. He contacted Antonin Holy, the drug's inventor, in Czechoslovakia and requested a small amount of the compound. When Holy refused to send the drug, David found a San Francisco chemist with the equipment and chemicals needed to synthesize the drug. Now, he was testing it on the rabbits—along with several other promising anti-CMV compounds—to determine its basic toxicity.

"It's like performing your own animal studies," I said. Images of Rob Springer came to mind.

"You might say that. It's not a perfect animal model. But with the rabbits, I can at least gauge a drug's basic level of toxicity before I decide to use it."

He paused and wiped his hands on a cloth. "The animals that go blind are sold to a dealer in Oakland. None are destroyed."

Later, David and I chatted over teriyaki chicken and chow mein at a restaurant in Chinatown. He only picked at his food. I could tell that his appetite was waning. "We've been through so much together," he started. "I can't believe it's been two years already."

"I know," I said. "This thing has dragged on so long. How did you know you were first losing your sight?"

"It's hard to describe. It started with those damn cotton wool spots. Like patches or puffs of clouds in the retina is how one ophthalmologist described it to me. But they were stable and my vision wasn't adversely affected. Then I started to notice that my field of vision in the left eye narrowed, my vision became blurry . . . almost as if someone had pulled a curtain over a portion of my sight. But that's just the mechanical part of it. Losing your sight is like losing a part of your soul."

There was a pause. He looked down at his plate and said quietly, "I used to be so strong. I was able to fight this so much more easily in the beginning. It's harder now. Even my vocal tone has changed. I don't have authority in my voice now."

"You're still strong. A lot stronger than most everyone else," I reminded him.

"You know, if I completely lose my sight from this thing, it's going to be harder to fight," he went on. "My morale just isn't going to be as strong."

I wondered how I would cope with blindness. "Don't worry," I reassured him. "We'll get the new drugs. There's always retinal transplants. If you can reconstitute your immune system somewhat, the retinitis will disappear on its own, just the way it did in Dwyer's thymic transplant experiment."

"This disease strips you of your freedom," he said. "It strips you of your honor."

Tears formed in his eyes. He gripped my hand. "You don't know how hard it is to tell your child that her father may not be around much longer. What happens if my wife gets sick too? Will my child go through life knowing both her parents died of AIDS?"

We fell silent for a long moment.

"Thank you, Paul. Thank you for being a friend."

On July 10, 1990, David lost the sight in his left eye. He nevertheless managed to maintain a bright and cheerful façade, but I could tell he was torn apart inside. And I could see fear stamped on the faces of his wife and daughter. Yet even in the midst of his own tragedy and confronting almost certain total blindness, David was selfless, supporting others who were even less fortunate than he. While in San Francisco, we visited a man who was dying of CMV in the lungs, and David held his hands and offered words of encouragement. He made conference calls with others in Los Angeles who had CMV retinitis.

On one level, I realized how dissimilar David and I were in certain ways. He was a straight yuppie, married, a political conservative. My own politics were far to the left. Yet we had formed an inseparable bond, an unlikely friendship forged not so much by social similarity or background but by a passionate desire to outlive a hideous plague, a resolution to be among the earliest survivors.

I was consistently amazed how HIV changed gay male relationships, for better and for worse. One of my mother's acquaintances, a schoolteacher named Richard Adams, was gay. He and his lover, Jack, lashed out at each other and fought constantly. It was remarkable that the two had managed to remain together for so long. But when Richard was diagnosed with AIDS in August 1990, their fighting ceased. They became an astonishingly happy couple, reaffirmed their love at the Metropolitan Community Church in Fort Lauderdale, and even tried to adopt a child. Perhaps it was guilt that played a role in the transformation, perhaps the impending knowledge that time had suddenly made a definitive claim on one of them.

Not so positive a change was experienced by Rodney and Billy. For years, Rodney had avidly pursued Billy, attracted to his rugged good looks, swimmer's build, and magnetic smile. In fact, Rodney secretly worshiped Billy, placing his picture on the wall above his dresser and fantasizing that Billy loved him as fully as he loved Billy. Billy didn't feel the same toward Rodney and insisted that their friendship remain platonic. In 1987 Billy was diagnosed with AIDS. Rodney offered to move in and help care for him. Billy refused. Six months later, Rodney was himself diagnosed with AIDS. Realizing that Rodney had substantial assets and insurance policies in Billy's name, Billy agreed to move in with him, even pretending to love him. When Rodney died two years later, he left everything to Billy, including a large house in Key West and $100,000 in insurance dividends. To this day, Billy lives in the ornate Key West mansion, caught in the terminal stages of AIDS, and facing his own demise—secure but alone.

And then there was Philip. Since 1979, he had faithfully taken care of three lovers who had succumbed to AIDS. But when he was diagnosed with the disease in March 1988, his own lover moved out and ended their three-year relationship. "I just can't cope with the burden," Philip's lover told me the day he left. In September 1990, Philip died alone in a hospice in downtown Miami.

My cognitive impairment seemed to be worsening. It was becoming harder and harder for me to organize my thoughts. I often substituted an incorrect word in conversation, particularly toward the end of sentences. For example, instead of saying, "I want to go to the store," I would say, "I want to go to the football." I was embarrassed by my frequent verbal *faux pas* and was becoming introverted and silent. And I experienced disorientation with regard to time. When I awoke in the mornings, I often did not know the day of the week or the date. I was unable to remember at what point a task stopped *or* started. My memory was shot; I was unable to remember the time of appointments, people's last names, or where I'd placed objects in the house.

Much to my frustration, most of the standard neurological tests continued to reveal no significant pathology. My spinal fluid was essentially normal in all parameters. Both my CT (computerized tomography) and MRI brain scans were normal, as was the standard EEG.

More advanced technologies, however, revealed subtle changes. The SPECT scan measures regional cerebral blood flow with a modified high-resolution camera that rotates 360 degrees around the brain and produces color images of areas with reduced blood flow. Mine revealed decreased flow to the basal ganglia, the left temporal lobes, and even the frontal lobes, and a patch of low intensity at the junction of the pons and cerebellum, in a brain structure known as the locus coeruleus. These lapses in the locus coeruleus and the left and right frontal lobes were especially significant, one neurologist explained. The locus coeruleus projected to the right frontal lobe with heavy concentrations of norepinephrine, an excitatory neurotransmitter that was thought to be linked to selective attention, concentration, and motivation—all cognitive processes that had been especially affected in my own case.

Like the SPECT, the BEAM (brain electronic advanced mapping) scan produces a color map of the brain's electrical activity. My scan showed abnormally slow delta and theta waves, sometimes associated with decreased concentration and verbal spontaneity.

In spite of all they revealed, the tests provided only vague clues about the parts of my brain that were not performing optimally and the ways in which they were malfunctioning. They neither provided specific information about the concentration of neurochemicals that might be depleted at certain sites, nor did they identify neural connections or receptors that might be blocked. Indeed, looking at the human brain with SPECT, BEAM, and even PET (positron emission tomography) was not dissimilar to gazing at the bottom of a shallow pond filled with muddy water and attempting to discern the intricacies of the surface below.

In short, no measure of my memory or cognitive ability could fully assess the damage that had been done to my brain and its true impact on my mental well-being.

Time was running out. I knew some radical tack would be required to cure AIDS or at least develop an effective maintenance therapy. It had become strikingly clear that once the CD4 cells fell and remained at values below a certain level, spontaneous immune reconstitution was unlikely, even with the help of the most potent antivirals. Full-scale immune reconstitution was necessary. My own

CD4 count had fallen to an all-time low of 65. I knew that there was a real chance I would cross over the line to full-blown AIDS.

It occurred to me that by using a technique not dissimilar to that in lymphocyte transfusion therapy, it might be possible to harvest an AIDS or ARC patient's remaining CD4 cells, grow them in glass or plastic, and then treat them with some genetic vector that could assure their long-term survival and even confer antiviral resistance to those still in the body that had not been treated. It may have sounded like science fiction in the fall of 1990, but various elements were already in place to make it happen.

Cytotoxic cells, a subpopulation of CD8 cells, are known to have definitive antiviral properties. Patients who remained stable as ARC or HIV-positive asymptomatics for years often had high levels of CD8 cells. Scientists now hypothesized that the cells exerted some type of protective effect, perhaps by suppressing the reproduction of HIV or abolishing the harmful cytokines produced in response to it. In a preliminary experiment following five treatments of autologous (the patient's own) CD8 cells, four of six patients showed partial resolution of hairy leukoplakia and partial regression of Kaposi's sarcoma.

And in a landmark experiment, NIH researchers R. Michael Blaese, W. French Anderson, and Kenneth Culver successfully propagated the CD4 lymphocytes of a five-year-old girl with inherited immune deficiency disease called SCID/ADA (severe combined immunodeficiency/adenosine deaminase) and, moreover, had treated them with a gene from a healthy cell spliced onto a retroviral vector. The researchers were able to produce short-term clinical remission.

The implications of the NIH researchers' experiments were obvious. Like a defective gene, HIV contributed to a loss of CD4 lymphocytes, which might be replaced with propagated cells containing bioengineered genetic vectors that would guarantee their long-term survival and proliferation. Designing and implementing such an experiment for AIDS, however, posed unique and even overwhelming theoretical problems. A portion of the CD4 cells harvested from an AIDS patient would contain active or latent HIV virus that would certainly multiply when the cells were cloned in the test tube. Some method would have to be developed to purge the cells of both active and latent virus, or effectively eliminate those virus-ridden cells prior to cell expansion.

Interleukin-2 was also known to be an efficient means of multiplying the cells in the SCID/ADA experiment and in cancer therapies, but its use in a potential AIDS experiment was less than desirable because CD4 cells grown in its presence typically died within forty-eight hours and did not cause the cells to be fully viable. Some other, more efficient chemical means of cell propagation would be required, one that would guarantee the cells' long-term survival *in vitro* and provide specific immunological memory.

Also, stem cells (cells from which *all* cells, including immune cells and CD4 cells, are derived), even more than peripheral cells, would seem preferable to use in the expansion process. But did an AIDS patient have enough of them left to make the experiment work? And even if he or she did, wouldn't it be necessary to stimulate their differentiation into mature lymphocytes prior to reinfusion?

Finally, once the cells were infused back into the body of an AIDS patient, ensuring their survival would be doubly problematic when compared to the ADA cells. In the case of AIDS, the cells would be reinfused back into a patient who had other cells rife with HIV and potentially harmful cytokines circulating around in the peripheral blood and tissues, cells that could potentially reinfect the newly cloned lymphocytes and destroy them within weeks of reinfusion. Some method would have to be developed to ensure the cells' long-term survival once reinfused.

For the next several weeks, I spent hours speaking on the telephone with researchers at biotechnology firms such as Oncogene in Seattle and Pacific Biologies Research in Berkeley. I pitched the potential AIDS treatment to them, got their feedback, and listened to their critiques of what might go wrong in each procedure, hoping against hope that I would find someone who had already considered the questions I currently contemplated and who had formulated a solution. It was becoming increasingly difficult for me to organize my thoughts and carry on a fast-paced conversation during those discussions, and I often found myself stammering in mid-sentence or losing my train of thought. It wasn't easy to understand the ideas some of the people discussed, and I frequently found myself asking them to repeat themselves.

Finally, a scientist at a laboratory in Chicago recalled that a Ph.D. candidate named Michael Gruenberg had proposed just such an idea to treat AIDS in 1988. I tracked Gruenberg down in Minneapolis, where he indicated that he had in fact proposed a process to restore immunocompetence in AIDS patients by expanding autologous CD4 and CD8 cells in specially designed artificial capillary bioreactors. Gruenberg agreed to send me a copy of his dissertation, completed for his Ph.D. in bioengineering.

In his thesis, Gruenberg neatly laid out a step-by-step plan to harvest white blood cells from AIDS patients and purify CD4 lymphocytes and anti-HIV CD8 lymphocytes. The plan also detailed a process whereby the purified CD4 lymphocytes could be purged of both latent and active HIV infection. Finally, an instrument and process was described that was capable of expanding the viral-free CD4 lymphocytes and the anti-HIV CD8 lymphocytes from a starting population of 1 million to nearly 100 billion cells.

Gruenberg's plan addressed many of the problems I had anticipated. And it confirmed my impression that IL-2 might not be the best growth mechanism for the CD4 cells. Instead, he suggested using anti-CD29 monoclonal antibodies, which he obtained from a researcher in Japan and which in several studies had been shown to be effective catalysts for the proliferation of the cells.

In a pilot experiment, Gruenberg presented evidence that CD4 cells taken from a late-stage AIDS patient could be successfully purified and expanded under his protocol and that these cells were functionally active and could restore normal natural killer cell function *in vitro*. These expanded CD4 cells were also shown by a sensitive p-24 antigen assay to be free of HIV. The purified and expanded CD8 cells were shown to have been capable of lysing autologous CD4 cells infected with HIV *in vitro*. In the pilot study the cells were not reinfused into the patient, and therefore it was impossible to determine if they would survive or maintain a functional viability in the human body.

Gruenberg proposed that a clinical protocol should involve giving an initial infusion of 100 billion lymphocytes and making the number of anti-HIV CD8 cells greater than the number of CD4 cells. He theorized that at the initial cellular infusion the CD8 cells would serve to reduce the viral burden of the patient, and that after reduction of the viral load, large numbers of CD4 cells could be infused to transfer immunocompetence back to the patient. In this manner, Gruenberg hoped that the restored immunocompetence would enable the patient to survive as an asymptomatic carrier.

In an updated conclusion to his dissertation, written after the completion of his pilot study, Gruenberg proposed additional strategies to ensure the protocol's success based on new findings in immunology. He suggested that the purified, viral-purged CD4 cells could be further purified to ensure the infusion of Th1 cells, a specific type of CD4 cells. Recent research had shown that the Th1 subset are the effectors in delayed hypersensitivity reactions while another subtype of CD4 cells, Th2 cells, may provide unwanted immunosuppression. Further, Gruenberg suggested that the infusion of a subset of CD4 cells known as *naive* cells would be preferable to using large numbers of cloned *memory* cells. Only reconstruction with naive cells would allow the immunocompromised patient to "relearn" his or her immune repertoire. And Gruenberg reported on recent studies that described specific markers of naive cells that would allow them to be distinguished from memory cells.

Further, in a pilot experiment using a novel, hollow-fiber cell-culture technology he helped develop, Gruenberg successfully purified, propagated, and virally purged the lymphocytes of a healthy patient and an HIV-positive patient. The cells were not reinfused.

With all the potential solutions that Gruenberg had worked out, problems still remained. Simultaneously reinfusing CD8 cells with the newly propagated CD4 cells would confer some resistance against reattack but provide no means of long-term survival.

Most important, CD4 cells were not generic and homogeneous. CD4 cells bore receptors that recognized specific peptides of specific organisms. The potential number of different specificities was in the hundreds of thousands. Each subtype worked against a specific type of pathogen. An AIDS patient with five CD4 cells circulating in each cubic millimeter of his or her peripheral blood hardly had enough variety, I was sure, to produce a full complement of heterogeneous lymphocytes active against a broad spectrum of pathogens, once expanded, even with the use of the naive cells. Possibly, a source of CD4 cells could be found that could guarantee a supply of more diverse cell types. A lymph node or even a tissue culture from the spleen, I hypothesized, represented two possibilities.

The use of stem cells that had been extracorporeally activated to express CD4 was yet another possibility. Indeed, it might be difficult to find a lab with the expertise and resources to accomplish the project, and that would be willing to work with HIV-infected cells. And if such a lab *could* be found, the scientists there would almost certainly demand that it undergo institutional-review-board approval and file an investigational new drug application with the FDA.

Other questions remained, one immunologist reminded me. Would the cells somehow change their surface characteristics once reinfused and be ineffective? Even if they did survive for an extended period, would the lymphocytes maintain a functional viability? Would the patient inherit various lymphotoxic cytokines along with the newly propagated cells, cytokines that could undermine the positive effect of the newly infused cells? And perhaps most important, would the simultaneous reinfusion of CD8 cells provide an effective antiviral cover for the viral-free CD4 cells?

I sent a copy of the dissertation to a dozen mainstream AIDS researchers and to David, along with a letter expressing my belief in the idea. I cautiously explained that the protocol was fraught with problems and that there was no guarantee that it would work at all. I also explained that as a means of full-scale immune reconstitution, the protocol had numerous theoretical and practical advantages over some of the other methods, including thymic transplant therapy. In lymphocyte transfusion therapy, the cells came from a donor and because of their genetic dissimilarity might have less probability of long-term viability. The cells in lymphocyte expansion therapy, however, are one's *own* and might, have a better chance of long-term survival. And even if the CD4 lymphocytes did not survive forever, perhaps they could be reinfused continuously over a three- to six-month period, creating a maintenance therapy in much the same way that insulin was used to treat chronic diabetes. It was a very long shot.

"I have a well-written screenplay; now I need a workable shooting script," I joked in a letter to David.

He called me the following day and revealed that his health had deteriorated but that he wanted to help with the project. "How fast could you get lymphocyte expansion up and running?" he asked.

"I don't know," I replied. "As fast as I can."

The following day, I received a wire for several thousand dollars. And a note in David's handwriting that simply said, "Make it happen!"

CHAPTER 14

LAB CULTURES

W hen I received the money that David had wired, I placed it, along with money that Luiz had contributed, in a special fund. The money would barely cover the start-up costs involved in mounting the lymphocyte expansion project—expenses such as photocopying, postage, and phone bills. But at least it would allow me to develop the project somewhat.

But how could I make this ambitious undertaking happen? I was only one boy at war. I had no formal training as a researcher, no way to scale the walls of Jericho. I had nothing but my own personal initiative and a subtly undermined left brain. It would have to be enough.

The first step was to find a laboratory—preferably one already involved in similar research—that had the facilities and human resources to successfully implement the complex series of steps Gruenberg had outlined. I needed a lab director who would be sympathetic to the objectives of the project—someone willing to enlist the aid of a wide variety of consultants if necessary, and work with both an institutional review board and the FDA to get the project approved. Finding both an appropriate setting and a cooperative director by calling individual labs—those capable of harvesting and expanding lymphocytes—would be like finding a needle in a haystack. I needed to reach the largest possible audience without delay.

After some deliberation, I decided to take out display ads in *Biotechnology News* and *Hybridoma*. Both would be read by the administrative personnel I needed to reach. Each half-page ad cost three hundred dollars and ran for a month.

LAB WANTED

FOR AUTOLOGOUS CD4/CD8 EXPANSION

Biotech lab with capability of identifying, harvesting, and expanding CD4 memory cells from AIDS patients' peripheral blood. Contact Paul Sergios at 305-555-2368.

Within the first week of the ad's appearance, there were no responses. In the second week, I received a call from a researcher who had been involved in LAK (lymphocyte activated killer) cell therapy for cancer. It was he who suggested that I contact Paul McClellan, an assistant professor of pharmacology and toxicology and the manager of the hybridoma laboratory at a university in Virginia.

Finding Dr. McClellan proved to be a pivotal turning point in the success of the project. He managed a small lab replete with an inverted tissue-culture microscope, culturing facilities, cell-separation equipment, and additional support facilities for medium preparation, flow cytometry, nucleic-acid synthesis, and human-tissue acquisition. More important, McClellan was knowledgeable in lymphocyte propagation. For the last two years, he had published widely on the most effective techniques for cell harvesting and growth. He had been involved in experiments that investigated the feasibility of propagating CD4 lymphocytes in AIDS patients and was the principal investigator on a project called "T Cell Expandability in AIDS." Like Gruenberg, he had formulated a step-by-step plan to successfully harvest and grow the cells, using blood from several AIDS patients. And like Gruenberg, he had not actually reinfused the cells into a patient in a clinical trial but was actively looking for the chance to do so. Our plan to do a Phase 1 clinical trial with three AIDS patients and three ARC patients provided him with the opportunity. It was a perfect match.

At the same time, David managed to find a doctor in San Francisco willing to supervise the reinfusion of the lymphocytes and serve as the pilot project's sponsor and principal investigator. The physician had been a longtime friend and ally of David's and instantly agreed to lead the lymphocyte expansion experiment. This was important for McClellan, since we'd had trouble finding a doctor in Virginia willing to serve as principal investigator. Many were involved in their own clinical studies; others simply didn't want to get involved in a maverick project that was risky and fiscally speculative.

In *Good Intentions,* Bruce Nussbaum concludes that only a few of the top American pharmaceutical companies understand the drug development system in America; small, creative firms stand little chance of succeeding in the current market or in dealing with the complex web of relationships among the FDA officials and NIH researchers who regulate drug development. Principal investigators and members of NIH committees, Nussbaum contends, often have agendas that are at odds with those of research-and-development executives in private industry. And certain companies simply lack an understanding of the logistics of the process.

Larry Kramer points out, too, in *Reports from the Holocaust,* that the FDA is actually a passive organization. Everything must be presented *to* it in a rigorous and organized fashion. Nowhere in the administration is there a mechanism for actively helping a small company that doesn't have the technical expertise or resources of a Burroughs Wellcome to maneuver through the IND and NDA maze.

To some extent, I found all of this to be true in my attempts to assemble the lymphocyte expansion project. Some companies seemed to share ideological and philosophical scientific viewpoints with key, top-level governmental scientists, and, on a more practical level, seemed to have better relationships with the FDA. These companies tended to be organized in the processing of paperwork, understood the precise and often mind-boggling requirements of drug development at the FDA, had already obtained cross-reference file numbers for products, were familiar with the IND process, and were able to provide the agency with everything it needed.

I also helped write a first draft of an IND application for the lymphocyte expansion project, based on Gruenberg's dissertation and copies of INDs I had been given for other, similar protocols. McClellan offered numerous suggestions for rewrites. I had been suffering from pain that radiated from my shoulders and chest down my arms, diagnosed by one doctor as HIV neuropathy. It was difficult to manipulate my fingers on the keyboard. And my impaired concentration and memory made it harder for me to keep my place and compose intelligent copy. The document, running into hundreds of pages, was extremely complex. Every piece of equipment, every reagent, every process used in the experiment had to be dissected and described in depth. The document contained about twenty sections, each with headings such as "Chemistry, Manufacturing and Control Data" and "Facilities and Investigators Data." There were flowcharts detailing each step, layouts of laboratories, and diagrams of reagents. What at one time would have taken me days now took weeks.

By December 10, 1990, I had a final version of an IND that detailed the procedure. McClellan revised it further and submitted it to the FDA.

In *Surviving AIDS*, Michael Callen argues vehemently that no AIDS patient—not even an asymptomatic one—should ever take AZT. "A healthy, asymptomatic HIV seropositive person taking AZT is like someone who detonates a thermonuclear warhead to rid his or her home of cockroaches," he writes.

Callen cites a number of reasons why AZT should be avoided at all costs. He points out that the modest CD4 cell increases typically seen in the first weeks of AZT therapy usually taper off and return to normal within sixteen to twenty weeks. On higher doses of the drug certain patients may, in the interim, pay a high price in bone-marrow toxicity. According to Callen, a French study of AZT, published in *Lancet*, which used a methodological design and execution that was superior to the American AZT trial and tracked patients over a longer period of time, established that "the benefits of AZT are limited to a few months for ARC and AIDS patients."

Callen further argues that AZT has no ability to control the reactivation of latently infected cells and that the decline in p-24 antigen, commonly seen with AZT therapy, occurs despite little or no change in the amount of free virus in the blood or its ability to culture HIV from latently infected lymphocytes. Contrary to the popular belief, he says, AZT does not extend life by preventing opportunistic infections; the increases in survival time for PWAs are most likely due to PCP prophylaxis—including aerosolized pentamidine therapy—and *not* AZT. Furthermore, some researchers have suggested that prolonged AZT therapy may increase the chance of an AIDS patient's developing lymphoma and may also cause impotence. Most important, the virus can begin mutating to evade the drug, becoming resistant to AZT within months of a patient's starting treatment. Researchers had found that such viral resistance appears as early as six months in late-stage patients and twelve months in early-stage patients.

Finally, Callen points out, AZT is a DNA chain terminator and holds the potential to destroy immature bone-marrow precursor cells, including white and red blood cells. To quote his mentor Dr. Joseph Sonnabend, "AZT is simply incompatible with life." My own experience with the drug, when I used it in combination with ddI and ddC, was that it did produce some short-term clinical and immunological benefit.

The truth about AZT, I suspected, was that it addressed one

distinct but perhaps relatively unimportant aspect of the disease's pathogenesis. At low doses and for a limited period of time, it probably did buy some time and improve the quality of life for PWAs, but it also required careful patient management to monitor its toxicity and might be made more effective in combination or rotation with ddI or ddC. In fact, most studies had shown that AZT did prolong survival and improve patients' condition, at least in the short term. However, Callen, Sonnabend, and other critics alleged that researchers developed AZT to the exclusion of other promising HIV antivirals. In 1990, more than 75 percent of all NIH-sponsored AIDS trials involved some combination of AZT therapy.

A former gymnast, Luiz Vasquez often enjoyed an occasional romp on the pommel horse or trampoline in the backyard of his South Miami home. Recently, however, the trampoline hadn't seen much activity, and Luiz now rarely visited the gym. He had been plagued by bouts of fatigue, a marked loss of energy, uncontrollable diarrhea, and oral thrush that would not respond to nystatin or other anti-fungal therapies. Worse still, Luiz watched as his CD4 cell count inexorably fell. The panoply of drugs he tried had not seemed to stop the rapid cell decimation.

In July 1990, Luiz told a friend, "I think the end is near. I just don't feel right these days."

Those of us who were friends with Luiz knew he had another problem to deal with—his lover, Stuart. Handsome and magnetic, Stuart had managed to beat the odds for the past six years. Although addicted to both cocaine and alcohol, he had nevertheless managed to function, maintaining his high-paying administrative position with the City of North Miami. He had been in and out of treatment clinics without success and was now growing worse. Luiz had been caught up in Stuart's dizzying spirals, which had been draining him both financially and emotionally; most recently, he was confronted with Stuart's erratic behavior and bizarre outbursts. We could see that he was torn between his need to free himself from this self-destructive behavior and his desire to lend his lover sustenance. Though his head told him what to do, he could not find it in his heart to force Stuart out.

Luiz had heard about a researcher in Morristown, New Jersey, named Emil Bisaccia. Dr. Bisaccia was about to publish a study documenting the effects of extracorporeal photophoresis in five ARC patients whose immunological parameters were similar to Luiz's own. Luiz literally waited at the door to the medical library when the article documenting Bisaccia's study arrived in August 1990. Rumor had it that the results had been extremely positive.

Indeed, as Luiz read the article, he learned that some apparently remarkable things had happened to the treated patients. Lymphadenopathy disappeared in all five. Four of them experienced improved delayed hypersensitivity reactions. And most important, four of them demonstrated statistically significant rises in the percentage of their CD4 cell counts, with one patient experiencing a 300 percent increase after six months of treatment.

Luiz already knew that photophoresis was dependent on a drug called 8-MOP (8-methoxypsoralen), which became active only when exposed to ultraviolet light. The drug, found naturally in a family of plants that grow along the Nile River, was originally discovered by the ancient Egyptians, who recognized its ability to make the skin more sensitive to sunlight. In modern photophoresis, blood is removed from a patient's body and the white blood cells are separated from the red, much like our leukophoresis procedure. The white cells are passed through a column in a centrifuge-like device and exposed to a specific frequency and dose of ultraviolet light. The light activates the 8-MOP, which integrates into the cells' DNA and "turns on" its healing properties. The blood is then returned to the patient.

Luiz was excited and uplifted by the promising results. He contacted Bisaccia and requested a spot in the researcher's Phase 2 protocol, which would include twenty more ARC patients and was currently under way at Morristown Hospital. Bisaccia, however, had filled all the spots.

Luiz contacted researchers who managed a photophoresis laboratory at the University of Miami, but none were willing to try the experimental therapy on him. At the same time, the FDA issued a statement to the forty-four sites across the nation that managed photophoresis labs, warning them not to use the therapy in HIV disease. Luiz remained undaunted. He wrote cover letters to the medical directors of all forty-four sites, asking them to include him in any potential pilot studies of photophoresis in AIDS therapy. He finally found a physician in Dayton who was willing to give the therapy a try.

One evening six months later, Luiz called me on the phone. "It doesn't seem to have had any positive effect at all," he said. "What are we going to do now?"

On New Year's Eve 1990, Luiz made one of the most difficult decisions in his life. He had invited Stuart to a series of New Year's Eve parties. Stuart, however, was nowhere to be found. Later, friends confessed they'd seen him free-basing on the streets of Miami. Concerned about Stuart's whereabouts but unwilling to allow his disappearance to spoil his own New Year's, Luiz attended the parties alone and then returned home.

At five o'clock in the morning, he was awakened by the sound of Stuart's anguished screams and an incessant pounding on the front door. Before Luiz could go downstairs in the art deco mansion that had been their home for the last six years, Stuart had broken one of the windows to get in, instantly triggering the alarm. A policeman arrived moments later.

Luiz gazed sadly at his lover standing in the living room, barely able to hold himself up, obviously stoned, and realized the scenario was a familiar one that had been played out over and over again. He'd had enough. Summoning the bravest and toughest instincts he could find, he told the policeman, "I don't know this man—this cocaine addict and obvious alcoholic. I want him off my property."

Stuart pleaded with Luiz to allow him to stay, but Luiz was firm in his insistence that Stuart leave immediately and never return. Early in the new year, Luiz heard that Stuart was admitted to another treatment program, this one in Coral Gables. Luiz matched his emotional housecleaning with the real thing: he cleared out all of Stuart's belongings, sending them to a sister who lived in North Miami. They spoke only sporadically after that.

"There was a definite correlation between the fall of my CD4 cells and the problems I was having with Stuart," Luiz later confided. "The stress and worry he constantly put me through seemed to perpetually further harm my immune system. I only wish I had had the strength to become independent six years ago."

Lenny Kaplan's Fight for Life Buyers' Club continued to prosper. People from as far away as St. Louis and Minneapolis came to Fort Lauderdale to take advantage of his supervised administration of trichosanthin. He also sold such drugs as oral interferon and levamisole, monitored patients' clinical progress and laboratory changes, and published his findings in such publications as the New York *Native*.

Apart from the Fight for Life Buyers' Club, Kaplan engaged in a variety of activist pursuits. Among his many crusades was the creation of an ACT UP chapter in Broward County that continued to fight for social change on the AIDS front, and serving as head of an advocacy group for inmates with AIDS. He often visited local prisons, provided PWAs with information and support, and attempted to secure them AZT and pentamidine, basic medications that they were often denied. When two prisoners died from AIDS within a day of each other, Kaplan argued that PWAs in prison should be free to spend their final days with relatives.

One of the inmates was Dale Renner, a thirty-five-year-old former female impersonator who had had a sex-change operation before contracting AIDS. She had been a popular and colorful figure in the gay communities of Texas and Florida and had won major awards for her drag performances. After being diagnosed with AIDS, the well-liked Renner took a turn for the worse. She was serving a seven-year sentence for burglary and possession of cocaine.

Kaplan helped fund a trip to Florida for Renner's mother, Beverly Barker, who lived in Plano, Texas. Barker was a vibrant woman with green eyes and a compelling style of speaking. She had always supported her child's controversial life-style and "had loved him equally as a son as well as a daughter." Her only wish was to be able to take her daughter home to die. She wrote letters to the governor's office, prison officials, and the judge who sentenced her daughter—all to no avail. While in Fort Lauderdale, she made one final attempt to persuade officials to release her daughter. They denied her request. Renner ultimately died in jail.

Barker visited my mother's home for dinner one evening, about two weeks before her daughter's death. Her eyes welling with tears, she said, "It wasn't as though it was an unreasonable request. My daughter couldn't even walk and had wasted away to skin and bones. I held her in that jail cell, told her how much I loved her. But I so wanted to have her home in the end . . ."

Like Luiz, I realized that my own health was continuing to deteriorate. While in the past I had not suffered from major symptoms, I now experienced numbness and a painful tingling in my arms, chest, and legs. "Peripheral neuropathy and parethesias related to general HIV infection," Dr. John Kantor, my primary care physician, assured me. "Elavil may provide symptomatic relief but nothing can cure it." At times the pain was excruciating, not unlike tiny pinpricks all attacking simultaneously in the most unpredictable spots.

I still experienced problems with my memory and concentration, despite the use of such drugs as nimodipine, which researchers thought might have some effect on one of the causes of HIV dementia. My energy level was considerably diminished. Thrush bloomed in my mouth and throat.

• • •

David Wilson attended a one-day conference in Washington, D.C., on immune reconstitution and met with researchers individually, pitched our lymphocyte expansion project, and got their feedback. He had lost sight in one eye, had a fever of 102 degrees, and felt nauseous. He couldn't hold down much food and frequently got diarrhea when he did. His digestive system seemed to be progressively dysfunctional, and he was losing the use of his arms.

He phoned me the morning after the conference from his hotel room. His vision had deteriorated to the extent that he could not see the numbers on the phone. He also had difficulty reading abstracts from the conference he had just attended. But his memory was still sharp, his voice strong. And he insisted we call researchers around the world in an attempt to obtain samples of some of the newer antiviral medications discussed at the conference. We spent the morning phoning Paris and Budapest and succeeded in locating several new drugs. In my heart, I felt we were both doomed, that it was too late for the drugs to be effective for us. But I agreed to make the calls.

David's commitment at that moment was especially significant in light of his own personal problems, which I learned about only after his death. His Jacksonville business was on the verge of bankruptcy; he had probably spent his last dime on the calls and faxes we sent. But he remained undaunted. He told me of his plans to travel to Los Angeles to enroll in a trial of passive immunotherapy in the office of Dr. Michael Roth.

In June 1991, the Centers for Disease Control announced that 100,000 people had now died of AIDS. Their report elucidated an almost unbelievable reality: AIDS was now the leading cause of death among the country's young adults.

The previous December, Ellen Cooper resigned from her

position as Director of Antiviral Drug Development at the FDA. Citing the stress endemic to the job, she asked to be transferred to another position in the agency. Cooper told the *Wall Street Journal* that her stress was exacerbated by an erosion of support from within the Department of Health and Human Services. She charged that some officials leaked preliminary data to activists "feeding the frenzy" for earlier drug approval while at the same time publicly blaming the FDA for its inaction. Cooper's resignation came just months before ddC and ddI—as well as several other AIDS drugs—would be ready for approval. Some activists contended that her sudden departure would be "disastrous" for the continued approval of new drugs.

In March 1991, a federally appointed committee determined that the FDA was grossly overextended, underbudgeted, housed in inadequate quarters, and shackled by bureaucratic constraints. The committee, a fifteen-member advisory panel chaired by Senator Edward M. Kennedy, determined that the agency simply was not equipped to carry out its basic mandates and called for major reforms. They concluded that the FDA needed more money, power, and status within the federal government. But they did not request a large infusion of money, emphasizing instead the agency's need to set new priorities, streamline its operations, and improve its mid- and upper management.

In what was perhaps one of the boldest activities of the AIDS underground to date, a Washington State chemist announced the formation and creation in June 1991 of a laboratory that would manufacture anti-HIV medications and a network that would distribute them to large numbers of AIDS patients across the country with even greater speed and efficiency than the buyers' clubs. The project was the brainchild of Jack Gerhardt, among the most charismatic and outgoing of all the underground AIDS personalities I had known. He was a tall, handsome man whose personal uniform usually consisted of a T-shirt, jeans, and a black leather jacket.

Gerhardt excelled in chemistry in high school, but just as he graduated, he found himself immersed in the counterculture. "I got stuck in the sixties and decided to party until I was thirty," he told the San Francisco *Examiner.* Although he did obtain a B.A. degree, his real education—the one he was to later draw upon in his battle against HIV—was obtained producing mind-altering drugs in underground labs. By the age of twenty-four, he had opened a legitimate chemical supply company, a small mail-order business, and several counterculture-oriented retail shops.

During the sixties, Gerhardt experimented with MDA, Ecstasy, and various other chemicals. Some he made himself. When clean syringes were not available, he shared with friends. When he turned thirty, Gerhardt began to notice minor but recurring problems with his health—chronic lymphadenopathy and fungal infections, for example. Realizing that he might be suffering from the early effects of HIV, he reappraised his life-style.

Both he and his wife, Sheila, had always dreamed of leaving the rat race and moving to the country. Realizing that their time might be limited, they now resolved to make their dream come true. Gerhardt closed his businesses, sold his waterfront house, and purchased a bucolic but rundown ranch in eastern Washington. The move took nearly two years. By the time they prepared for their final move, the blood test for HIV had been developed. An appointment with their doctor confirmed what they had previously suspected: both tested positive. As they walked away from their waterfront Seattle home for the last time, Gerhardt made a final gesture of farewell: he flushed two thousand dollars' worth of cocaine down the toilet.

Although they had both already started on low doses of AZT, the couple seldom thought about HIV as they began the process of restoring the ranch and learning the rudiments of farming. Over the course of the next two years, they rebuilt the old house and transformed the once-drab property into a thriving alfalfa farm. The new life-style agreed with them; they found themselves in better physical and spiritual condition than ever before.

When Sheila became sick one cold January evening, Gerhardt rushed her to the nearest emergency room, about forty miles away, where she discovered that she not only had a flu but was also pregnant. Gerhardt and his wife agonized for months about the decision to have the baby, questioning whether they had the right to subject a newborn infant to the risk of HIV infection. Studies had shown that up to 30 percent of the babies born to HIV-positive women would also be HIV-positive. After much deliberation, they chose to have the child, and six months later Sheila gave birth to a healthy, HIV-negative baby girl.

In October 1989, Gerhardt experienced what he perceived at the time as simply a bad flu. His fever rose to 104 degrees, and he began having night sweats and experiencing numbness in his arms. Within a week, this had progressed to extreme pain and weakness. In desperation, Sheila drove him to an HIV clinic in Seattle. EMG testing confirmed peripheral neuropathy as well as liver and kidney damage. Although the physicians said the problems were caused by HIV-induced autoimmunity, they offered no treatment other than narcotics. Within a month, Gerhardt had lost more than forty pounds, his muscles had shriveled, and he was often too weak to feed himself. He realized that if he continued to follow his doctors' advice and do nothing, his productive life would be over. He would have to find a treatment himself.

He began scouring the medical literature and, as I myself had earlier read almost every abstract ever written on AIDS. He spent long hours on Medline, the computerized medical database, which he accessed using his home computer. His wife drove him to the local university, where she helped him pore through articles, making photocopies of the relevant ones.

Within a couple of weeks he had designed a protocol that suggested a rationale for the combined use of ddC and a short course of high-dose D-penicillamine followed by several other agents (anabolic steroids and levamisole). It was his hope that the regimen would both control the virus and stop the autoimmune reaction to it.

He acquired the ddC from a pharmaceutical supply company and put it in capsules himself. The D-penicillamine and the other drugs were obtained from a sympathetic physician. Although the synergy of the drugs did not produce a clinical cure, they effectively arrested his decline. His energy returned and within a couple of months he had gained back much of his weight. He copied the protocol and distributed it to PWAs across the country. He immersed himself in his fight with a vengeance.

During the following sixteen months he developed contacts with other chemists, some of whom worked inside several of the nation's larger pharmaceutical companies. These "moles" copied and supplied him with the structure and early data for drugs that were still under development. Sometimes they were even able to get him a sample of the drug itself. In other cases, persons involved in studies would divert small samples of their drug to him. Gerhardt would then employ nuclear magnetic resonance imaging to analyze the unpublished structure. Finally, he would acquire the chemicals to synthesize the compound in his modest lab. In that process, Gerhardt vowed that until HIV is completely controllable, he would use all his resources, background, and knowledge to help himself and others survive.

"All my expertise prepared me for this," Gerhardt said. "You set up a lab. You make the drug. Only now, you don't make people high. You make them well."

In 1990, having experienced positive results with his own blood chemistries, Gerhardt produced a batch of Imuthiol and made it available to buyers' clubs, including those in Los Angeles and Dallas. He also supplied small amounts of HPMPC (an antiviral nucleoside analog used against herpes) and a variety of other compounds for David Wilson to use in his animal studies.

By July 1991, Gerhardt's lab had grown. He and another chemist had succeeded in producing modest quantities of both d4T (an anti-HIV-replication dideoxynucleoside analog) and soluble melanins. In addition, he had been able to develop a procedure for inexpensive, large-scale extraction of hypericin, a drug derived from the Saint-John's-wort herb. Gerhardt also revealed that he would be working on trying to produce the Roche drug TAT soon.

Gerhardt's decision to first develop d4T and hypericin was strategic; d4T was being exclusively developed by Bristol-Myers, the same company that owned the rights to and was supervising the monitoring trials of ddI. Insiders observed that the company might not vigorously promote d4T if ddI were approved for widespread use by the FDA in the fall of 1991, even if d4T proved more effective. Expanded Phase 2 trials of d4T were slated for the winter of 1991. (The company claimed that it wanted to make d4T its primary drug for AIDS and would commit millions to this end.) But the drug might not be licensed for years. Thus, a huge underground market existed for the more advanced nucleoside analog, which was perhaps safer and even more effective than AZT. As for hypericin, it had only been available underground in the Yerba Prima health-food formulation, which contained only 0.014 percent hypericin and which was probably ineffective as an anti-HIV therapeutic. Gerhardt's formulations were up to 98 percent pure hypericin.

Gerhardt's simple lab stands in stark contrast to the multimillion-dollar facilities of Burroughs Wellcome and Merck. Gerhardt estimates he poured $30,000 of his own savings into running the facility in 1990 alone. It was, of course, a far cry from what the giant drug companies spent on their labs, but like the larger companies, he found himself spending a great deal of time and money on the research and development of drugs that ultimately showed no promise when tested in people.

Gerhardt admitted to violating patent laws by synthesizing the experimental drugs. But he was quick to add that he was not stealing anything. "I'm not competing with marketed products, because most of the drugs I make have not yet been approved by the FDA," he said.

He also told me he was in the process of setting up an even larger lab in central California, one that would be far more advanced and contain such equipment as a 72-liter reaction vessel with a reflux condenser, a Brinkman rotary evaporator, and a walk-in fume hood. All of this would allow him to expand production and mass-produce drugs in the near future that he could now create only in moderately large quantities.

In addition to manufacturing and distributing drugs on the underground, Gerhardt told me, he was working with several physicians across the country, including Bernard Bihari in New York and a doctor in Texas. In cooperation with Alex Conn, the research-and-development executive at Pacific Biologics in Oakland, Gerhardt was supplying hypericin to these doctors at a discounted price; they in turn were enrolling patients in their own clinical trials to assess the drug's basic toxicity and effectiveness. In a short period of time, Gerhardt hoped to determine the drug's optimum doses and preliminary efficacy. He also sold the drug directly to PWAs and buyers' clubs.

With the opening of his own lab and distribution system, Gerhardt had advanced to a new level a concept that until then had been informally implemented only in the underground: the large-scale synthesis and production of new anti-HIV therapeutics. While Steve Gavin and Rob Springer produced small batches of such drugs, and Jim Corti, Ron Woodruff, and Derek Hodel found sources of the compounds in international markets and imported large quantities of them, neither faction gained the ability to actually manufacture large quantities of the more sophisticated drugs.

More important, Gerhardt's plans called not only for the drugs to be tested under the auspices of community physicians in observational tracking studies, but also for the drugs to be made available for sale to patients—even before the trials were complete—through buyers' clubs and his own network. It assembled many of the best ideas and intentions of parallel track, the CRI, and the underground studies, and in so doing, redefined the self-empowerment of the patient. It provided expanded access to new medications for PWAs while at the same time finding the means to gather reliable and replicable data quickly, outside the traditional system.

Gerhardt told me that his laboratory, located in the Washington mountains some sixty miles from his ranch, was under the professional direction of several chemists, one of whom was formerly with the NIH. "I can't tell you his name," Gerhardt said, "but he has a broad-based background in the synthesis of both nucleoside analogs and polypeptides." He went on to say that every piece of material produced in the lab was subjected to analysis and scrutiny by an outside firm for purity and lack of toxins.

In addition to opening his underground lab, distribution network, and testing system, Gerhardt created DATA—Direct Action for Treatment Access—with activist and journalist Steven Fowkes. Its mission, according to Fowkes, was to promote access to lifesaving drugs and therapies by providing information on unapproved drugs and therapies, political advocacy at the congressional level, and scientific investigation into promising therapies that were being neglected by the mainstream medical establishment. Ultimately, I became a member of DATA's medical advisory board and a regular contributor to its publication *Forefront*.

Gerhardt and Fowkes added that the buyers' clubs had themselves become overly political and sometimes offered products for sale that had long been known to be ineffective, or only marginally so. Through its newsletters and drug fact sheets, DATA would not only provide detailed and comprehensive information on new medications to doctors and patients but would also gauge the quality of the services and products offered by the various buyers' clubs. The whole purpose, according to Gerhardt, was not to create dissension, but rather to foster unity in an underground that had become increasingly disorganized and filled with friction.

Ironically, while Gerhardt was planning to unify the underground, legislation was being proposed that threatened to shut it down completely or at least threaten its widespread existence. The threat came in the form of two proposed congressional bills with what appeared to be contradictory and (ironically) disparate goals. The first, proposed by new FDA Commissioner David Kessler, was HR-2597, which would essentially grant police power to the FDA.

Under the new law, the FDA would have the power to conduct searches without a warrant and take all manner of police and law enforcement action without the need for judicial authorization. It could conceivably enter a health-food store, doctor's office, or other establishment and seize any goods or records it chose. It would have the power to subpoena and require any person to appear before its staff and produce any records it demanded—all without judicial oversight. The FDA could, further, impose huge civil penalties— between $250,000 and $1 million—for each act that violated either its own arbitrary rules or those of the Food, Drug and Cosmetics Act. Finally, under the bill, any food, drug, or cosmetic could be destroyed by the FDA at its sole discretion. And buyers' club presidents and underground AIDS drug developers, including Gerhardt, would be under constant scrutiny by federal officials under the new legislation.

The second bill, HR-2872, was called the Access to Lifesaving Therapies Act. Written by San Francisco ACT UP activist and DATA vice president Jim Driscoll, it would allow pharmaceutical companies to obtain licensing and to market experimental drugs after the drugs had completed Phase 1 trials and shown promise of efficacy and manageable toxicity. The drugs could be withdrawn from the market at any time if they proved unsafe or ineffective in Phase 2 or Phase 3 studies. The bill, sponsored by Congressman Tom Campbell of California, would therefore provide incentives for fledgling companies to develop drugs and would allow them to compete with their larger counterparts by reducing the cost necessary to develop the drugs.

Driscoll, a Shakespearean scholar who became an AIDS activist in an attempt to find treatments for his friend Dave Olson, was sharply critical of the current system of providing patients with drugs. In a *Wall Street Journal* op-ed piece, he wrote: "The shortcomings of our present Band-Aid system of 'expanded access' giveaways, which compel pharmaceutical companies to offer experimental drugs free to select patients, underscore the need for a new approach." Expanded access has failed to provide early or wide access to breakthrough drugs. Like the drug underground, it enables primarily affluent, well-educated patients to obtain these drugs, and thus it discriminates against minorities, the poor, and people outside major cities. Even the best-informed patients with the finest health care are often stymied because rigid, FDA expanded-access protocols arbitrarily exclude many who might benefit. Furthermore, drug companies resist giving away drugs on expanded access. Worst of all, the prospect of its daunting costs inhibits private research on lifesaving drugs with limited markets. Representative Campbell's proposal for expedited approval, which provides coverage for these drugs by health-insurance plans, would expand market incentives for drug development. Indeed, by making AIDS research much more attractive to drug companies, HR-2872 could create a privately financed "Manhattan Project" for AIDS.

While the Campbell bill would put more drugs in the hands of AIDS and ARC patients much faster than is currently possible, it would also spell disaster for the underground suppliers of such medications. Drugs that were once bought in New York or San Francisco storefronts could now be procured with a doctor's prescription in the local pharmacy. Needless to say, Gerhardt and others in the underground vehemently opposed the draconian HR-2597. Surprisingly, however, the same people supported the Campbell bill.

"The most important thing is for AIDS patients to have immediate and unrestricted access to promising new medications," Gerhardt told me. "The proprietary interests of underground drug kingpins, including myself, must remain subordinate to this. Furthermore, there will always be some market for drugs through the underground."

Approval was finally granted to ddI on July 19, 1991, but it almost didn't happen. By and large, most of the government researchers believed that ddI could maintain the health of HIV-infected people—at least for a while. But some members of the committee that had reviewed the data found statistical discrepancies in the analysis of the Phase 2 study. Pressure from activists—and an early review of the Phase 3 data, which was considerably less ambiguous—finally caused the drug to be approved.

I had long attempted to prepare myself for David Wilson's death. I knew it was inevitable. But nothing could fully prepare me for the fateful call that came from David's roommate, Tony, in San Francisco on June 7, 1991. David had succumbed to CMV. The technology he had hoped would save his life had not come in time.

I bowed my head in silence for several moments. David Wilson, the young man with the boyish looks and boundless energy, had finally succumbed to the battle he had fought hardest and longest to win.

On the evening of March 12, 1991, Luiz Vasquez experienced an uncontrollable spasticity in his upper arms and chest. He tried to sleep but awoke in the middle of the night with a painful headache and a terrifying numbness. He could barely walk. He was rushed to a Miami hospital, where he was diagnosed with toxoplasmosis, one of the most devastating of all AIDS infections. Over the next several days, Luiz remained paralyzed in more than 90 percent of his body. He couldn't get out of bed or eat. Status epilepticus, he knew well—a consequence of the toxoplasmosis. He was given a variety of drugs. His condition gradually improved, and he was discharged in ten days.

The tests that the FDA had requested on the lymphocyte expansion project would not be completed anytime soon. The principal investigator's interest and enthusiasm had waned, and the project seemed in danger of stagnation, caught in a mire of bureaucracy and indifference. I received responses from 75 percent of the mainstream researchers who had reviewed the protocol. Most called it unfeasible.

One researcher told me, "You have a probing mind and a strong will—tempered by rationality and common sense. All of those are necessary to cure AIDS. The reality is, successfully pulling off the experiment you propose in 1991—with or without genetic vectors—would be like staging a moonwalk for the first time in 1961 and having it go off without a hitch." Perhaps lymphocyte expansion and gene therapy *did* represent an unrealistic "moonwalk." But even the most promising "do-able" therapies were not being tested rapidly enough. On April 29, 1991, Hoffmann-La Roche announced plans to indefinitely postpone trials of its TAT-inhibitor, considered by many to be among the more promising anti-HIV therapeutics. Researchers at Johns Hopkins University in Baltimore, where the trial was about to begin, were described as shocked by the news. A spokesman for Hoffmann-La Roche was quoted in the *AIDS Treatment News* as acknowledging that there was no "scientific reason" to halt the trial. He claimed that the company had reviewed its entire antiviral program and had chosen to pursue the development of ddC while "aggressively" seeking another pharmaceutical company as a partner to continue TAT development. Insiders put it more pointedly: "A hugely expensive drug. A relatively small market and no guarantee of profit. Why take the risk alone?" However, on July 1, 1991, after much community pressure, Hoffmann-La Roche restarted the trial. Yet I knew the scenario would repeat itself in the coming months. Cultural inertia, the dogmatic ego and myopia of scientists immersed in their own agendas, the attitude of the American pharmaceutical industry—which believed that it was more profitable to develop a new antihistamine than an HIV antiviral drug—and a society that had long ago pledged its basic indifference would prevent most therapies from being quickly developed.

• • •

In the end, Luiz pursued every available option with a passion. He researched therapies and procured drugs with an even greater ambition than David Wilson, it seemed to me. Between July and October 1991, Luiz traveled all over the world in search of drugs and treatments that held the potential to restore his damaged immune system.

In Zurich, he participated in a protocol designed by the Swiss physician Stuart Roka. Roka created a formulation extracted from nearly a score of plants and herbs that purportedly possessed strong immunomodulatory properties, and then combined the injections of the substance with ozone treatments. Luiz spent a week in an elegant Scandinavian clinic where he gained weight—but not CD4 cells. Doctors there administered an immune globulin preparation derived from the serum of pigs. The project's principal investigator, Kurt Osther, believed that the "porcine antibodies" held the potential to raise CD4 cell counts. After completing a small trial with half a dozen AIDS patients and achieving marginally encouraging results, the doctor offered the therapy to Americans at a clinic in Copenhagen at a cost of $10,000.

Luiz also obtained Dr. Daniel Zagury's new adjuvant, a vaccine that contained inactivated alpha-interferon, selected HIV antigens, and stabilized RNA-free HIV pseudovirus. Zagury had unleashed a media frenzy at the Seventh International AIDS Conference in Florence in 1991 when he presented the data on this treatment, with graphs and charts that depicted the gradual but complete restoration of patients' immune systems. He also visited Dr. Michael Scolaro in Los Angeles, who was participating in a study in which subjects were inoculated with a vaccine that contained putative, non-pathogenic strains of HIV. According to George Pieczenik, a co-principal investigator of the study and an executive at the Immuvax Corporation, the non-pathogenic HIV variants could displace or out-compete virulent HIV at the molecular level.

In short, none of the therapies seemed capable of bringing Luiz's immune system up from ground zero. In October, he was hospitalized with disseminated CMV infection. A mutual friend called to inform me that Luiz's condition was deteriorating rapidly. I visited him on November 11, 1991, in the same South Miami hospital where he had cared for so many patients over the years. We had not communicated much in the months before his illness, and I felt a need to see him again.

He was propped up on a pillow. His complexion was remarkably vibrant, but he was clearly dying. A translucent oxygen mask covered his face. He breathed in and out with massive convulsions, fighting and gasping for every breath. The CMV that had invaded his lungs was now unstoppable. I could tell his body was in a state of collapse. His heart, however, continued to beat strongly, almost defiantly.

Medicines that had once hung on the IV hook over his bed had now been removed; only a bag of Versed remained, helping to relieve his discomfort and pain. It had also placed him in a twilight mental state. He was not aware of my presence.

His mother grasped his hand by his bedside. She seemed emotionally drained yet continued to move nervously in her chair crying, "Luizito . . . Luizito . . ." Someone had placed a cross at the foot of the bed; a religious icon was there as well. Luiz's sister performed a prayer in the corner of the room.

On the nightstand across from his bed, I noticed the familiar spiral notebook into which Luiz had meticulously copied information on the wide variety of therapies he had pursued throughout the world. There was a recent letter from the manufacturer of a new CMV drug, indicating their willingness to send the medication.

I watched him breathe through the mask, struggling for every last breath. His expression seemed stubborn and resolute.

I left the hospital after about an hour.

Early that evening, I received a call. Luiz had died of complications of pulmonary CMV. A few days before, he was visited by his ex-lover Stuart. Talking without rancor or bitterness, Stuart opened his heart, sharing his sorrow for all the unhappiness he had caused Luiz. Luiz also talked almost continually, sharing emotions he had never discussed before.

In those moments, everything between them was complete.

THE DUCK POND REVISITED

Activists hoped that Magic Johnson's and Arthur Ashe's disclosures of their HIV status would galvanize the nation's disparate groups, spur broad public support for AIDS research, ignite even more ambitious and effective education and prevention campaigns, and lead to promising new treatments. But Johnson's resignation from the Presidential Commission on AIDS in September 1992, followed by Ashe's death less than five months later, only reinforced the overwhelming sense I had of the government's apathy.

It was ironic that it took the illness of mainstream sports figures whose influence penetrated all levels and segments of society to increase awareness when, for the last decade, hundreds of thousands of ordinary citizens were silently dying.

And I also found it disturbing that few corporations planned to retain Magic as their spokesman but chose instead to incorporate him into educational campaigns and public service announcements that would prove more palatable to advertisers. As an attorney for one of the corporations put it, "You can't afford to take the chance that a fairly large population might look upon Magic's conduct as not exemplary."

By the end of the century, according to projections by the Harvard-based Global AIDS Policy Coalition, Magic Johnson would be but one of 110 million people worldwide infected with HIV, the fastest-growing among them women and teenagers.

One morning in November 1991, I awoke and noticed a patchy red rash that started at the center of my spine and extended around my left side and underneath my left pectoral, stopping midline at my chest. Within days, small clusters of blisters had developed, causing a stinging, burning pain.

"Classic herpes zoster," Dr. Kantor said. "Otherwise known as shingles. Very likely, the needle sticks you felt as early as six months ago were an early sign of the zoster reactivation."

Shingles results from a reactivation of the herpes zoster (chicken pox) virus that lies dormant in nerve roots and can re-emerge later in life, typically spreading with painful blisters across the nerves of the chest wall. It can happen even in healthy persons without HIV. In fact, I had had both shingles *and* chicken pox as a teenager. Possibly, Dr. Kantor hypothesized, my weakened immune system had allowed the virus to gain a foothold.

"It's not necessarily an opportunistic infection," he assured me. "You're going to get through this without complications." He increased my dose of oral acyclovir, which I had been on as a preventive measure for the last six months, as it had previously shown efficacy in the treatment of shingles in adults. Unfortunately, Dr. Kantor's optimistic prognostication did not come true.

On the evening of December 5, 1991, I awoke with a 105-degree fever and a crushing headache. I felt delirious, I found it difficult to walk, and my mind was completely clouded. I was disoriented. The pain along the intracostal nerve had become excruciating.

My next-door neighbor, also a friend, asked me if I knew where I was.

I tried to speak, but it was as if I was trying to articulate an abstract thought in vain.

"What's *wrong?*" he asked. There was more stammering on my part. Bob was more frustrated than frightened.

With agonizing slowness, I managed to blurt out, "The acyclovir didn't work . . ."

"You're burning up with fever," he observed. "Can you understand me at all?"

I nodded, but couldn't manage much else. It was as if a curtain had been drawn over the mechanism in my brain responsible for speech, yet there was still something left that allowed me to convey the message that the herpes virus had progressed and the medication was no longer effective.

My friend called my mother and Dr. Kantor, then rushed me to the emergency room of the hospital. After a spinal tap, an MRI of my brain, and an EEG, a neurologist on staff diagnosed disseminated herpes zoster. Evidently, the virus had crossed the blood/brain barrier into the spinal fluid and had produced an encephalopathic meningitis. I was immediately placed on a high-dose treatment of intravenous acyclovir. I was transferred to the HIV ward, which was on the top floor and was immaculate. Each patient had his own room and an impressive view of the city. The quality of care was surprisingly good.

I knew from my past research that an experimental drug David and I had tried was effective for both hepatitis and herpes zoster. I had a package of ampules left. Of course, the drug had not yet been approved by the FDA and was prohibited in the hospital. A nurse I had known from the Compound Q study therefore agreed to give me daily intramuscular injections. He stole into my room at midnight, when the nurses were on a break, and gave me the shots.

Within three days, the rash began to heal and my mental state cleared somewhat, although I still suffered from the general problems in concentration and memory that had plagued me years earlier. And it was still difficult for me to maintain my balance.

I sat up in bed throughout those days, tried to concentrate on television, listening to the voice of the hospital page operator, who summoned doctors to patients' bedsides. Occasionally I would hear the voice utter in the most unemotional tone, "Code blue . . . Code blue," which meant that someone on the floor was dying.

By the fifth day of the treatment, I was out of bed and walking the halls of the ward. A patient was being rolled down the corridor in a wheelchair. He stared blankly ahead, as if unaware that he even existed. I wondered if my end would be this way.

I continued down the corridor and happened to glance into the room of another patient. There, sitting up in bed, was Scott Yageman.

I knocked once. "May I come in?"

Scott looked up. "Well! Imagine seeing you here, stranger. Come in and close the door."

I entered the room and shut the door behind me.

I was struck by how pale and thin he looked. He had never appeared so gaunt. He had lost at least fifteen pounds.

"Is it all right if I sit here?" I asked, indicating the chair by his bed.

He grinned. "If you're not afraid of catching something."

"What are you in for?"

"PCP. My first bout. Dr. Simon says we caught it early. There shouldn't be any complications." He let forth a hoarse, hacking dry cough. An IV had been set up over his bed. Pentamidine dripped into his veins.

"I thought you were on aerosolized pentamidine," I said.

"I was," he replied. "And Bactrim. They stopped working. I'm what's called a 'breakthrough.' Some breakthrough! What about you?" he asked.

"Disseminated zoster. It got into my central nervous system. I had a raging headache and fever when I came here. But I seem to be getting better."

"That's good. You should be out in no time. I haven't seen you in so long . . . I heard from Joe Radish that you were working on that lymphocyte cloning project."

"Lymphocyte *expansion*," I corrected him. "It's been a major undertaking."

"Do you think it's going to work?" He looked at me with real sadness in his eyes.

"I can't say. If it does, you'll be one of the first to know."

"I can't believe the nurses on this floor. They refuse to stay near me for very long. They seem to be afraid. This is 1991—aren't they even partially enlightened?" he asked. "You can't catch PCP like you can TB . . ." He coughed again. "Maybe you'd better not get too close," he joked.

"I'm probably more a danger to you than you are to me," I said. "Zoster can be contagious."

There was an awkward silence between us.

"Well," he said slowly, "looks like we both crossed over. Into full-blown AIDS, that is."

I considered his point. "Yeah, it looks like it."

"Remember how we used to sit in the lobby at Dr. Mayer's and watch all the people with PCP—and crypto—and toxo—and say, 'It'll never be us . . . We'll never be *that* sick . . .' Looks like we were wrong."

"Yeah . . . I know," I said.

Then he paused, as if the painful recollection had been replaced by a happier one. "But we had such fun," he said. "Remember when Susan accidentally substituted potassium for heparin in Rick Andrews's ozone treatment? His skin turned purple!" He began laughing uncontrollably, but his laughter was interrupted by the cough again, this time more severely.

"Poor Rick's potassium levels must have been out of sight," I added. "And the time the doctor from Bulgaria unexpectedly visited the clinic to see a classic American experimental center for unproven HIV medications including ozone. Susan told Mayer the man looked *officious*. Mayer caught a glimpse of him and was certain he must be from the FDA. He hid in his office for an hour!"

This broke us both up. We started to laugh again.

"Have you had many visitors?" I asked him.

"Not many. My parents were down from Orlando. But there

haven't been too many." Then, after another pause, "Four guys I used to drive died last week. All on the same day."

I looked into his eyes and I knew the horrible possibility he contemplated.

"You think they'll ever find a cure?" he asked.

"Sure," I said. I could see his eyes water. "Sure."

There was another pause.

"I heard David Wilson died," he said.

I nodded, looking downward, avoiding his stare. The gathering silence was punctuated by Scott's cough.

"I don't want to die," he said slowly.

Tears fell on his hospital gown. "I don't want to seem like a child. But there's still so much I want to do. I watched so many people die . . . You'd think I'd be used to it by now." He caught his breath. "I'm scared—I'm very scared." I grasped his hand. He coughed again and then raised himself up a few inches on his pillow, wiping his eyes. "I'm sorry."

"It's all right," I answered.

"You don't seem as afraid as I am."

"Maybe I'm not."

"Why?"

"I don't know." How could I explain the change I had experienced in the last few months? "I suppose I'm more afraid of *decay* than of death itself. I don't want to turn into a corpse before I die, watching my skin rot."

We sat in silence for several moments longer. Outside the room, the sounds of the hospital corridor filtered in: carts being wheeled, the beep of an oscilloscope, the placid voice of the page operator.

After several more minutes, he fell into a light sleep. I watched him breathe deeply for several more moments. I rose and left the room.

Scott's prediction was correct. Five days later, I was discharged from the hospital. The rash had almost completely healed and the headache had diminished greatly. I was still dizzy, though, and walking was laborious.

My disability insurance, I learned, had been approved.

Jack Gerhardt called. He had a surge of energy and a renewed sense of enthusiasm. He had succeeded in synthesizing the TAT-inhibitor, a new antiviral agent that might hold considerably more promise than any of the approved drugs currently available.

I gave him lukewarm words of encouragement and hung up the phone. It all seemed futile to me now. In how many voices had I heard the fire, the drive, that had become extinguished by the disease? How many had given of themselves so valiantly like Gerhardt? Luiz Vasquez . . . David Wilson . . . Rob Springer?

My mother stayed with me and brought me food. She had been so strong throughout my illness, always maintaining a calm veneer. But now I could see an unmistakable fear in her eyes.

One day, I felt an urge to return to the duck pond. My mother had warned me not to go. "Dr. Kantor says you have to stay in bed for at least ten more days," she reminded me. But I felt a nagging desire to revisit the spot, the only one that could offer solace. I shrugged into my overcoat and drove down the old road toward the pond.

It had rained earlier, so the shiny surface of the road was slick and treacherous. I braked for an animal that darted into the beam of my headlight. The sudden sway of the car reminded me of the dizzy feeling the swing used to give me down at the pond.

I parked my car on the embankment and slowly made my way to the edge of the pond. The pain in my chest was still intense, and there was a numbness in my arms. I walked with a limp, feeling like a tightrope walker struggling to maintain my balance on an especially difficult wire. I tried to suppress the pain I felt, to push it back.

In some respects the pond was exactly as I remembered it. But there were perceptible differences. I studied the scene of my childhood playground. The arches of the bridge that had once seemed so grand now appeared unimposing and even rundown. A ficus tree grew out of the fireplace well from which smoke once streamed. The giant white pillars of the gazebo were riddled with graffiti spraypainted by a neighborhood gang. Only one or two mallards remained, hovering under the trees. The pond looked empty and stark.

The Walden Pond of my youth had changed. But my inner Walden Pond had changed as well. I stared up at the patterns of the massive, interconnected seagrape trees and tried to focus on the peacefulness of the slowly swaying leaves. The tangled boughs only served to remind me that my mind had become more and more like those crazy, illogical branches, a convoluted picture of mental disarray.

Two men emerged from behind the bushes, one pulling up his Levis, each heading in a separate direction toward his car.

I stared into the water and then closed my eyes tightly, trying to focus on the Sunday afternoons I had spent there with my mother as a child, the times in high school when Pete and I had made love in the dark. I tried to picture myself as a teenager, standing by the duck pond, to manipulate the image and hold on to it. But because of my dementia, I could not.

I opened my eyes and moved closer to the edge of the bridge, looking down into the water and studying my reflection. The water rippled over the image of my face, distorting it.

I continued to stare at the brackish water of the pond. It was dusk and the setting sun cast a haunting, romantic glow. My gaze caught a stray shaft of light in a corner of the pond. Like a barely visible candle flame flickering in its final moments, the light danced on the surface of the water. It seemed to me that the water somehow fought to preserve the light, trying to rouse it to new life. In the end, I knew, biotechnology and man would triumph over disease, and young people would no longer suffer.

I turned away from the pond and started back to my car, pulling my overcoat tightly around me, ready to face the gathering dark.

NOTES

CHAPTER 2

Page 17 On GRID: The coining of the term GRID is documented in Randy Shilts, *And the Band Played On* (New York: St. Martin's Press, 1987), p. 121.

The full range of early theories on the disease is documented in Shilts, *And the Band Played On.*

19 On the primary immune response and immunological memory: When any of the CD4 lymphocytes "see" an antigen for the first time, the reaction that follows is a *primary immune response,* in which specific CD4 cells must recognize their antigen and produce alarmlike chemicals, such as Interleukin-2. The primary immune response can be slow, where days can pass between the onset of the infection and the start of a specific reaction. However, on its second encounter with the same antigen, the body's immune system is better prepared, since first encounters lead to the recognition of the invader. They also cause a geometric increase in the number of CD4 lymphocytes— promoted by Interleukin-2—with the capacity to recognize this invader. This state of heightened preparedness, called *immunological memory,* is the basis upon which all vaccines function. Vaccines are a small amount of a specific disease-causing organism (i.e., antigen) in an inactivated or harmless form, which produces a primary immune response. This ensures immunological memory and a redoubled response to the antigen, should it subsequently enter the bloodstream in a dangerous active form. See P. Sites et al., *Basic and Clinical Immunology* (Los Altos, Calif.: Lange Medical Publications, 1989), pp. 78, 89.

20 In the healthy immune system: From P. Sites et al., *Basic and Clinical Immunology* (Los Altos, Calif.: Lange Medical Publications, 1989), pp. 78, 89.

21 On AIDS-related infections: In addition to the major opportunistic infections, people with AIDS can develop chronic disorders that are not neces-

sarily life-threatening but are nevertheless painful, discomforting, and cause great suffering. These include oral hairy leukoplakia—white patches on the tongue thought to be linked to Epstein-Barr virus. Thrush, a white patchy fungus *(Candida albicans)*, may also appear on the tongue; in systemic candidiasis, the *Candida* fungus can spread into the esophagus, causing difficult and painful swallowing, or into the intestines, resulting in diarrhea. Anemia, a reduction in the number of red blood cells, can be caused by certain viruses (such as paroviruses) and some medications, and can result in fatigue. Increased levels of tumor necrosis factor, an immunoregulatory protein produced by white blood cells, may cause weight loss; it may play a role in the AIDS-defining disorder known as "wasting syndrome," in which a patient sustains marked weight loss. A variety of organisms can cause chronic but not life-threatening diarrhea. Antibodies that the body makes against a specific microbe, after HIV infection occurs, mistakenly attack the body's own platelets, resulting in immune thrombocytopenia, or decreased platelet counts; a reduction in the number of platelets—which are essential for the process of blood clotting—can result in impaired clotting, manifested as easy bruising, nosebleeds, and blood in the urine. The early immune response to AIDS itself can produce recurring fevers, associated with the release of fever-inducing molecules by HIV-stimulated white blood cells.

The depressed cell-mediated immunity associated with AIDS can also result in certain types of abnormal cell growth and cancers such as B-cell lymphoma or Kaposi's sarcoma. The latter is a skin cancer often seen in HIV patients; its true cause remains unknown.

Finally, AIDS can cause dementia. In its earliest stages, it can be nonfatal, unprogressing, and chronic. It is characterized by lapses in short-term memory, difficulty in concentrating, and impaired abstract reasoning; apathy and changes in behavior; and mild motor symptoms, such as clumsiness and slowed responses.

The humoral immune system: Willheim, *Fundamental Immunology*, p. 80.

Page 23 On naltrexone background: A long-term follow-up study with naltrexone showed that 60 percent of the patients responded to treatment, experiencing drops in alpha-interferon levels and fewer opportunistic infections than the non-responders. However, there were no significant increases in CD4 cell counts or other immunological parameters in the "responders." Bernard Bihari et al., *Fifth International Conference on AIDS*, Montreal, 1989, abstract M.C.P. 62.

25 The CDC's responsibilities: information provided by the Centers for Disease Control, Atlanta, Georgia.

26 The disease was probably sexually transmitted: The Operation Protocol 577 report specifically indicated that the variable most strongly associated with illness was a larger number of male sex partners per year. Compared to a control group of healthy male homosexuals, patients with KS and PCP were also more likely to have had prior exposure to syphilis and hepatitis B, to have been treated for enteric parasites, and to have used various illicit substances. Harold Jaffe et al., "National Case Control Study of Kaposi's

Sarcoma and *Pneumocystis carinii* Pneumonia in Homosexual Men: Part 1," *Annals of Internal Medicine* 99 (August 1983), p. 2.

A subsequent report showed that infected patients were more likely to have a reversal of the T-helper to T-suppressor ratio, higher levels of IgG antibody when compared to controls, and higher concentrations of antibodies to cytomegalovirus and Epstein-Barr virus. Martha Rogers et al., "National Case Control Study of Kaposi's Sarcoma and *Pneumocystis carinii* Pneumonia in Homosexual Men: Part 2," *Annals of Internal Medicine* 99 (August 1983), pp. 151–58.

27 AIDS survival rates: Richard Rothenberg et al., "Survival with AIDS: Experience with 5833 Cases in New York City," *New England Journal of Medicine* 317, no. 21 (November 19, 1987), p. 1297; and George Lemp et al., "Trends in the Length of Survival for AIDS Cases in San Francisco," *Fourth International Conference on AIDS,* Stockholm, 1988, abstract.

The analysis of another cohort of 288 seropositive homosexual men in San Francisco who were seropositive when the study began showed that 22 percent developed AIDS after three years of observation. Another 19 percent developed clinical symptoms of infection and an additional 24 percent showed signs of immune suppression. The study projected that 50 percent of the men will develop AIDS within six years of observation and that many more will develop AIDS in subsequent years. A. R. Moss et al., "Seropositivity for HIV and the development of AIDS or AIDS related conditions: Three year follow up of the San Francisco General Hospital cohort," *British Journal of Medicine* 296 (1988), pp. 745–50. More recent data predict the possibility that 100 percent of persons infected with HIV will develop AIDS within thirteen years after initial infection. Reported in National Academy of Sciences, "HIV Infection and Its Epidemiology," *Confronting AIDS: Update 1988* (National Academy of Sciences Press, 1988), pp. 33–55.

Progression from ARC to AIDS: J. L. Fahey et al., "Diagnostic and Prognostic Factors in AIDS," *Mount Sinai Journal of Medicine* 53 (1986), pp. 657–63.

CHAPTER 3

33 On modification of gay sexual practices: The dynamics and true etiology of male promiscuity are discussed in Donald Symons, *The Evolution of Human Sexuality* (New York: Oxford University Press, 1979). Indeed, male promiscuity, the desire of the male for novel excitement and variety in sex, evolved for specific reasons related to the guarantee of reproductive success. It seems absurd and archaic to me to ascribe a moral judgment to behavior that almost certainly had its roots in physiological and biological processes.

32 On transmission of HIV: At least one recent study has shown that HIV cannot be transmitted by saliva, perspiration, or tears. And another, the San Francisco Men's Health Study, showed that men who engaged only in oral sexual contact had a 1% incidence of HIV transmission. But there still remains controversy about the potential of saliva to transmit HIV.

33 Rates of rectal gonorrhea had plummeted: from data compiled by the City of San Francisco Health Department.

On the closure of bathhouses: The fourteen San Francisco bathhouses affected by Silverman's decision all reopened within a matter of hours, forcing the city to go to court. Seven weeks later, a state superior court judge ruled that the baths could remain open, but under strict requirements that included closing the private rooms and routine monitoring to prevent high-risk behavior. Michael Helquist, "Court Allows Bathhouses to Re-open," *Coming Up!* (December 1984), p. 7.

As Dennis Altman notes, the decision to close the baths reflected a problem of balancing two equally legitimate concerns of public policy: the preservation of civil rights and privacy, and the safeguarding of public health. Dennis Altman, *AIDS in the Mind of America* (New York: Anchor Press/Doubleday, 1986), p. 153.

Page   34 "Federal Official Says He Believes Cause of AIDS Has Been Found," *New York Times*, April 22, 1984.

      35 Montagnier on the American announcement: Dominique Lapierre, *Beyond Love*, translated from the French by Kathryn Spink (New York: Warner Books, 1991), p. 264.

According to the *New York Times*, March 2, 1992, lawyers for the Pasteur Institute are now "seeking to reverse that agreement and recover from Washington payments of $20 million plus future royalties" as a result of a new U.S. Federal inquiry into possible perjury and product fraud on the part of Dr. Robert Gallo and his colleague Dr. Mikulas Popovic."

      36 Gallo and HTLV-III pictures: "What's Next in the Gallo Case?" *Science* 254, p. 944.

Montagnier on Gallo's misrepresentation: Lapierre, *Beyond Love*, p. 269.

Flossie Wong Stahl, *Cell* 227 (1985), pp. 759–62. The results of the French studies were first published in an article by Barre-Sinoussi et al., "Isolation of a T lymphotropic virus from patients at risk for AIDS," *Science* 220 (1983), pp. 868–72. Gallo's studies were first published in Robert Gallo et al., "Frequent Detection and Isolation of HTLV-III from patients with AIDS and at risk for AIDS," *Science* 224 (1984), pp. 500–503.

A chronology summarizing the course of AIDS research that had been developed by Gallo and Montagnier was published in *Nature* in 1987. See "The Chronology of AIDS Research," *Nature* 326 (1987), p. 171.

The controversy over who first discovered the virus is best summarized by John Crewdson and by Lapierre in *Beyond Love*. In 1991, Gallo acknowledged that a culture of a virus taken from an AIDS patient probably became contaminated with a virus sent to him from the Pasteur Institute. See Philip J. Hilts, "US Scientist Confirms Mixup in AIDS Virus Study," *New York Times*, May 31, 1991.

      37 On pathogenesis: A. B. Rabson, *AIDS: Pathogenesis and Treatment*, J. A. Levyu, ed. (New York: Dekker, [n.d.]); A. G. Dalgleish, *Nature* (London) 312 (1984), p. 763; P. J. Maddon et al., *Cell* 47 (1986), p. 333.

On post integration of HIV: J. Sodroski et al., *Nature* 322 (1986), p. 470; J. D. Lifson, et al., *Science* 232 (1986), p. 1123.

On syncytia formation: J. A. Levy et al., *Virology* 147 (1985), p. 441; D. Ho et al., *Journal of Clinical Investigation* 77 (1986), p. 1712; S. A. Salahuddin et al., *Blood* 68 (1986), p. 281.

On infection of macrophages on autoimmune: D. Klatzmann et al., *Immunology Today* 7 (1986), p. 291.

200 billion to 300 billion CD4 cells: John Dwyer, *The Body At War: The Miracle of the Immune System* (New York: New American Library, 1988), p. 131.

Once the CD4 cells fall: ibid., p. 131.

39 1984 AIDS statistics: from the Centers for Disease Control's *Morbidity and Mortality Report*, April 1, 1984, p. 15.

40 On moralistic dogmas: Some gays found it difficult not to internalize the guilt assigned to them by conservative religious pundits and reinforced by a new psychiatric orthodoxy that suggested that gay promiscuity was a sign of immaturity and self-hate. The most insidious attack was the suggestion that there were those who were innocent victims of AIDS and those who fully deserved it, and that all homosexuals belonged in the second category.

Rejecting the moralistic rhetoric, many gays had come to understand that the desire for sexual variety is a quirk of human nature and, even in the age of AIDS, had found mechanisms to develop models for committed relationships that were not necessarily monogomous.

41 Theories on origins of the virus: Robert Gallo, *Virus Hunting: AIDS, Cancer and the Human Retrovirus* (New York: HarperCollins, 1991), p. 227.

Ribavirin's effect on HTLV-III: John McCormick, "Ribavirin Suppresses Replication of Lymphadenopathy-Associated Virus in Cultures of Human Adult T Lymphocytes," *Lancet*, December 15, 1984, pp. 1367–69.

42 Ribavirin fact sheet background: The ribavirin/isoprinosine protocol fact sheet was the brainchild of Sam Murdoch, a Texas attorney who suffers from Parkinson's disease and who had sought out a wide variety of treatments for his own condition. Murdoch was not HIV-positive himself but had seen many of his friends succumb to AIDS.

In 1984, Murdoch obtained copies of Vernon Smith's *Clinical Applications of Ribavirin* and *Ribavirin: A Broad Spectrum Anti-Viral Agent*. Based on information in these compendiums, along with discussions with Dr. R. Canonico, a U.S. Army virology researcher, he formulated the intermittent protocol. "That seditious little fact sheet I wrote in 1984," Murdoch said, "was actually one of the pioneering efforts of the AIDS drug underground and marked the start of informal research." In subsequent months, after numerous patients had followed the protocol with the help of their individual physicians, Martin Delaney and Joe Brewer of Project Inform obtained a copy and used it as the basis for their own monitoring trial of ribavirin and isoprinosine, BARIG.

In 1987, Murdoch turned his interest to an aloe vera extract called carrisyn, which had been investigated as an antiviral agent against measles virus and herpes type I. It was Bill McAnalley at the Dallas-based Carrington Laboratories who first recognized carrisyn as the active ingredient in aloe vera and who helped lead an open label pilot study of the drug. Murdoch worked with Carrington to create his own brand of the aloe vera juice product, which he named the De Veras Beverage and labeled with the disclaimer "Contains Stabilized Aloe Vera Juice with Pulp . . . NO Medical Claims Made." He sold it directly through his own company and through the L.A. Nutritional Products Buyers' Club to PWAs at a cost of $10 a bottle. While no one was cured by taking the substance, many reported slight increases in CD4 cells and improved energy levels.

Most recently, Murdoch has worked with Dr. Robert Mayer in Miami to create an ozone-based vaccine (see Chapter 9). Sam Murdoch, personal communication, 1992; Sam Murdoch, "AIDS: The Disease and Its Therapy," unpublished manuscript, 1984; H. R. McDaniel et al., "A clinical pilot study using carrisyn in the treatment of AIDS," *American Society of Clinical Pathologists,* New Orleans, 1987, p. 120; H. R. McDaniel et al., "A Favorable Response of HIV-1 infected patients to Oral Acemannan," unpublished manuscript.

Page 44 On the price increase of Ribavirin: The actual cause of the price increase in ribavirin was linked to the collapse of the peso, the renewal of ICN Pharmaceutical's three-year price agreement with the Mexican government, and the burgeoning demand for the drug among AIDS patients, which in the history of the underground consistently forced all drug prices to increase. Sam Murdoch, personal communication, April 14, 1992.

45 On driving through customs: A ruling passed in May 1988, the "Personal Import Policy," allowed patients to import a three-month supply of any drug from any country in the world provided that the drug was for his or her own personal use, would not be resold, and would be taken under the supervision of a physician. However, at the time John and I obtained ribavirin and isoprinosine from Mexico, this policy was not yet in effect. After it was, PWAs who made the trip to Mexico and back in subsequent months simply placed their drugs on the dashboard and provided the customs agents with invoices showing the true quantity, and were not given any trouble.

Dextran sulfate was the first drug to be allowed into the country through the Personal Import Policy. Subsequent to the policy's implementation, all packages of dextran sulfate and, later, all other experimental drugs were labeled as follows: "This package contains tablets for personal use by the addressee. It is not for commercial distribution. It is being used under the supervision of Dr. ———. It does not pose a safety risk. Thank you for allowing this to pass into the United States." However, the Personal Import Policy was consistently broken by PWAs and people helping them. Many PWAs were simply not in a position to obtain the drugs themselves and they relied on others, such as Jim Corti and the buyers' clubs, who imported the drugs in large quantities and then redistributed them to the individual patients. Individuals who wanted to obtain the drugs in bulk quantities for themselves and their friends were still forced to find ingenious ways of smuggling them into the country.

46 Ribavirin and isoprinosine trial results: At the Third International Conference on AIDS, held in 1987 in Washington, D.C., principal investigators Peter Heseltine of Harvard University and Peter Mansell of USC/LA County Medical Center announced that in a Phase 2 placebo-controlled trial of ribavirin in 163 ARC patients, no subject among the 52 given 800 milligrams a day of ribavirin progressed to AIDS while 10 of the 56 subjects given a placebo did. Although no immunological improvement was noted in the treated subjects, the researchers concluded that ribavirin might potentially halt the disease's progress.

The results of this trial were questioned by FDA representatives who claimed that the study was biased because ribavirin was given to the healthiest patients and a placebo to the sickest, thus creating an unfair distribution of patients. An FDA analysis of the data found it "very unlikely" that subjects were assigned to drug and placebo groups purely by chance. Essentially, Ellen Cooper testified that, based on her analysis, sixteen patients who already had AIDS symptoms entered the test in violation of the protocol, and twelve were assigned to the placebo group. A statistician for the government said, "If you don't count the sicker patients, the treatment effect disappears." On the basis of these and other findings, the FDA refused to approve the drug for compassionate use in AIDS patients.

Investigator Mansell countered that using different statistical calculations, the differences in CD4 cell counts of the patients' condition did not account for all the differences in the results. Nor did chance. And that the dosage of Ribavirin was a "significant independent predictor" of whether the patient would progress to AIDS.

But negative results continued in other studies. Another Phase 2 double-blind palcebo controlled trial, ironically presented at the same conference as Heseltine's, showed that the drug had no detectable effect on levels of HTLV-III in patients' blood or positive benefits on patients' CD4 cell counts. A further trial reported by Spector and colleagues late in 1987 confirmed these results.

Richard Schulof at the George Washington Medical Center evaluated the combination of ribavirin and isoprinosine in an identical protocol to the one I had followed. Although both drugs seemed well tolerated, no immunological or virological improvements were noted. P. Heseltine et al., Report of Clinical Research, 1987, *Congressional Record* 35, no. 3, p. 616A (from a transcript of hearings of the House Subcommittee on Oversight and Investigations re regulatory activities of the FDA relating to the drug Virazole and its sponsor, ICN Pharmaceuticals, May 28, 1987); Heseltine, response to allegations (letter), *CDC AIDS Weekly,* July 6, 1987, p. 5; Smith et al., "A Phase 2 Placebo-Controlled Clinical Trial of Ribavirin," *Third International Conference on AIDS,* Washington, D.C., 1987, abstract, p. 271; S. Spector et al., "A Placebo-Controlled Clinical Trial of Ribavirin," Report of the International Conference on Antimicrobial Agents and Chemotherapy, October 27, 1987, p. 326; and K. Johnson et al., *Fourth International Conference on AIDS,* Stockholm, 1988, abstract 3571.

Two major double-blind placebo-controlled trials of the use of isoprinosine against HIV infection have been reported in the literature. In one, isoprinosine showed no effect on disease progression compared to placebo.

The second study, conducted in Sweden, showed that 2 of 412 isoprinosine patients progressed to AIDS as compared to 17 of 421 placebo recipients, a difference considered statistically significant. However, no difference in the decrease in CD4 cell count or p-24 antigen level was detected. A follow-up to these results showed that after another six months on the drug, 37 more subjects had progressed to AIDS: 73 percent were from the placebo group and only 27 percent were from the group on the drug. However, there was still no apparent clinical benefit or significant increase in CD4 cells.

In addition, a small study in HIV-seropositive men who were given a combined dosage regimen of both ribavirin and isoprinosine showed that the drugs produced no increases in CD4 cell counts, DTH skin test reactions, or other immune functions. M. Loveless et al., *Fifth International Conference on AIDS,* Montreal, 1989, abstract W.B.P. 288: p. 288; C. Pedersen et al., "The efficacy of isoprinosine in preventing AIDS in persons with HIV infection," *New England Journal of Medicine* 322, no. 25 (1990), pp. 1757–63; and S. Schulof, "Clinical, Virologic and Immunologic Effects of Combination Therapy with Ribavirin and Isoprinosine in HIV-Infected Homosexual Men," *Journal of AIDS* 3 (1990), pp. 485–92.

Page 46 Fauci's medical background: "Anthony S. Fauci, MD," *HIV* 1, no. 1, p. 2.

Fauci and roles of NCI and NIAID in clinical trials: Bruce Nussbaum, *Good Intentions: How Big Business and the Medical Establishment Are Corrupting the Fight Against AIDS* (Boston: Atlantic Monthly Press, 1990), p. 145.

47 Kramer's attack on Fauci: Larry Kramer, "An Open Letter to Dr. Anthony Fauci," *Village Voice* 33, no. 22 (May 31, 1988), pp. 18–20.

50 HPA-23 background: HPA-23—famous because the actor Rock Hudson had traveled to the Pasteur Institute to receive it—is, like AZT, a reverse transcriptase inhibitor. In the early 1980s, researchers at the NCI found that HPA-23 had some inhibitory effects on reverse transcriptase of the mouse leukemia retrovirus in tissue culture assays. However, the drug has shown little or no inhibitory effect on HIV RT in culture. Clinical trials in Paris have been ongoing since 1984 but have not produced noteworthy results, and the drug is not currently studied in the United States.

60 On the federal AIDS budget: The $20 million allocated by Congress in 1985 was only a fraction of the total Public Health Service Budget for AIDS, which allocated and reallocated funds among the CDC, NIH, NAIAD, NIMH, and various other agencies. The budget expended for AIDS in fiscal year 1982 was only $5.5 million. It increased to $28.7 million in fiscal year 1983, $61.4 million in 1984, and up to $108.6 million in fiscal year 1985. Sandra Panem, *The AIDS Bureaucracy* (Cambridge, Mass.: Harvard University Press, 1988), p. 83.

The NIH and AIDS research: Raymond Keith Brown, in *AIDS, Cancer, and the Medical Establishment* (New York: Robert Speller, 1986), refers to the National Institute of Health as "a bastion of conservatism that has poured billions of dollars down the avenues of orthodoxy and scientific fashion and has operated with guidelines that protect the conventional while discouraging originality or independence."

Robert Gallo described the NIH as an impressive, sprawling, plush green campus in Bethesda and noted that the *Scientist* "hailed the NIH as the crown jewel" of the U.S. government's biomedical research enterprise that employs no less than 10 percent of the world's top 100 most cited biomedical scientists.

A more objective analysis would show that the NIH is a large medical campus that sprawls over 300 acres of what was once Bethesda, Maryland, farmland. Its 64 buildings are home to hundreds of research laboratories and offices, a 540-bed research hospital, a large medical library, and the largest staff of scientists and doctoral-level biomedical researchers gathered at any one place in the world.

The NIH is organized into thirteen separate institutes specializing in different groups of diseases. The largest and best known of these is the National Cancer Institute, where Gallo's Laboratory of Tumor Cell Biology is located. Next in order of size is the National Heart, Lung and Blood Institutes. The third-largest is the National Institute of Allergy and Infectious Diseases (NIAID), where most of the AIDS research programs are conducted, under the direction of Dr. Anthony Fauci.

In the mid-1980s, some scientists came to believe that the NIH was beginning to view the challenge of AIDS research as theirs alone—that the problem would ultimately be solved by NIH scientists, and that the NIH wanted to maintain a dominant, singular presence in the field of AIDS.

And AIDS activists charged that the NIH actually stood for "Not Interested in Homosexuals," that it had produced only one drug, AZT, in ten years of research, and that under more careful scrutiny, the NIH was overwhelmed by a variety of problems—ranging from the conservative bias of modern science to low government-scale salaries, organizational stagnation, and institutional inbreeding, all of which undermined its ability to conduct innovative AIDS research. Paul Varnell, "NIH in Turmoil—Accused of Folly and Possible Fraud by Activists," *The Weekly News*, August 7, 1991, p. 26.

61   Today, fifty-two sites in the system: From NIAID, *AIDS Clinical Trial Units* (ACTUs), a list of NIAID's clinical trial sites and principal investigators.

CHAPTER 4

64   Broder's cancer research background: Dominique Lapierre, *Beyond Love*, translated from the French by Kathryn Spink (New York: Warner Books, 1991), p. 233.

On *in vitro* effects of Suramin: H. Mitsuya et al., "Suramin protection of T cells *in vitro* against infectivity and cytopathic effect of HTLV-III," *Science* 126 (1984), pp. 172–74.

On early AIDS Suramin studies: S. Broder et al., "Effects of Suramin on HTLV-III/LAV infection presenting as Kaposi's Sarcoma or ARC," *Lancet* 1985, pp. 627–30.

65 Cheson and suramin studies: Denise Grady, "Look, Doctor, I'm Dying, Give Me the Drug," *Discover,* August 1986, pp. 78–86.

Wolfe and problems with suramin: Nussbaum, *Good Intentions: How Big Business and the Medical Establishment Are Corrupting the Fight Against AIDS* (Boston: Atlantic Monthly Press, 1990), p. 23.

Cheson and problems with suramin: Grady, "Look, Doctor," p. 85.

Premature deaths with suramin: Nussbaum, p. 23.

66 Kidney damage and muscle weakness: Nussbaum, *Good Intentions,* p. 23.

Deaths during the study: Grady, "Look, Doctor," p. 85.

Suramin study results: The study also noted that suramin, at doses of 0.5, 1.0, and 1.5 grams given weekly for up to six months to 41 AIDS or ARC patients produced no regression of KS. Although six patients became HIV-culture-negative during the trial, all but one of these six had disease progression. Decreases in the numbers of total CD4 cell counts were noted in ARC and AIDS patients. L. D. Kaplan et al., "Lack of Response to Suramin in Patients with AIDS and ARC," *American Journal of Medicine* 82 (March 23, 1987), pp. 615–20.

67 Underground dextran sulfate protocol: Rob Springer, "A protocol for the combined use of dextran sulfate and AZT," unpublished manuscript, June 1985.

68 DTC background: DTC was very similar to a drug called levamisole, an immunomodulator that proved useful in treating certain cancers in Europe and which was approved by the FDA for certain cancers in 1991. Because levamisole was unpatentable, the Merieux Institute in 1985 created its own product, Imuthiol.

Dr. Jean-Marie Lang and colleagues in cooperation with the Merieux Institute reported on an eight-month clinical trial in France in which 83 asymptomatic or symptomatic ARC patients received either one weekly oral dose of 10 milligrams per kilogram of DTC or a placebo. The authors of the article, which stirred broadened interest in the drug in the United States, concluded that "DTC might increase the number of T cell precursors responsive to T cell differentiation signals, might inhibit HIV enzymatic pathways and even act as an intracellular 'scavenger' of cytotoxic free oxygen radicals." J.-M. Lang et al., "Randomized Double-Blind Placebo-Controlled Trial of DTC in HIV Infection," *Lancet,* September 24, 1988, pp. 702–05.

69 Springer on metal-chelating agents: Pompidou et al., "In vitro replication of HTLV-III in infected lymphocytes by DTC and isoprinosine," *Lancet,* 425, 1985, p. 73; and D. W. Hutchinson, "Metal chelators as potential antiviral agents," *Antiviral Research* 8 (1985), p. 193.

"I encoat each tablet": There were companies in southern California and elsewhere capable of enterically coating the capsules. But most required a huge minimum order of capsules, volume that Springer was not able to provide.

71 The 1978 article to which Springer referred was N. F. Moore et al., "Interaction of Vascular Stomatitis Virus with Lipid Vesicles: Depletion of Cholesterol and Effect on Virion Membrane Fluidity and Infectivity," *Journal of Virology* 27, no. 2 (1978), p. 320.

HIV, cholesterol, and AL-721: Lyte et al., "A special lipid mixture for membrane fluidization," *Biochimica et Biophysica Acta* (1985), pp. 133–38.

AL-721 inhibiting HIV *in vitro:* P. Sarin et al., "Effects of a Novel Compound (AL-721) on HTLV-III Infectivity In Vitro" (letter), *Lancet* 313, no. 20 (November 14, 1985), pp. 1289–90. (The background of AL-721 is explained more fully in Chapter 5 of this book, pp. 91–93.)

AL-721 study of 60 people in Israel: *Baltimore Jewish Times*, October 9, 1985.

72 DNCB background: The grass-roots guerrilla clinic movement for the manufacture and distribution of DNCB was pioneered in 1984 by Jim Henry, a San Francisco AIDS patient who helped establish a national DNCB information phone line to disseminate information on DNCB to interested persons. The network also included individuals in each city who actually prepared large doses of the drug and distributed it to HIV and KS patients, in a similar manner as Springer.

There was renewed interest in DNCB in 1990 when the role of dendritic cell infection was specified as an important part of the pathogenesis of HIV. Several studies are in progress. Stricker et al., "Topical DNCB: A Feasible and Economical Treatment for AIDS?" unpublished manuscript, 1990.

74 On Jerome Horwitz: Because Horwitz never patented the drug, he never shared in any of the profits. Nussbaum, *Good Intentions,* p. 178.

75 AZT research at Max Planck Institute: Linda Wastila et al., "The History of AZT," *Journal of Clinical Research and Pharmacoepidemiology* 4 (1990), pp. 25–37.

76 In *Beyond Love,* Dominique Lapierre's comprehensive history of AIDS medicine, Sam Broder is quoted as saying, "The directors of Burroughs Wellcome were afraid of not getting the necessary finances from their directorship to see that kind of venture through to its conclusion. And even if they managed to come up with a drug, they weren't a hundred percent sure that the operation would one day be commercially profitable. I couldn't hold it against them. More than anything else, I wanted that enterprise to be profit making. Not because of any personal devotion to capitalism, but for the simple reason that a commercial failure would have the effect of putting all the other pharmaceutical laboratories off researching an anti-AIDS medicine." *Beyond Love,* p. 281.

It was named BW509 because it was the 509th compound to be screened for anti-HTLV-III activity by Burroughs Wellcome, and dubbed "Compound S" because it was the nineteenth compound in the batch to be screened and S is the nineteenth letter in the alphabet. Wastila, "History of AZT," p. 40.

Broder and BW509: Nussbaum, *Good Intentions,* pp. 7–30.

NOTES

Page 77 AZT tolerance levels: R. Yarchoan et al., "Administration of AZT, an Inhibitor of HTLV-III Replication, to Patients with AIDS or ARC," *Lancet,* March 15, 1986, pp. 575–80.

Results of Phase 1 AZT trial: Yarchoan, ibid., and Grady, "Look, Doctor," p. 81.

78 Finding thymidine for AZT study: Wastila, "History of AZT," p. 46.

79 Protocol for the Phase 2 AZT trial: "A Protocol to Evaluate the Efficacy of AZT," AZT Working Collaborative Group, 1986.

80 Gottlieb's database search of PCP cases: Randy Shilts, *And the Band Played On: Politics, People and the AIDS Epidemic* (New York: St. Martin's Press, 1987), p. 43.

On Gottlieb's attempt to publish AIDS article: Gottlieb found resistance to his conclusions in the attitude of the *New England Journal of Medicine*'s editor, Arnold Relman, who insisted that he provide thorough documentation on the patients' immunological conditions, and who published the article only after six months' delay. Gottlieb's article actually first appeared in the June 5, 1981, Centers for Disease Control, *Morbidity and Mortality Report.* A faction of Gottlieb's colleagues suggested that a virus of some sort could be at work, perhaps cytomegalovirus (CMV) or a strain of the herpes group, two viruses commonly found in gay men. But Gottlieb was not convinced that CMV alone was the cause. Perhaps, Gottlieb reasoned, something had triggered the activation of the viruses, turning them lethal. Gottlieb performed a massive literature search on CMV and immune suppression, hoping to find some clues. Gottlieb's article first appeared in M. S. Gottlieb et al., *New England Journal of Medicine* 305 (1981), pp. 1425–31. In New York at the end of July 1981, Dr. Alvin Friedman-Kien reported the occurrence of Kaposi's sarcoma during the previous thirty months in twenty-six homosexual men. Eight of the patients had died within twenty-four months of the diagnosis. His report, published exactly two months after Gottlieb's, confirmed what Gottlieb had seen as well: in seven of the KS patients, there were unusual opportunistic infections including pneumonia and toxoplasmosis of the brain. See Centers for Disease Control, *Morbidity and Mortality Report,* volume 30, no. 25 (July 3, 1981), p. 1.

80 Gottlieb and AmFAR: Shilts, *And the Band Played On,* p. 59.

82 On subjects who cheat in clinical trials: The phenomenon of "cheating," in which subjects lie about their true condition to gain admittance to a clinical trial and/or take other experimental medications forbidden by the protocol, is not uncommon. People with life-threatening illnesses, especially PWAs, did engage in this kind of behavior, and it sometimes confounded the results of the trial.

Some activists contended that allowing the more aggressive patients to have other means of obtaining treatment, such as through expanded-access programs and buyers' clubs, would eliminate this population of individuals from participation in Phase 1 and 2 clinical trials of the new drugs. Those patients who did sign up for the trials might be more cooperative and less apt to cheat, the activists reasoned.

85 Withholding AZT and use of placebo: Wastila, "History of AZT," p. 28.

86 Krim on AZT compassionate use: Grady, "Look, Doctor," p. 83. All Krim quotes in this chapter are taken from this article.

87 Weiss's 1985 congressional subcommittee hearing: Krim's testimony also addressed the problem of the lack of laboratories capable of assaying promising compounds, the lack of adequate public education campaigns for HIV prevention, and an end to discrimination against homosexuals. From *Federal and Local Governments' Response to the AIDS Epidemic; Hearings before a Subcommittee of the Committee on Government Operations*, 99th Cong., 1st sess., July 3, 1985, p. 236.

Side effects in Phase 2 AZT trial: Nussbaum, *Good Intentions*, p. 159.

88 The American AZT trial: There was speculation that the data from the Phase 2 AZT trial, in which I had taken part, may have been misinterpreted. From the beginning, it was apparent that AZT produced harmful side effects. In the Los Angeles arm of the trial, at least 50 percent of the subjects experienced major decreases in their total white blood cell counts and, most notably, drops in their red blood cell counts and hemoglobin levels, signs that AZT was killing healthy bone-marrow cells at a rapid pace. There was a mounting campaign among physicians at some sites to close the study down.

It was the University of Miami's Dr. Margaret Fischl who argued for the drug then, convincing the group to persevere. The anemia, Fischl was sure, was not related to an aplastic process and could be corrected with blood transfusions. Six months later, when none of the subjects died of anemia and nineteen of the placebo recipients died, while only one of the AZT-treated patients died from AIDS-related causes, it was Fischl again who helped spearhead the effort to get early approval of the drug from the FDA.

When a federal review team was sorting through the Phase 2 trial data, however, they found one puzzle after another. Immediately after the study was terminated in September 1986, patients who had been on placebo were switched to AZT. Even so, in the following three months, thirteen more people from the original placebo group died, and there were seven deaths among those who had been on AZT from the beginning. Suddenly, the mortality differential between the two groups didn't look quite so dramatic—not nineteen to one, but less than two to one.

Members of the FDA committee collectively noted that at 18 to 24 weeks on the drug, patients' health started declining. Committee Chairman Dr. Itzhak Brook told a packed meeting room, "I was struck by the fact that AZT does not stop deaths. Even those who were switched to AZT still kept dying." Brook added that numerous confounding variables could have entered into the early phase of the study and skewed the results, producing falsely positive data. Many of the subjects, he pointed out—and as I well knew—were not compliant during the trial and were taking other antiviral and immunomodulatory therapies obtained on the underground. Still others, Brook correctly guessed, may have traded halves of capsules so that if one were on placebo and the other on active drug, both would be getting at least a portion of AZT.

Nonetheless, the committee concluded, even with the confounding variables, the initial mortality differential was undeniably impressive. If AZT brought even three to six months for AIDS patients and possibly more for those with ARC, it was a valuable addition to the AIDS pharmacopoeia. Fischl denied that anyone on the committee questioned the legitimacy of the data. She told me, "I was not aware at any time there were any questions about the quality of the data or the research ... on the part of Ellen Cooper or anyone else." But others were not so easily convinced of the solidity of the AZT research design. Dr. Joseph Sonnabend conducted his own investigation into Fischl's research. Sonnabend was concerned because there was no detailed information about what had actually killed the patients who had been taking the placebo; no autopsies had been performed and the exact opportunistic infection or neoplasm that caused death was not isolated. And Sonnabend found another inconsistency: The causes of death provided to the FDA did not match those in the article on the research Fischl had published in the *New England Journal of Medicine.* Sonnabend conjectured that because of the overt changes in red blood cell counts and MCV values, which had never been whited out or hidden on the lab sheets, researchers knew instinctively who was on placebo and who was on active drug, despite the "double-blind" design of the experiment, and thus certain patients may have been neglected or treated differently by investigator clinicians.

And in October 1987, a year after Fischl's study ended, Dr. Gordon Dickinson, Fischl's research collaborator at the University of Miami, presented the results of his own study of patients receiving long-term AZT treatment. During their first six months on the drug, patients did in fact show clinical signs of improvement: weight gain and increased energy levels. They also experienced slight rises in their total CD4 cell counts and clear-cut drops in p-24 antigen. But after six months, the patients began losing weight and their CD4 cells returned to baseline or sub-baseline values. Many developed life-threatening opportunistic infections. Most of the patients at the highest dose of the drug suffered from anemia or granulocytopenia. Dickinson, like other researchers across the globe, concluded that AZT's value was mainly short-term and that its dose required careful monitoring and alteration. The Phase 2 study, which ended after only seven months, was not able to assess the drug's long-term value. Elinor Burkett, "The Queen of AZT," *Miami Herald Tropic Magazine,* September 23, 1990, pp. 8–15; Margaret Fischl, personal communication, April 10, 1992.

Page 88 AZT Phase 2 study results: The results of the Phase 2 study in which I took part showed that 19 placebo recipients and 1 AZT recipient died during the study. Opportunistic infections developed in 45 subjects receiving placebo, as compared to 24 receiving AZT. Karnofsky ratings (patient self-ratings of quality of health) increased significantly among AZT recipients. There was a statistically significant increase in the number of CD4 cells noted in subjects receiving AZT. And skin-test anergy was partially reversed in 29 percent of the subjects receiving AZT, versus 9 percent of those on placebo.

M. A. Fischl et al., "The Efficacy of AZT in the Treatment of Patients with AIDS and ARC," *New England Journal of Medicine* 317 (July 23, 1987), pp. 181–91.

89 Treatment IND background: While a regular IND permit authorized safety studies in small numbers of people, a treatment IND permit allowed, through the granting of a new drug application (NDA), more widespread use of drugs that had been established as safe and possibly effective but which had not been fully approved for the mass market.

CHAPTER 5

90 On safe sex education: Apart from the surgeon general's 1987 pamphlet, it was not until 1991 that state and federal public health officials began to consider the need for more aggressive approaches to safe-sex education, including the distribution of condoms in high schools and the education of females in the negotiation of safe-sex techniques.

91 Effect of egg lipids on cholesterol in cell walls: Lyte et al., "A special lipid mixture for membrane fluidization," *Biochemica et Biophysica Acta* 812 (1985), pp. 133–38.

Change in brain cells of mice: Published in Rivnay et al., "Enhancement of the Response of Aging Mouse Lymphocytes by In Vitro Treatment With Lecithin," *Mechanisms of Aging and Development* 23 (1983), pp. 329–36.

Effect of AL-721 on heroin withdrawal and memory: M. Shinitzky et al., *Physiology of Membrane Fluidity* (Boca Raton, Fla.: CRC Press), p. 101.

Patent for Al-721: M. Shinitzky et al., "Lipid Fraction for Treating Disease," U.S. Patent no. 4,474,773, October 2, 1984.

These AL-721 studies by Samuel were reported in I. Yust et al., "Reduction of Circulating HIV Antigens in Seropositive Patients After Treatment with AL-721," *Israeli Journal of Medical Science* 26 (1990), pp. 20–26.

Gallo's *in vitro* studies of AL-721: P. Sarin et al., "Effects of a Novel Compound (AL-721) on HTLV-III Infectivity In Vitro" (letter), *Lancet* 313, no. 20 (November 14, 1985), pp. 1289–90.

92 Lippa's Phase 1 study of AL-721: M. H. Grieco et al., "Open Study of AL-721 in HIV-infected subjects with generalized lymphadenopathy syndrome," *Third International Conference on AIDS*, Washington, D.C., 1987, abstract T.P. 223. Follow-up published in *Antiviral Research*, 1988, pp. 177–90.

Evaluation of AL-721 in animal studies: L. Antonian et al., "AL-721, a Novel Membrane Fluidizer," *Neuroscience and Biobehavioral Reviews* 11 (Winter 1987), pp. 399–413.

Evaluation of Phase 1 AL-721 study, and vote against further testing: Bruce Nussbaum, *Good Intentions: How Big Business and the Medical Establishment Are Corrupting the Fight Against AIDS* (Boston: Atlantic Monthly Press, 1990), p. 148.

Mildvan's Phase 1 dose-escalating trial: ibid.

Page 93 Results of Mildvan's study: D. Mildvan et al., "An Open Label Dose Ranging Trial of AL-721 in Patients with PGL and ARC," *Journal of AIDS* 4, no.
10 (October 1991), pp. 945–51.

Results confirmed by British study: Peters, *Lancet*, March 3, 1990, p. 545.

Decline of interest in AL-721: Nussbaum, *Good Intentions*, p. 326.

Weizmann Institute agrees to treat May with AL-721: K. Coughlin, "Musi-
cian defies 'death sentence' with help of AIDS Drug from Israel," Newark
Star-Ledger, December 2, 1986, p. 31.

May's account of his treatment with AL-721 first appeared in "AL-721
and the Deadly Silence," *AIDS Treatment News*, no. 21 (January 2, 1987), p.
2.

94 Researchers shared AL-721 formula: Steve Gavin, personal communication,
November 11, 1991.

May's search for company to make AL-721: ibid.

95 On the American Roland version of AL-721: Insiders speculated that the
American Roland product, which Hannan and Callen distributed, bore little
resemblance to the AL-721 made in Israel. Later, though, the health club
obtained the product through other sources, versions which were closer to
the real thing.

May's concern about preparation and availability of AL-721: Shirley May,
personal communication, March 4, 1992.

95 May and AL-721 made by "Nick": ibid.

AL-721 in South Africa: ibid.

96 Lippa's analysis of underground AL-721: Arnold Lippa conducted an analysis of eight underground samples of AL-721, provided by two AIDS patients. The analysis evaluated their phospholipid content and purity. It
showed that only one sample had a PC:PE ratio that was acceptable and
within the correct limits. From a memo from Claire Klepner to Dr. Arnold
Lippa, March 16, 1987.

Concerned that many of the samples might be subject to bacterial
contamination and incorrect manufacturing, Dr. Mathilde Krim wrote a
letter to Dr. Anthony Fauci, urging him to speed the development of ATEU
trials with AL-721. Ultimately, those trials never materialized. Letter from
Dr. Mathilde Krim to Dr. Anthony Fauci, May 4, 1987.

Shinitzky published his most recent studies on the reduction of antigens in
Shinitzky et al., "Suppression of HIV antigenaemia by AL-721" (letter),
Lancet, May 26, 1990, p. 1281.

97 On Gavin's early activities in the underground: Steve Gavin, personal
communication, January 11, 1990.

98 The obscure Russian article was U. E. Zaitseva et al., "Aminonucleosides
and their Derivatives: Synthesis of Amino $-2'-3'-$ Dideoxynucleoside
Triphosphate," translated from *Bioorganicheskaya Khimiya* 10, no. 5 (May 2,
1983), pp. 670–81.

The article by University of Michigan researchers was Glinkski et al., "Nucleoside Synthesis," *Journal of Medicinal Chemistry* 12, no. 1 (1978), pp. 108–09.

"There's no question . . .": Gavin, personal communication, January 11, 1990.

Gavin's efforts to obtain ddC: Jules Parnes, personal communication, March 15, 1989.

99 Gavin and ddI: David Wilson, personal communication, November 12, 1989.

On the underground researchers of the mid-1980s: It is important to note here that although the underground researchers of the mid-1980s were aggressive and hardworking, they were not inherently innovative. Almost every lead they pursued came from a mainstream American or European researcher. At no point did the underground researchers "discover" a novel compound of their own that showed efficacy and gained popularity. In part, this was due to the fact that none of the underground researchers had *in vitro* screening systems or technology to identify such novel compounds.

100 Broder on the AIDS drug underground: Nussbaum, *Good Intentions*, p. 21.

101 "Many individuals . . .": Donald Abrams, "Alternative Therapies in HIV Infection," *AIDS* 4 (December 1990), p. 1179.

102 Background on history of FDA: The FDA emerged from obscurity while it was part of the Agriculture Department when Congress passed the Food, Drug and Cosmetics Act in 1938 in response to more than one hundred deaths that resulted from faulty production of sulfanilamide. This legislation required that new drugs pass safety tests and that relevant data be submitted to the government for clearance prior to licensing; it also expanded the meaning of the term "adulteration," sought greater guarantees of purity of all substances, and extended the law to cover cosmetics for the first time.

In the following years, the American pharmaceutical industry grew exponentially. Whole new classes of drugs entered the marketplace. Many of these drugs were of such complex makeup and had so many potential adverse effects that it was impossible to devise a label that informed the consumer of all the pertinent information. As a result, Congress passed the Durnham-Humphrey Amendment in 1951, exempting certain drugs from the labeling requirements. Instead, these drugs were to be dispensed only under the supervision of a doctor and were available to the consumer only by prescription. This was the basis for the present system.

In 1962, Thalidomide, a sedative for expectant mothers, caused congenital deformities in several thousand British and German infants. The full force of the tragedy was averted in the United States because the drug had not been administratively cleared through the FDA. As a result of this narrow escape, the Kefauver-Harris Amendment to the 1938 Act was pushed through Congress, changing the course of the FDA and its role in American medicine. This amendment gave police powers to the FDA, allowing the agency to make and enforce decisions on drug safety autonomously. More crucial, it gave the FDA the right to demand proof of efficacy, in addition to proof of safety, prior to drug licensing.

The 1962 revision of the law spelled out strict new procedures for drug clearance, recording and reporting experience with new drugs, drug labeling, factory inspection, manufacturing controls, drug patents, and control of information and advertising to physicians. New regulations required relatively long and exhaustive animal testing and human testing, with more difficult approval procedures. The liability, as measured in dollars required to discover and develop a new drug in the United States, was an increase from an average of $6.5 million in 1961 to more than $70 million in 1981. To advance a new drug from investigational status to consideration for approval by the FDA—through trials similar to those I participated in for AZT and Ampligen—could take up to ten years. As a result, the United States began to lose its postwar leadership in the development of innovative drugs. What evolved was a close-knit clique involving the larger drug companies, the FDA, and large academic medical centers that could administer the studies. Smaller companies either went out of business or formed alliances with larger companies that could compete in the marketplace and pay the billions of dollars required to put the drugs through the clinical trials. In the first ten years after the 1962 revision of FDA regulations, the U.S. pharmaceutical industry failed to introduce any new drugs for the treatment of heart disease, high blood pressure, or lung diseases—three of the major causes of death and disability in the United States.

Despite the implementation of the strict new rules for drug safety in the United States, tragedies involving FDA-approved drugs still occurred. The deaths of more than 100 patients around the world due to the FDA-approved anti-arthritis medication Oraflex and the deaths of 852 patients injected with the heart drug epinephrine are only two examples of the failure of the system to protect the public against adverse effects. Meanwhile, it denied U.S. citizens access to new drugs that had become available in other countries until many years after they had been approved and tested overseas. What resulted was a plethora of Mexican cancer clinics and a thriving black market, with mail-order pharmacies springing up all along the U.S. borders with Mexico and Canada and in Europe. Raymond Keith Brown, *AIDS, Cancer, and the Medical Establishment* (New York: Robert Speller, 1986), p. 147.

Page 103 Testing drugs for FDA approval: "The Drug Approval Process," *AIDS Medicines in Development*, Pharmaceutical Manufacturers Association, Summer 1989, p. 5.

$230 million over the course of a twelve-year period: ibid.

Five out of every four thousand: ibid.

IRB: Richard Thompson, "Protecting 'Human Guinea Pigs,' " in *New Drug Development in the United States* (Washington, D.C.: U.S. Food and Drug Administration, revised, 1990), p. 18.

104 Treatment IND background: Treatment IND was a creation of Frank Young, an effort to make investigational drugs available more quickly to

those who met specific criteria. Although AZT was distributed through this mechanism to larger numbers of patients prior to its approval, activists argued that Treatment IND was actually a sham and would not, in any significant way, speed the approval of potentially promising agents.

On personal importation policy: In truth, the Personal Import Policy was consistently broken by PWAs and drug importers. Many PWAs were simply not in a position to find sources and order the drugs they needed themselves, so they relied on buyers' club presidents and importers to purchase and import large quantities of the medications from foreign markets (much larger quantities than the law allowed). These importers then redistributed the drugs to patients in the United States.

On personal importation policy: From a document dated July 20, 1988, from the FDA Director of Regional Operations, directed to regional and food directors, import branch managers, and compliance directors. Reprinted in James Johnson, *How to Buy Almost Any Drug Legally Without a Prescription* (New York: Avon Books, 1990), p. 24.

105 Compassionate Use IND: Thompson, "Protecting 'Human Guinea Pigs,' " p. 18.

James on the mainstream system of drug research: John S. James, "The Drug Trials Debacle, Part II: What to Do Now," *AIDS Treatment News*, no. 78 (May 5, 1989), p. 4.

106 Harrington on government-sponsored clinical trials: ACT UP testimony before the Interim Report to the National Committee to Review Current Procedures for Approval of New Drugs for Cancer and AIDS (Lasagna Committee), May 2, 1989. Mark Harrington, personal communication, January 7, 1991.

107 Cooper's professional background: Philip Boffey, "At Fulcrum of Conflict, Regulator of AIDS Drugs," *New York Times*, August 19, 1988, p. A-12.

108 Cooper on the early approval of ddI: Jonathan Kwitny, *Acceptable Risks* (New York: Simon & Schuster, 1992), p. 410.

109 Cooper as scapegoat: Boffey, "At Fulcrum of Conflict."

21 percent using unapproved or unconventional treatment: Greenblatt et al., "The heavy utilization of medications by patients attending an AIDS clinic," *Report of the 29th International Conference on Antimicrobial Agents and Chemotherapy*, Houston, September 1989, abstract 110.

Up to 52 percent: From the San Francisco Men's Health Study (1990), unpublished personal communication.

110 Three years after decreasing our doses: The study that established the 600-mg/day dose as being equally effective and significantly less toxic than the 1,200-mg/day dose was: Margaret Fischl et al., "A randomized controlled trial of a reduced daily dose of zidovudine in patients with AIDS," *New England Journal of Medicine* 323, 15 (1990), pp. 1009–14.

112 AZT price: from a press release of the Burroughs Wellcome Company, 1987.

Page 113 Burroughs Wellcome's defense of AZT price: Nussbaum, *Good Intentions,*
p. 176.

Prediction of first-year earnings from AZT: ibid.

Successful effort to get AZT price reduced: ibid., p. 321.

On Burroughs Wellcome lawsuit: In 1991, the PWA Health Group of New
York filed a lawsuit against Burroughs Wellcome, asking a federal court to
invalidate the patent the company held on AZT, thus stripping the company of its exclusive right to manufacture and sell it, and allowing other
drug companies to produce and market the compound.

The federal government also wanted to break Burroughs Wellcome's
monopoly on AZT and encourage lower-priced competition to manufacture the drug. On May 28, 1991, a spokeswoman for the NIH indicated that
NCI investigators should have been named co-inventors on the AZT-
related patents issued to Burroughs Wellcome. Burroughs Wellcome maintained that *its* scientists were the first to use AZT for the treatment of HIV
infection, and that "this creative insight" is the basis for the patent granted
in 1988. Although Burroughs Wellcome acknowledges that there were
outside collaborators, the company remains firm in its assertion that they
were not co-inventors. But scientists in the NIH claimed that doctors there
applied state-of-the-art laboratory analysis (Broder's assay) in early 1985 to
evaluate its possible therapeutic value and that "the intellectual and scientific contributions made by NCI to the evaluation of AZT were essential
components to the invention of AZT therapy for AIDS." Nevertheless, the
NIH itself did not file the lawsuit; it was the People with AIDS Health
Group whose action would set the stage for the resolution of the issue.

Ultimately, though, a U.S. Circuit Court judge dismissed the case.
The judge's dismissal hinged on the existence of litigation in North Carolina between Burroughs Wellcome and Barr Laboratories, a manufacturer
of generic drugs. In that litigation, Barr also attempted to have Burroughs
Wellcome's patents declared invalid, so that it could market its own generic
version of AZT. Under a license awarded to Barr by the NIH, the company
holds the government's rights, if any, to the inventions concerning the
anti-AIDS uses of AZT. Insiders speculated that it was the PWA Health
Group's action that set the stage for the positive action in Barr's litigation.

115 Effects of dextran sulfate on AZT: R. Ueno et al., "Dextran Sulfate, a Potent
Anti-HIV Agent in Vitro Having Synergism with AZT," *Lancet,* August 22,
1987.

Subsequent studies of dextran sulfate: H. Mitsuya et al., "Dextran Sulfate
Suppression of Viruses in the HIV Family: Inhibition of Virion Binding to
CD4 + Cells," *Science* 240 (April 29, 1988), pp. 646–49.

116 On Corti's importation of dextran sulfate: Corti later revealed to me that he
found it difficult to obtain the preferred brand of dextran sulfate—KOWA
—in the spring of 1988. There was speculation that someone in the American government or the ACTG system had asked pharmacies in Japan to stop
selling the drug to Corti, who had become known to AIDS patients as "the
Dextran man." Corti ultimately found another source of the KOWA brand

in Bangkok and imported the drug from that country. Jim Corti, personal communication, May 10, 1989.

118 Dr. Michael Scolaro background: Michael Scolaro was a Los Angeles physician with a large AIDS and ARC practice who consistently tried a variety of alternative therapies. Corti had worked for him in the past and had kept in continuous contact with him. Scolaro reported in the February 12, 1988, *AIDS Treatment News* that more than 60 percent of the thirty patients he monitored who had used dextran sulfate for at least two months had shown dramatic improvements in lab tests and some increase in CD4 cell counts.

CHAPTER 6

125 Hay "released the anger . . .": Carolyn Reuben, "Healing Your Life with Louise Hay," *East West*, June 1988, pp. 35–41.

129 Louise Hay, *You Can Heal Your Life* (Carson, Calif.: Hay House, 1987).

Excellent summaries of the most recent research in psychoneuro-immunology are provided in Dr. Bernie Siegel's *Love, Medicine & Miracles* (New York: Harper and Row, 1988), and Dr. Deepak Chopra's *Quantum Healing: Exploring the Frontiers of Mind/Body Medicine* (New York: Bantam Books, 1989).

CHAPTER 7

132 Herve Guibert, *To the Friend Who Did Not Save My Life* (New York: Collier, 1991), p. 78.

135 I actually visited a CFIDS specialist in Los Angeles who, without being able to entirely rule out the syndrome, explained that my laboratory parameters were not consistent with CFIDS.

136 HIV dementia's array of symptoms: B. Navia et al., "The AIDS dementia complex as the presenting or sole manifestation of HIV infection," *Annals of Neurology* 44 (1988), pp. 65–9.

HIV dementia as early manifestation of AIDS: This trend may have changed. Early in the epidemic, a significant percentage of new AIDS diagnoses were made only on the basis of symptoms of HIV dementia. These newly diagnosed people often suffered from HIV dementia but no other AIDS-related condition. By 1991, many clinicians reported that they no longer saw people who had only HIV dementia. They suggested that HIV dementia had increasingly become a disease of late-stage AIDS in which people also suffered from multiple infections and neoplasms. Exactly why this occurred is unclear, although the early introduction of AZT and other antivirals may have stemmed the prevalence of the condition in some patients. Derek Link, "AIDS Dementia Complex," *GMHC Treatment Issues* 6, no. 2 (1991), p. 4.

137 Singer's studies of patients with HIV dementia: E. Singer et al., "Cerebrospinal Fluid and Blood Markers in HIV Seropositive Individuals," *Fifth International Conference on AIDS*, Montreal, 1989, abstract Th.B.P. 236; and E. Singer

et al., "Neuro-Performance Measurement and Memory Profiles of Disability in HIV Seropositive Individuals," ibid., abstract Th.B.P. 292.

Page 139 On mandatory screening: At least two of the nation's leading ethicists have argued against universal mandatory screening and suggest that any potential benefits would be outweighed by the consequences of the invasion of the individual's privacy. The researchers note that there are special exceptions: special settings such as blood banks and health-care settings involving the open wounds of patients. The researchers conclude that anonymous testing based on moral obligation without legal coercion offers the greatest protection for the confidentiality of test results and the greatest protection of the rights of the individual. Ronald Bayer et al., "HIV Antibody Screening: An Ethical Framework for Evaluating Proposed Programs," *JAMA* 256 (October 3, 1986), pp. 1768–74.

140 On syphilis and AIDS: Harris Coulter, *AIDS and Syphilis: The Hidden Link* (Berkeley: North Atlantic Books, 1987; reprinted in 1990 by B. Jain Publishers, Paharganj, New Delhi). Quoted passages: "Like AIDS, . . ." (p. 23); "The advent of oral antibiotics . . ." (p. 25).

141 Positive reaction to syphilis disappeared: D. Johns et al., "Alteration in the Natural History of Neurosyphilis by Concurrent Infection with HIV," *New England Journal of Medicine* 346, no. 25, pp. 1569–72.

Edmund Tramont, *New England Journal of Medicine* (June 18, 1987).

143 CDC's recommendation on treatment of syphilis: Due in part to Coulter's and others' warnings about misdiagnosis and mistreatment of syphilis, the Centers for Disease Control published "A Recommendation for Diagnosing and Treating Syphilis in HIV-Infected Patients," in its October 7, 1988, *Morbidity and Mortality Report*. The report recommended that when clinical findings of syphilis are present in an HIV-infected person but the blood tests for syphilis are negative, other tests such as the FTA-AB (fluorescent treponemal antibody absorption), dark stain, and examination of biopsy tissue should be used; and it also recommended treatment of infected patients with long courses of intravenous penicillin.

144 Caiazza's published findings: Stephen Caiazza, "Chronic Sphirochetal Infection and the Pathogenesis of AIDS," *Quantum Medicine* 1, no. 1 (January 1988), pp. 117–21. The theory is also explained in Caiazza's self-published book: *AIDS: One Doctor's Struggle* (Highland Park, N.J.: Caiazza, P.O. Box 4523, 1989).

Caiazza's self-treatment: Stephen Caiazza, personal communication, February 5, 1988.

On my own penicillin treatment: One year later, I did undergo the treatment in Florida. I experienced no improvement in my memory or concentration.

145 On the cause of Dr. Caiazza's death: The true cause remains somewhat of a mystery. Several individuals told me they believed that Caiazza, buckling under the intense pressures of the medical establishment, which opposed his controversial views on AIDS, may have committed suicide.

146 Ineffectiveness of dextran sulfate given orally: Investigators at Johns Hopkins University gave 18 healthy, uninfected men either a single 1,800-milligram oral dose or a single 225-milligram or 300-milligram intravenous dose of dextran sulfate. For the drug given orally, less than 1 microgram of the drug per milliliter of blood and less than 0.5 percent of the drug was evident in urine samples. By contrast, intravenous dextran sulfate produced 26 to 35 micrograms of the drug per milliliter of blood and 25 to 29 percent of the drug in urine. D. Abrams et al., "Oral Dextran Sulfate in the Treatment of AIDS and ARC," *Annals of Internal Medicine* 110 (1989), pp. 183–88.

Results of clinical trial of oral dextran sulfate at San Francisco General Hospital: D. Abrams et al., ibid.

Ineffectiveness of dextran sulfate given intravenously: Anecdotal reports from physicians monitoring patients taking dextran sulfate indicated no significant toxicity but no changes in CD4 cell counts or p-24 antigen levels. "Dextran Sulfate," *GMHC Treatment Issues* 1, no. 2 (December 31, 1987), p. 5.

Pentosan-polysulfate background: A two-year clinical trial of pentosan-polysulfate indicated that the drug, despite its apparent *in vitro* activity against HIV, produced little clinical improvement or increase in CD4 cell counts in ARC or AIDS patients. B. Ruf et al., "Two-Year Clinical Trial With Pentosan-Polysulfate in HIV-Infected Patients," *Fifth International Conference on AIDS,* Montreal, 1989, abstract W.B.P. 300.

Imuthiol background: According to news reports, a senior executive at Institute Merieux International said that while Imuthiol did not produce harmful effects, neither did it show benefits. The executive went on to state: "The initial results, while not yet fully understood, are unfavorable to the product and inconsistent with the results observed in earlier trials (which showed much higher increases in CD4 cells in a small group of ARC patients). Pending further investigation of these results, after informing the Health Authorities concerned, Pasteur Merieux International has decided to suspend clinical and commercial use of DTC."

At least one American study, involving 389 patients (107 AIDS and 282 ARC), was unable to replicate the French results. While there were 62 percent fewer opportunistic infections in the group treated with Imuthiol, equal numbers of patients died in both groups. Average CD4 cell counts remained stable in both groups. E. Hersch et al., "A randomized, double-blind placebo-controlled trial of DTC in patients with ARC or AIDS," *Sixth International Conference on AIDS,* San Francisco, 1990, Abstract S.B. 498.

A Scandinavian study found that the drug produced no improvements in CD4 cell counts of PHA responses in 15 HIV-seropositive asymptomatic men. M. Hording et al., "Lack of Immunomodulating Effect of DTC on HIV-Positive Patients," *Journal of Immunopharmacology* 12, no. 2 (1990), pp. 145–47.

In April 1990, the FDA denied the manufacturer's application for Treatment IND status for Imuthiol; however, the drug was approved in New Zealand.

Page 149 How neurotransmitters operate: M. Hutchison, *Megabrain: New Tools and Techniques for Brain Growth and Mind Expansion* (New York: Ballantine Books, 1986), p. 259.

Effect of Peptide T on CD4 receptors: C. Pert et al., *Proceedings of the National Academy of Sciences* 83 (1986), pp. 9254–8; and D. Brenneman et al., "Peptide T Prevents GP120 Induced Neuronal Cell Death In Vitro: Relevance to AIDS Dementia," *Drug Development Research* (1988).

Peptide T trial results: In a small clinical trial of Peptide T in Sweden which began in 1986, subjects with HIV-related dementia experienced subjective improvements in memory and concentration and significant positive changes in their MRI brain scans. Further, the subjects experienced decreases in their cerobrospinal fluid levels of beta-2 microglobulin, a surrogate marker thought to be possibly elevated in patients with HIV dementia. A. Sonnerberg et al., "Treatment of Four Patients with Peptide T: A Pilot Study," *Fourth International Conference on AIDS*, Stockholm, 1988, abstract 3102.

But controversy over Peptide T erupted at the Third International Conference on AIDS in Washington, D.C., in 1987, when Dana Farber Cancer Institute researchers William Haseltine and Joseph Sodroski announced that, despite repeated testing, they were unable to reproduce the *in vitro* results reported by Pert and her colleagues. The researchers disputed Pert's conclusions that Peptide T blocks the gp120 and that the region of gp120 specified by Peptide T interacts with the cellular CD4 molecule. Haseltine flatly told the Boston *Globe:* "Peptide T does not work." (Pert responded to the charges by pointing out that Sodroski created experimental conditions inapplicable to *in vivo* conditions by using high concentrations of HIV as well as target cells with high receptor densities.)

Despite all the controversy, a Phase 1 trial of the drug, in 1987, continued at USC, co-sponsored by the NIH and led by Dr. Peter Heseltine (the principal investigator of the controversial ribavirin study). Heseltine's results showed that while CD8 cell counts increased in many patients, there were no other significant immunological changes such as improvements in CD4 cell counts or DTH skin tests. P. Heseltine et al., "Peptide T Phase 1 Study: Immuno/Virologic Results," *Sixth International Conference on AIDS*, San Francisco, 1990.

In a separate unpublished study made in July 1989 Peter Bridge reported treating twelve HIV-seropositive moderately neuropsychiatrically impaired men with a range of doses of Peptide T. After twelve weeks, only one person continued to be classified as neuropsychiatrically impaired; but there were no significant changes in immunological or virological parameters. P. Bridge et al., "Improvement in AIDS Patients on Peptide T" (letter), *Lancet*, July 1989, pp. 226–27.

A 1988 study of Peptide T, on thirty-two HIV-positive patients, used the intranasal method of administration at the Fenway Community Health Center in Boston and showed that Peptide T produced an improvement in HIV-related cognitive dysfunction, a reduction in fatigue, and statistically significant weight gain, with some significant changes in mean CD8 cell counts but none in mean CD4 cell counts. K. Mayer et al., "Phase 1 Study on Intranasal Peptide T," *Fourth International Conference on AIDS,* Stockholm, 1988.

151 Improvements reported using Peptide T: It must be noted that the mainstream Peptide T trials that reported positive results in these areas used the intranasal and intravenous methods of administration, not subcutaneous. However, insiders have speculated that subcutaneous administration of between 2 and 5 milligrams a day produced adequate blood levels, as effective as intravenous, and that the drug effectively crossed the blood/brain barrier. Alan Field, personal communication, January 2, 1991.

On Corti's importation of Peptide T: Corti flew to Copenhagen and picked up 15 grams of Peptide T at a cost of $10,000. He worked with a pharmacist in Los Angeles to prepare the Peptide T in a special mist for intranasal administration. After the third pickup, a Carlsburg executive refused to sell Corti any more of the drug. The company had entered into a deal with the U.S. government to supply the drug for government-sponsored trials. Corti convinced the company to supply the drug by sending it through Paris, to lessen the suspicion that it was being used on the American underground. But shipping it through Paris meant increased taxes and a higher price passed on to PWAs. So Corti worked with a nonprofit foundation in London that could bring drugs into England without paying the value-added tax. In this way, the price of Peptide T was kept more reasonable. Jim Corti, personal communication, March 7, 1991.

On Woodruff's acquisition of Peptide T: Ron Woodruff, personal communication, November 5, 1990; and "Suit Says FDA Blocks Vital AIDS Drug," Associated Press report, December 6, 1990.

152 On Retrogen: Later, Dr. Paul Ki at Washington Biolab in Ames, Iowa, developed a product similar to Ampligen, which he called Retrogen. He distributed small amounts of the drug to physicians across the country and tracked patient response to the medication. Paul Ki, personal communication, November 4, 1988.

CHAPTER 8

154 On *in vitro* effects of Ampligen: D. C. Montefiori et al., "Antiviral activity of mismatched double-stranded RNA against HIV *in vitro,*" *Proceedings of the National Academy of Sciences* 84 (1987), pp. 2985–89.

On the Phase 1 Human Trials of Ampligen: William Carter et al., "Clinical Immunological and Virological Effects of Ampligen, a Mismatched Double-Stranded RNA, in Patients with AIDS or ARC," *Lancet,* June 6, 1987, pp. 1286–92.

Du Pont sponsors Phase 2 clinical trial: "Researchers to Present Preliminary Research on Ampligen," *Wall Street Journal,* December 4, 1987, p. 42.

Protocol of Phase 2 clinical trial: "A Multicenter Controlled Study of the Efficacy and Safety of Ampligen in Patients with AIDS Related Immune Dysfunction," Protocol AM0101/CBA.AR001, HEM Research Inc., February 1, 1988.

Page 156 On David Wilson's true identity: David Wilson was not his real name. It was a name he created for himself for use on the underground. At the request of several individuals, I have maintained his anonymity here.

157 On change in sexual behavior: "Gay Males Altering Sexual Behavior, Researchers Report," *American Medical News,* July 7, 1984; and W. Winkelstein et al., "The San Francisco men's health study: Reduction in human immunodeficiency virus transmission among homosexual/bisexual men, 1982–86," *American Journal of Public Health* 76 (1987), pp. 685–9. While gay men altered their sexual behavior early in the epidemic, heterosexuals did not. At least two studies published in 1992 showed that over two-thirds of sexually active heterosexual young people did not practice safe sex.

159 Levin's HIV video: Alan S. Levin, "HIV as a Chronic, Manageable Disease Process," videotaped presentation, January 1988.

On surrogate markers: The true value of surrogate markers in gauging disease progression or even a treatment's efficacy has recently been questioned. P-24 antigen and beta-2 microglobulin have produced especially questionable results in these regards. According to some researchers, only CD4 levels and other measures of immune function seem to be valuable surrogate markers.

160 Transfer factor background: Transfer factor, an immunomodulator, is a polypeptide secreted by lymphocytes activated by antigens during the process of cell-mediated immunity. When nonactivated lymphocytes come into contact with transfer factor, they are specifically activated against the same antigen that activated the lymphocyte producing the factor. Levin produced his own transfer factor by using leukocytes from HIV-seropositive individuals with high antibody concentrations to HIV antigens pooled with transfer factor prepared from the serum of healthy subjects and extracting the transfer factor by dialysis. A preliminary report showed that transfer factor restored delayed hypersensitivity reactions in six of seven previously anergic AIDS patients. However, the patients demonstrated unchanged CD4 cell counts and function. J. T. Carey et al., "Augmentation of Skin Test Reactivity and Lymphocyte Blastogenesis in Patients with AIDS Treated With Transfer Factor," *Journal of the American Medical Association* 257, no. 5 (February 6, 1987), pp. 651–5.

Levin on HIV therapy: Alan S. Levin, "The Treatment of HIV-Positive Asymptomatic Individuals," unpublished manuscript, 1987; and "Dr. Levin Developing New Drug," *Positive Outlook,* the newsletter of Positive Action Healthcare, Spring 1988, p. 1.

163 On the results of the Ribavirin tracking project: The results of Project Inform's ribavirin tracking project were not published in a scientific journal. However, they were published in a report issued to the community. The results showed that "two-thirds of those in the monitoring program asserted subjectively that their rate of deterioration from HIV slowed, stopped or reversed while on treatment." *A Report to the Community: HIV-infected People Self Medicating with Ribavirin and Isoprinosine Purchased in Mexico.* Project Inform, 1987.

Passive immunotherapy: Critics have indicated that the clinical value of administering anti-p-24 neutralizing antibodies has not been established and that the true protective value of these antibodies is suspect. Moreover, the immune-system improvements seen in patients treated with passive immunotherapy were mixed. The one obvious, undeniable benefit—lack of occurrence of opportunistic infections—could be due as much to the fact that the patients received high concentrations of antibodies against a broad spectrum of pathogens, not just HIV, from the serum of the donors, causing such opportunistic infections as toxoplasmosis and cryptococcal meningitis, and that it was these neutralizing antibodies that were producing the effect. G. Jackson, "Passive Immunoneutralization of HIV in patients with advanced AIDS," *Lancet* (1988), pp. 647–51; and A. Karpas et al., "Long-term follow-up on the effects of passive immunization in patients with ARC and AIDS," *Sixth International Conference on AIDS*, San Francisco, 1990, abstract SB.499.

164 Ampligen development discontinued: Michael Waldholz, "Du Pont Raises Dust by Ending Venture," *Wall Street Journal*, September 1, 1988.

Phase 2 Ampligen trials closed: Gina Kolata, "Poor Results Bring End to Anti-AIDS Drug Study," *New York Times*, October 15, 1988.

In December 1989, however, businessman E. Paul Charlap formed an investor group to buy 27 percent of the Ampligen's developer, HEM Research, and to sponsor further clinical trials with the drug in patients with HIV disease.

Some researchers believed that Ampligen had been ineffective because it had been given in too low a dose, and because it was administered in plastic bags (the chemists claimed that a substance on the inside of the bags lessened the drug's true effectiveness). The subsequent study of Ampligen in AIDS used doses of up to 700 milligrams, and subjects were given the drug directly from glass ampules. Even with this dosing regimen and method of administration, the drug failed to produce promising results and all trials were closed. But researchers continued to study the drug's effects on Chronic Fatigue Immune Dysfunction Syndrome (CFIDS), and a clinical trial completed in the fall of 1991 showed that the drug did seem to have some positive impact on CFIDS. "Against all odds, E. Paul Charlap bets on Ampligen, forsaken by others," *Wall Street Journal*, December 28, 1989, p. B-6.

165 MMI results: Z. Lurhuma et al., "The Results of MM1, an antiviral agent in the treatment of AIDS," translated from *Egyptian Medical Journal*, July 1988.

Travel to Zaire for MM1: Barry Gingell, "MM1," *GMHC Treatment Issues* 2, no. 7, pp. 11–12.

Sale of homes to raise money: John Scafutti, personal communication, October 15, 1988.

166 Resistocell: Dr. Karl von Weldt, personal communication, June 1988.

170 Major histocompatibility system: *Basic and Clinical Immunology* (Los Altos, Calif.: Lange Medical Publications, 1980), pp. 52–7.

Donor matching: ibid., p. 58.

Page 171 Hauptman's transfusion therapy study: Stephen S. Hauptman et al., "Immune Reconstitution Following Allogenic Lymphocyte Transfusions in Patients with AIDS," Cardeza Foundation and Department of Medicine, Jefferson Medical College of Thomas Jefferson University, unpublished manuscript, October 1987.

172 Failure of transfusion therapy: Stephen Hauptman, personal communication, November 14, 1988.

173 Efficacy of ddI without AZT's side effects: R. Yarchoan, "In vitro activity against HIV and favorable toxicity profile of ddI," *Science* 245 (1989), pp. 412–15.

On distribution of underground ddI: Although I was not directly involved with the distribution of underground ddI, I was in constant contact with David Wilson as these events took place, and kept an accurate log of dates and events. Later, prior to his death, during an extensive unpublished interview, David Wilson himself confirmed the validity of this story. In March 1992, the story was independently corroborated by Orlando AIDS activist Alfredo Martinez, who assisted in the bookkeeping of the project.

176 First drug in parallel track program: Malcolm Gladwell, "AIDS Drug Policy Switch Is Proposed," Washington *Post,* May 19, 1990.

177 On Fauci's hearing: *Therapeutic Drugs for AIDS: Development, Testing, and Availability,* Hearings Before a Subcommittee of the Committee on Government Operations, April 28–29, 1988, pp. 367–74.

Number of AIDS cases in U.S. by November 1988: *AIDS Weekly Surveillance Report,* Centers for Disease Control, Atlanta, November 7, 1988.

CHAPTER 9

179 Ozone use in Germany: J. LaRaus, ed., *Medical Applications of Ozone* (Norwalk, Conn.: International Ozone Association, 1985).

180 Horst Kief, "The Treatment of AIDS and ARC Patients with Ozone," translated from the German medical journal *Erfahrungsheilkunde* 37, no. 7 (July 1988).

180 On the administration of ozone: Ozone was never injected directly into the bloodstream in adults. Researchers had established that it could cause harm if administered this way and thus evolved the major autohemotherapy method. LaRaus, *Medical Applications of Ozone.*

Ozone's moderate *in vitro* activity: K. Wells et al., "Inactivation of HIV Type I by Ozone in Vitro," unpublished manuscript, SUNY Health Science Center, Syracuse, NY, 1991.

Another researcher's results: M. Carpendale and J. Freeberg, "Ozone Inactivates Extracellular HIV at Non-Cytotoxic Concentrations," *Antiviral Research* 16 (1991), pp. 281–92.

182 Infinitesimal doses of typhoid vaccine: Katie Leishman, "Mr. Catapano's Breakthrough," *City Week,* July 18, 1988.

183 Using the vaccine on AIDS patients: Salvatore Catapano, "A Treatment for the Remission of Symptoms Associated with AIDS," unpublished manuscript, June 1988.

On typhoid vaccine data: Salvatore Catapano, "A Process for the Treatment and Remission of AIDS," U.S. Patent no. 4,711,876, December 8, 1987.

Catapano's licensing agreements: Leishman, "Mr. Catapano's Breakthrough."

Catapano's typhoid vaccine protocol: Catapano, "A Treatment."

Data on vaccines: J. I. Colon, "The Efficacy of a Polyantigenic Immunoregulator in the Treatment of Patients Infected With HIV," unpublished manuscript, 1983.

T. Aoki and H. Miyahoshi, "Staphage Lysate and Lentinan as Immunomodulators in Clinical and Experimental Systems," in E. M. Hersh, ed., *Augmenting Agents in Cancer Therapy* (New York: Raven Press, 1981).

A. Alan, "Polio Vaccine in the Treatment of AIDS," *Clinical Immunology and Immunopathology* 43 (1987), pp. 277–80.

184 Suggestion of typhoid vaccine as HIV "cure": Catapano, "A Treatment."

Detecting syphilis: ibid.

185 San Francisco doctor's early data: Louis Mehl, personal communication, January 1989.

186 Few of the drugs—even ozone—produced consistent improvements: Ozone, I suspected, was highly virucidal and even capable of inactivating HIV as the *in vitro* studies had shown. But it did not work effectively in HIV disease through the major autohemotherapy method, I knew, in the same way that it seemed to work for hepatitis B and herpes. HIV was a disease that manifested itself in cells throughout the body including the spleen and the Langerhans cells as well as the peripheral blood. Simply removing a single liter of blood, ozonating it, replacing it, and then repeating this for 30 consecutive days could hardly affect the bulk of the process, even with ozone's apparent ability to recruit other cells once reinfused. Perhaps, I reasoned, ozone therapy would be better practiced in HIV treatment using a heart-lung machine so that a larger amount of blood could be processed quickly, but even this posed problems: under such conditions, it would be difficult to maintain optimal concentrations of the gas, toxicity could easily result, and certain sites of action still would not be accessible. Moreover, if the true pathogenesis of HIV was linked to some factor other than viral load, such as cytokine mediation, then ozone would prove to be of limited value, no matter what method of administration was used.

Later, in 1991, Mayer worked with Sam Murdoch in a different application of ozone. The pair explored the possibility of creating an autologous vaccination of ozone for HIV-infected patients. Murdoch believed that a vaccine for intramuscular injection could be prepared using a small portion of the patient's blood that had been treated with ozone. A Canadian study had used just such a vaccine in a dozen ARC patients and had shown some promising results. A. Garber et al., "Ozone Therapy in AIDS: Summary of Findings," Ottowa General Hospital, unpublished manuscript, January 1990.

Murdoch wrote in an unpublished manuscript about the ozone vaccine: "The beneficial long-term effects of the procedure result primarily from the immune response of the patient, including the anamnestic response to the perceived viral invasion, the production of antibodies and the consequent alteration of the immunological memory, rather than any effects of the ozone gas upon the HIV microbes." S. Murdoch, "An Autologous Vaccination of Ozone for HIV," unpublished manuscript, July 1991.

Several mainstream researchers have attempted to design a vaccine specifically against HIV by using recombinant core and envelope proteins. These individuals include Dr. Jonas Salk of the Salk Institute and Lt. Col. Robert Redfield of the Walter Reed Army Institute of Research. However, early clinical trials with both vaccines have not produced exceedingly promising results. Salk reported in A. Levin, et al., "Immunization of HIV-Infected individuals with inactivated HIV immunogen," *Sixth International Conference on AIDS*, 1:204, Abstract TH.A.337, 1990. Redfield reported in R. Redfield, et al., "A Phase 1 Evaluation of the Safety and Immunogenicity of Vaccination with Recombinant gp160 in Patients with Early HIV Infection," *NEJM* 324, no. 24, June 13, 1991, p. 1677–84.

And at the 1992 International AIDS Conference, Dr. Jonas Salk surprised delegates by announcing that all vaccine strategies used to treat HIV-infected persons, including his own HIV Immunogen, were misguided. He announced that he had conceived an entirely new approach to developing an AIDS vaccine for already infected persons. Salk made the controversial claim that treatments that cause the body to produce antibodies to HIV as in standard vaccines not only won't work but may hasten the progression of the disease. Salk made the radical proposal that a model AIDS vaccine should *suppress* production of antibodies and ultimately cause a rapid increase in the CD4 Th1 cell line. From the Sacramento *Bee*, July 21, 1992.

Page 186 Patients in different stages: There are actually strictly defined demarcations known as "Walter Reed Classification Stages" which define the various phases of the illnesses medically. They range from early asymptomatic at stage 1 to full-blown AIDS at stage 6. The stages are based on CD4 cell counts, DTH skin test responses, and clinical presentation of symptoms.

187 HIV is highly mutagenic: Some researchers have suggested that antigenic diversity or increases in numbers and diversity of genetically distinct strains of the virus might correlate with disease progression and severity. Martin Nowak et al., "Antigenic Diversity Threshholds and the Development of AIDS," *Science* 54 (November 15, 1991), pp. 963–69.

189 Characteristics and potential reversibility of KS: Robert Gallo, *Virus Hunting: AIDS, Cancer and the Human Retrovirus* (New York: Basic Books, HarperCollins, 1991), p. 263.

KS's true pathogenesis: ibid., p. 264.

193 Compound Q results: M. S. McGrath et al., "GLQ223: an inhibitor of HIV replication in acutely and chronically infected cells of lymphocyte and mononuclear phagocyte lineage," *Proceedings of the National Academy of Sciences* 86 (1989), pp. 2844–48.

194 Compound Q (GLQ223) patent: J. Lifson et al., "A Method of Inhibiting HIV," U.S. Patent no. 4,795,739, January 3, 1989.

CHAPTER 10

195 Trichosanthin and related compounds: H. W. Yeung et al. in *Advances in Chinese Medicinal Materials Res.* (Singapore: World Scientific Publishers, 1985).

Testing compounds' HIV activity in macrophages: "An Interview with Michael McGrath," San Francisco General Hospital AIDSFILE, Spring 1989; and Richard Goldstein and Robert Massa, "Compound Q: Hope and Hype," *The Village Voice,* May 30, 1989, p. 30.

196 McGrath and Yeung's compounds: ibid.

The patent's explanation of trichosanthin's anti-HIV activity: J. Lifson et al., "A Method of Inhibiting HIV," U.S. Patent no. 4,795,739, January 3, 1989.

197 Use of tricosanthin in abortion: J. Cui, "Intra-amniotic injection of crystal trichosanthin for induction of labor in second trimester pregnancy," *Journal of the Second Shanghai Medical University* 1 (1987), pp. 37–39; and S. W. Tsao and H. W. Yeung, "Selective killing of choriocarcinoma cells in vitro by trichosanthin," *Toxicon* 1 (1986), pp. 831–40.

GLQ223 developed by GeneLabs: Goldstein and Massa, "Compound Q."

198 "Informational blackout": "Compound Q: The Real Story," *PI Perspectives,* November 1989.

Phase 1 study of GLQ223: The results of the Phase 1 study were published in J. Kahn et al., "The safety and pharmacokinetics of GLQ223 in subjects with AIDS and ARC," *AIDS* 4 (1990), pp. 1197–1204.

Trichosanthin studied by Dr. Cui in Shanghai: H. W. Yeung, personal communication, February 20, 1989.

200 Detailed information on trichosanthin's effects: H. W. Yeung, "The immunomodulatory and antitumor activities of trichosanthin, an abortifacient protein isolated from Tian-Hua-Fen," *Asian Pacific Journal of Allergy and Immunology* 4 (1986), pp. 111–20.

Instructions for taking the drug: "Trichosanthin Injection" (package insert, translated from the Chinese).

201 Verification of the correct and pure version of trichosanthin: Martin Delaney, personal communication, March 30, 1989.

203 Why the firm fired him: Scott Yageman, personal communication, February 2, 1989.

"I'll be damned . . .": Elinor Burkett, "Patient Heal Thyself," Miami *Herald,* October 18, 1989.

Page 204 First dose of Compound Q given in the U.S.: Contrary to what was reported elsewhere, we did not first inject Scott Yageman with the drug before sending it for analysis of its purity and stability.

205 Trichosanthin could be immunosuppressive: H. W. Yeung, "trichosanthin."

212 Jim Corti arrived from Los Angeles: Contrary to what was reported in Jonathan Kwitny's *Acceptable Risks* (New York: Simon & Schuster, 1992), we had our own protocol in place long before Corti arrived. At no time did our nurse volunteers get "cold feet" about helping with the study. Nor did we ask for Corti's assistance. It was Corti himself who insisted on coming to Miami to observe the injections and also to transact an ongoing deal with David Wilson on ddI. Furthermore, Corti did not inject some patients with saline and others with sterile water in an effort to see what method worked best. The patients were given the drug with no dilution, as per the instructions from China.

213 100 ampules for $100 apiece: Corti returned once to the factory during the height of the Tiananmen Square conflict and purchased another 150 ampules at a slightly reduced price. Jim Corti, personal communication, August 2, 1989.

214 Preliminary protocol and results: Paul Sergios, correspondence to Martin Delaney, including "A Phase 1 Study to Evaluate the Safety and Efficacy of Trichosanthin in ARC Patients," May 1, 1989.

Byers's preliminary animal studies on trichosanthin: V. Byers et al., "A Phase 1-2 study of trichosanthin treatment of HIV disease," *AIDS* 4, no. 12 (1990), pp. 1189–1195.

McGrath's studies: Jonathan Kwitny, *Acceptable Risks*, p. 255.

215 We would conform to the national effort in every way: On May 16, 1989, Delaney faxed me a copy of the protocol that we and the other sites would follow ("A Treatment Program Using Trichosanthin in Patients with HIV Disease," unpublished protocol, May 1989), along with new case-report forms. There was also a lengthy narrative confirming that the objectives of the study were "to provide a body of documented, scientifically valid experience of the safety and efficacy of trichosanthin in HIV infection over a 90-day period."

The case-report forms lacked blanks for subjects to provide two pieces of key information, including whether or not they had any history of thrush or oral candidiasis or had developed it during the course of the study. Moreover, Delaney had excluded two major outcome variables that had been part of our original protocol: the DTH skin test reactions, and an additional complex measure of immune function, PHA blastogenesis. I assured Delaney that we would follow the protocol but that we would not drop the two additional variables we had originally included. We would perform the latter test at our own lab in Miami. I further noted my belief that the drop rate of 1½ hours was too slow and that 45 minutes was probably preferable. Contrary to what was reported in *Acceptable Risks*, at no time did we break compliance with the study or incorrectly fill out the case-report forms.

217 AIDS patient in Kansas: Goldstein and Massa, "Compound Q."
San Francisco patient: Kwitny, *Acceptable Risks*, p. 290.

218 Robert Parr: ibid., p. 290.

Levin on Compound Q neurological risks: "Compound Q: The Real Story,"
PI Perspective, November 1989.

219 Six other patients: "Preliminary Results of Compound Q Treatment Protocol," press release from Project Inform, September 20, 1989.

220 One patient at San Francisco General Hospital: Kahn indicated that he did
administer Decadron, having previously received a memo from Levin and
Waites indicating their experience with Chinese Q. But Kahn noted that the
drug did not seem to have a measurable impact on the patient's condition.
Kwitny, *Acceptable Risks*, p. 281.

On deaths by trichosanthin: There was also controversy surrounding the
death of one of Barbara Starrett's patients in New York. The controversy
is well summarized in Kwitny, *Acceptable Risks*, pp. 455–60.

Bazell went public: "NBC Nightly News" with Tom Brokaw, June 27, 1989.

The *Sun-Sentinel* carried the story: Nancy McVicar, "AIDS patients go
underground for drug tests," Fort Lauderdale *Sun-Sentinel*, June 28, 1989.

221 Abrams on underground tactics: Frank Browning, "The Question of Q," *In
Health*, September/October 1990, p. 57.

Reiter on "assertiveness of PWAs": Burkett "Patient Heal Thyself."

Volberding on the underground: Gina Kolata, "AIDS Drug Tested Secretly
by Group Critical of FDA," *New York Times*, June 28, 1989.

Kramer on Martin Delaney: Gina Kolata, "Critics Fault Secret Effort to
Test AIDS Drug," *New York Times*, September 19, 1989.

222 Delaney's memo: Martin Delaney, letter to Mathilde Krim, September 21,
1989.

FDA bans trichosanthin: Nancy McVicar, "FDA orders ban on import of
drug from China," Fort Lauderdale *Sun-Sentinel*, August 4, 1989.

Peck's FDA request: Carl Peck, letter to Martin Delaney, August 10, 1989.

223 "It's all about power . . .": Browning, "Question of Q."

Preliminary presentation of the Miami study's results: We also published
our data separately in the *European Journal of Clinical Investigation* 22, no. 2
(February 1992), pp. 113–22.

224 Delaney's presentation in San Francisco: Martin Delaney, speech given at
the Metropolitan Community Church, San Francisco, September 19, 1989.

225 On the percentage of CD4 cells: The absolute number of CD4 cells (the T4
cell count or CD4 cell count) is calculated by multiplying the percentage of
CD4 cells (0–50) by the patient's total white blood cell count and then
multiplying this figure by the percentage of lymphocytes. Many researchers
now believe that the *percentage* of CD4 cells—one of the three components
used to calculate the absolute CD4 cell count—may be far more accurate than
the absolute number in predicting disease progression and response to

therapy in clinical trials, since it tends to be uninfluenced by routine shifts in the white count or lymph count. Most clinical trial results published in journals now "separate out" or differentiate between the absolute CD4 cell count changes patients experienced and the percentage of CD4 cell counts. Later, however, we performed an analysis of the percentage of CD4 data on our twenty subjects and found that statistically significant increases occurred only in subjects who started with percentage CD4 cell values of 16 or greater.

Early patients given prednisone: Anthony Pinching, "Early Studies of Trichosanthin: What do they show?" *AIDS* 4, no. 12 (December 1990), pp. 1289–91.

Page 226 Reiter on Compound Q: Burkett, "Patient Heal Thyself."

Meeting with FDA, October 6, 1989: This discussion is recounted from detailed notes I took at the meeting.

On Dr. Paul Rothman's breaking compliance: Exactly why Paul Rothman's L.A. group broke compliance is unclear. He told me, in a separate conversation, that he did not observe any of the positive changes in p-24 antigens or CD4 cells observed at any of the other sites. (Some insiders speculated that this was due to the extremely slow drip method he used, not the ineffectiveness of the drug.) But there was also speculation that he was pressured by his conservative partners to end the trial. Paul Rothman, personal communication, October 14, 1989.

227 The NAMES Project AIDS Memorial Quilt background information provided by The NAMES Project Foundation, San Francisco, Calif.

229 On Wall Street disruption: "Five Protest Cost of AZT at Stock Exchange," *New York Times,* September 15, 1989.

On AZT price reduction: Andrew Miller, "Burroughs Cuts AZT Price 20 Percent," *Outweek,* October 1, 1989, p. 12.

230 FDA approved sale of ganciclovir to PWAs: Bruce Nussbaum, *Good Intentions: How Big Business and the Medical Establishment Are Corrupting the Fight Against AIDS* (Boston: Atlantic Monthly Press, 1990).

On Mark Harrington's demands: ACT UP testimony before the Interim Report to the National Committee to Review Current Procedures for Approval of New Drugs for Cancer and AIDS (Lasagna Committee), May 2, 1989.

With regard to the Harrington manifesto's demand for using other endpoints in evaluating drugs, many smaller pharmaceutical companies simply could not afford the costlier and more lengthy clinical trials in which death was used as an endpoint of a drug's true effectiveness. This was another reason why activists argued for the use of surrogate markers and not death as an endpoint.

CHAPTER 11

233 Fletcher on the underground Compound Q study: Gina Kolata, "Critics Fault Secret Effort to Test AIDS Drug," *New York Times,* September 19, 1989.

Bayer's criticism of the study: Ronald Bayer, "The ethics of research on HIV/AIDS in community-based setting," *AIDS* 4, no. 12 (December 1990), pp. 1287–88.

234 Levin's defense of the study: Kolata, "Critics Fault Secret Effort."

235 Protocol for Phase 2 study of GLQ223: Vera Byers et al., "GLQ223 Protocol," November 27, 1989.

    According to one source, James Kahn was upset by the Levin–GeneLabs alliance. He believed that the study might negatively affect enrollment in his own, ongoing trial of GLQ223 at San Francisco General Hospital. Other investigators in the ACTG system also came out against Delaney and Levin. Despite all this, GeneLabs submitted its proposal to the FDA in December 1989. Ellen Cooper arbitrarily decided to cut the number of patients treated from 100 to 10, and to keep the dose at 16 micrograms—far lower than that now thought to be effective. Kahn's study was dosing up to 100 micrograms and even higher. After some pressure from activists, Cooper agreed to approve the original protocol. Jonathan Kwitny, *Acceptable Risks* (New York: Simon & Schuster, 1992), p. 321.

236 60 percent stabilized or increased: Kwitny, ibid., p. 330.

    Use of Compound Q continued: Derek Hodel et al., "Quid Pro Q," *Notes From the Underground*, March 1991, p. 1.

237 Percentage of lymphocytes and macrophages infected: H. E. Harper et al., *Proceedings of the National Academy of Sciences* 83 (1986), p. 772.

    Theory of cytokine production: Fauci also pointed out that although cytokines such as tumor necrosis factor and IL-6 increase the expression of HIV, the immune system had a number of natural factors that decrease HIV expression. One of the most important is transforming growth factor beta (TGF-b). Clearly, Fauci reasoned, therapeutic strategies needed to be directed at finding ways to maintain increased levels of TGF-b, which might exert some long-term protective effect in persons infected with HIV. Anthony S. Fauci, "The Role of Endogenous Cytokines in the Regulation of HIV Expression," *HIV* 1, no. 1, pp. 3–6.

    Dendritic cells and Langerhans cells: S. E. Macatonia et al., "Dendritic cell infection, depletion and dysfunction in HIV-infected individuals," *Immunology* 71 (1990), pp. 38–45.

238 Montagnier on mycoplasma as AIDS co-factor: Steve Sternberg, "US AIDS Expert Raps Rival's Two-Germ Theory," *Atlanta Constitution,* June 21, 1991, p. B-4.

    Duesberg against HIV as cause of AIDS: Peter Duesberg, "HIV and AIDS: Correlation but not Causation," *Proceedings of the National Academy of Sciences* 86 (February 1989), pp. 755–64.

    Duesberg also argued that the overuse of drugs was the more likely cause of AIDS, in his article "The role of drugs in the origin of AIDS," *Biomedicine and Pharmacotherapy* 46 (February 1992), pp. 3–15.

    As early as 1984, Dr. Joseph Sonnabend also argued for an alternative model to explain the disease, part of which he described in his article "A

Multifactorial Model for the Development of AIDS in Homosexual Men,"
Annals of the New York Academy of Sciences 437 (1984), p. 177.

Gallo on Duesberg's assertions: Robert Gallo, *Virus Hunting: AIDS, Cancer
and the Human Retrovirus* (New York: Basic Books, HarperCollins, 1991), pp.
287–91.

Page 240 Parallel track program: Kenneth Bacon, "US Moves to Help Critically Ill
Get New AIDS Drugs," *Wall Street Journal,* May 21, 1990, p. B-6A.

241 "We have the spontaneity . . .": Elinor Burkett, "Patient Heal Thyself,"
Miami *Herald,* October 18, 1989.

242 Underground Compound Q clinics: Hodel, "Quid Pro Q."

243 On the arrest of Stephen Herman: Jim Carlton, "Orange County Physician
Charged with AIDS Quackery," Los Angeles *Times* (Orange County edition), January 12, 1990.

On the scientific soundness of the Hermans' theories: The Hermans' theories were not without mainstream scientific precedent. Some researchers
have speculated that another drug may also have this antiviral potential:
GCSF, or granulocyte colony stimulating factor (Neupogen), which increases the neutrophil counts of AIDS patients and is most commonly used
to counter the neutropenia of other drugs and treat secondary infections in
HIV. These researchers suggested that, through a process called antibody-
dependent cell-mediated cytotoxicity, GCSF may activate the neutrophil
to kill HIV-infected cells through antiviral antibodies and the production of
bacteria-killing molecules called defensins. Cocita Gayle Baldwin et al.,
"Factors Enhance Neutrophil Cytotoxicity Toward HIV-Infected Cells,"
Blood 74, no. 5 (October 1989).

But recent studies have shown that GCSF does not produce significant increases in the percentage of CD4 cells in HIV-infected patients or
increases in the patients' total lymphocyte counts. Satoshi Kimura et al.,
"Efficacy of recombinant granulocyte colony stimulating factor on neutropenia in patients with AIDS," *AIDS* 4, no. 12 (December 1990), pp. 1251–54.

244 On the Hermans' providing intravenous supplies: Jules Parnes, personal
communication, October 12, 1989.

The Hermans' account of Viroxan therapy results: Stephen Herman et al.,
"VIROXAN: A Novel Superoxide Generating Compound With Broad
Spectrum Anti Infective and Immunomodulatory Applications in the Clinical Management of Chronic, Inflammatory and Autoimmune Diseases,"
unpublished manuscript, October 1989.

245 Viroxan's ineffectiveness and side effects: Parnes, personal communication,
October 12, 1989.

Allegations of death: Carlton (as in Note 19).

The charges against Herman: Lily Dizon, "Doctor Who Created AIDS
Drug Charged," Los Angeles *Times,* February 15, 1991.

246 Herman insisted publicly: ibid.

246 Action by California Medical Board: Jack Cheevers, "Judge Revokes Doctor's License in AIDS Quackery Case," Los Angeles *Times,* December 11, 1991.

247 On the continual underground use of Viroxan: Scott Beatty, personal communication, December 15, 1991.

Herman sentenced and fined: Mark Pinsky, "Developer of 'AIDS Drug' Is Sentenced," Los Angeles *Times* (Orange County edition), January 9, 1992.

CHAPTER 12

250 Events that led to founding New York PWA Health Group: Tom Hannan, personal communication, March 31, 1990.

251 Sold $1 million worth of AL-721: ibid.

Three companies in California: "AL-721 Workalikes: Where to Get Them," *AIDS Treatment News,* no. 30 (September 1987), p. 1.

252 The CRI pentamidine trial: Joseph Sonnabend et al., "A Trial of Aerosolized Pentamidine (AP) for Prophylaxis of *Pneumocystis carinii* Pneumonia (PCP) in AIDS," *Fifth International Conference on AIDS,* Montreal, Abstract C.639, p. 665.

In 1991, the CRI was reorganized as the CRIA (Community Research Initiative on AIDS).

On the CRI's participation in the underground study: Sonnabend, Callen, Hannan, and the New York CRI were invited to participate in the underground study of Compound Q, but Sonnabend and Callen declined, citing the fact that the study was not FDA approved. Only Hannan chose to assist in the New York arm of the project, independently helping Dr. Barbara Starratt there. Tom Hannan, personal communication, March 30, 1990.

253 The New York Buyers' Club under Hodel's direction: Derek Hodel, personal communication, August 12, 1992.

On early buyers' clubs: From 1987 to 1989, before Corti formed his Los Angeles Buyers' Club, there was a club known as the Nutritional Products Buyers' Club in Los Angeles run by Doug Cooper, which sold AL-721 workalikes, Monolourin, and the DeVeras Beverage. Nutritional Products Buyers' Club fact sheet, 1987.

254 An FDA representative told activists: Derek Hodel et al., "Crackdown Crackup," *Notes from the Underground,* no. 12 (November/December 1991), p. 1.

255 Activist support and demonstrations for ddI and ddC: Jim Driscoll, personal communication, June 14, 1992.

Freehill's citizen's petition to the FDA: Barry Freehill, letter to the Food and Drug Administration, September 1990.

AZT combined with ddC: T. C. Meng et al., "Combination Therapy with Zidovudine and Dideoxycytidine in Patients with Advanced Human Immunodeficiency Virus Infection," *Annals of Internal Medicine* 166, no. 1 (January 1, 1991), pp. 13–19.

Page   256   Corti and suppliers of ddC: Jim Driscoll, personal communication, June 14, 1992.

More ddC customers for buyers' clubs: Gina Kolata, "Patients Turning to Illegal Pharmacies," *New York Times*, November 3, 1991.

The FDA tests samples of ddC from buyers' clubs: Lisa Krieger, "Underground AIDS drug under probe," San Francisco *Examiner*, January 30, 1992, p. 1.

Consequences of FDA's tests: Correspondence from Dr. Randolph F. Wykoff to Derek Hodel and others, published in *Notes From the Underground*, no. 14 (March/April 1992), p. 4.

257   Corti's newly formulated ddC: Driscoll, personal communication, June 14, 1992.

On continued sales of ddC: Even after ddC's approval, when availability was no longer an issue, buyers' clubs continued to stock the drug, for another issue became strikingly relevant: price. While the drug was available for $30 to $50 for a bottle of 100 pills through the buyers' clubs, its average retail cost was $170.

Woodruff's involvement in litigation over Peptide T: "Suit Says FDA Blocks Vital AIDS Drug," Associated Press, December 5, 1990. Also, "AZT patent overturned, *Notes From the Underground* 14 (March/April 1992), p. 6.

258   David had crossed the line from ARC to AIDS: Originally, an HIV-seropositive person was classified as having AIDS only if he or she had suffered from at least one opportunistic infection, neoplasm, or Kaposi's sarcoma. People with persistent generalized lymphadenopathy and/or other minor symptoms of HIV infection, such as thrush and weight loss, were classified as having ARC (AIDS-Related Complex). In 1991, the Centers for Disease Control broadened the classification of AIDS to include any HIV-seropositive person with fewer than 200 CD4 cells, whether or not that person had experienced opportunistic infections or KS.

259   Alzheimer's compared to HIV dementia: Stephan Buckingham et al., "Essential Knowledge about AIDS Dementia," *Social Work*, March-April 1988, pp. 112–15.

Clinical symptoms of HIV dementia: ibid. and B. A. Navia et al., "The AIDS Dementia Complex," *Annals of Neurology* 19 (June 1986), pp. 517–24.

CHAPTER 13

265   Research by Ho and his colleagues: M. Li et al., "Inhibitory Effect of Chinese Herbal Medicines on HIV Infection In Vitro," *Sixth International Conference on AIDS*, San Francisco, 1990, abstract Th.A.237, pp. 179.

266   Relman on Delaney's Compound Q data: Nancy McVicar, "AIDS activist, researcher clash over test results," Fort Lauderdale *Sun-Sentinel*, June 23, 1990.

Dwyer's thymic tissue experiments: John Dwyer et al., "Transplantation of Thymic Tissue in AIDS," *Archives of Internal Medicine* 147 (March 1987), pp. 513–17.

267 Dwyer's conclusions about thymic transplants: John Dwyer, personal communication, June 24, 1990.

Thymic peptide's background: There were also a variety of "thymic peptides," synthesized hormone-like products secreted by the thymus, which some researchers believed might help immature, precursor cells develop into fully competent immune cells. We tried a variety of them, including thymic humoral factor, thymosin, and thymopentin. None produced any significant increases in CD4 cells. The thymic peptide research is described in Derek Link, "Thymic Peptides: An Overview," *GMHC Treatment Issues*, July 1992, p. 1.

268 Results of Cummins' oral alpha-interferon study: D. Koech et al., "Low dose oral alpha interferon therapy for patients seropositive for HIV," *Molecular Biotherapy* 2 (June 2, 1990), pp. 91–5. Within weeks of the news reports about the spectacular results achieved with oral alpha-interferon, underground AIDS drug dealers and buyers' club presidents began scrambling to obtain a steady source of the drug. By August 1, 1990, the Dallas Buyers' Club, the Fort Lauderdale Fight for Life Buyers' Club, and the New York PWA Health Group were all offering a version of oral alpha-interferon for sale, although no club's version of it was exactly the same as the drug Koesch had used in Kenya. Evidently, Kemron was in short supply, no buyers' club presidents resorted to obtaining products such as Roferon, made at Interferon Sciences in Nutley, N.J., and Interferon A, made by Roche Labs in New Brunswick, N.J. David and I actually obtained the true drug from Hayashaburu Laboratories in Japan, but it failed to produce any improvement in our symptoms or CD4 cell counts. The drug was later debunked as an HIV treatment.

On the SCID mouse: J. Michael McCune et al., "The SCID/HU mouse: murine model for the analysis of human hematolymphoid differentiation and function," *Science* 241 (1988), pp. 1632–39.

269 Logistical and theoretical barriers to human immune system transplant: John Dwyer, personal communication, March 15, 1991.

274 Significance of CD4 cell count: In 1991, Sam Broder and Robert Yarchoan presented what some considered to be a significant discovery. Broder, Yarchoan, and their colleagues at the National Cancer Institute had gone back through the records of every patient treated with an antiviral drug in the NCI's own HIV studies since 1985. The analysis of all this data showed that as long as CD4 cell counts were kept above 50, patients survived. Only one patient had died with a CD4 count above 50. And no patient on AZT with a CD4 cell count of over 50 had ever developed lymphoma. The results provided support for the use of CD4 cells as a valuable surrogate marker for treatment efficacy and for gauging disease progression.

275 CD8 cell treatments: R. Herberman et al., "Adaptive Therapy With Purified CD8 Cells in Patients with HIV Infection," *Report of the American Society of*

Hematology Annual Meeting, December 6, 1991; and N. Klimas et al., "A Phase 1 Ex Vivo CD8 Cell Augmentation, Activation and Reinfusion Trial—Clinical Observations in Six HIV-Positive Subjects," *American Society of Hematology Annual Meeting,* December 6, 1991.

Experiment on girl with SCID/ADA: This pediatric disease is caused by the lack of the gene that "codes" (or provides the blueprint for) adenosine deaminase (ADA), an enzyme that breaks down toxic biological products. In the rare cases of ADA-deficient children, both the gene and the enzyme are missing. As a result, toxins accumulate in the bloodstream, killing essential CD4 and B cells and deactivating the immune system in much the same way that HIV destroys the immune system in AIDS. With little or no defense against disease, even in germ-free environments, victims usually died early in childhood—like the famous boy who was kept in a plastic bubble. ADA injections directly into their bloodstream could not help, since the ADA deteriorated within minutes. A long-acting form of the drug required multiple, expensive infusions and was equally ineffective.

Blaese, Anderson, and Culver extracted viable CD4 cells from the young patient and then cloned them in the test tube using interleukin-2, increasing their number to more than one billion. They exposed the newly propagated cells to mouse leukemia retroviruses into which human ADA genes had been spliced. The retroviruses were rendered harmless by genetic engineering but maintained the ability to penetrate the cell nucleus and insert retroviral DNA into the cells' own chromosomes. The retroviruses were in a sense the "vectors," the stripped-down conveyer-belt vehicles that would deliver the genes to their target. The retroviruses invaded the CD4 cells and burrowed into the CD4 cell DNA (much the way HIV invades CD4 cells), carrying the good ADA gene with them. (The retroviral vector had the desired gene spliced directly into its nucleus.) This began the process of transduction, in which cells designed to receive the gene made contact with the gene-boosted vector and became assimilated. The billion or so CD4 cells—now equipped with the new ADA gene—were reinfused into the patient.

Several months later, the researchers confirmed that ADA genes were being expressed in the patients' blood and that the needed enzyme was being produced. The patients' immune systems had been restored, at least in the short run. Researchers cautioned that the children could not be considered permanently cured; they would have to return monthly for at least two years to the NIH, where doctors would infuse them with more engineered CD4 cells and monitor possible toxicities.

Critics pointed out that in order for the experiment to be 100 percent successful, stem cells and not mature lymphocytes would have to be used. For logistical reasons, the researchers settled on using mature lymphocytes from peripheral blood and not stem cells, which had proven virtually impossible to identify and harvest from bone marrow. Recently, however, scientists had developed a technique whereby the cells *could* be identified and harvested in high numbers. Subsequent experiments with gene therapy in ADA would almost certainly make use of the stem cells, not mature lymphocytes. K. Culver et al., "Lymphocyte Gene Therapy," *Human Gene*

Therapy 2 (1991), pp. 107–9; Robin Marantz Henig, "Dr. Anderson's Gene Machine," *New York Times,* March 31, 1991, Section 6, p. 31; "Elusive Quarry: Researchers are closing in on the stem cell," *Scientific American,* September 1991, pp. 22–23; and prospectus of the Systemix Corporation, Palo Alto, Calif., 1990.

Page 277 Gruenberg's dissertation: Michael Gruenberg, "A Process for Isolating and Expanding Viral Free CD4 and HIV-Specific Killer Cells from AIDS Patients," Ph.D. diss., Columbia Pacific University, 1990, revised 1992.

CHAPTER 14

283 Pharmaceutical companies and the drug development process: Bruce Nussbaum, *Good Intentions: How Big Business and the Medical Establishment Are Corrupting the Fight Against AIDS* (Boston: Atlantic Monthly Press, 1990), p. 296.

Kramer on passivity of FDA: Larry Kramer, *Reports from the Holocaust* (New York: St. Martin's Press, 1988), p. 233.

284 IND application for the lymphocyte expansion project: In the experiment we designed, CD4 and CD8 cells would be removed from both peripheral blood and lymph node tissue. Stem cells would also be harvested and lymphoid stem cells isolated. CD4 naive cells and CD8 cytotoxic cells would be isolated. Cells positive for p-24 and gp120 could be removed from the sample. Both the CD4 helper and CD8 cytotoxic cells would be activated and expanded to clinically relevant numbers. After screening again for HIV, the cells would be reactivated and cultivated further. The cells would be grown and reinfused on a monthly basis. AZT, ddI, and ddC would be given in rotation. Paul Sergios et al., "Cellular Immunotherapy of AIDS with Autologous Effector Lymphocytes Propagated in vitro," unpublished protocol, 1990.

Callen's reasons against taking AZT: Michael Callen, "The Case Against AZT," in *Surviving AIDS* (New York: HarperCollins, 1990), pp. 203.

285 French study of AZT: Dournon et al., "Effects of Zidovudine in 365 Consecutive Patients with AIDS or ARC," *Lancet* 2 (December 3, 1988), p. 1297.

Callen further argues: Callen, "The Case Against AZT."

Prolonged AZT therapy and chance of lymphoma: According to Sam Broder, three of the nineteen original Phase 1 patients developed lymphomas between one and two-and-a-half years since starting AZT. Robert Yarchoan et al., "Clinical Pharmacology of Zidovudine and Related Dideoxynucleosides," *New England Journal of Medicine,* September 14, 1989, pp. 726–35.

Viral resistance to AZT: D. Richman et al., "Zidovudine resistance of HIV," *Review of Infectious Disease* 12 (1990), pp. 507–12.

AZT is a DNA chain terminator: Callen, "The Case Against AZT."

286 AZT at low doses and in combination with ddI and ddC: Researchers recently found that patients who started with CD4 cell counts of 60 or

higher who took lower doses of AZT (150 mg/day and .015 mg/kg/day of ddC) saw increases in CD4 cells of up to 120 cells, and that these increases remained stable for up to one year. Margaret Fischl, T.C. Meng et al., "Combination Therapy with Zidovine and Dideooxycytidine in Patients with Advanced Human Immunodeficiency Virus Infection," *Annals of Internal Medicine* 166, no. 1 (January 1, 1991), pp. 13–19.

And the underground researcher Jack Gerhardt suggested the following sample rotation schedule of AZT, ddI, and ddC: weeks one and two, AZT at 100 milligrams, four times a day; weeks three and four, ddC at 0.75 milligrams, three times a day; weeks five and six, ddI at 162 milligrams, two times a day; weeks seven and eight, follow weeks one and two and repeat. Jack Gerhardt, "Nucleoside Antiviral Rotation for HIV," *Forefront,* October 1990, p. 1.

AZT prolonging survival and improving condition: T. Creagh-Kirk et al., "Survival Experience Among Patients with AIDS Receiving Zidovudine," *Journal of the American Medical Association,* November 25, 1988.

Three other studies demonstrated that at various dosages, AZT did delay disease progression in asymptomatic and ARC patients but did not demonstrate any survival benefit. M. Fischl et al., *Annals of Internal Medicine,* 112 (1990), pp. 727–37; J. D. Hamilton et al., *New England Journal of Medicine,* (1992), pp. 437–43; and P. Volberding et al., *New England Journal of Medicine* 322, no. 14 (1990), pp. 941–9.

Page 287 Results of Bicaccia's study: Emil Bisaccia et al., "Extracorporeal Photophoresis in the Treatment of ARC: A Pilot Study," *Annals of Internal Medicine* 113 (1990), pp. 270–75.

Photophoresis and 8-MOP: Richard Edelson, "Light-activated Drugs," *Scientific American,* August 1988, pp. 68–75.

289 Efforts to allow PWAs in prison to die at home: Nancy McVicar, "Deaths of Inmates Spur Drive," Fort Lauderdale *Sun-Sentinel,* September 27, 1989, p. 1-B.

291 Cooper's resignation from FDA: Marilyn Chase, "Top Regulator of AIDS Drugs Quits Her Post," *Wall Street Journal,* December 24, 1990.

292 FDA evaluated by committee: Edward Kennedy, chair, Hearing Before the Committee on Labor and Human Resources, United States Senate, 102d Congress, 1st session, March 6, 1991.

293 "I got stuck in the sixties . . .": Lisa Krieger, "Notes from the Underground," *IMAGE* magazine, San Francisco *Examiner,* September 15, 1991, pp. 16–21.

The Gerhardts' background and personal history: Jack Gerhardt, personal communication, March 15, 1992.

294 Percentage of babies born HIV-positive: Studies have also shown that a certain percentage of infants born HIV-positive actually seroconvert, or turn HIV-negative, over time. These infants have seemed to maintain a normal immune system and researchers predict that they will develop normally as adults. "European collaborative study: Mother-to-child transmission of HIV infection," *Lancet,* November 5, 1988, pp. 1039–43; and from a report by Dr. Stephen Joseph in the Kenneth D. Blackfan Lecture cited

in C. Levine et al, "The Ethics of Screening for Early Intervention in HIV Disease," *American Journal of Public Health* 79, no. 12 (December 1989), pp. 1661–67.

294 Gerhardt's illness and search for information about AIDS: Gerhardt, personal communication, March 15, 1992.

Gerhardt's protocol: Jack Gerhardt, "A Protocol for the Combined Use of D-Penacillamine and ddC," unpublished manuscript, March 1988.

295 Contacts with other chemists: Jack Gerhardt, personal communication, March 15, 1992.

"All my expertise prepared me . . .": Marilyn Chase, "Popular AIDS Treatment Is Illicit Copy of Hoffmann-La Roche's New Drug, DDC," *Wall Street Journal,* July 12, 1991.

d4T and hypericin: d4T, like other nucleoside analogs such as AZT and ddI, inhibits HIV replication by inducing premature viral DNA chain termination. Preliminary *in vitro* data has established that it might be much more effective and at the same time less toxic than AZT, ddI, or ddC. Early human studies would seem to confirm this research. D4T produced CD4 increases and decreases in p-24 antigen for a much longer period of time than would be expected with the approved nucleosides. Toxicity (paresthesis and neuropathy) was seen only at the highest doses. The latest randomized study of the drug enrolled 152 patients, comparing three different dosages. Approximately 40 percent to 50 percent of the subjects experienced an improvement in their CD4 cell count. Only six subjects had to discontinue the drug because of toxicity. There was an incidence of peripheral neuropathy of 12 percent to 16 percent. Michael Ravitch, "d4T Overview," *GMHC Treatment Issues,* November 1992, p. 1.

Hypericin is an aromatic polycyclic dione found in the herb *Hypericum triquetrifolium,* or Saint-John's-wort. It occurs in the plant at levels of only one part per thousand, so previously developed extraction procedures have proven too expensive and cumbersome for large-scale production. The ongoing trials at New York University have tried to overcome this problem by using synthetic hypericin, which still costs several thousand dollars a gram. Gerhardt solved the problem by developing an entirely new way to purify it from the herb. *In vitro,* hypericin has been shown to inhibit the assembly and budding of HIV virions from infected cells—possibly by direct inactivation of assembled virus particles at the cell membrane. Other researchers have suggested that hypericin inhibits protein kinase C, a molecule essential to viral reproduction. M. Browne et al., "Phase 1 study of D4T in patients with AIDS and ARC," *Sixth International Conference on AIDS,* San Francisco, 1990, abstract S. B. 456, p. 200; and F. Valentine et al., "Synthetic Hypercin . . . ," *Seventh International Conference on AIDS,* Florence, Italy, 1991, abstract W.A. 1022.

296 d4T in parallel track: In October 1992 d4T was made widely available to patients as part of a parallel track program. Those who were unable to take part in the formal clinical trials of the drug and who could not tolerate the approved HIV drugs or who were no longer receiving benefit from them were eligible for the parallel track study. "d4T Parallel Track

Study, Patient Information Sheet," Bristol-Myers Squibb Company, October 1992.

Gerhardt on his lab, on synthesizing and distributing experimental drugs, on working with physicians, on providing expanded access. Gerhardt, personal communication, March 15, 1992.

Page 298 HR-2597: "A Bill to amend the Federal Food, Drug and Cosmetic Act to enhance the enforcement authority of the Food and Drug Administration, and for other purposes," introduced by Representative Henry Waxman of California, June 7, 1991.

299 HR-2872: "A Bill to provide for the expedited approval of drugs or biologics for individuals in need of treatment for a life-threatening disease or seriously debilitating illness," introduced by Representative Tom Campbell of California, co-authored by Jim Driscoll, ACT UP Golden Gate, July 11, 1991.

Campbell bill background: In June 1992, Representative Campbell was defeated in his bid for the Republican senatorial nomination, leaving the "Access to Life Savings Therapy Act" an orphan in the House. However, by September 1992, the bill had 115 sponsors, some of whom expressed strong interest in being original sponsors for an amended version of the bill. Activists hope the bill will be introduced to the next Congress in February 1993. The bill's Senate sponsors also plan to reintroduce it there.

Driscoll's critique of current system: James Driscoll, "Why We Need Congressional Legislation to Speed Approval for AIDS Drugs," *BETA,* November 1991, pp. 7–8; and James Driscoll, "Consumer Protection Could Kill AIDS Patients," *Wall Street Journal,* March 6, 1991, p. 22.

300 "The most important thing . . .": Gerhardt, personal communication, March 15, 1992.

Approval for ddI: "FDA Committee Votes DDI Approval," ACTG/FDA Antiviral Drugs Advisory Committee Meetings, Washington, D.C., July 14–19, 1991, minutes summarized in *Highlights,* July 1991.

302 Hoffmann-La Roche stops developing TAT-inhibitor: John S. James, "TAT-Inhibitor Trials Cancelled: Business Reasons Cited," *AIDS Treatment News,* no. 127, p. 5.

On continuation of trial: Fowkes, personal communication, January 10, 1992.

306 On Magic Johnson's announcement: "Johnson may lose his magic," Associated Press, November 8, 1991.

307 On AIDS projections: N. McVicar, "AIDS: Numbers Still Climbing," Fort Lauderdale *Sun-Sentinel,* September 19, 1992.

GLOSSARY:
The Language of AIDS

ABSOLUTE CD4 CELL COUNT (T4 count): The number of "helper" CD4 lymphocyte cells in a cubic millimeter of blood. The CD4 cell count declines as HIV infection progresses and is frequently used to monitor the extent of immune suppression in HIV-infected people.

ADJUVANT: Any substance that enhances the immune-stimulating properties of an antigen or the pharmacologic effect of a drug; usually, an ingredient added to a vaccine to increase the production of antibodies by the immune system. Certain vaccines contain adjuvants.

AIDS CLINICAL TRIALS GROUP (ACTG): A group of fifty-two university-based research centers, each with its own principal investigators, that conducts clinical trials on anti-HIV therapeutics.

AIDS-RELATED COMPLEX (ARC): A term used to describe a variety of symptoms and signs found in many people with HIV infection, including recurring fevers, weight loss, swollen lymph nodes, and fungal infections.

ANEMIA: An abnormal deficiency of red blood cells, of hemoglobin, or of total blood volume. It may be caused by AZT as well as other drugs or medical conditions.

ANTIBODY: A molecule in the blood or other body fluids that is generated in reaction to a specific antigen (a microorganism or a foreign protein or polysaccharide) and that tags, neutralizes, or destroys the antigen, thus providing immunity against it or its toxins. Most antibodies are proteins known as immunoglobulins, which are produced and secreted by B lymphocytes in response to stimulation by antigens or, in some cases, occur naturally.

ANTIGEN: Any macromolecular substance—a microorganism such as a virus or bacteria, or a foreign protein or polysaccharide—which, when introduced into the body, is capable of inducing an immune response and eliciting the production of a specific antibody or specifically sensitized T lymphocytes, or both. Only a specific portion of the antigen molecule—known as the antigenic determinant—combines with the antibody or a specific receptor on a lymphocyte.

ANTIGENIC DRIFT/ANTIGENIC DIVERSITY: The chance variations in a virus's antigenic structure over a period of time.

ASSAY: An analysis of a substance to determine its characteristics or components, or of a drug to determine its biological or pharmacological potency.

AUTOIMMUNITY: The condition in which an individual's immune system reacts against its own tissues. One theory of the pathogenesis of AIDS suggests that the body's own immune system somehow attacks and destroys itself.

B CELL (or B lymphocyte): One of the two major classes of lymphocytes—CD4 cells are the other—that together comprise the immune system's chief mechanism of resistance to a wide range of antigens, i.e., bacteria, viruses, and other potential causes of disease. B cells are the principal components of the body's humoral immune response to an invading antigen. (CD4 cells are involved primarily in cell-mediated immunity.) The humoral response is activated when B cells—assisted by macrophages and directed by helper CD4 cells—react to a specific antigen by multiplying and forming plasma cells, which produce vast amounts of a specific antibody against that antigen. The antibodies bind with the antigens, marking them for destruction by other cells or neutralizing or destroying them directly. Some of the B cells become memory B cells, which will produce more antibodies against the antigen if there is ever a recurrence.

BETA-2 MICROGLOBULIN: A protein tightly bound to the surface of many nucleated cells, particularly those of the immune system. Elevated beta-2 microglobulin levels occur in a variety of diseases and cancer. While elevated levels are not specific to HIV, there is a correlation between this marker and the progression of HIV disease.

BIOAVAILABILITY: The degree to which a drug is absorbed into the bloodstream and is thus physiologically active.

BLASTOGENESIS: The transformation of small lymphocytes into larger blastlike cells capable of undergoing mitosis, induced by PHA (phytohemagglutinen), antigens to which the cell donor has been immunized, and leukocytes from an unrelated individual. It is a measurement of the strength of a patient's cell-mediated and humoral immune response *in vitro*—as important a measure of immune system condition as absolute CD4 cell counts. Blastogenesis levels are typically low in persons with AIDS.

BLOOD/BRAIN BARRIER: The protective physiological barrier between the brain's blood vessels and its tissues, which restricts the passage of some substances into the brain. Drugs for treating HIV must be composed of molecules small enough to cross this barrier.

BLOOD UREA NITROGEN (BUN): The amount of nitrogen present in blood urea. Used as a rough indication of kidney function and helpful in the diagnosis of kidney failure and gastrointestinal bleeding.

BONE MARROW: Soft tissue located in the cavities of the bone where certain blood cells, including erythrocytes, leukocytes, and platelets are formed from maturing stem cells.

BUYERS' CLUB: Organization that makes available for sale anti-HIV medications, some of which are still experimental.

CASE-REPORT FORMS: Forms used in a clinical trial to document a patient's condition and response to therapy.

CD4 CELLS (or CD4 lymphocytes): T lymphocytes that bear CD4 receptor molecules on their surfaces, and that are often referred to as "helper T cells" because of the role they perform in the immune system. CD4 cells regulate all aspects of immune function by coordinating the activities of the phagocytes, the killer T cells, the B cells, and other immune cells. When the body is invaded by an antigen, CD4 cells identify it and then secrete substances called lymphokines, which activate the production of the appropriate antibody by the B cells, or dispatch killer T cells to the site of infection. The CD4 receptor is the principal site where HIV binds to uninfected cells, and CD4 lymphocytes are the primary cell type killed by HIV. Normally, CD4 helper cells make up about 60 percent of the T cells, and thus an average of 45 percent of the body's total number of lymphocytes.

CD8 CELLS (or CD8 lymphocytes): T lymphocytes that bear CD8 receptors on their surface, and consisting of two different types. CD8 killer cells (or cytotoxic T cells) attack and destroy invading antigens or infected cells, assisted and directed by CD4 helper cells. CD8 suppressor cells turn off the immune response after the antigen has been successfully controlled and destroyed. Normally, CD8 cells make up about 30 percent of the T cells, and thus an average of 22.5 percent of the body's total number of lymphocytes. In HIV infection there is some increase in the number of CD8 cells, in addition to the acute reduction in CD4 cells.

CELL-MEDIATED IMMUNITY: One of the two main branches of the immune system (the other is humoral immunity). In the cell-mediated immune response to the invasion of the body by an antigen—i.e., bacteria, viruses, parasites, etc.—helper T cells (CD4 lymphocytes) first identify the antigen and then dispatch killer T cells (cytotoxic CD8 lymphocytes) to the site of infection; the killer T cells then attack and destroy the invading antigens or the infected cells. It is this branch of the immune system that is under siege in AIDS patients.

CELL PROPAGATION: The growth or multiplication of cells.

CLINICAL TRIAL: A formal investigation of an experimental drug in humans, usually conducted by a research institution.

CO-FACTORS: Bacteria, viruses, or characteristics of a patient that may increase the advancement of a disease or the chances of becoming ill.

COMMUNITY RESEARCH INITIATIVE (CRI): The national organization of groups of doctors and researchers working with community activists to mount and implement clinical trials, usually outside of traditional mainstream research but with IRB approval and IND filing.

CRYPTOCOCCOSIS: An infection caused by the yeastlike cryptococcus fungus, which begins in the respiratory tract and often spreads to the meninges (the membranous lining of the brain and spinal cord) as well as the kidneys, liver, spleen, joints, and skin. It is a common opportunistic infection in AIDS. Coughing or breathing problems may the first indication of the pulmonary infection, which is usually mild; but once it is disseminated, it can invade the central nervous system and cause meningitis, with symptoms of headache, blurred vision, confusion, and slurred speech. It is fatal if left untreated. Amphotericin B and fluconazole are two drugs used to treat cryptococcal meningitis.

CYTOKINES: Non-antibody proteins that are produced and released by lymphocytes or macrophages in response to a specific antigen, and that orchestrate a wide range of immunologic functions and host defenses. Certain cytokines, including tumor necrosis factor, may actually upregulate the expression of HIV.

CYTOMEGALOVIRUS (CMV): A virus related to the herpes virus family. CMV infections may occur without any symptoms or may result in mild flulike symptoms of aches, fever, sore throat, or enlarged lymph nodes. Severe CMV infections, such as those seen in AIDS, can result in infection of the retina (retinitis), liver (hepatitis), or lungs (pneumonia). Ganciclovir is the drug of choice for treating CMV: others are in development, including triclonal antibodies, FIAC (fiacitabine), and HPMPC (an antiviral nucleoside analog).

DELAYED HYPERSENSITIVITY REACTIONS (DHR): An immunological test to gauge the strength of the immune system, in which antigens are injected subdermally (just underneath the skin) and a response of swelling (induration) or redness (erythema) is recorded 12 to 48 hours later. In AIDS, no responses are typically seen, since the immune system's ability to react to the antigen is compromised. Hypersensitivity refers to the body's exaggerated immune response to a foreign substance; hypersensitivity reactions are classified as immediate (caused by antigens that induce an antibody response) or delayed (caused by natural infection, viral vaccination, or antigen injection, inducing a T-lymphocyte response). Delayed hypersensitivity is another term for cell-mediated immunity.

DIMETHYLSULFOXIDE (DMSO): A free radical acceptor and antioxidant used in drug delivery systems to treat bladder infections and sports injuries. Typically applied directly to skin, and can penetrate into tissue. Reduces darkening effect in bruises. May somehow affect Glutithione levels in HIV patients.

DNA: A nucleic acid that is the carrier of genetic information in all cellular organisms and the DNA viruses. HIV can insert its own DNA into a cell's DNA and use cellular mechanisms for its own replication.

ENDPOINTS: Specific conditions resulting from experimental drugs which indicate that the drugs in a clinical trial should be stopped. Usually endpoints are severe toxicity or disease progression, but sometimes death is used as an endpoint.

ENVELOPE: A natural covering or membrane, such as the protective coat surrounding the protein shell of a virus or retrovirus. The HIV envelope is lipid-coated and is composed of two protein units: gp120 and gp41. Gp120 is the knoblike protein on the HIV envelope that binds to the CD4 receptor on a cell's surface.

GENE: A segment of the DNA molecule that carries the code for producing a protein or enzyme linked to a specific cell function.

GENOME: The DNA code for a particular organism, consisting of the complete set of genes in the chromosomes of that organism.

GLIAL CELLS: Non-neuronal cellular elements of the peripheral and central nervous system formerly thought to be supportive cells but now known to be involved in metabolic processes, since they are interspersed between neurons and blood vessels. The disruption of glial-cell function is thought by some researchers to be at the heart of AIDS dementia.

HELPER-SUPPRESSOR RATIO: The ratio of CD4 to CD8 cells in the body. The T lymphocytes of most healthy people consist of about 60 percent CD4 cells and 30 percent CD8 cells, a ratio of 2 to 1. In HIV-infected people, there is a severe decrease in the number of CD4 cells, frequently to half the normal level or less, and there is some increase in the number of CD8 cells, resulting in a ratio of 1 to 1 or even lower. (Although a drop in this ratio also occurs in other viral infections, it is caused not by a loss of CD4 cells—a sign of serious disease—but solely by an increase in CD8 cells, which is a normal protective mechanism.)

HERPES VARICELLA ZOSTER VIRUS (HVZ): A virus that causes chicken pox in children and may reappear in adulthood as herpes zoster. Herpes zoster is also known as shingles and usually causes very painful blisters on the skin above the involved nerve pathways.

HIV (human immunodeficiency virus): The retrovirus isolated and recognized as the etiologic agent of AIDS. HIV is classified as a lentivirus in a subgroup of the retroviruses. Also known as HTLV-III or LAV.

HIV-RELATED DEMENTIA (or HIV dementia): Chronic intellectual impairment, loss of mental capacity with organic origins. Various mechanisms have been postulated to explain its causes. In HIV, infected macrophages are thought to release toxins that contribute to the loss of neurons. Another theory is that the envelope protein gp120 often crosses the blood/brain barrier and indirectly kills neurons, resulting in dementia. Still another argues that it is caused by the hyperactivation of specific NMDA–glutamate receptors and the abnormal uptake of calcium into neurons.

HORMONE: A complex chemical substance that is secreted by a specific organ structure in one part of the body and then transported to another part of the body, where it has a specific regulatory effect on the activity of a certain organ or organs or a group of cells.

HUMAN LEUKOCYTE ANTIGENS (HLA): The body's main group of histocompatibility antigens, which are proteins in the immune system that affect organ transplant rejection and susceptibility to certain diseases. They act as genetic markers that identify cells as part of the body, thus preventing attack by the immune system. In tissue transplant operations HLA markers between donor and recipient are closely matched to prevent rejection of the transplant. Some groups of HLAs are essential for the function of the T lymphocytes called natural killer cells, acting as their guides in recognizing foreign antigens and abnormal (virus-infected or tumorous) cells.

HUMORAL IMMUNITY: One of the two main branches of the immune system (the other is cell-mediated immunity). In the humoral immune response to the invasion of the body by an antigen—i.e., bacteria, viruses, parasites, etc.—B cells, assisted by macrophages and directed by helper T cells, multiply and form plasma cells, which produce vast amounts of a specific antibody against that antigen. The antibodies bind with the antigens, marking them for destruction by other cells or neutralizing or destroying them directly.

IMMUNE SYSTEM: The body's complex network of cells, cell products, and cell-forming tissues that protects it from pathogens and other foreign agents or substances by recognizing them, neutralizing them, and recalling the response later when confronted with the same challenge. Its two principal components are the humoral response (based on B lymphocytes and the production of antibodies) and the cell-mediated response (based on T lymphocytes and the production of natural killer cells and phagocytes).

IMMUNOMODULATOR: Any agent, substance, or drug that triggers, enhances, or diminishes the body's immune system—i.e., an adjuvant, immunostimulant, or immunosuppressant.

IMMUNOTOXIN: A plant or animal poison (usually a protein) that is bound to an antibody or antigen and used to destroy specific target cells. An example of immunotoxins with the potential to kill HIV-infected cells is pseudomonas-exotoxin-

CD4 conjugate. In its ability to selectively destroy HIV-infected macrophages, Compound Q functions like an immunotoxin, but it is actually in a class of drugs known as Ribosome Inhibitory Protein.

IN VITRO (i.e., in glass): The term used to refer to an artificial environment created outside a living organism—for example, a test tube or culture plate—used in experimental research to study a disease or biological process.

IN VIVO (i.e., in life): The term used to refer to studies conducted within a living organism.

INFORMED CONSENT: Permission from a patient or subject to perform a specific test or procedure, obtained before performing the procedure or admitting the subject to a research study, clinical trial, or drug trial, in order to protect the subject. It usually consists of a document describing the experiment and the associated risks and benefits to the subject.

INSTITUTIONAL REVIEW BOARD (IRB): A committee consisting of physicians, lay people, clergy, and attorneys that initially approves and periodically reviews an experimental protocol in order to ensure that the rights of human subjects are being protected. Every institution that conducts or supports biomedical or behavioral research involving human subjects must, by federal regulation, have an IRB overseeing its research.

INTERFERON: A term used to describe a family of 20 to 25 glycoproteins that cause a cell to become resistant to a wide variety of diseases, by inhibiting the synthesis of viral RNA and proteins and by enhancing T-cell activity and NK cell cytotoxic activity. Cells infected by almost any virus will produce interferons in response. Synthesized interferon has been shown to interfere with the budding of the HIV virus but has not produced promising results when given as an anti-HIV therapeutic.

INVESTIGATIONAL NEW DRUG (IND) APPLICATION: A request that clinicians or investigators must file with the FDA before beginning Phase 1 clinical trials of a drug. If the results of Phase 1, 2, and 3 clinical trials are successful, a sponsor wishing to market the drug must also file a new drug application (NDA) with the FDA.

KAPOSI'S SARCOMA (KS): A vascular tumor of the cells of the blood vessel wall. It usually appears as brownish-pink to purple spots on the skin, beginning at the feet or ankles, but may also occur internally in addition to being independent of cutaneous lesions. A syndrome of KS was detected in certain populations of men in Eastern and Central Europe and was known to have an indolent course; however, in HIV, the disease is far more aggressive and lethal. Researchers speculate that although the cancer is common in HIV patients, it is caused by an organism unrelated to HIV, and perhaps related to basic fibroblast growth factor, although the exact pathogenesis has not been elucidated. No treatments have yet emerged with significant success of curing KS, although chemotherapy, interferon, radiation therapy, and topical substances have all shown some marginal efficacy in slowing down the disease at early stages in certain persons.

KILLER T CELLS (or cytotoxic T cells or CD8 killer cells): T lymphocytes that attack and destroy invading antigens or infected cells, assisted and directed by CD4 helper cells. Killer T cells are the primary weapon of the body's cell-mediated immune response.

LANGERHANS CELLS: Dendritic cells in the skin that carry surface receptors for immunoglobulin and are thought to pick up antigen and transport it to the lymph nodes. HIV can infect this cell line.

LEUCOCYTE: White blood cell.

LYMPH NODES: Small, mostly bean-size organs of the immune system, located along the lymphatic vessels and distributed widely throughout the body; they are often enlarged in AIDS. Lymph fluid flows through the lymph nodes, which act as filters, trapping microorganisms and other antigens that have entered the body through the bloodstream. They also produce lymphocytes and certain antibodies to neutralize or destroy the antigens.

LYMPHOCYTE: Any of a group of white blood cells formed in lymphatic tissue throughout the body (e.g., lymph nodes, spleen, thymus, and sometimes bone marrow). The two principal types of lymphocytes are B cells and T cells.

LYMPHOCYTE EXPANSION: An experimental procedure in which a patient's lymphocytes are extracted from the blood and propagated to large numbers *in vitro*.

LYMPHOCYTE TRANSFUSION: An experimental therapy for AIDS in which CD4 lymphocytes are harvested from a patient's first-degree relative (sibling or parents) and reinfused into the patient, much like a transfusion of normal red blood cells.

LYMPHOKINES: Substances secreted by CD4 lymphocytes in response to specific antigens; they help direct and regulate the immune response by stimulating the activity of monocytes and macrophages, activating the production of the appropriate antibody by the B cells, and dispatching killer T cells to the site of an infection. Interleukin-2 is a lymphokine.

LYMPHOMA: A tumor of the cells of the lymph system; it is usually cancerous and is commonly seen in AIDS. Treatment includes chemotherapy and radiation therapy.

MACROPHAGE: A scavenger cell involved in the initial ingestion and processing of large particulate antigens before interaction with lymphocytes; it is part of the cell-mediated immune system. Some macrophages bear CD4 receptors on their surface and, consequently, are susceptible to infection, although not death, by HIV. They may thus serve as long-term reservoirs for HIV infection.

MAJOR HISTOCOMPATIBILITY COMPLEX: A group of genes that controls the production of the body's histocompatibility antigens and is thus the chief determinant of tissue type and transplant compatibility. *See also* HUMAN LEUKOCYTE ANTIGENS.

MONOCLONAL ANTIBODY: An artificially produced antibody, derived in the laboratory from a single clone of a B lymphocyte in order to neutralize a particular antigen. They are highly specific, and react to a precise segment or configuration of a protein.

MYCOBACTERIUM AVIUM INTRACELLULARE (MAI): A bacillus that can cause an infection of most internal organs, but especially the lungs. When present in the intestinal tract, MAI can cause diarrhea and wasting. MAI is one of the most common opportunistic infections in AIDS. Several drugs, including Rifabutin, have shown efficacy in treating MAI.

MYCOPLASMA: Small bacterialike microbes that are able to reproduce and metabolize outside of cells. They have a membranous envelope and are capable of taking on an extreme variability of form (both size and shape). Neither viruses nor bacteria, they are commonly found as contaminates in laboratory experiments but recently have been isolated in the peripheral blood and tissues of patients with AIDS. Some researchers have recently proposed that mycoplasmas—and not HIV—are the chief cause of CD4 cell death in AIDS, but this idea has been refuted by other researchers.

NATURAL KILLER CELLS: Large granular lymphocytes, indirectly related to but different from killer T cells. Natural killer cells can destroy a broad variety of target cells—mostly virus-infected cells and tumor cells—without first being activated by other immune system components (such as antibodies). Although they are not the primary cell line attacked by HIV, their numbers and function are often deficient in AIDS patients.

NEUROPATHY: Any abnormal condition, functional disturbance, or pathological change in the peripheral nervous system. In HIV disease, neuropathy can manifest as numbness, pain, or tingling, most frequently in the fingers and feet.

NEUTROPHIL: A type of white blood cell that plays a central role in defending the body against infection by engulfing and killing foreign microorganisms.

NEW DRUG APPLICATION (NDA): An application required by the FDA prior to a drug's final approval and marketing, and which summarizes all the data that has been accumulated about it.

NUCLEOSIDE ANALOGS: Drugs or synthetic compounds similar to any one of the four basic components of DNA or RNA, but slightly different in structure so as to possess different properties. These drugs work by preventing DNA from becoming elongated. AZT, ddI, and ddC are nucleoside analogs that have been found to inhibit replication of HIV (in which DNA elongation is essential).

OPPORTUNISTIC INFECTION: An infection caused by any microorganism that normally does not cause disease in healthy humans but which does become pathogenic when the host's immune system is compromised, as in AIDS.

ORPHAN DRUGS: A group of drugs that have been approved for use in another country but are not approved or marketed in the United States, usually because the American market is considered too small to make them financially profitable.

P-24 ANTIGEN: A core protein of HIV. Elevated levels of serum p-24 occur during viral replication and are sometimes used as surrogate markers of an antiviral drug's efficacy.

PARALLEL TRACK: A system of distributing experimental drugs prior to their full licensing, after they have undergone Phase 1 testing, to patients who are unable to participate in ongoing clinical efficacy trials. The first drug to be available to AIDS patients through parallel track was ddI.

PATHOGENESIS: The specific mechanism by which a disease originates, develops, and causes damage to the body.

PCP: *See* PNEUMOCYSTIS CARINII PNEUMONIA.

PENTAMIDINE: A drug used to treat and prevent PCP, a common opportunistic infection in AIDS. Pentamidine is most often taken in aerosolized form and inhaled.

PEPTIDES: Two or more chemically linked amino acids; the constituent parts of proteins. In the brain, certain peptides—such as dopamine, endorphins, enkephalins, and serotonin—are essential neurotransmitters involved in mood states, learning, and memory. Several essential pituitary hormones are also peptides.

PERCENTAGE OF CD4 CELLS: The percentage of CD4 lymphocytes compared to the total number of lymphocytes. Some researchers believe that this marker is more significant than the absolute CD4 cell count.

PERSISTENT GENERALIZED LYMPHADENOPATHY: Chronically swollen, firm, and possibly tender lymph glands, commonly seen in HIV infection.

PHA: A mitogen that stimulates T lymphocytes. In the laboratory, it can be used to test the reactivity and stimulation potential of an AIDS patient's CD4 cells.

PHARMACOKINETICS: The action of drugs in the body over a certain period of time, including their distribution throughout the body, binding sites, metabolism, and elimination, as well as the rates at which these activities occur.

PHARMACOLOGY: The field of study dealing with drugs, their sources, appearance, chemistry, pharmacokinetics, modes of action, and uses.

PHOTOPHORESIS: Experimental AIDS treatment in which a patient's blood, first enriched with a drug called 8-MOP, is temporarily shunted out of the body, subjected to ultraviolet light, then reinfused. Photophoresis has shown efficacy in treating cutaneous T-cell lymphoma and mycoses fungoides. Its potential mode of action in HIV is not well understood.

PLACEBO-CONTROLLED TRIAL: A study that uses an inactive substance, often a sugar pill, against which an investigational drug is compared for efficacy. In such a study, usually half the subjects receive a placebo, the other half active drug. In a double-blind, placebo-controlled trial, neither the subject nor the researcher knows who is getting which agent.

PNEUMOCYSTIS CARINII PNEUMONIA (PCP): A parasitic fungal infection of the lungs, one of the most common life-threatening opportunistic infection in AIDS patients. Pentamidine is used to treat and prevent PCP, along with Bactrim and Septra.

POLYANIONIC SUBSTANCES: Drugs or compounds that specifically interfere with virus absorption or attachment into the host cell. Dextran sulfate and suramin are two drugs in this category.

PRINCIPAL INVESTIGATORS: The head researchers of a clinical trial at an institution—for instance, at an ACTG medical center.

PROTOCOL: Detailed research plan outlining a clinical trial's hypothesis, rationale, and objectives, and specifying the drug involved, the dosage levels, methods of administration, duration of treatment, and potential side effects. The protocol also explains the criteria for inclusion and exclusion: who may or may not be considered as study participants.

PSYCHONEUROIMMUNOLOGY: The field of study dealing with how the mind influences the body, especially the immune system, through a complex network of hormones, peptides, and neurochemicals. It has the theoretical potential of harnessing the mind's power to fight disease.

PWA: Person with AIDS.

RETINITIS: A medical term describing inflammation of the retina. CMV is capable of causing a serious form of retinitis in AIDS patients, which often leads to blindness.

RETROVIRUS: A class of viruses that includes HIV. Retroviruses are so named because they carry their genetic information in RNA, rather than DNA, and the RNA information is then translated backward into DNA through reverse transcriptase.

REVERSE TRANSCRIPTASE: An enzyme essential to retroviruses that transcribe their viral RNA into DNA. AZT and other nucleoside analogs inhibit the reverse transcription process in HIV disease.

RNA (ribonucleic acid): One of the two complex proteins that carry genetic instructions within a cell for the control of the cell's chemical activities, or that assist in the decoding of these instructions. Retroviruses, including HIV, encode their genetic information in RNA rather than DNA, and the RNA information is then translated backward into DNA.

SCID (severe combined immunodeficiency disorder): A group of rare congenital immune system disorders in which the body's humoral and cell-mediated immunity are both impaired. When an antigen invades the body of a patient with SCID, there is no production of antibodies to fight it or T lymphocyte response against it; a SCID patient also lacks immunoglobulins, which would normally prevent a vaccine from causing a fatal infection or a blood transfusion from resulting in graft-versus-host disease. Researchers have transplanted a human immune system with SCID into a mouse (referred to as a SCID mouse), enabling them to accelerate the pace of animal studies in the development of new drugs.

SCID MOUSE: A mouse that lacks a normal, working immune system because of a condition known as the Severe Combined Immune Deficiency (SCID). By transplanting human fetal thymus, bone marrow precursor cells and spleen tissue, researchers have been able to actually build a functional *human* immune system into the mouse. The SCID/HU mouse has allowed researchers to accelerate the pace of animal studies in new drug development by providing a human model in the laboratory.

SEROCONVERSION: The development of detectable specific antibodies in the blood as a result of infection or immunization.

SITE OF ACTION: The organ structure, tissue, or a cell type in the human body that a drug must reach at sufficient concentrations to achieve its desired effect.

SKIN TEST REACTIONS (same as DTH): A test in which an antigen is injected beneath the skin to determine the reaction of the body to a substance. Can be used to evaluate the strength of a person's immune system. Typically in AIDS studies, four common antigens are injected subdermally. A red bump, or erethema, that appears at the injection site forty-eight hours later is indication of a positive response.

STEM CELLS: Cells from which all blood cells are derived, often located in the bone marrow. A certain class of stem cells called lymphoid stem cells gives rise to T lymphocytes.

SURROGATE MARKERS: A term used in clinical research trials for biologic events, determined by laboratory tests, that may predict a patient's clinical outcome or indicate whether a drug is effective. The p-24 antigen, beta-2 microglobulin, and CD4 cell count are all surrogate markers that have been used in clinical trials for AIDS drugs.

SYNCYTIA: A dysfunctional clump of cells that have fused together. HIV-infected cells can fuse with non-HIV-infected CD4 cells, forming syncytia, and compounding the destruction of CD4 cells.

T CELL (or T lymphocyte): One of the two major classes of lymphocytes (B cells are the other), which together comprise the immune system's chief mechanism of resistance to a wide range of antigens, i.e., bacteria, viruses, and other potential causes of disease. The T cells are the principal components of the body's cell-mediated immune response to an invading antigen. (B cells are involved in humoral immunity.) There are several different kinds of T cells, each of which functions in specific ways to control and execute the immune response. The role of killer T cells (also called cytotoxic T cells) is to attack and destroy the antigens or the infected cells. They are assisted and directed in this process by helper T cells—called T4 or CD4 cells, because of the CD4 receptor molecule on their surface—which coordinate the activities of the phagocytes, the killer T cells, the B cells, and other immune cells. T4 cells identify the antigen, and then dispatch the killer T cells or activate the production of the appropriate antibody by the B cells. There are also suppressor T cells, which turn off the immune response after the antigen has been successfully controlled or destroyed. Killer T cells and suppressor T cells both bear the CD8 receptor molecule on their surface, and are thus both referred to as T8 or CD8 cells. Some T cells become memory T cells, which will reactivate the cell-mediated immune response against the antigen if there is a recurrence. Normally, about three-quarters of the body's white blood cells are T cells, of which 60 percent are killer or suppressor T cells and 30 percent are helper T cells.

THRUSH: A fungal infection of the mouth and throat, common in AIDS, caused by *Candida albicans* and marked by white patches on the tongue or in the throat cavity.

THYMIC TRANSPLANT THERAPY: An experimental therapy for AIDS in which human thymic tissue is transplanted; it did not produce positive results in preliminary trials.

THYMUS: A lymphoid organ in the upper chest cavity where T cells mature. It reaches its maximal development at about puberty and then appears to shrink or become rudimentary, resulting in a steady decrease of its immune function throughout adulthood.

TOXICITY: The degree to which a drug or antigen is poisonous or harmful to the body. Phase 1 clinical trials determine how much drug can be given safely without producing toxic effects.

TOXOPLASMOSIS: A disease resulting from infection with the protozoan parasite *Toxoplasma gondii*. In patients with AIDS and other immune disorders, it frequently causes severe encephalitis (inflammation of the brain), and may also involve other organ systems, including the heart, lungs, and testes.

TRANSACTIVATOR (TAT): A regulatory gene of HIV that controls the rate of viral reproduction. A new class of drugs that inhibit TAT may show promise in treating HIV disease.

UNDERGROUND STUDY: A clandestine study implemented by volunteer researchers and physicians outside the walls of traditional research. Underground studies do obtain subjects' informed consent but do not file for treatment INDs or use IRBs.

VACCINE: A substance that contains inactivated antigenic components from an infectious organism, which stimulates an immune response against that antigen and protects the body against future infection by that organism.

RESOURCES

INFORMATION ON TREATMENTS
AND CLINICAL TRIALS

Write or call for subscription rates

American Foundation for AIDS
  Research
733 Third Avenue
12th floor
New York, NY 10017
(212) 682-7440
Publishes quarterly *Treatment
  Directory*

John S. James
P.O. Box 411256
San Francisco, CA 94141
1-800-873-2812
Publishes twice monthly *AIDS
  Treatment News*

Gay Men's Health Crisis
129 West 20th Street
New York, NY 10011
(212) 337-1950
Publishes monthly *Treatment Issues*

Project Inform
347 Delores Street
San Francisco, CA
1-800-822-7422
Publishes quarterly *P.I. Perspectives*

DATA
P.O. Box 60637
Palo Alto, CA 94306
(415) 949-0919
Publishes quarterly *Forefront*

BUYERS' CLUBS

Write for current product and price
list.

PWA Health Group
150 West 26th Street
Suite 201
New York, NY 10001
(212) 255-0520

Dallas Buyers' Club
3527 Oak Lawn Ave
Suite 117
Dallas, TX 75219
(214) 528-4460

PWA Health Alliance
370 E. Prospect Street
Oakland Park, FL 33334
(800) 447-9242

Healing Alternatives Foundation
1748 Market Street
Suite 204
San Francisco, CA 94102
(415) 626-2316

This is only a partial list. There are AIDS organizations that can provide information and support services in almost every American city.

INDEX

(an asterisk denotes a pseudonym)